BIBLICAL AND NEAR
EASTERN STUDIES

William Sanford LaSor

BIBLICAL AND NEAR EASTERN STUDIES

Essays in Honor of William Sanford LaSor

edited by
Gary A. Tuttle

William B. Eerdmans Publishing Company
Grand Rapids, Michigan

255 Jefferson Ave. S.E., Grand Rapids, Mich. 49503

Printed in the United States of America

Library of Congress Cataloging in Publication Data

Main entry under title:
Biblical and Near Eastern Studies.
"A select bibliography of William Sanford LaSor": p. 276.
Includes indexes.
CONTENTS: Bruce, F. F. The Davidic Messiah in Luke-Acts.—Carmignac, J. Hebrew translations of the Lord's Prayer—an historical survey.—Epp, E. J. Jews and Judaism in the Living New Testament. [etc.]
1. Bible—Criticism, interpretation, etc.—Addresses, essays, lectures. 2. Semitic Philology—Addresses, essays, lectures. 3. LaSor, William Sanford—Addresses, essays, lectures. 4. LaSor, William Sanford—Bibliography. I. LaSor, William Sanford. II. Tuttle, Gary A. III. Title.
BS540.B4457 220.6 77-10797
ISBN 0-8028-3500-7

CONTENTS

PREFACE

The essays in this volume are presented to honor William Sanford LaSor, master pedagogue, careful scholar, devoted churchman and solicitous friend, on the occasion of his sixty-fifth birthday. Over half of the contributors are former students of Dr. LaSor, whose dates of graduation (1952-1972) span almost his entire career at Fuller Theological Seminary. The other contributors are academic colleagues and friends whose own careers have intersected with LaSor's at diverse times and places. That this group comprises New Testament, Old Testament and Semitics scholars of international repute is an important index of the range of LaSor's academic interests and a measure of his scholarly competence.

Nearly every *Festschrift* has a lengthy history, and this one is no exception. Plans to produce a volume were formulated in June 1975 and solicitation of articles began on 1 August. Advice I had received suggested that securing contributions would be difficult because of the immensely busy schedule which is the nemesis of every academician. However, to my delight, and as an indication of the respect in which LaSor is held, positive responses began coming in within ten days. And, in fact, everyone contacted that month and asked to contribute agreed to do so. I was also warned that I should not expect more than 70-80% of those who had agreed to contribute to follow through, and actually produce an article. It is a tribute to the integrity of the contributors and the providence of God that only one found it impossible to fulfill his obligation.

In considering the nature of the volume through which Dr. LaSor would be honored, a decision was made not to develop the book around a particular theme. It was felt the volume would have more integrity if its unity were defined in terms of Dr. LaSor's own interests. Thus its unity is organic, reflective of the heart and mind which has in some measure nurtured each of the contributors. And it is because of Dr. LaSor's wide-ranging interests and abilities that his students have been equipped to enter such a diversity of specialties.

There are many people without whose cooperation, participation and encouragement this project would not have been brought to fruition. Pride of place among these acknowledgments must, of course, go to the contributors whose cordiality and faithfulness have been most gratifying. A *Festschrift* is one of the very few ways available to scholars to honor one of their own in a significant, enduring and public way. My thanks, then, to the Wm. B. Eerdmans Publishing Company and its competent staff for allowing us the opportunity. A modest subsidy was provided by Fuller Theological Seminary to underwrite the expenses associated with retyping various MSS, and photocopying, a practical help I gratefully acknowledge. Gratitude is due also to my colleagues, Rabbi David Wortman and Professor James Bradley, who were of considerable help in unraveling various bibliographic knots. Finally, my patient wife, Janice, has given unstintingly of her considerable secretarial and editorial skills to aid the diversity of MSS on their intricate way toward stylistic conformity. Janice was Dr. LaSor's secretary in 1971-72, and as each of us has sought to do him honor in an area of our special competence, so has she. While her work is a fitting tribute to Dr. LaSor, it has been of special service to me, and I am most thankful for her skill and constancy.

GARY A. TUTTLE
New Haven, CT

PRINCIPAL ABBREVIATIONS

(The designation N followed by a number—e.g. [N 4]—enclosed in parentheses or square brackets, refers to the preceding NOTE in the same essay where complete bibliographic data are given. Abbreviations particular to individual essays are given in the first note of those essays.)

AASOR	—Annual of the American Schools of Oriental Research
AB	—Anchor Bible
'Abot R. Nat.	—*'Abôt de Rabbi Nathan*
AfO	—*Archiv für Orientforschung*
Ag. Ap.	—Josephus, *Against Apion*
AHW	—W. von Soden, *Akkadisches Handwörterbuch*
AJBA	—*Australian Journal of Biblical Archaeology*
AJSL	—*American Journal of Semitic Languages*
Akk.	—Akkadian
ANET	—J. B. Pritchard, ed., *Ancient Near Eastern Texts Relating to the Old Testament*
AnOr	—Analecta Orientalia
Ant.	—Josephus, *Antiquities*
AOAT	—Alter Orient und Altes Testament
AOS	—American Oriental Series
Ar.	—Arabic
Aram.	—Aramaic
ARM(T)	—Archives royales de Mari (transcrite et traduite)
ArOr	—*Archiv orientální*
AT	—*The Complete Bible: An American Translation*
ATAbh	—Alttestamentliche Abhandlungen
b.	—born
BA	—*Biblical Archaeologist*
BASOR	—*Bulletin of the American Schools of Oriental Research*
BDB	—F. Brown, S. R. Driver and C. A. Briggs, *Hebrew and English Lexicon of the Old Testament*
BH[3]	—R. Kittel, ed., *Biblia Hebraica,* third edition.
BJRL	—*Bulletin of the John Rylands Library*

BSOAS	—*Bulletin of the School of Oriental and African Studies*
BZ	—*Biblische Zeitschrift*
BZAW	—Beihefte zur ZAW
c.	—circa
CAD	—*The Assyrian Dictionary of the Oriental Institute of the University of Chicago*
CAH	—*Cambridge Ancient History*
CBQ	—*Catholic Biblical Quarterly*
CD	—Cairo (Genizah text of the) Damascus (Document)
CTM	—*Concordia Theological Monthly*
d.	—died
D (-stem)	—qiṭṭēl
DibHam	—Dibrê Hamm^{e}'ôrôt (=Les paroles des luminaires)
E	—English (verse reference when different from Hebrew)
EA	—El-Amarna (text references from J. A. Knudtzon, *Die El-Amarna-Tafeln* [Leipzig: Hinrich, 1915])
ETL	—*Ephemerides theologicae lovanienses*
ETR	—*Etudes théologiques et religieuses*
EvQ	—*Evangelical Quarterly*
EvT	—*Evangelische Theologie*
G (-stem)	—qal
H (-stem)	—hiqṭîl
HAT	—Handbuch zum Alten Testament
Heb.	—Hebrew
HSAT	—Die Heilige Schrift des Alten Testaments
HtD (-stem)	—hitqaṭṭēl
HSM	—Harvard Semitic Monographs
HTR	—*Harvard Theological Review*
IB	—*Interpreter's Bible*
ICC	—International Critical Commentary
IEJ	—*Israel Exploration Journal*
Int	—*Interpretation*
JANES	—*Journal of the Ancient Near Eastern Society of Columbia University*
JAOS	—*Journal of the American Oriental Society*
JB	—*Jerusalem Bible*
JBL	—*Journal of Biblical Literature*
JBR	—*Journal of Bible and Religion*
JCS	—*Journal of Cuneiform Studies*
JESHO	—*Journal of the Economic and Social History of the Orient*
JETS	—*Journal of the Evangelical Theological Society*
JJS	—*Journal of Jewish Studies*
JNES	—*Journal of Near Eastern Studies*
JPOS	—*Journal of the Palestine Oriental Society*

JPSV	—*Jewish Publication Society Version*
JQR	—*Jewish Quarterly Review*
JSJ	—*Journal for the Study of Judaism in the Persian, Hellenistic and Roman Period*
JSS	—*Journal of Semitic Studies*
JTS	—*Journal of Theological Studies*
J.W.	—Josephus, *Jewish Wars*
KB	—L. Koehler and W. Baumgartner, *Lexicon in Veteris Testamenti libros*
KHC	—Kurzer Hand-Commentar zum Alten Testament
KJV	—*King James Version*
LBP	—*Living Bible Paraphrased*
LCL	—Loeb Classical Library
LTK	—*Lexikon für Theologie und Kirche*
LXX	—Septuagint
MA	—Middle Assyrian
MB	—Middle Babylonian
MRS	—Mission de Ras Shamra
MS(S)	—Manuscript(s)
MT	—Masoretic Text
N (-stem)	—Niqṭal
NAB	—*New American Bible*
NEB	—*New English Bible*
NIV	—*New International Version*
NJV	—*New Jewish Version*
NTS	—*New Testament Studies*
OIP	—Oriental Institute Publications
Or	—*Orientalia*
PL	—J. Migne, *Patrologia latina*
PRU	—*Le Palais royal d'Ugarit*
4Q176	—4QTanḥumim, quotations from Psalms, Isaiah, Zechariah with fragments of comments, from Qumran cave 4
11QBer	—Bᵉrākôt (Blessings) from Qumran cave 11
4QFlor	—Florilegium (or Ecclesiastical Midrashim) from Qumran cave 4
1QH	—Hôdāyôt (Thanksgiving Hymns) from Qumran cave 1
$1QIs^a$	—Isaiah scroll, first exemplar, from Qumran cave 1
1QM	—Milḥāmā^h (War Scroll) from Qumran cave 1
$4QpIsa^c$	—Pesher (commentary) to Isaiah, third exemplar, from Qumran cave 4
$4QpPs^a$	—Pesher (commentary) to Psalm 37 from Qumran cave 4
1QS	—Serek hayyaḥad (Rule of the Community, Manual of Discipline) from Qumran cave 1
11QtgJob	—Targum to Job from Qumran cave 11

RA	—*Revue d'assyriologie et d'archéologie orientale*
RB	—*Revue biblique*
REJ	—*Revue des études juives*
RevQ	—*Revue de Qumrân*
RHA	—*Revue hittite et assianique*
RHR	—*Revue de l'histoire des religions*
RLA	—*Reallexikon der Assyriologie*
RSO	—*Rivista degli studi orientali*
RSR	—*Recherches de science religieuse*
RSV	—*Revised Standard Version*
SBL	—Society of Biblical Literature
SBLDS	—SBL Dissertation Series
Syr.	—Syriac
TDNT	—G. Kittel and G. Friedrich, ed., *Theological Dictionary of the New Testament*
TDOT	—G. J. Botterweck and H. Ringgren, ed., *Theological Dictionary of the Old Testament*
TEV	—*Today's English Version*
TToday	—*Theology Today*
TZ	—*Theologische Zeitschrift*
UF	—*Ugarit-Forschungen*
Ug.	—Ugaritic
UG 5	—*Ugaritica* 5
UT	—C. H. Gordon, *Ugaritic Textbook*
Vg.	—*Vulgate*
VT	—*Vetus Testamentum*
VTSup	—Supplements to VT
WTJ	—*Westminster Theological Journal*
ZA	—*Zeitschrift für Assyriologie*
ZAW	—*Zeitschrift für die alttestamentliche Wissenschaft*
ZDMG	—*Zeitschrift der deutschen morganländischen Gesellschaft*
ZKT	—*Zeitschrift für katholische Theologie*
ZNW	—*Zeitschrift für die neutestamentliche Wissenschaft*

WILLIAM SANFORD LASOR— A PERSONAL TRIBUTE

DAVID ALLAN HUBBARD

When William Sanford LaSor arrived at Fuller Seminary in the fall of 1949, he was in the midst of what some might call his third career. For nearly ten years he had served Presbyterian pastorates in Ocean City, New Jersey and Scranton, Pennsylvania. Then, during World War II, he donned the uniform of a Navy chaplain with a tour of duty that took him across the heart of China ministering to the personnel on the weather stations during one of the strangest expeditions in Naval history. His teaching career began in 1946 at Lafayette College, Easton, Pennsylvania, where he was called to set up a new department of religious studies.

This third career in teaching and scholarship had been in the making for years. Always an outstanding student, LaSor had graduated from high school in Philadelphia at age fifteen and had matriculated at Princeton Theological Seminary at nineteen, following his graduation from the University of Pennsylvania. When he received his Bachelor of Theology degree with honors at Princeton in 1934, he had simultaneously completed a Master of Arts program at Princeton University in comparative religion. In 1943 he completed a Th.M. at Princeton Seminary with biblical theology as the specialization.

His almost boundless capacity for hard work enabled him to earn his Ph.D. in Akkadiology in 1949 at the Dropsie College for Hebrew and Cognate Learning while teaching full-time at Lafayette. At Fuller, LaSor repeated that pattern by successfully pursuing a doctorate in theology at the University of Southern California (1956) despite a teaching load that has always included more than the expected number of courses. Comparative religion, pastoral studies, Semitic literature and philology, and New Testament—in each of those areas LaSor completed an advanced degree. The amazing breadth of this intense and prolonged program of higher education has greatly enriched his teaching through the years.

Though in a sense teaching is Dr. LaSor's third career, he would see it as a specific expression of his first and only calling—Christian ministry. He has never ceased to be a pastor. The churchmanship which he learned from his parents—his father was a Presbyterian elder, his mother a strict daughter of the Scottish church—has been built into his bone and marrow. It shows itself in the teaching ministry he conducts in scores of congregations in Southern California and in the popular books he has written, like his *Men Who Knew God* and *Men Who Knew Christ* and his highly successful lessons on Acts, *Church Alive!* Above all, this concern for the church has been evident in his commitment to the training of ministers. The lavish effort that he put into the teaching of the biblical languages, Hebrew, Aramaic and Greek, has had one aim—the preparation of men and women to be effective communicators of the Christian faith as it is taught in the Scriptures. Something like 2,000 persons at Fuller alone have benefited directly from the language courses which LaSor has supervised and the handbooks he has developed. Much of the motivation for the teacher's zeal has been the pastor's heart.

Similarly, Professor LaSor has never ceased to be a chaplain. For twenty-five years after his discharge from the Navy he maintained an active relationship in the Naval Reserve, including enthusiastic involvement in the National Military Chaplains' Association. Most importantly, he has been instrumental in the recruiting and training of several dozen military chaplains at Fuller, the first of whom, Dick Carr, has recently been named Deputy Chief of Chaplains for the Air Force. More than once we have had students come to the Seminary who were the spiritual sons and daughters of our chaplains, and who themselves then looked to LaSor to encourage them in the faith as he had their "fathers."

Something of Bill LaSor's churchmanship can be seen in the difficult story of his relationships with the United Presbyterian Church. A Presbyterian, born, bred, educated and ordained, he had come to Fuller high with hopes that the Los Angeles Presbytery would receive him into fellowship and grant him permission to "labor outside the bounds of Presbytery" (the technical term for work done by Presbyterian elders outside of Presbyterian congregations and agencies). Feelings ran strong among many of the leaders of the Presbytery that Fuller Theological Seminary, as an interdenominational organization with no official tie to any churchly body, might prove divisive to Presbyterian causes. After five years of discussion and ecclesiastical litigation, the painful decision was rendered: LaSor and three other colleagues would have to choose whether to leave Fuller or to surrender ordination in the Presbyterian Church. Even after leaving his church and receiving ordination in the Reformed Episcopal Church, Dr. LaSor labored extensively to encourage and assist Fuller students who felt called to serve as Presbyterian pastors. Years of patient effort to establish a working agreement between the Los Angeles Presbytery and the Seminary came to fruition on February 14, 1967, when, fittingly, LaSor was the first faculty member to be received into Presbytery membership, where his heart had been during the long years of exile from the church that had nurtured him.

Generations of students testify to Dr. LaSor's effectiveness as a teacher. While demanding in his standards, LaSor has always been supportive in his teaching procedures. His classes have benefitted since the beginning from the arduous efforts and organizing gifts that have resulted in major syllabi for virtually every course. His largest contribution to the pedagogy of his students has been the inductive handbooks in biblical Hebrew and New Testament Greek (keyed to Acts). The motivation for an inductive approach to study was sharpened by his years of study at Dropsie under the master Semitic philologist, Cyrus H. Gordon. LaSor and I arrived at Fuller at the same time—I as a first-year student, he as an associate professor of Old Testament. For the five years of our work together, I watched the development and refinement of the inductive method of teaching Hebrew. Then, as now, every ministerial student at Fuller was required to take basic courses in Hebrew. LaSor chose the book of Esther as the biblical text, a happy choice for three reasons: (1) it attested all the high-frequency vocabulary of the Old Testament (except *'ĕlôhîm* and *gābô^ah*); (2) it contained the feminine verbs and adjectives not always found in other narratives of the Bible; and (3) it was relatively free of theological issues which so often seduce students from careful study of grammar and vocabulary. The verdict on the success of the inductive method, in which grammatical instruction is based on actual reading rather than the learning of cold paradigms and abstract syntactical principles, is not unanimous. Yet an overwhelming majority of the students who have persevered would testify to its benefits in aiding memory and in providing incentive for study. The widespread use of LaSor's method and materials beyond the walls of Fuller means that he now has many students who have never enrolled in his classes.

Those of us who sat under his tutelage in work for advanced degrees owe him a special debt. He is a mentor both patient and perceptive. We have learned that the forbidding signs on his door, which seek to protect his time and control his appointments with students, are there not because he is hard-hearted, but because he is kind-hearted. The amount of time he is prepared to give away to inquisitive students knows almost no bounds. I can remember asking questions whose answers required the time to browse and discuss a shelf of books. Yet I never felt he regretted the cost.

His impatience with theories that did not face facts, with generalizations drawn from secondary sources, with philology more whimsical than scientific, with sloppy documentation, with attempts to shortcut the tedious tasks of scholarship, present an unforgettable model to all who have worked with him. His appreciation of our insights, even when they were really neither new nor good, stimulated us to harder, better work. His confidence in our fledgling abilities as scholars and teachers steadied us through many a storm of uncertainty. And there must be half a hundred or so of his students—who learned to teach by watching him and by teaching biblical languages under his supervision—who are serving the faith by teaching on every continent. They would testify to his twin gifts of inspiration and example. Even more, they would testify that Bill LaSor encouraged them not to copy him in either thought or style, but to teach in their own ways.

His interests as a scholar have ranged widely: Semitic philology, Old Testament historical-geography, the Dead Sea Scrolls and their voluminous bibliography, and more lately Old Testament Theology. Working regularly in the texts of two dozen languages, he has demonstrated the importance of comparative philological studies and has rightly criticized the shabby etymological work to which even competent semitists sometimes resort. When the new edition of *The International Standard Bible Encyclopedia* appears, confidence in its integrity will be heightened by the knowledge that Professor LaSor has edited over 1500 of the articles in the area of archaeology.

LaSor's style as a teacher and minister has been enriched by his amazing versatility. His interests range from music (he enjoys playing the electronic organ in his home), to travel (nine trips to the Middle East have increased his appreciation of and sensitivity to biblical settings), to photography which has enriched his lectures through the years and brought enjoyment and enlightenment to countless congregations.

His nearly thirty years at Fuller have left their permanent stamp on our institution. Alumni from the early years will remember how singlehandedly he kept us in touch with the Seminary by editing and writing *Theology, News and Notes,* which now looks much more sophisticated and professional than did the mimeographed sheets that used to pour from LaSor's typewriter twenty years ago, but is no more heartily welcomed by Fuller's sons and daughters than was its austere and stimulating predecessor. The registrar and other administrators will recall that the puzzles of scheduling classes in an interlocking curriculum were not usually solved until LaSor's mental computer began to weigh the variables and eliminate the conflicts. The hundreds of missionaries and national pastors who have graduated from Fuller's School of World Mission ought not forget that it was Dr. LaSor who headed the committee that laid plans for the founding of that school in 1965. The Seminary's relationship with members of the Jewish community—both academic and religious—has been measurably strengthened by the ties that LaSor has fashioned.

Sometimes by gentle wooing and at other times by blunt confrontation, Bill LaSor has shared his common sense with the Seminary. He came in our third year as the seventh professor. As a pillar faculty member he shares significant credit for the Seminary's growth and maturity.

Throughout his ministry LaSor has been sustained and supported by the love of his family. Elizabeth Vaughan LaSor (Betsy) has been a partner to him for more than forty years. Their four children—William Sanford LaSor, Jr., Elizabeth Ann LaSor, Frederick Eugene Vaughan LaSor and Susanne Marie LaSor Whyte—have blessed and strengthened their relationship. Nine grandchildren promise to bring joy and satisfaction to these years of maturity.

Through his dedicated teaching and his thoughtful writing, William Sanford LaSor has created a host of debtors throughout the Judeo-Christian world. This word of appreciation and these scholarly essays may help pay interest on that indebtedness.

I. New Testament Studies

1

THE DAVIDIC MESSIAH IN LUKE-ACTS

F. F. BRUCE

While Dr. LaSor is best known as a Hebraist and an Old Testament specialist, he has not excluded the Greek language or the New Testament from his scholarly exploration. His *Handbook of New Testament Greek: An Inductive Approach Based on the Greek Texts of Acts* and his commentary on Acts, *Church Alive!* bear witness to his interest and competence in the latter fields. It is a pleasure for one who first entered the world of biblical and New Testament scholarship with a study of Acts to share in this tribute of admiration and friendship to Dr. LaSor with a brief survey of one aspect of the use of the Old Testament in Luke-Acts.

I. Luke's Nativity Narrative

One of the most noteworthy negative features in Jesus' allusions to his identity or rule is the absence of any appeal to the promises attached to the house of David. He did not repudiate the designation "son of David" when it was given to him by others,[1] but on the only occasion when he himself is recorded to have raised the subject, it was to point out the inadequacy of the designation "son of David" for one whom David recognized to be his lord.[2] (There is nothing to suggest that his riposte to the Pharisees who criticized his disciples for plucking and eating some ears of grain on the sabbath, "Have you not read what David did. . . ?" implies that if David could override the law on occasion, so *a fortiori* could the son of David.)[3]

When Jesus was challenged by the high priest, at his appearance before the Sanhedrin, to say whether or not he was the Messiah, he acknowledged that, if this was the title on which his judges insisted, he had no option but to lay claim to it. But he went on immediately to show in what sense he claimed it by using the transcendent imagery of apocalyptic and not the language in which the hope of the restoration of the Davidic monarchy was traditionally couched.[4]

Yet, if it is plain that Jesus did not use this language of himself, it is equally plain that others used it of him, and that from an early date. When Paul introduces his letter to the Christians of Rome with a reference to Jesus' being "descended from David according to the flesh,"[5] he is probably not using the terminology which he found most congenial but adapting the words of a Christian confession which he assumed would be as familiar in Rome as he knew it to be in the Eastern Mediterranean. When he expresses his own insight into the identity of Jesus, he uses different language,[6] but by the same token he knew the language quoted in Rom 1:3 to be primitive—the language used by some who were in Christ before himself. This is confirmed by the testimony of non-Pauline writings of the New Testament, and not least by that of the writings of Luke.

The nativity narratives of both Matthew and Luke attest Jesus' descent from David, but Luke's narrative does so with special emphasis. Luke indicates that both Jesus and his forerunner were born into a circle of pious people who looked for the near fulfillment of the ancestral hope of Israel and associated that fulfillment with the coming of the long-expected prince of the house of David. In this regard they show a striking affinity with the pious circle from which, a few decades earlier, the Psalms of Solomon came, with their reprobation of the Hasmonean usurpers who had "laid waste the throne of David," and their earnest prayer that God would soon raise up the rightful heir to that throne to put down the oppressors of Israel and restore his people's fortunes. The prophecies of the wealth of nations being brought to enrich the city of God would then be realized, but above all Jerusalem would once again be known as the city of righteousness: "for all will be holy, and their king is the anointed Lord."[7] Commentators generally regard this last phrase (*christos kyrios*) as a Greek mistranslation of the lost Hebrew original (*m^{e}šî^{a}ḥ YHWH*), but this is doubtful. If YHWH had been the Hebrew wording, the translators had ample precedent in the Septuagint to guide them to its proper rendering *christos kyriou*. We must bear in mind the occurrence of the same phrase *christos kyrios* in the angelic message to the shepherds near Bethlehem[8] (although this has also, but unconvincingly, been explained as a comparable mistranslation).

Luke's record introduces the Davidic motif when he tells how, six months after the announcement of the impending birth of John the Baptist, the angel Gabriel came to Nazareth to make a similar announcement to Mary, "a virgin betrothed to a man whose name was Joseph, of the house of David."[9] Here, as in Matthew's record,[10] it is Joseph who is said to have been of Davidic descent: all that can be known of Mary's family must be inferred from the statement that she was related to John's mother Elizabeth, who belonged to "the daughters of Aaron."[11] Luke leaves his readers in no doubt that Jesus was conceived while his mother was still a virgin, but that in law Joseph was his father; hence in law Jesus ranked as a son of David, while by divine providence he was marked out as *the* son of David in whom the age-long promises were to meet their fulfillment. Hence Gabriel speaks thus to Mary about her coming son:

> He will be great, and will be called the Son of the Most High;
> and the Lord God will give to him the throne of his father David,
> and he will reign over the house of Jacob for ever;
> and of his kingdom there will be no end.[12]

It is not difficult to recognize in these words an echo of various Old Testament passages, such as Isaiah's oracle of the prince of the four names, whose government will be established without end "upon the throne of David, to uphold it with justice and with righteousness from this time forth and for evermore."[13]

The same note is struck in Zechariah's song of praise at the birth of his son—the more surprisingly, as Zechariah was a priest and did not belong to the royal line which was the subject of the Davidic promises. Yet in the birth of John he greeted a token of what was shortly to be fulfilled in the royal line:

> Blessed be the Lord God of Israel,
> for he has visited and redeemed his people,
> and has raised up a horn of salvation for us
> in the house of his servant David,
> as he spoke by the mouth of his holy prophets from of old. . . .[14]

We may discern this note again in the angels' good news to the shepherds: "to you is born this day in the city of David a Saviour, who is Christ the Lord (*christos kyrios* 'the anointed Lord')."[15] Why in the city of David? Because, as Luke tells us in his own prosaic narrative, in pursuance of a census decree of the Roman Emperor, Joseph "went up from Galilee, from the city of Nazareth, to Judea, to the city of David, which is called Bethlehem, because he was of the house and lineage of David, to be enrolled with Mary, his betrothed, who was with child."[16]

A similarly matter-of-fact datum, albeit in another genre, is provided by Luke in his genealogical table which traces Jesus' lineage back through Joseph to David (and beyond David to Abraham and Adam)—not, however (as in the Matthean genealogy), through the succession of kings descended from David (Solomon and his heirs) but through Nathan, another son of David, and his completely obscure descendants.[17] Whatever significance there is in this curious fact does not lie on the surface; anyone undertaking to lay it bare must explain at the same time why Luke's line coincides with the more illustrious line in the persons of Shealtiel and Prince Zerubbabel.[18]

After the genealogy, however, no mention is made of Jesus' Davidic descent throughout the whole Gospel of Luke except once, incidentally, by the blind man of Jericho.[19] Remarkably enough, Luke's description of the triumphal entry into Jerusalem suppresses the reference to "the kingdom of our father David" which Mark's parallel narrative puts on the lips of the pilgrim crowd.[20] Like an underground stream, nevertheless, the Davidic motif emerges into the light of day again when we come to the apostolic preaching in Luke's second volume. Its absence from the record of Jesus' ministry deserves to be invested with all the importance which is attached, in current gospel criticism, to the "criterion of dissimilarity."

II. Pentecost in Jerusalem

Of the speeches in Acts there are two in particular which insist that Jesus was descended from David and that in him the divine promises made to or through

David were realized: Peter's speech in Jerusalem on the day of Pentecost and Paul's speech in the synagogue of Pisidian Antioch. Although there are differences in detail between the two speeches in their deployment of the Davidic theme, they share sufficient common ground to suggest that both draw upon an early pattern of Christian preaching which maintained that the resurrection of Jesus fulfilled certain well-known scriptures. Of these scriptures, the sixteenth psalm figures in both speeches.

Peter's speech in Jerusalem begins by explaining the phenomena that have amazed his audience—those attendant on the descent of the Spirit—in terms of the prophecy of Joel 2:28–32; then he goes on to announce that Jesus of Nazareth, so recently put to death in that city, has been raised from the dead. Peter and his associates can bear first-hand testimony to his resurrection, and in it they see clearly the fulfillment of the hope expressed in Ps 16:10:

> thou wilt not abandon my soul to Hades,
> nor let thy holy one see corruption.[21]

By common consent this psalm was ascribed to David; what then could be the meaning of the confidence to which these words of David give utterance? We might say today that, whoever the author was, he was voicing his assurance that God would deliver him from death in some critical situation. But this would not satisfy the hermeneutical principles underlying the application of the words in Peter's speech: however many deliverances from death the psalmist experienced, one day death caught up with him, so that his soul was given over to Hades and his body did undergo corruption. (The exegesis here depends on the Greek rather than the Hebrew text: 'corruption,' Greek *diaphthora,* renders Hebrew *šaḥat* 'the pit,' which stands in synonymous parallelism with *šᵉʾôl* 'Hades.')

The interpretation of the passage in Peter's speech extracts the last ounce of significance from the words, for they were the words of a prophet. The oracle entitled "the last words of David" opens with the claim:

> The Spirit of Yahweh speaks by me,
> his word is upon my tongue[22]

—and everything in the Psalter spoken by David, or attributed to David, is understood in the light of this claim. Every word must be given its full weight, and so the confidence expressed in Ps 16:10 is referred not to an occasional deliverance from death but to absolute deliverance, such as Jesus experienced. The words, then, cannot be applicable to David, since he "died and was buried, and his tomb is with us to this day."[23] Yet they were spoken by him, and spoken in the first person singular; this must therefore be one of those places where the messianic Spirit spoke in the prophets, "predicting the sufferings of Christ and the subsequent glories."[24] David, by the Spirit, spoke not *in propria persona* but as the mouthpiece of his greater son, the Messiah, who as a matter of now attested fact "was not abandoned to Hades, nor did his flesh see corruption."[25]

But if Jesus' resurrection, to which his followers were witnesses, declared him to be the Messiah, then other oracles which, by general agreement, pointed to the Messiah must have come true of him. When Jesus, in debate with the scribes during Holy Week, asked how the Messiah could be David's son if David by inspiration called him "my lord," it was accepted by him and them alike that Ps 110:1 ("Yahweh's oracle to my lord: 'Sit at my right hand. . . .' ") was a prophetic utterance of David and that the person invited to sit at God's right hand was the Messiah.[26] Peter, having affirmed Jesus to be the Messiah, can now go on to affirm that these words must therefore apply to him (as they could obviously not apply to David): "Being therefore exalted at the right hand of God, and having received from the Father the promise of the Holy Spirit, he has poured out this which you see and hear. . . . Let all the house of Israel therefore know assuredly that God has made this Jesus . . . both Lord and Messiah (*kyrios* and *christos*)."[27]

The primitiveness of the use of Ps 110:1 as a *testimonium* to the exaltation of Jesus is seen by the way in which it crops up in so many strata of the New Testament. Once again, Paul's evidence in his letter to the Romans is important, for his reference in Rom 8:34 to "Christ Jesus. . . , who is at the right hand of God, who also makes intercession for us," is probably (like his reference to Jesus' Davidic descent in Rom 1:3) taken from an early confession of faith.[28]

III. At Pisidian Antioch

The Davidic-Messiah group of *testimonia* is by no means the only one found in the speeches in the early chapters of Acts—we may think of the combination of the Servant-of-Yahweh theme with the Prophet-like-Moses theme in Peter's speech in the temple court in Acts 3:13–26[29]—but Luke may have reasons of his own for putting it in the forefront of the apostolic preaching. The next outstanding occasion on which the Davidic-Messiah theme is emphasized in the apostolic preaching is in Paul's synagogue address at Pisidian Antioch.

This address begins with an outline of the mighty acts of God in the history of Israel from the Exodus to the rise of David.[30] This outline, as the late George Ernest Wright pointed out, summarizes the Old Testament *kerygma,* Israel's salvation-history as it was recited in the national worship.[31] A good example of this is presented by Psalm 78, which surveys Yahweh's dealings with the nation from the days of Egypt and the wilderness until

> he chose David his servant . . .
> to be the shepherd of Jacob his people,
> of Israel his inheritance.[32]

But, whereas the psalmist sees the rise of David and his dynasty, with the establishment of the sanctuary on Zion, as the climax of salvation-history,[33] Paul treats it as a stage on the way to the real climax, for he moves directly from David to Jesus, the son of David: "Of this man's posterity God has brought to Israel a Saviour, Jesus, as he promised."[34] Then follows an outline of the New Testament *kerygma* which, as regularly in the gospel tradition, finds its inception in John's baptismal ministry[35] and its culmination in the death and resurrection of Jesus.

After the reference to those who were eyewitnesses of the risen Christ come the *testimonia*. One has not hitherto been used in Acts[36]—the oracle of Ps 2:7, in which Yahweh addresses his anointed one with the acclamation:

> Thou art my Son,
> today I have begotten thee.

This is adduced as a *testimonium* to God's "raising" of Jesus[37]—not, probably, to his being raised from the dead but to his being raised up as Israel's deliverer (just as, earlier in the address, God is said to have "raised up David to be their king"[38]). In the original Lucan account of Jesus' baptism this may well have been the precise wording of the heavenly voice (it is so read in the Western text).[39] The occasion indicated in the present context is best taken similarly as the baptism of Jesus; it was then that (as Peter put it in the house of Cornelius) "God anointed Jesus of Nazareth with the Holy Spirit and with power."[40] (It might be argued against this that Paul himself thinks of the *resurrection* as the occasion when Jesus was "designated Son of God in power,"[41] but the phrase "in power" there may be understood by way of contrast with his being "crucified in weakness."[42] It was the Son of God that was crucified as truly as it was the Son of God that was raised from the dead—but in being raised from the dead he was effectively shown to be the Son of God.)

One of the *testimonia* adduced at Pisidian Antioch for the resurrection of Jesus is Ps 16:10, as it had been in Jerusalem at the first Christian Pentecost.[43] But at Pisidian Antioch it is associated interestingly with Isa 55:3 where God, restoring his people after exile, promises to give them "the holy and sure blessings of David."[44] Both in Hebrew and in Greek these two *testimonia* are linked by a common term: we have here an instance of the rabbinical interpretative principle *g*^{e}*zērā*^{h} *šāwā*^{h} ('equal category'). In the Hebrew text *ḥāsîd* ('holy one') in Ps 16:10 is cognate with *ḥasdê* ('covenant mercies') in Isa 55:3; in the Septuagint the same adjective *hosios* is used in both places (in the masculine singular in the former and in the neuter plural in the latter). This provided sufficient ground to join the two in a common exegetical schema. If Jesus, the son of David, was the "holy one" of God who was saved from undergoing corruption, his resurrection was the means by which God kept his undertaking to fulfill for his people the covenant mercies promised to David and his dynasty. As Paul expresses it in 1 Cor 15:25, Jesus, having been raised from the dead, must reign until God "has put all his enemies under his feet."[45]

Is this speech at Pisidian Antioch genuinely Pauline? The point that might particularly give us pause is the statement in it that, after his resurrection, Jesus "for many days appeared to those who came up with him from Galilee to Jerusalem, who are now his witnesses to the people."[46] Here at least Luke is reproducing the general terms of the apostolic preaching rather than Paul's distinctive witness: we may be sure that at this point Paul would say, and indeed did say, "Last of all... he appeared also to me."[47]

But the Pauline authenticity of the speech is not put in question by the emphasis which it lays on the Davidic motif, in contrast to the absence of such emphasis in Paul's letters. This is synagogue evangelism, not Christian instruction, and Paul could have taken the cue for his address from the contents of one or the other of the scripture lessons for the day.[48]

Of the *testimonia* adduced thus far, two have unmistakable reference to the king of Israel and the other (Isa 55:3) explicitly mentions David. Ps 2:7 and Ps 110:1 both preserve divine oracles of reassurance and victory addressed to the king, perhaps forming part of the enthronement liturgy. The former certainly[49] and the latter probably[50] were understood as messianic before the beginning of the Christian era; when Jesus was identified with the Messiah, therefore, it was a foregone conclusion that they should be interpreted with reference to him. The same is true of the mention of the covenant mercies promised to David in Isa 55:3. Once Jesus was acknowledged to be the son of David *par excellence,* these covenant mercies were seen to be secured in him, the more so if the end-time David of that context, given as "a witness to the peoples,"[51] was recognized to be the same person as the suffering and triumphant Servant of chapters 42–53.

Psalm 16, on the other hand, made no reference to any king, and there is no evidence that it was thought of as messianic in any sense before the apostolic age. Its enlistment as a *testimonium* is the result of exclusively Christian insight or inspiration. It was in the light of the Easter event that the appropriateness of the psalmist's confident hope of preservation from death to the resurrection of Jesus was appreciated. Since the psalm was traditionally Davidic, the conclusion was not far to seek that this confident hope was voiced by David through the spirit of prophecy, and came historically true in the experience of great David's greater Son.

IV. The Gentile Mission

There is one further messianic *testimonium* in Acts which will repay attention. Towards the end of the book of Amos there is an oracle relating to the Davidic dynasty which proclaims that, although that dynasty has fallen on evil days, its past glories are nevertheless to be restored. In the heyday of David's imperial power he had extended his sway over the Edomites and other neighboring ethnic groups. These became not only David's vassals but also subjects of Yahweh, whom David worshiped and by whose grace he won his victories.[52] The "shields of the earth" thus belonged to the God of Israel; by his name the subject nations were called.[53] Hence the prophecy of restoration says:

"In that day I will raise up
  the booth of David that is fallen
and repair its breaches,
  and raise up its ruins,

and rebuild it as in the days of old;
that they may possess the remnant of Edom
and all the nations who are called by my name,''
says Yahweh who does this.[54]

The Septuagint rendering of this oracle provides a good example of the spiritualizing tendency of that version. Instead of a program of renewed imperial expansion it presents a picture of religious conversion:

''In that day I will raise up David's fallen tent
and rebuild its wreckage
and raise up its ruins,
and rebuild it as in the days of old;
that the remnant of mankind may seek out,
even all the nations on whom my name has been called,''
says the Lord who does this.

The most crucial change here is the vocalization of *'dm* as *'ādām* ('mankind') instead of *'ĕdōm* ('Edom'); this has changed the whole tone of the oracle. Here it is reinterpreted so as to convey a promise like that of Isa 55:3–4, where the fulfillment of the covenant mercies promised to David brings hope for the world at large, in keeping with Israel's mission to impart the knowledge of the true God to her neighbors. The reading of the verb *yîr^{e}šû* ('may possess') as *yidr^{e}šû* ('may seek') may have been due to a scribal slip, but it helps the reinterpretation. Whereas ''the remnant of Edom'' was the object of the verb ''may possess'' in the original text,[55] ''the remnant of mankind'' becomes the subject of the verb ''may seek out'' in the Greek version, while the unexpressed object of this verb is probably to be understood as ''me'' (the Lord). The point of the Greek version then is that, thanks to the witness of Israel, the nations will seek the God of Israel and become his subjects.

The Hebrew text was used as a *testimonium* in the Damascus Document, where ''the booth of David'' is identified with ''the booth of the king'' in Amos 5:26 (a revocalization of ''Sakkuth your king'') and the two oracles together are interpreted of the restoration of the law to its place of supremacy in the assembly of the saints (the Qumran community).[56] This denudes it of all messianic significance in the proper sense.

The Greek text is used as a *testimonium* in Luke's account of the Council of Jerusalem. Here the apostles and elders meet to consider the terms on which Gentile believers in Jesus may be enrolled among the people of God in this new age. They listen to arguments on this side and that, until James the Just sums up the sense of the meeting. He expresses approval of Peter's exhortation, based on personal experience, not to impose on the Gentiles conditions which God himself had manifestly not required, for ''with this,'' he says, ''the words of the prophets agree, as it is written:

'After this I will return,
and rebuild David's fallen tent;

I will rebuild its ruins
and I will set it up,
that the rest of mankind may seek the Lord,
even all the Gentiles who are called by my name,'
says the Lord, who has made these things known
from of old.''[57]

Apart from minor changes at the beginning and the end of the quotation,[58] this is essentially the Septuagint rendering. Now the object sought by the remnant of mankind is made explicit: it is the Lord. But now the rebuilding of David's fallen tent has a more precise relevance than was possible for the pre-Christian Greek translator and spiritualizer. The ''remnant of mankind,'' i.e., the non-Jewish nations, by hearing and obeying the gospel of Christ, are yielding allegiance to the Son of David. The Son of David is extending his sovereignty over a wider empire than David himself ever controlled, and extending it by the persuasion of love, not by force of arms. This and similar Old Testament oracles are now receiving a more detailed and literal fulfillment than either the Hebrew prophets or even their Greek interpreters could have envisaged.[59]

V. A Davidic Compilation

These messianic *testimonia* in Acts do not stand in isolation from one another. They bear witness to the exegetical activity which was vigorously pursued in the early church—more particularly, to the compilation of a body of texts linked in their original setting by a common reference to David and his line (whether expressly or by implication) and in their new setting by their appropriateness to the saving work accomplished by Jesus, the Son of David, both in his earthly experience and in its far-reaching sequel. This compilation of Davidic *testimonia* is attested in other New Testament documents,[60] but pre-eminently in Luke's nativity narrative and in the speeches in Acts. So basic is it in the Lucan writings that references to David's enemies in the Psalter can be applied, without any need for justifying argument, to the enemies of Jesus—whether to Judas Iscariot[61] or to ''Herod and Pontius Pilate, with the Gentiles and the peoples of Israel.''[62]

If, as I have argued elsewhere,[63] the speeches in Acts are not Lucan compositions *in toto,* but are based on material substantially earlier than Luke's own literary activity, then this Davidic strand of Christian interpretation is so much the more primitive: it represents one of several creative lines of Old Testament exegesis to which the Christ-event gave rise in the earliest days of the church's existence.[64]

NOTES

1. Cf. Mark 10:47–48; Matt 15:22.
2. Mark 12:35–37.
3. Mark 2:25–26; cf. 1 Sam 21:1–6.

4. Mark 14:61–62.
5. Rom 1:3.
6. Paul had access to a corpus of Davidic-Messiah *testimonia* but made little use of it. In Rom 15:12 he quotes Isa 11:10, a prophecy regarding the "root of Jesse," with reference to the Gentile mission rather than to the identity of Jesus. In v 9 he has similarly quoted Ps 18:49 = 2 Sam 22:50 without the contextual mention of David. The phrase "descended from David" in 2 Tim 2:8 is repeated from Rom 1:3.
7. *Pss Sol* 17:5–36.
8. Luke 2:11.
9. Luke 1:26–27.
10. Matt 1:1–16,20.
11. Luke 1:5.
12. Luke 1:32–33.
13. Isa 9:6–7.
14. Luke 1:67–79.
15. Luke 2:10–11.
16. Luke 2:1–5. In Matt 2:5–6 the birth in Bethlehem is viewed as fulfilling the oracle of Mic 5:2.
17. Luke 3:23–38; contrast Matt 1:6ff. For Nathan (Luke 3:31) cf. 2 Sam 5:14; 1 Chr 3:5.
18. Luke 3:27 (cf. Matt 1:12), where "rhesa" probably represents Aram. *rēšā'* 'prince,' the title of Zerubbabel, not a separate name.
19. Luke 18:38–39.
20. Luke 19:38, as against Mark 11:9–10. But Luke replaces Mark's "Blessed is he who comes . . ." with "Blessed is the King who comes. . . ."
21. Acts 2:16–28, especially vv 25–28. The superscription in MT and LXX alike designate Psalm 16 (LXX 15) as Davidic.
22. 2 Sam 23:2.
23. Acts 2:29.
24. 1 Pet 1:11.
25. Acts 2:31.
26. Mark 12:35–37.
27. Acts 2:33–36.
28. Cf. Heb 1:3, etc.; 1 Pet 3:22.
29. Cf. J. A. T. Robinson, "The Most Primitive Christology of All?" in *Twelve New Testament Studies* (London: SCM, 1962): 139ff.
30. Acts 13:16–41.
31. G. E. Wright, *God Who Acts* (London: SCM, 1952): 70–81.
32. Ps 78:70–71.
33. Ps 78:67–72.
34. Acts 13:23.
35. Cf. Acts 1:22; 10:37.
36. The first two verses of Psalm 2 are quoted and interpreted in Acts 4:25–28; cf. p. 15 with n. 62 below.
37. Acts 13:33.
38. Acts 13:22.
39. Luke 3:22 (cf. *RSV* margin).
40. Acts 10:38.
41. Rom 1:4; cf. Mark 9:1.
42. 2 Cor 13:4.
43. Acts 13:35.
44. Acts 13:34.
45. In fulfillment of Ps 110:1.
46. Acts 13:31.
47. 1 Cor 15:8.
48. For the reading of "the law and the prophets" see Acts 13:15.
49. Cf. *Pss Sol* 17:26, where Ps 2:9 is applied to the expected Davidic king.
50. There are messianic overtones, drawn from Psalm 110, in the proclamation of Simon as "leader and high priest forever" in 1 Macc 14:41ff.
51. Isa 55:4.

52. Ps 18:43–50.
53. Ps 47:3,9.
54. Amos 9:11–12.
55. This is plain from the presence before *šᵉʾērît* ('remnant') of the accusative prefix *'et,* to which LXX here offers no equivalent.
56. CD 7:14ff.
57. Acts 15:16–18.
58. These minor changes may be the result of conflation of *testimonia* in a collection; the wording at the beginning of the quotation resembles that of Jer 12:15, and the wording at the end resembles that of Isa 45:21.
59. C. C. Torrey argued that even the MT could have served James' purpose, "since it predicted that 'the tabernacle of David,' i.e., the church of the Messiah, would 'gain possession of all the nations which are called by the name [of the God of Israel]' " (*The Composition and Date of Acts* [Cambridge, MA: Harvard University, 1916]: 38–39).
60. Cf. Rev 5:5; 22:16; Heb 1:5,13; 5:5–6. The ascription to Jesus of the perpetual priesthood of Melchizedek's order announced in Ps 110:4 (an ascription not found in the New Testament outside Hebrews) is based on the recognition that the oracle in that verse must be addressed to the same person as the oracle in v 1 (i.e., the Davidic king).
61. Cf. the quotation in Acts 1:20 of Ps 69:25 and Ps 109:8 (both traditionally Davidic psalms). For other *testimonia* drawn from Psalm 69, see John 2:17; Rom 15:3.
62. Acts 4:27, interpreting Ps 2:1–2.
63. F. F. Bruce, *The Acts of the Apostles* (London: Tyndale, 1951): 18ff.
64. Cf. C. H. Dodd, *The Apostolic Preaching and its Developments* (London: Hodder & Stoughton, 1944): 17ff.; *According to the Scriptures* (London: Nisbet, 1952): 28ff., 104–06, *et passim.*

2

HEBREW TRANSLATIONS OF THE LORD'S PRAYER: AN HISTORICAL SURVEY

JEAN CARMIGNAC

I. The Sources

Faced with the proposition of studying all Hebrew versions of the Lord's Prayer, our first task is to locate the various translations. The following are the main avenues that have been explored.

1. The first place to look is obviously the Hebrew versions of Matthew, the gospel in which the standard text of the prayer occurs (6:9–13). The list I have compiled is almost certainly not complete, but it covers every major attempt at rendering the whole gospel into Hebrew. My list of translators (or editors) is as follows: Shem Tob ben Shafrut, Sebastian Münster, Jean Cinqarbres, Jehan du Tillet, Marco Marini(?), Elias Hutter, Domenico Gerosolimitano, Georg Mayr, Giovanni-Battista Jona, William Robertson, Rudolph Bernhard, Johannes Kemper, Simon Rosenbaum, Ezekiel Raḥabi, Richard Caddick, Thomas Yeates, The London Society for Promoting Christianity amongst the Jews, William Greenfield, Robert Young, Elias Sołoweyczyk, Franz Delitzsch, Isaac Salkinson and J. M. Paul Bauchet. Though many of these translations have never been published, quite a number have gone into second and later editions which have, in some cases, been significantly revised.

Next should be mentioned the harmonies that reduce all four gospels to a continuous narrative. Of these I have noted translations by Thomas Lydyat, Isaac-Louis Caignon and Alfred Resch.

Included last in this section are translations of the shorter version of the Lord's Prayer in Luke 11:2–4. As this paper is concerned with the standard form of the prayer, our attention will be limited to those parts of it in Luke which agree with Matthew. There is, however, a further complication arising from the fact that before the appearance of critical editions (a fairly recent phenomenon) translators mostly relied on the *textus receptus,* which falsifies the version in Luke by filling it out with interpolations from Matthew.

We should note here that some translations of Matthew into Hebrew seem to be no longer extant. Among the lost versions must be counted those by Simon

Atumanos, Erasmus-Oswald Schreckenfuchs, Hotaris, Christian-Gottlieb Unger and one by an anonymous professor at Lausanne c. 1725.

2. As the most important of all Christian prayers the Our Father may perhaps be sought in the Hebrew translations of various prayer books such as *Le pieux hébraïsant* by Paul-Louis-Bernard Drach. Unfortunately books like this are often published anonymously and tracking them down in catalogues can be a monumental task. Furthermore, since many of these translations exist only in manuscripts which have never been published, investigations (whether they are in private or in public libraries) can be seriously hampered, on the one hand because of inadequate cataloguing, and on the other because of the small degree of importance attached to them. As a result important translations remain buried in spite of considerable and protracted efforts on my part to rediscover them.

3. Primers and other Books of Hours form a particular class of these works of devotion. Chief among these is the Officium Parvum or Little Office of Our Lady which for many centuries enjoyed a particular vogue among Catholics. Other devotions of a similar nature would include, for instance, the Little Office of the Sacred Heart and the many Little Offices of particular saints. Translations of these into Hebrew were frequently attempted, but since they are based on the public liturgical office many of them follow the pattern of the Roman office in which the Lord's Prayer is said *sub silentio* and many of these primers simply omit the rest of the words. The following is far from being a complete list of these Little Offices, and in fact I doubt if a complete list can ever be drawn up. The ones of which I have made use are those translated by Cesare Mainardi (of Vallombrosa), Francesco Donati, Honoratus Peyer im Hof (in the library of St. Gall), Dei Fioghi, Gennaro Sisti and J. M. Lara.

4. The Book of Common Prayer has been translated into Hebrew for the benefit of converts to Anglicanism, and each of these translations repeats the Lord's Prayer several times, sometimes with and sometimes without the doxology. The three translations that I know are those made by Abraham ben Jacob ha-Levi, Christian-Hermann-Friedrich Bialloblotzky and Christian Czerskier.

5. Since the recent permission for them to say mass in Hebrew, Catholic priests in Israel have produced translations that naturally include the Lord's Prayer, and there are others still in preparation according to Pinchas Lapide (*Hebräisch in der Kirchen* [Neukirchen: Neukirchener Verlag, 1976]: 110–20).

6. From the sixteenth century onward a number of catechisms (Catholic, Protestant and Anglican) have been translated into Hebrew.[1] All of these contain the Lord's Prayer, and catalogues of them may be found in J. C. Wolf, *Bibliotheca Hebraica* 1 (Hamburg and Leipzig: Liebezeit, 1715): 1065–67; *The British Museum: General Catalogue of Printed Books* 35, cols. 328–44; and *The Na-*

tional Union Catalog, Pre-1956 Imprints 99, pp. 87–103. In spite of these catalogues it is difficult to draw up a complete list and even more difficult to find the books themselves, even in major libraries. Among those to which I have had access are the catechisms translated by I. Tremellius, J. Claius, C. Neander, G. Mayr, T. Ingmethorpe and G. B. Jona.

7. As far as I know, there have been only two attempts at a Life of Christ in Hebrew: P. Levertoff and J. Klausner. Only the second translated the Lord's Prayer.[2]

8. There is still a possibility that the Lord's Prayer in Hebrew may occur in some of the controversial works published by Jews and Christians; a lot of this material, however, comes out in very small editions and sometimes so badly printed as to be nearly illegible. The possibility of anyone even attempting to list all these tracts would be seriously hampered by the fact that many libraries have never catalogued their Hebrew titles. The most useful references for the moment will be found under "Polemics and Polemical Literature" in the *Encyclopaedia Judaica* 1 (Jerusalem: Keter, 1972): 690. This is an area, however, where I am fully aware of the gaps in my information.

9. Hebrew grammars often provide Old Testament passages for exercise, and those by Christians sometimes include Hebrew versions of the Lord's Prayer. The number of Hebrew grammars by Christians is very considerable; see *The Jewish Encyclopedia* 6 (New York: Funk & Wagnalls, 1904): 73–77. So far I have consulted all Hebrew grammars published earlier than 1608 that are held by the Bibliothèque Nationale in Paris. Most of them use already existing translations, but there are some grammars that are not in the Bibliothèque Nationale, and there are probably others that have never been printed: consequently I may well have missed several translations that could be of particular interest.

10. Some MSS have a translation of the Lord's Prayer inserted by the copyist or even by a reader. As these MSS are often quite old, these translations can be particularly valuable, and they show that a knowledge of Hebrew was not as rare as we have been led to think among medieval Christians.[3] However, so many MSS are either inadequately catalogued or not catalogued at all that we can expect discoveries to go on being made in this group for some time to come.

11. Among the most obvious places to look are those books that give the Lord's Prayer in as many translations as possible. The earliest of these was published by Conrad Gesner in 1555. Most such books include a version in Hebrew; in fact, quite a number give several, and often provide examples written in "rabbinic" or in "samaritan" characters. These specimens of the Lord's Prayer in a variety of languages are a commonplace, and a great many catalogues have been published that aim at giving as complete a list as possible.[4] All these collections, however, are much less helpful than one might think, as their authors know as much

Hebrew as they do of the other 100, 200, 500 or 1,200 languages they display, and so they usually include translations that have already been published. In addition to introducing several misprints, they hardly ever give a reference to the source of the translation.

In making this survey of the various avenues I have explored in order to collect as many Hebrew versions as possible of the Lord's Prayer,[5] I have indicated the areas where I am aware of gaps in my information. If these remain unfilled for the moment, it is due more to lack of time than to want of trying. May I take this opportunity to assure all readers how much I should like to hear from them if they know of any other translations or if they happen to come across any in the future. A first history of these translations is bound to be incomplete, and I would very much like one day to bring it up to date. Anyone able to supplement the work already done will earn my deepest gratitude. Meanwhile, I remind readers that this is only a first stage of the survey and I crave their indulgence for all its lacunae.

II. TEXTS

1. Ninth Century

Düsseldorf, Landes- und Stadtbibliothek, D1, folio 216vo

According to H. Dausend,[6] this MS, which is a sacramentary coming from Essen, was copied (as regards folios 14–215) during the pontificate of Adrian II (864–872), but from folio 216 the date is slightly later. The errors that have crept into the Latin transcription of the Lord's Prayer in Hebrew show that neither the transcription nor the translation can be by the scribe, who must have been copying an earlier text. P. Lapide suggests[7] that this translation might have been made in the region around Lyons c. 835, the date when Agobard, bishop of Lyons, complained about Jewish influence,[8] or alternatively that it might have been made by Bodo,[9] who had been deacon at the court of Louis I the Pious (= the Débonnaire) and who, having learned Hebrew, became a Jew in 839. The text of the transcription in Latin was edited by Robert von Nostitz-Rieneck (*ZKT* 12 [1888]: 728–33) and by Joseph Schulte (*BZ* 6 [1908]: 48).[10]

Latin text:	In Hebrew characters:
Auinu . sebassamaim .	אבינו שבשמים
cudessatehe . semah .	קודש תהיה שמך
tauo . Bemalchuthah .	תבוא במלכותך
tehe . rokonagkauassa .	תהיה רצונך
amaim . uba . arez .	כבשמים ובארץ
Lah . hemehenu . thamia . tenlanu . haggeon	לחמנו תמיד תן לנו היום

2. Ninth and Tenth Centuries

Hospital zu Cues bei Bernkastel an der Mosel, *Psalterium Cusanum,* folio 64

The MSS bequeathed by Nicolas Cardinal de Cusa to the Hospital of this town have been studied by F. X. Kraus[11] and J. Marx.[12] The one in which we are interested is a psalter which has been described by C. Hamann.[13] Kraus dates the psalter to the ninth century, Hamann to the early tenth, while Marx says it could be either ninth or tenth. There are two points in which I would disagree with Hamann in his restoration of the Hebrew text: (1) Where the MS reads *IBUA* (1. 3) he corrects to *tbw'*. However, though the masculine form *ybw'* ('may it come') does not agree with the feminine *mlkwtk* ('your kingdom') this is a mistake that sixteen other translators have made (see p. 61). The Latin scribe might have misread *T* as *I*, but, as there is no way of telling whether he did or not, it seems better to take the reading as it stands. (2) Following the suggestion of Hermann Strack, Hamann inserts *lb'ly* after *mnyḥym* and so produces a reading similar to that published later in 1537 by Sebastian Münster. It seems to me more probable, however, that the translator into Hebrew wrote *ḥy(y)bynw* ('the offenders against us'), and that a copyist has read this as *ḥwbwtynw,* his eye having been misled by the appearance of this word in the preceding stich. This remains a hypothesis, whatever its degree of probability, and it should not prevent the text from being printed as it stands in the MS.

Latin text:	In Hebrew characters:
ABINU SEBACAMAIM	אבינו שבשמים
ACADEC AT SIMAK	הקדש את שמך
IBUA MALCOTHAK	יבוא מלכותך
VIHI HEPHZHAK	ויהי חפצך
KABASSAMAIN VBA ARES	כבשמים ובארץ
LEHEM SILANV TAMID TENLANV HIC IOM	לחם שלנו תמיד תן לנו היום
VAHANNA HLANV HOBOTINV	והנח לנו חובותינו
KAMOSEANV MANIHIM HOBOTINV	כמו שאנו מניחים חובותינו
VAALTO LIKAOTANV BINITSEIOM	ואל תוליך אותנו בנסיון
VAATSILINV MI RE	והצילנו מרע

3. and 4. Twelfth and Thirteenth Centuries

Oxford, Bodleian, Or 62 (olim 159) folio 3

In his *Catalogue of the Hebrew Manuscripts in the Bodleian Library* 1 (Oxford: Clarendon, 1886): cols. 14–15, no. 88, Adolf Neubauer describes this MS as "Ezekiel with interlinear translation and another in the margin . . . squ(are) char(acters) (not a Jew's hand) with vowel points; the Latin char(acters) seem to be of the 12th century." However, in the copy of the catalogue annotated by Sir Edmund Craster, who was Librarian of the Bodleian from 1931 to 1945, a note in the margin opposite "12th" reads "probably 13th century."[14] At the end[15] of the MS there is added a translation of the Lord's Prayer into Hebrew, but although the hand is similar to that of the MS they are not by the same writer. A later hand has made corrections to the Lord's Prayer and then made a second copy of it incorporating not only these corrections but others as well. It is obvious that each of the two translators has worked from the Latin and has been influenced by its forms, e.g.: "regnum" (neuter), "voluntas" (feminine), "sicut et nos," "nos inducas.'' They would seem to belong to the same ''school'' as the copyist of the MS itself.

First text:

אבינו אשר בשמים
יקדש שמך
יבא מלכתך
יהא חפצך
כאשר בשמים ובארץ
לחמנו יום יום תן לנו היום
ונח לנו את־חובותינו
כאשר ואנו נוחנו לחיבותינו
ואל אנו הבאת בנסיון
כי הצילנו מרעה אמן

Second text:

אבינו אשר בשמים
יתקדש שמך
יבא מלכותך
תעשה חפצך
כאשר בשמים ובארץ
לחמנו יום יום תן לנו היום
וסלח לנו את־חובותינו
כאשר ואנו מניחים לחובינו
ואל אנו תביא בנסיון
אבל הצילנו מרעה

5. Fourteenth Century (?)

Oxford, Bodleian, Hebr. f 15, document 1, folio 356

This is a Jewish apologetic work in Hebrew that cites gospel passages in order to refute them. It begins with the invocation of Ps 51:14: ''You, O Lord, will open my lips, and my mouth shall declare your praise,'' and then immediately after it adds the Lord's Prayer, which a later hand has provided (in the margin) with a rather unusual doxology.

The MS is a collection of disparate documents. In their *Catalogue of the Hebrew Manuscripts in the Bodleian Library* (Oxford: Clarendon, 1906) Adolf Neubauer and A. E. Cowley say about the third of these documents (vol. 2, cols. 202–03, no. 2790), which is dated 1525, that it is written in ''modern Ital(ian) curs(ive) char(acters),'' while the first document (the one with the Lord's Prayer) is written in ''old Ital(ian) curs(ive) char(acters).'' On this basis we might assign it roughly to the 14th century. The Italian provenance is confirmed by the title of the paragraph which concerns us: *wzh nwsḥ hmyśśh* ('This is the text of the Missa'). An identical translation is given in the Hebrew grammar published by Johannes Setzerius Lauchensis at Haguenau ex Academia Thomae Anshelmi (n.d.). The translations (see below, texts 10 and 11) given in München Clm 28.233 and by Aldo Manuzio are very similar.

אבינו שבשמים
יתקדש שמך
יבא מלכותך
יעשה רצונך
כבשמים גם בארץ
לחמנו התמידי תן לנו היום
ומחול לנו אשמתנו
כאשר אנחנו מוחלים לאשר אשמו לנו
ואל תביאנו לידי נסיון
אבל תצילנו מרעה אמן

שמלכותך שלך והכח והוד וההדר לעולם ועד עולם[16] אמן

6. C. 1380

Shem Tob ben Isaac ben Shafrut, *Eben Boḥan*

The number of copies in manuscript of Shem Tob ben Shafrut's major work, entitled *Eben Boḥan,* is fairly large,[17] but no critical edition of it has yet appeared. In chap. 12 he gives a translation of the entire Gospel of Matthew, including, therefore, the Lord's Prayer. The work was completed in Spain c. 1380 and revised by the author in 1385 and again c. 1400.[18] As I have been able to consult only three MSS, the text given here is not definitive. The MSS I have seen are: (1) Leiden, Cod. Or. 4766 (= Hebr. 28), p. 421; (2) Oxford, Bodleian, OPP. ADD. 4° 72, folio 163vo; (3) Oxford, Bodleian, MICH 119, folio 69ro. I shall refer to these MSS as: L (= Leiden), O (= Bodleian, OPP), M (= Bodleian, MICH). As L is generally considered the best, I give its text and note any variants from it by the other two MSS.

אבינו שבשמים[19]
יתקדש שמך
ויתברך מלכותך
רצונך יהיה עשוי
בשמים ובארץ
לחמנו תמידי[20] תן היום לנו[21]
ומחול[22] חטאתינו
כאשר אנחנו מוחלים לחוטאים לנו
ואל תביאנו לידי נסיון
ושמרנו מכל רע אמן

7. C. 1400

Georges de Rahyn: Tours, Bibliothèque Municipale, no. 95, folio 72ro

Among the MSS in the library of Tours are those collected by a rather interesting personality, Georges d'Esclavonie.[23] Born at Rahyn in Dalmatia, he went to study in Paris, where he remained from 1381 until 1403; he was then appointed Canon Penitentiary at Tours, where he died 13 May 1416. In a copy of Jerome's Latin version of the psalter he wrote out a translation of the Lord's Prayer in Hebrew and added various notes in Croatian for which he used the Glagolitic script. The Lord's Prayer is given twice—first in Latin characters, then in Hebrew. It is almost certain that Georges de Rahyn was not the translator, and the version he gives is probably one that was in use toward the end of the fourteenth century. Moreover, the Latin transcription does not always correspond with the Hebrew, and the Hebrew, as he gives it, includes a number of obvious mistakes.

Latin text:	Hebrew text:
Abynu schaschamaym	אבינו שבשמים
tythquadasch schymcha	תתקדש שמך
ybounu malchuscha (malchuthesa[24]*)*	יבואנו מלכותך
iehi ratzonach	יהי רצונך

kabaschamaym bearetz . . .	כבשמים בארץ . . .
Lachmenu temydi ten lanu hayom	לחמנו תמידי תן לנו היום. . .
uslach lanu chobothenu	וסלח לנו חובותינו
kemo scheanu solchym lechaiabanu	כמו שאנו סולחים לחייבנו
veal tebyenu bnisáyon	ואל תביאנו בניסיון
abal chàlcenu meraah Amen	אבל חלצנו מרעה

8. Fifteenth Century

Vaticano Ebraico 100, folio 8vo–9ro

This Vatican MS,[25] which contains the four gospels (and so includes the Lord's Prayer), is particularly interesting; its author lived in Crete during the fifteenth century, and translated the gospels into Hebrew from a Catalan original. That he was proficient in Hebrew is perfectly clear, and yet the text exhibits a number of flagrant mistakes. P. Lapide is driven to suppose a situation in which a Jew, requested (or even forced) by a Christian to produce a translation, has deliberately sabotaged his own work. It is true, however, that there does seem some uncertainty whether this MS is the original holograph or only a later copy.

אבינו שבשמים
שמך יהיה מקודש שהוא קדוש
ויבא למלכותך
רצונך תעשה
בשמים ובארץ
תן לנו לחם כל יום שהוא מסעד חיינו
והנח לנו חובותינו
כי אנחנו מניחים למחוייבינו
ואל תנהיגנו בנסיון
אבל תשמרנו מכל רע אמן

9. 1477

Peter Schwar(t)z (= Petrus Nigri, sometimes given as Petrus Niger): München, Bayerische Staatsbibliothek, Clm 23.818, folio 330vo

Petrus Nigri was a Dominican, possibly of Jewish descent.[26] In 1476–77 he composed an *Explanation of the Psalms* in Latin, at the end of which he appended translations into Hebrew (but written in Latin characters) of the Benedictus, the Nunc Dimittis, the Magnificat, the Pater, the Ave Maria, the Credo and the Gloria Patri. It is not clear if he was the translator of all of these, or whether he merely copied them; he may even have collected them from different sources. At all events the translation he gives of the Lord's Prayer was later to influence Kilian Leib (see text 15).

Latin text:	In Hebrew characters:
Abinu asscher baschamaim	אבינו אשר בשמים
niqdasch schimcha	נקדש שמך
kische iabo malchutcha	כי שיבוא מלכותך
ihjeh rezoncha	יהיה רצונך

ken baschamaim ken baarez	כן בשמים כן בארץ
lahamenu iom iom ten lanu hajom	לחמנו יום יום תן לנו היום
umhol lanu[27] *hafonotenu*	ומחל לנו עוונותינו
kaasscher anu mohalim onavotenu	כאשר אנו מוחלים עונותינו
ve lo tabinu lemazzah	ולא תביאנו למסה
ki im tinzerennu mikkol[28] *rah Amen*	כי אם תנצרנו מכל רע אמן

10. 1501

München, Bayerische Staatsbibliothek, Clm 28.233, folio 230 vo

This particular page of the MS on which the Lord's Prayer appears in Hebrew is dated 1501. The MS was part of the library of the humanist Kaspar Amman. The text is clearly linked to that of Bodleian Hebr. f 15 (see text 5).

אבינו שבשמים
יתקדש שמך
יבא מלכותך
יעשה רצונך
כבשמים ובארץ
לחמינו הרמידי[29] תן לנו היום
ומחול לנו אשמתינו (חובותינו)
כאשר אנחנו מוחלים לאשר אשמו לנו
ואל תביאנו לידי נסיון
אבל הצילינו מרע אמן

11. October 1507

Aldo Manuzio

Aldo Manuzio (b. 1446/47, d. 1515)[30] was a Venetian printer who published a Latin grammar in February 1502 (= 1501 in the Venetian calendar). At the end he added an ''Introductio perbrevis ad hebraicam linguam,'' and this he also added at the end of the Greek grammar by Constantin Lascaris which he published in 1503. He republished them in October 1507 with the title *Aldi Manutii Romani Institutionum Grammaticarum Libri Quatuor,* and in this, as an exercise for the reader, he introduced the Lord's Prayer in Hebrew. Lacking a Hebrew font in movable type, he had a xylograph produced which provides, above each Hebrew word, both its pronunciation and its Latin translation. This short Hebrew grammar went through many editions, a new one appearing as early as April 1508; sometimes it was published on its own and sometimes as an appendix to either the Latin or the Greek grammar.

François Tissard and the Paris printer, Gilles de Gourmont,[31] who were in the habit of forging Aldine editions, brought out their own pirated version of the grammar dated 29 January 1508. In this edition the only differences from the authentic Aldine lie in the vocalization, which in some places they have changed for the better but in others for the worse. This Paris edition lacks a title and begins with a letter from Franciscus Tissardus *ad Franciscum Valesium*, which is followed immediately by a dialogue in which the participants are called

Prothumopatris and Phronimus. Like the original Aldine, the Tissard text also went through many editions, and was itself pirated by other printers. Among this proliferation of grammars the Aldine version of the Lord's Prayer turns up in the following: Agathius Guidacer(i)us, *Grammatica Hebraicae Linguae* (n.d.; probably c. 1520); the Greek grammar of Lascaris with the rudiments of Hebrew (Venice: Melchior Sessa and Petrus de Ravanis, 17 Oct. 1521); the Aldo Manuzio, *Institutionum Grammaticarum Libri Quatuor* (Venice: Franciscus Bindoni and Maphaeus [*sic*] Pasini, August 1538); a new edition of the Greek grammar of Lascaris with the rudiments of Hebrew and the Lord's Prayer (Basel: Jean Oporin, June 1547); Charles Estienne, *Alphabetum Hebraicum* (Paris, 1559). The Aldine Lord's Prayer is also given in Latin transcription in the MS that once belonged to the library of Joannes Eck, a parish priest who was also professor at and rector of the Ingoldstadt University from 1510 to 1543 (this is now codex MS 800 [4th document], folio 78vo in the Universitätsbibliothek of Munich, and it may well be in Eck's own handwriting).

This Aldine Lord's Prayer is almost identical with that given in Bodleian Hebr. f 15 (text 5); the only differences occur in stich 9, which has been made to correspond more closely to the Latin "et ne nos inducas in tentationem."

אבינו שבשמים
יתקדש שמך
יבא מלכותך
יעשה רצונך
כבשמים גם בארץ
לחמינו התמידי תן לנו היום
ומחול לנו אשמותינו
כאשר אנחנו מוחלים לאשר אשמו לנו
ואל אותנו תביא לנסיון
אבל הצילנו מרעה אמן

12. 8 March 1508

Johann Pfefferkorn

What is probably the only copy of this broadsheet in the world now belongs to the Niedersächsische Staats- und Universitätsbibliothek at Göttingen, where it is shelfmarked "2° Theol pol 564/81." Printed by Johann Landen at Cologne and dated 8 March 1508, it gives translations into Hebrew of the Pater, Ave Maria and Credo, together with interlinear transcription and Latin back-translation. The author leaves us in no doubt about his identity: "Hoc opus editum a Johanne pefferkorn (*sic*) olim iudeo nunc christiano anno mee (*sic*) regenerationis tercio." Pfefferkorn was born 1469 and died sometime after 1521 (see *Encyclopaedia Judaica* 13, cols. 355–57). His translation has many points of originality, but it must have been the typesetter who introduced the confusion between *wb'rṣ* and *wb'ryz* (1. 5).

אבינו אשר אתה בשמים
יתקדש שמך

לבא אתנו מלכותך
ריצונך יעשה
כבשמים ובאריז (= ובארץ)
לחם התמידים תן אתנו היום
ומחל לנו אשמתנו
כאשר אנחנו מחלים לחייבין
ואל תנהלנו לניסיון
רק גאל אתנו מכל רע אמן

13. 1513

Matthäus Adrianus

According to J. and B. Prijs,[32] an edition of the *Introductio utilissima hebraice discere cupientibus* by Aldo Manuzio was brought out at Basel by J. Froben in 1518, dated 15 March; it was republished in February 1520. In these editions there is added to the original text, "Oratio dominica, Angelica salutatio, Salve regina. Hebraice. Mattheo Adriano equite aurato interprete." According to Giambernardo De-Rossi,[33] an earlier edition had been brought out at Tübingen in 1513 entitled "Oratio Dominica, Magnificat, Symbolum Apostolorum, aliaeque Preces heb. et lat. interprete Matthaeo Adriano." I have not so far been able to consult any of these editions, but the Hebrew version of the Lord's Prayer was reprinted (using the Froben title) in an *Alphabetum Hebraicum* published by Petrus Vidovaeus at Paris in 1531, and again in another *Alphabetum Hebraicum* published by Joannes Tornaesius at Lyons in 1549.

Matthäus Adrianus[34] was a Spanish Jew who, having become Christian, was appointed professor of Hebrew at Heidelberg, Louvain and Wittenberg. He greatly helped to spread the knowledge of Hebrew in germanic countries. A meticulous copy of Matthäus Adrianus' version was made soon after 1552 by Mariano Vittorio in MS 8856 of the Bibliothèque de l'Arsenal at Paris (folio 7 vo); it is exact down to the smallest details of spelling. The same version was adopted by Wigandus Happellius in his *Linguae Sanctae Canones Grammatici* (Basel: T. Guerin, 1561).

אבינו שבשמים
יתקדש שמך
יבא מלכותך
יהי רצונך
כבשמים ובארץ
לחמינו תמידי תן לנו היום
והנח לנו חובותינו
כמו שאנו מניחים חובינו
ואל תביאנו בנסיון
אלא הצלנו מֵרע אמן

14. May 1514

Johann Boeschenstein

Johann Boeschenstein (b. 1472, d. 1532)[35] published a pamphlet dated "Auguste (= Augsburg) ex officina Erhardi oeglin (*sic*) mense Maio Anno

M.D.XIIII (*sic*).'' It has no particular title and begins with the words, ''bšm 'rb'h 'wtywt'' ('in the name of the tetragrammaton,' lit. 'the four letters'), and continues, ''Contenta in hoc libello nuper a Ioanne boeschenstein esslingensi edita: Elementale introductorium in hebreas litteras teutonice et hebraice legendas. Decem precepta Exodi XX. Oratio dominica Math VI, Luce XI. Salutatio angelica Luce primo. Simbolum apostolorum. Canticum Marie Luce I. Canticum Simeonis Luce 2. An(tiphona) Veni Sancte. An(tiphona) Salve regina. Canticum zacbarie (*sic*) Luce I.'' The Lord's Prayer in Hebrew is printed on page B2 (*sic*), and this identical translation also occurs in J. Boeschenstein's more formal Hebrew grammar, *Hebraicae Grammaticae institutiones,* published in December 1518.

אבינו שבשמים
יתקדש שמך
תבא מלכותך
יהי רצנך
כבשמים ובארץ
לחמינו תמידי תן לנו היום
ומחול לנו חובותינו
כמו שאנו מוחלים חובינו
ואל תביאנו בניסיון
אלא היו[36] הצלינו מרע אמן

15. C. 1516–1520

Kilian Leib(?): Berlin, Staatsbibliothek Preussischer Kulturbesitz, Orientalabteilung, MS Or. Oct. 148, folio 130ro

The contents of this MS[37] are: (a) a Passover ritual (folios 1 to 15ro); (b) extracts from the Talmud (folios 15vo to 17vo); (c) the grammar of Qimḥi in Hebrew with a German translation (folios 24 to 120); (d) Hebrew translations of the following: Grace before meals, Pater, Ave Maria, Credo, Magnificat, Nunc Dimittis and Benedictus (folios 126–132). On folio 120vo at the end of Qimḥi's grammar the translator gives his name as Kilian Leib.[38] Leib was the prior of Rebdorf; he was born 23 February 1471 at Ochsenfurt am Main, entered the monastery in 1486, became prior in 1503 and died 16 July 1553. The exact date at which he translated the grammar of Qimḥi and made (or copied) these translations of Christian prayers is uncertain, but it could very likely have been between 1516 and 1520, which were the years in which we know he showed an interest in Qimḥi and rabbinic literature.[39] After this date his time would have been fully taken up with his anti-Luther polemics and the work involved in writing first his *Annales Majores*[40] and then his *Annales Minores,*[41] and he would have had little leisure for Hebrew scholarship. The Kilian Leib translation of the Lord's Prayer is clearly based on the one by Petrus Nigri (see text 9), which he has altered only slightly.

אבינו שבשמים (או אשר בשמים)
נקדש שמך
כשיבא מלכותך

יהיה רצונך (או יהי)
כן בשמים כן בארץ
לחמינו יום יום תן לנו היום
ומחול לנו עוננותינו (ענונותינו)
כאשר אנו מוחלים לחטאים נגדינו
ולא תביאנו לניסיון
כי־אם תנצרינו מרע אמן

16. 1520

Sebastian Münster

Sebastian Münster[42] was born 1489 at Ingelheim, and died at Basel 23 May 1552. Having been a student of Elias Levita, his *Epitome Hebraicae Grammaticae* was published in August 1520 by Johann Froben at Basel. Among the exercises he gives are translations into Hebrew of: Pater Noster, Ave Maria, Credo, Magnificat, Nunc Dimittis, Benedictus and Salve Regina. His version of the Lord's Prayer, which is very close to that of Boeschenstein (see text 14), was inserted into the *Precationes aliquot celebriores e sacris Bibliis desumptae ac in studiosorum gratiâ lingua Hebraica, Graeca, et Latina in Enchiridij formulam redactae,* which Sebastian Gryphius published at Lyons in 1538,[43] and which in 1544 Jacques Bogard republished in Paris.[44] The same translation of the Lord's Prayer was also used by Petrus Artopoeus for his *Christiana Elementa Trilinguia,* published in March 1544 at Basel by Henricus Petri. It was also written out by Rupert Re(g)nauld in what is now the Epernay MS 45, folio B, though in the last petition he has written *'bl* in place of *'l'*. An anonymous hand has also copied it (with a few mistakes) in MS 4473 of the Bibliothèque Mazarine at Paris, p. 3.

אבינו שבשמים
יתקדש שמך
תבא מלכותך
יהי רצונך
כבשמים ובארץ
לחמנו תמידי תן לנו היום
ומחול לנו את־חובותינו
כאשר ואנחנו מוחלים לחובינו
ואל תביאנו בנסיון
אלא הצילנו מרע אמן

17. C. 1520 or 1530

Hebrew translation of Matthew by an Italian Jew

Sebastian Münster (see text 16) published *Evangelium secundum Matthaeum in lingua Hebraica, cum versione latina atque succinctis annotationibus Sebastiani Munsteri* (Basel, March 1537; the Lord's Prayer occurs on p. 63). In his epistle dedicating the work to the king of England, Sebastian Münster points out that though he is responsible for the translation into Latin, he has edited the Hebrew from a MS in a tattered condition, which he had acquired "many years ago" from some Jews. He had in fact already made use of this MS when quoting

Matt 5:1–18 in his *Isagoge Elementalis (sic) Perquam Succincta in Hebraicam Linguam,* which Froben had published at Basel in 1535. However, no trace of it appears in any of his earlier works, so it is possible that "many years ago" may mean no more than three or four. This is the first of all translations of Matthew into Hebrew ever to have been printed, and it achieved a phenomenal success.[45]

In 1553 Jehan du Til(l)et, the bishop of Saint-Brieuc, was on pilgrimage in Rome, where he met some Jews who had another MS of this Hebrew version of Matthew. He published it in 1555; it was printed by Martin Le Jeune (together with a translation into Latin made by Jean Mercier) under the title *Evangelium Hebraicum Matthaei, recens e Judaeorum penetralibus erutum, cum interpretatione Latina, ad vulgatam quoad fieri potuit, accommodata*. The MS on which it was based is now Hebr. 132 of the Bibliothèque Nationale in Paris, where, as may be seen, it is in an excellent state of preservation, and where the great accuracy of Jehan du Tillet's edition may be checked. Consequently any preference should go to this MS (or the edition based on it) rather than to the Hebrew translation published by S. Münster which relied on a MS that was not only in a poor condition then, but which has now been lost, so that we can no longer check the points at which its readings needed to be guessed.

In 1879 a new edition of the Jehan du Tillet text was brought out by Adolf Herbst, who collated it with Münster's text and noted all the many variants, but erroneously he attributed the translation itself to Shem Tob ben Shafrut.[46] Who in fact the translator was is not yet known. At the most we can say that he *may* have been an Italian Jew, who probably lived c. 1520–30, a date that is suggested by the fact that this is the first translation to include the doxology, which began to spread in the West only after 1516 (see below, p. 69).

The text of the Lord's Prayer printed here is that of Paris MS 132, which is exactly as given by J. du Tillet; all the S. Münster variants (other than purely orthographic ones) are given in the notes.[47]

אבינו שבשמים
יתקדש[48] שמך
תבוא מלכותך
יעשה רצונך
כבשמים ובארץ
את־לחמנו תמידי תן לנו היום
וסלח לנו את־חובותינו
כאשר אנחנו מוחלים[49] לבעלי חובותינו
ואל תביאנו לידי נסיון[50]
אלא הצילנו מכל רע[51]
כי לך המלוכה[52] והגבורה[53] וכבוד לעולם ולעולמי[54] עולמים אמן

18. 1 May 1526

Alfonso de Zamora

Alfonso de Zamora (1474–1531) was a Spanish Jew[55] baptized in 1506. He was the first professor of Hebrew to be appointed at Salamanca, and was one of the collaborators of Cardinal Jimenez (or Ximenez) on the celebrated Polyglot. In 1526 on Tuesday the first of May he published in Academia Complutensi (= Alcalá de Henares) in edibus Michaelis de Eguia his *Introductiones Artis grammatice Hebraice nunc recenter edite*. Among the exercises in the grammar he included the Pater and Ave in Hebrew. In another work, the *Brevis tractatus de Orthographia Hebraica,* he included Hebrew translations of the epistle to the Hebrews (probably the first time ever that work appeared in that language!), of the Credo and of the Salve Regina.

At least two other writers used the Zamora version of the Lord's Prayer in Hebrew: Martin del Castillo (*Arte Hebraispano. Grammatica de la Lengua Santa en Idioma Castellano* [Leon de Francia (= Lyons): Florian Anisson, 1676]: 316) and Lorenzo Hervas (*Saggio Pratico delle Lingue* [Cesena: Gregorio Biasini, 1787]), who, however, inverts the word order in stich 6.

אבינו שבשמים
יתקדש שמך
יבא מלכותך
יעשה רצונך
כמו בשמים גם בארץ
לחמנו תמידי תן לנו היום
וסלח לנו אשמותינו
כמו שאנו סולחים לאשמינו
ואל תביאנו בנסיון
אך הצילנו מרעה אמן

19. 1548

Theodor Buchmann (= Bibliander)

Theodor Buchmann (or Bibliander; 1504–64)[56] is still considered, for his time, the most able of Hebrew scholars in Switzerland. In his *De Ratione communi omnium linguarum et literarum commentarius* (Zurich: Christoph Frosch, 1548): 234–35, he gives a Hebrew translation of the Lord's Prayer, printed in Latin characters. This is the first translation to notice that there is a threefold wordplay in petitions 5 and 6 (see below, pp. 62–64).

The Bibliander version was written out on three occasions by Jacques Cellier (1583/1587, 1593, 1597) in three different MSS that have intrigued me for some time.[57] It was also the example preferred by at least two other writers: Claude Duret, *Thresor (sic) de l'Histoire des Langues de cest Univers . . .* (Cologny: Société Caldoriene, 1613): 405; and Léonard Richard, *Manuel des Langues Mortes et Vivantes, Contenant . . . l'Oraison Dominicale en 190 langues* (Paris: Mansut, 1839): 38, no. 75.

Latin text:	In Hebrew characters:
Abinu aschär basschamaim	אבינו אשר בשמים
ijkkadesch schimcha	יקדש שמך
thabo malchuthcha	תבוא מלכותך
thiheiäh retzoncha	תהיה רצונך

chemo basschamaim chen bearätz	כמו בשמים כן בארץ
lahhemenu thamid tithen lanu haijom	לחמנו תמיד תתן לנו היום
uattihssa lanu mascheotheinu	ותשא לנו משאותינו
chemo anahhenu noseini (=noseim) lehhobeinu	כמו אנחנו נושאים לחובינו
uelo thebienu lenissaion	ולא תביאנו לנסיון
äla hatzzilenu min hara Amen	אלא הצילנו מן הרע אמן

20. 1553

Johannes Isaac Levita

Johannes Isaac Levita[58] was born a Jew, became a Protestant in 1546 and a Catholic in 1547. His Hebrew grammar, *Absolutissimae in Hebraicam Linguam Institutiones Accuratissime in Usum studiosae iuventutis conscriptae* (Köln: A. Orpheldius, 1553), which went through several editions, gives the Lord's Prayer in Hebrew as an exercise on p. viii.

אבינו שבשמים
יתקדש שמך
יבא מלכותך
רצונך יהיה
כבשמים כן בארץ
לחם חקינו תן לנו היום
וסלח לנו חטאותינו
כאשר אנחנו סולחים לאשר אשמו לנו
ואל תוליכנו לנסיון
רק פדה אותנו מרע אמן

21. 1554

Anonymous

After two editions of the *Precationes Aliquot Celebriores . . .* were published (1538 and 1544; above, p. 30), Martin Le Jeune (= Juvenis) published a third in 1554 and, though he kept the title unchanged, he made use of a new translation of the Lord's Prayer in Hebrew (p. 5) without, however, giving any indication of who the translator was. An almost identical translation is written on the flyleaf of MS Hebr. 1265 in the Bibliothèque Nationale of Paris. The MS (which is dated vaguely to the sixteenth century) omits the doxology given in this 1554 anonymous version, and inverts the order of *'nḥnw swlḥym* to *swlḥym 'nḥnw*.

אבינו שבשמים
יקדש שמך
תבא מלכותך
יעשה רצונך
כבשמים ובארץ
לחם חקנו תן לנו היום
וסלח לנו את־משאותינו
כאשר אנחנו סולחים לאשר נשו ממנו
ואל תביאנו בנסיון

אבל הצילנו מרע
כי לך המלכות וגבורה וכבוד לעולמים אמן

22. 1554

Immanuel Tremellius

Tremellius[59] was an Italian Jew born at Ferrara in 1510 who became a Catholic in 1540 and later turned Protestant. He died at Sedan in 1580. Chiefly known for his *editio princeps* of the New Testament in Syriac (Geneva, 1569), he also taught Hebrew first at Hornbach, then at Cambridge and lastly at Sedan. As early as 1554 he published a translation of Calvin's catechism into Hebrew, which came out at Strasbourg with the title: *spr ḥnwk bḥyry yh* ('The Book of the Education of the Elect of the Lord'). The idea of a Christian catechism in Hebrew was at that time something quite novel and he felt obliged to make a long apology for it in the preface; nevertheless the idea was taken up by a great many imitators and his own translation went through several editions, the latest being published in 1820 by Macintosh of London; in this edition the Lord's Prayer in Hebrew is printed on pp. 78–79. The Tremellius version also occurs in at least three catechisms, one grammar and two MSS.[60]

אבינו שבשמים
יתקדש שמך
תבוא מלכותך
כאשר נעשה רצונך בשמים
כן יעשה בארץ
הטריפנו את לחמנו לחם חקנו דבר יום ביומו
וסלח לנו את־חובותינו
כאשר אנחנו סולחים לחובינו
ואל תביאנו ביד מסה
כי־אם הצילנו מהרע
כי לך הממלכה והגבורה וההוד לעולמי עד אמן

23. Post-1555

Paris, Alliance Israélite, MS 442, folio 5vo

No critical study has yet been made of this MS, hence its provenance and date remain uncertain. The contents are a translation into Hebrew of Matthew, Mark and part of Luke (up to 17:20). As it adopts the now standard division into chapters and verses it must be not only later than Stephen Langton, who introduced the chapter division at Paris in 1206, but later than Robert Estienne, who suggested the verse division in 1555.

אבינו שבשמים
יהיה שמך קדוש
מלכותך יבא
רצונך יהיה נעשה
בארץ כמו בשמים

תן לנו היום לחמנו שהוא טוב מכל המזוננו
סלח את־חטאינו
כמו שאנו סולחים לאותם שחטאו נגדינו
ולא תתן רשות לשטן להסטננו
ויצלו מכל רע אמן

24. 1568(?)

Marco Marini(?): Venice, Biblioteca Marciana, Manoscritti Orientali 216, folio 105

The MS[61] gives a translation into Hebrew of Matthew and Mark; it came from the convent of the Canons Regular of San Salvatore at Candiana near Padua. One of the canons in 1568 was that excellent Hebraist Marco Marini,[62] who was born at Brescia in 1542 and died 1594. To him we owe: (1) the first edition of Targum Yerushalmi; (2) a Hebrew grammar entitled *Gan Eden* ('The Garden of Delight') (Basel: Froben, 1580); (3) a Hebrew dictionary called *Tebat Noah* ('Noah's Ark') (Venice: Degara, 1593). Later in life he was appointed Censor in Rome for books in Hebrew.[63] One is strongly tempted to suppose that the translations in MS 216 were made by Marco Marini during his stay at Candiana in 1568; there is, however, no positive evidence to support this.

There are similarities between this version of the Lord's Prayer and those by S. Münster and J. du Tillet, but even so the points in which it differs from them are deliberate.

אבינו שבשמים
יקדש שמך
תבוא מלכותך
יהי רצונך
כבשמים ובארץ
לחמנו תמידי תן לנו היום
וסלח לנו את־חובותינו
כאנו סולחים לבעלי חובותינו
ואל תביאנו במסה
אלא הצילנו מרע
כי לך המלכות והגבורה והכבוד לעולם ועד אמן

25. 1574

Fridericus Petri (= Friedrich Peters)

Fridericus Petri[64] was born 10 March 1549 and died at Braunschweig in 1617. To him we owe the first published translation of Luke in Hebrew: *Evangelium D. Lucae hebraice conversum per M. Fridericum Petri Springensem*[65] (Vitebergae [= Wittenberg]: Iohannes Grato, 1574). Here the Lord's Prayer in Hebrew has been translated from the *textus receptus* of Luke 11:2–4, which is filled out from Matthew. So the translation given by Peters is as long as the text in Matthew, but conveys some specifically Lucan characteristics.[66]

אבינו שבשמים
יקדש שמך
תבא מלכותך
יעשה רצונך
כבשמים ובארץ
את לחמנו תמידי תן לנו יום יום
וסלח לנו חטאותינו
כי גם נחנו סלחים לכל חבל לנו
ואל תביאנו בנסיון
כי אם הצילנו מרע

26. 1591

Angelo Roccha a Camerino

Angelo Roccha[67] (1545–1620) was Director of the Vatican Press, and is responsible for the monumental *Bibliotheca Apostolica Vaticana*. . . (Rome, 1591) in which he has a chapter "De Oratione Dominica Variis Linguis" (pp. 365–76). In the Lord's Prayer as he gives it in Hebrew, the first part is taken from Aldo Manuzio (text 11) and the second from Münster (1537; text 17), from which, however, he omits the doxology and also (in two places) the particle *'t*. Not being a Hebrew scholar, it is unlikely that he was responsible for creating this hybrid, but the source which provided him with it ready-made has not been traced.

אבינו שבשמים
יתקדש שמך
יבוא מלכותך
יעשה רצונך
כבשמים גם בארץ
לחמנו תמידי תן לנו היום
וסלח לנו חובתינו
כאשר אנחנו סלחים לבעלי חובתינו
ואל תביאנו בנסיון
אלא הצלנו מרע אמן

27. 1591

David Wolder

David Wolder[68] (d. December 1604) followed up his Hebrew grammar, *Donatus Hebraicus*, with *Praxis Donati Hebraici, Sive Altera Pars Rudimentorum sanctae linguae continens Analysin Psalmi I et CXXXI Etymologicam, aliaq. lectionis Hebraicae exempla illustria* (Hamburg: Jacobus Wolff, 1591). One of the "exempla illustria" is the Lord's Prayer; it is a modified version of Tremellius (text 22).

אבינו שבשמים
יקדש שמך
תבוא מלכותך
יעשה רצונך בארץ

כאשר נעשה בשמים
את לחמנו תמידי תן לנו היום
וסלח לנו חובותינו
כאשר אנחנו סולחים לחובינו
ואל תביאנו למסה
כי אם הצילנו מהרע
כי לך הממלכה והגבורה וההוד לעולם עד אמן

28. 1593

Isaac ben Abraham min Troki

Isaac ben Abraham, born at Troki in Lithuania, was a famous author and a Qarait. His best-known work was written to stem the flood of conversions that he felt was affecting his contemporaries. He began this extensive book in 1593, the year before his death, and his disciple Joseph Malinovsky found little that needed adding in order to complete it. It is known as *Ḥizzûq 'Ĕmûnā*ʰ ('Strengthening of Faith'), and among the many passages it cites from the New Testament is the Lord's Prayer, discussed toward the end of chap. 10.[69]

The book became a huge success both in manuscript and print after being published by Joh. Christ. Wagenseil in his *Tela Ignea Satanae* 2 (Altdorf: J. H. Schönnerstaedt, 1681): 1–480;[70] it came out in Amsterdam 1705, Jerusalem 1845, Calcutta 1846, Johannesburg 1856, Leipzig 1857 and New York 1932. Manuscript translations exist in German, Spanish and Flemish; one in Yiddish was published in 1717, and in 1851 an abridgment in English (omitting, *i.a.*, the Lord's Prayer) was "printed but not published"; this was prepared by Moses Mocatta under the title *Faith Strengthened*.[71] A complete German translation was published with the Hebrew text by David Deutsch (Sohrau, 1865; 2nd ed. 1873). Many later anti-Christian writers drew on this polemic, most notably Voltaire.[72]

אבינו שבשמים
יתקדש שמך
יבא מלכותך
יעשה רצונך
בארץ כאשר בשמים
ותן לנו היום לחם חקינו
ומחול לנו חובותינו
כמו שגם אנחנו מוחלים לחייבים אלינו
ואל תביאנו לידי נסיון
והצילנו[73] מכל רע אמן

29. 1593

Elias Hutter

Elias Hutter (b. 1553/1554, d. between 1605 and 1609) began to teach Hebrew in 1577 and eventually brought luster to a number of universities by his learned writings.[74] In 1593 he published a short pamphlet for young students under the rather elaborate title *Kunstlich Neu ABC Buch. Darauss ein Junger Knabe die nötigsten vier Hauptsprachen Ebraisch, Griechisch, Lateinisch,*

Deutsch, Zugleich so leicht als ein alleine mit grossem vortheil lesen lernen kann . . . Durch Eliam Hutherum (Hamburg: Ernst Jandeck, 1593). The work, which was reprinted at Nürnberg in 1594, contained the following in each of the four languages advertised by the title: the Ten Commandments, Credo, Pater, Das Sacrament der heiligen Tauffe *(sic),* Das Sacrament des Altars, Der Morgen Segen, Der Abend Segen, Das Benedicite vor Tische, Die Zahlen.

The smallness of this 1593 pamphlet did not prevent it having a wide influence, and in particular the version of the Lord's Prayer appears in many of the books devoted to specimens of the prayer in a variety of languages, sometimes with slight variations and mistakes that have crept in, and often with the addition of the doxology taken from the 1537 text of S. Münster.[75] This 1593 Hutter version, oddly enough, is the one reproduced (with 50 others in diverse languages) in ceramic on the cloister walls of the Carmel of the Pater, built in 1869 on the Mount of Olives, Jerusalem. Two variants, however, have been adopted for the wall text: stich 6 has *tmydy* in place of *dbr,* and stich 8 adds *w'nw* after *k'šr*.

אבינו שבשמים
י קדש שמך
תבוא מלכותך
יהי רצונך
כאשר בשמים וכן בארץ
לחמנו דבר יום ביומו תן לנו היום
וסלח לנו את־חובותינו
כאשר סלחנו לבעלי חובותינו
ואל־תביאנו לנסיון
כי־אם הצילנו מרע אמן

30. 1599

Elias Hutter

When Elias Hutter undertook the editing of a polyglot New Testament, he decided to do the Hebrew version himself, and brought it out under the title *Novum Testamentum Dni Nri Jesu Christi Syriacè, Ebraicè, Graecè, Latinè, Germanicè, Bohemicè, Italicè, Hispanicè, Gallicè, Anglicè, Danicè, Polonicè. Studio et Labore Eliae Hutteri Germani. Noribergae, 1599.* This is the oldest translation of the entire New Testament into Hebrew now extant.[76] For Matt 6:9–13 he prepared a fresh translation of the Lord's Prayer.

This Hutter polyglot achieved considerable success, and became a quarry that supplied material for independent publications. Hutter himself published Matthew and Mark separately in 1599 and 1600 and then, in 1601, he published a tetraglot volume of the epistles and gospels for Sundays and feasts in Hebrew, Greek, Latin and German. The following year, 1602, he published a tetraglot of the entire New Testament in the same four languages. In one shape or another further editions followed in 1615, 1663 and 1732. Two revised editions came out in London with corrections and improvements; these were published in 1661 by

William Robertson and in 1798 by Richard Caddick, but in neither of these were any changes made in the Hebrew text of the Lord's Prayer.[77]

אבינו אשר בשמים
יקדש שמך
תבוא מלכותך
יהי רצונך
כאשר בשמים וכן בארץ
לחמנו דבר יום תן לנו היום
וסלח לנו את־חובותינו
כאשר אנחנו סולחים לבעלי חובותינו
ואל תביאנו בנסיון
כי אם הצילנו מרע
כי לך המלכות והגבורה והכבוד לעולם ועד אמן

31. 1599

Conrad Neander

Conrad Neander (or Neumann) is notable for several introductions to the study of Hebrew: 1586, a translation into Hebrew of the epistles for Sundays and feasts (a companion volume to the translation of gospel readings by Fridericus Petri); 1599, Hebrew translations of the Nicene and Athanasian creeds; a new translation of Luther's shorter catechism, *Der kleine Katechismus Luther's in's Hebräische übertragen, mit gramm. Noten; zugleichmit dem deutschen Originale von Luther, der lat. Uebersetzung von Joh. Sauermann und der griechischen von Mich. Neander* (Wittenberg, 1599); and *Catechesis Minor D. Martini Lutheri Quadrilinguis M. Johannis Claij . . . Correctio et Purior* (Wittenberg, 1599). In all these works he makes use of the same translation of the Lord's Prayer, which is basically that of Tremellius (text 22) but with some important modifications. In the Preface to the *Catechesis Minor* he declares that his primary aim has been to get back from rabbinic Hebrew to the pure Hebrew of the Bible.

אבינו בשמים (*sic*)
יקדש שמך
תבא נא מלכותך
יעשה רצונך
כבשמים כן גם בארץ
הטריפנו לחם חקנו דבר יום ביומו
וסלחת לעונינו
כמונו גם סולחים לחובינו
ואל תביאנו ביד המסה
כי־אם הצילנו מהרע אמן

32. 1600

Bertram Isaac Epstein: Vaticano Ebraico 311, p. 40^{ro-vo}

This is a manuscript translation of the Heidelberger Katechismus made for Frederic IV, the prince elector of the Palatinate.[78] The work, which is not particularly competent, has been dated by the translator, who designates himself as "Utriusq(ue) Medicin(a)e Doctorem," which so far remains the one biographical detail about him that has been recovered.

אבינו שבשמים
יתקדש שמך
תבא מלכותך
רצונך יהיה
כבשמים כן גם בהארץ *(sic)*
לחם תמידינו תן לנו היום
וסלח לנו חטאתינו
כאשר אנחנו סולחים לאשר אשמו לנו
ואל תוליכינו *(sic)* לידי נסיון
אלא פדה אותנו מהרע
כי לך המלכות הגבורה וההוד לעולמים אמן

33. 1609

Cesare Mainardi: Florence, Biblioteca Nazionale, Conv. Sop. K. 1.2+1.3+1.4

The Biblioteca Nazionale in Florence holds a number of Hebrew MSS (many of them written in a very beautiful hand) which once belonged to the abbey of Vallombrosa, which for a long time was a noted center for oriental studies.[79] The oldest of these MSS carry the name of Don Cesare Mainardi, abbot of Vallombrosa, who states that he "draughted" them in 1609 and that they were produced with the help of Don Amerigo de Gualterottis, who "did the ink work." The Hebrew translation of the Lord's Prayer is repeated, without any changes, on five separate occasions: twice in the hand of Cesare Mainardi himself, and three times in that of the novice master Don Lotario Bucetti, who adds the date 1779 to some of the copies he made.

אבינו שבשמים
יתקדש שמך
יבוא מלכותך
ויעשה רצונך
כאשר בשמים ובארץ
לחמנו התמיד תן לנו היום
וכפר לנו את עונותינו
כמו שאנו מכפרים לפושעים בנו
ואל תביאנו לידי נסיון
אבל הצילנו מכול רע אמן

34. 1613

Domenico Gerosolimitano: Vaticano, Neofiti 32

Domenico Gerosolimitano[80] began his translation of the four gospels into Hebrew in April 1613 and finished it on 12 December 1615. Born in Jerusalem c. 1533, he went successively, after lecturing in Galilee on talmudic subjects, first to Constantinople, then to Rome, where he became a Catholic c. 1573. For many years he filled the post of Censor for books written in Hebrew (some of his contemporaries thought him unduly lenient). He died in Rome c. 1620.

אבינו שבשמים
יתקדש שמך
תבא מלכותך
יהיה רצונך
גם בארץ כמו שהוא בשמים
תן לנו היום את לחם צורכינו
והרצה לנו את חובינו
כמו שנעזוב גם אנחנו את החייבים לנו
ואל תביאינו לניסיון
אך הצילינו מן הרעה
יען כי שלך הוא המלכות והגבורה וההדר לעולם עולמים

35. 1616

Francesco Donati

Francesco Donati,[81] a Dominican, wrote three treatises in Hebrew, entitled *tpwḥy zhb: Poma Aurea* (Rome: S. Paolini or A. Brugiotti, 1618). One of these is a catechism to which a number of Christian prayers is appended. Donati had finished his work on it by the beginning of 1616, but he does not make it clear whether he himself translated the prayers he is publishing or whether he has taken them from elsewhere. The work was republished at Rome in 1623, twelve years before Donati was killed by Muslims in April 1635.

אבינו שבשמים
יתקדש שמך
תבוא מלכותך
יעשה רצונך
כאשר בשמים כן בארץ
תן לנו היום את־לחמנו התמידי
וסלח לנו את־חובותינו
כאשר אנחנו סולחים לחובינו
ואל תביאנו בנסיון
אבל הצילנו מהרע אמן

36. 1620

Georg Mayr

Georg Mayr[82] (1564–1623) was a Bavarian who, as a Jesuit, spent practically the whole of his life teaching Hebrew. His Hebrew grammar (Augsburg, 1616) went through many editions and, in addition, he published in Hebrew a great variety of translations.[83] One of these is *šlwš hḥnwk: Petri Canisii . . . Catechismus Catholicus cum Interpretatione Graeca & Hebraica. Editus opera Georgii Mayr, Societatis Iesu* (Ingoldstadt, 1620; rpt. Dillingen: Vdalricum Rem, 1621). Mayr's translation of the Lord's Prayer seems to have been based to some extent on those of Tremellius (text 22) and Conrad Neander (text 31), both of whom had also translated catechisms into Hebrew.

Only a short time after publishing his translation of the Peter Canisius catechism, Mayr began his translation of the whole New Testament. This has never been published, but the original MS is in the Bibliothèque Nationale, Paris

(Hebr. 131). Its version of the Lord's Prayer is identical with that in the catechism except for three points: *yqdš* is corrected to *ytqdš; gm b'rṣ* is replaced by *wb'rṣ; lnsywn* is corrected to *lmsh*.

אבינו שבשמים
יקדש שמך
תבוא מלכותך
יעשה רצונך
כבשמים גם בארץ
לחמנו תמידי תן לנו היום
וסלח לנו את־חובותינו
כאשר גם אנחנו סולחים לחובינו
ואל תביאנו לנסיון
כי־אם הצילנו מהרע אמן

37. C. 1630

Thomas Lydyat: Oxford, Bodleian, Or. 253, p. 34

Thomas Lydyat[84] (1572–1646) was a graduate at Oxford, after which he became Rector of the little parish of Alkerton in Oxfordshire. During his life he achieved an extraordinary mastery of Greek, Hebrew, astronomy and chronography. He met a tragic end at the hands of Parliamentary soldiers while trying to preserve his library from destruction.[85] Among several preserved MSS is a harmony of the four gospels in Hebrew. Exactly when he wrote this cannot be determined, but it could well have been during his five years of imprisonment from 1627 to 1632. Everything we know about him suggests originality, and this is borne out by his Hebrew version of the Lord's Prayer, which is unlike any other.

אבינו אשר אתה בשמים
יקדש את שמך
תבוא[86] ממלכתך
יעש[87] את חפצך
אף בארץ כאשר בשמים
לחמנו די ליום הבה[88] לנו היום
וסלחת־נא לאשמינו
אנו אשר סלנחו[89] לאשמים עלינו
ולא תנהגנו[90] אל פח מסה
כי־אם חלצנו[91] מן הרשע
כי לך הממלכה והשלטון והכבוד להעולמים אמן

38. 1639

Giovanni Battista Jona

Jona[92] was born 28 October 1588 at Safed in Galilee. He was appointed lecturer in the Talmud after completing his studies. In 1625 he was baptized at Warsaw. From 1638 he lived in Rome where he held the post of professor of Hebrew. He died in Rome in 1668.

His Hebrew rendition of the gospels, which bore the title *Quatuor Evangelia*

Novi Testamenti ex Latino in Hebraicum sermonem versa ab Ioanne Baptista Iona (Roma: S[acra] C[ongregatio] Prop[agandae] Fidei, 1668), appeared in the year of his death, but from the approbations it is clear that the work was ready for the press in 1639; so, for whatever reason, publication was delayed for thirty years. In the Preface we are told that he drew on two sources: the *Eben Boḥan* of Shem Tob ben Shafrut (text 6) and the translation of Matthew published by J. du Tillet (text 17). However, as he makes the Vulgate his base, in the Lord's Prayer he gives the sense of Jerome's "panem nostrum supersubstantialem."

When in 1651 Propaganda decided to issue from their press in Rome an *Alphabetum Hebraicum Cum Oratione Dominicali, Ave Maria et Credo,* the version chosen for the Lord's Prayer was that of Jona, but with three modifications: (1) the more usual "panem nostrum quotidianum" is now represented by *lḥmnw tmydy;* (2) the phrase *lb'ly ḥwbwtynw* (taken from J. du Tillet) is altered to *lḥyybym lnw;* (3) stich 10 is rephrased: *whṣylnw mkl r'*.

Seven years later, in 1658, Propaganda brought out a Hebrew translation of Bellarmine's catechism: *Dottrina Cristiana Breve, Tradotta dalla Italiana nella lingua Hebrea*. This is explicitly attributed to Jona, and we find that the Lord's Prayer in it is Jona's 1651 *Alphabetum* translation unchanged except that *mkl r'* is corrected to *mhr'*.[93]

אבינו שבשמים
יתקדש שמך
תבוא מלכותך
יעשה רצונך
כאשר בשמים כן בארץ
לחמנו על הקיום תן לנו היום
ומחול לנו חובותינו
כאשר אנו מוחלים לבעלי חובותינו
ואל תביאנו לידי נסיון
אלא הצילנו מרע אמן

39. C. 1645

Félicien de Pont-Saint-Esprit: Marseille, Bibliothèque Municipale, no. 1060

This manuscript comprises a lengthy series of poems all devoted to gospel themes and collected under the title of *Paraphrases Sacrées*. The author, Félicien de Pont-Saint-Esprit, was a priest. Born in 1587 or 1588, he entered the Capuchins on 8 February 1609 and in 1639 became guardian of the friary at Uzès. He enjoyed a considerable reputation as a lenten preacher and died when nearly ninety years old on 5 February 1676.[94] The *Paraphrases Sacrées* seem to have occupied him from 1645 until 1657 and are prefaced with translations into Hebrew of the Pater (made from the Vulgate) and of the Ave Maria and Salve Regina. These versions appear to have been the work of someone still in the throes of learning the language, and they may well have been made by Father Félicien himself.

אבינו אשר בשמים
יקדש שמך

תאת מלכותך
היה חפצך
כמו בשמים ובארץ
לחמנו התמיד תן־לנו היום
וסלח לנו משאותינו
כמו ואנחנו סלחנו לחובינו
ואל תביא עלינו מסה
והצילנו מרע אמן

40. 1673

André Réal: Marseille, Bibliothèque Municipale, no. 24, p. 125

André Réal[95] wrote *Brevis ac facilis introductio ad linguam sanctam* (Lyons: J. Champion, 1646). Toward the end of his life he undertook the translation into Hebrew of the deuterocanonical books of the Old Testament (Tobit, Judith, Susanna, Wisdom of Solomon, Maccabees) and also of part of the New Testament (Luke, John, Acts). These were never published, and are now in the Municipal Library of Marseilles, but they deserve a better fate than simply to lie there gathering dust. André Réal's Hebrew version of the Lord's Prayer would appear to have been made from the Vulgate and thus he is the only known translator of Luke who is free from the influence of the interpolations by which the Greek *textus receptus* harmonizes Luke with Matthew.

אבינו
יקדש שמך
הביא מלכותך
לחמנו יום ביום תן נא לנו
וסלח לעוננו
כי נסלח לכל חובינו
ולא תוליכנו למסה

41. 1678

August Pfeiffer

August Pfeiffer (1640–98)[96] published a Hebrew grammar in Latin called *PAΔIOMAΘEIA sive Methodus Ebraea.* This had considerable success, three editions being published in Meissen (1678, 1680, 1685) followed by four in Leipzig (1689, 1694, 1702, 1707). His own translation of the Lord's Prayer occurs on p. 201 after a few pages (198–201) of notes explaining various philological points of interest. In stich 4 he gives *y'śh* as a possible alternative to *yhy*. In stich 6 he turns his attention to the word *mḥr* as attested by Jerome, but rejects it on the grounds that "non bene haec cohaerent: Panem crastinum da hodie." In stich 7 he hesitates between *slḥ* and *ś'* (< *nś'*) and again between *'šmwtynw* and *ḥṭ'ynw*. In stichs 7 and 8 he supplies a translation into Aramaic: *ûšᵉbuq lānâ' lᵉḥôbaynâ' hêᵏkᵉmâ' dᵉ ûp naḥnâ' šâbᵉqîn lᵉḥayyâbaynâ'*. Apart from one detail his doxology is taken from that produced by Sebastian Münster in 1537 (see text 17).

אבינו שבשמים
יקדש שמך
תבוא מלכותך
יהי רצונך
כבשמים גם כן בארץ
את לחם חקנו תן לנו היום
וסלח נא לנו לאשמותינו
כאשר גם אנחנו סולחים לכל אשר אשמו לנו
ואל תביאנו למסה
כי אם הצלנו מרע
כי לך המלכות וגבורה וכבוד לעולמי עולמים

42. 1703

Johan Kemper (= Moses ben Aharon Kohen miq-Qraqa): Uppsala, O. Hebr. 32, folio 14vo

Johan Kemper[97] was a Polish rabbi who was baptized in 1696 and lived in Sweden until his death in 1716. In 1703 he translated Matthew from Syriac into Hebrew and also wrote a commentary on that gospel. So far, unfortunately, neither work has been published. Kemper was deeply versed both in the Bible and in rabbinic literature; his version of the Lord's Prayer is comparatively original.

אבינו אשר בשמים
יקדש שמך
תבא מלכותך
יעשה רצונך
בארץ כאשר בשמים
לחם חקינו תן לנו יום יום
וסלח לכל אשמתינו
כאשר אנחנו סולחים לכל בעלי אשמתינו
ואל תביאנו לידי נסיון
ופדנו מכל רע
כי לך המלכות והכח והשבח לעולמי עולמים

43. 1705

Rudolf Bernhard (= Jacob Levi): Zürich, Or. 150, p. 23

Jacob Levi, a Jewish doctor at Prague, was baptized at Berne in 1694 and took the name Rudolf Bernhard. In 1705 he published a letter of exhortation to his Jewish brethren. This came out in Berne, but it is at Zürich that his most important works are now preserved, still in manuscript. These include three translations: the New Testament in Yiddish, the Heidelberg Catechism in Yiddish, and the New Testament in Hebrew with Yiddish commentary; this work, however, is not complete and stops at Luke 18:1. For his version of the Lord's Prayer he seems to have relied mostly on David Wolder (text 27).

אבינו שבשמים
יתקדש שמך

תבא מלכותיך
יעשה רצונך בארץ
כן יעשה בשמים
תן לנו היום לחם תמידי
וסלח לנו את־חובותינו
כאשר אנחנו סולחים לחובותינו
ואל תביאנו בנסיון
כי אם הצלינו מרע
כי לך הממלכה והגבורה וההוד לעולמי עולמים אמן

44. 1717

Abraham ben Jacob ha-Levi: Cashel (Ireland)

Abraham ben Jacob ha-Levi was born in 1656 in Poland and was baptized in Dublin on 2 June 1706.[98] Having been invited to translate the Book of Common Prayer into Hebrew, he completed it in 1717 between 15 May and 15 July. The original holograph is to be found at Cashel, but at least four MS copies of it are known: (a) Trinity College, Dublin, no. 1499; (b) the Diocesan Library, Cork; (c) Marsh's Library, Dublin; (d) Trinity College, Cambridge, F. 12.127 = Loewe 86. Particularly as regards the Lord's Prayer these four MSS exhibit some surprising variations. Here, however, we wish to record only the divergences attested in the nine occurrences of the Lord's Prayer in the Cashel MS. In 1829 Marianne Nevill wrote a limited edition of the prayer book ". . . in Lithiographic (*sic*) Ink . . . for the use of the Christian Israelites at Smyrna," but in this work[99] she saw fit to substitute the 1814 London Society version (text 52) of the Lord's Prayer for ha-Levi's.

אבינו שבשמים[100]
יתקדש שמך
תבוא מלכותך
יעשה רצונך
בשמים ובארץ[101]
תן לנו את־לחמנו דבר יום ביומו[102]
וסלח לנו את־כל[103]־פשעינו[104]
כאשר אנחנו סולחים לפושעים בנו
ואל תביאנו לידי נסיון
אבל הצילנו מרע[105]
כי לך היא המלכות והגבורה והכבוד לעולם ועד אמן[106]

45. 1727

Simon Rosenbaum: Uppsala, O. Hebr. 31, p. 7ro

This translation of the New Testament up to Gal 2:15 is in fact anonymous, but has been attributed to Simon Rosenbaum, the successor of Johan Kemper, by Hans Joachim Schoeps (*Philosemitismus in Barock* [N 97]: 119, n. 1 and 148–49), who proposes that it was written in 1727.

אבינו שבשמים
יתקדש שמך
תבא מלכותך
יהי רצונך
כבשמים כן בארץ
לחמנו תמידי תן לנו היום
וסלח לנו אשמתינו
כאשר אנו מסלחים לבעלי חייבי (*sic*) לנו.
ואל תביאנו לידי נסיון
כי־אם יצילנו מרע
כי שלך המלוכה הכח וההוד מעתה ועד־עולם אמן

46. 1730

Heinrich Christian Immanuel Frommann

H. C. I. Frommann, another Jewish convert to Christianity, was baptized at Gotha in 1722 or 1723.[107] Continuing his profession as a doctor, he became active in the Institutum Judaicum founded at Halle by Johann-Heinrich Callenberg. He spent 1730 and part of 1731 translating Luke into Hebrew. The work was still unpublished at his death on 2 January 1735, but that same year chaps. 1–12 came out, though chaps. 13–24 did not appear until two years later, in 1737. As in the case of Friedrich Peters (see text 25), Frommann relied for his Lord's Prayer on the *textus receptus,* which has incorporated some interpolations from Matthew into the Lucan text.

אבינו שבשמים
יתקדש שמך
תבא מלכותך
יהי רצונך
בארץ כאשר בשמים
את לחמנו דבר יום ביומו תן לנו בכל יום
וסלח לנו את חטאתינו
כי גם אנחנו סלחים לבעלי חבנו
ואל תביאנו לידי נסיון
כי אם הצלנו מכל רע

47. 1741

Isaac-Louis Caignon(?): Chantilly, Les Fontaines, MS not catalogued, pp. 10, 58

This MS is dated 1741 and probably was written in Normandy. The name of the author is written in both Hebrew and French, but the French has been so heavily erased that there is no possibility of deciphering it, even with chemicals; three of its letters would appear to read C–g–n. The Hebrew reads *qygnwn,* which might be Caignon, Coignon, Cuignon or even Caiganon, Coiganon, Cuiganon. As the name Caignon is attested in Normandy, it might as well be attached provisionally to the MS until further research solves the problem.

The MS is a sort of diatessaron drawing on all four gospels to produce a continuous narrative. The author makes grammatical mistakes, but has a good if bookish knowledge of Hebrew. By way of preface to the work he gives translations of the Pater, Ave Maria and Credo, where the text of the Lord's Prayer corresponds (minus the doxology) to Matt 6:9–13.

אבינו שבשמים
יקדש שמך
תבוא מלכותך
יהי רצונך
כבשמים ובארץ
את־לחם התושיה תן־נא לנו היום
ואת־חובינו שלחה לנו
כאשר משלחים אנחנו לחיבינו
ואל תביאנו במסה
אך הצילנו מרע
כי לך המלוכה והגבורה והכבוד לעולמים אמן

48. C. 1750–60

Ezekiel Ṙaḥabi: Cambridge University Library, 00–1–32

This MS was found at Cochin, India, in 1806 by Claudius Buchanan and presented by him to Cambridge University. It contains the whole New Testament in Hebrew translated by Ezekiel Rakibi, or rather Ṙaḥabi,[108] from the Syriac of the Peshitta. The translator (b. 1683, d. 1771) seems to have worked on it between 1750 and 1760. S. Schechter's judgment of him is as follows: "The translator performed his task very badly, his version being most inaccurate, and his Hebrew style and even spelling betraying an ignorance of the holy language unusual even with a Malabar Rabbi."[109]

ובכן צלו אתם לאביכם
ויתקדש שמו
תהא מלכותך
אמת ויצוב ומרוצה[110]
תחת השמים ואף על הארץ
תן לנו מזון דבר יום ביומו
ומחול לנו חובותינו
כמו שאנו מוחלין לחייבין
לא תביאנו ליד נסיון
אלא הצילינו מכל רע
לפי שמלכותך היא שלך וחילך ותושבחתך לעולם ועד

49. 1756

Bonifazio Finetti

In his *Trattato della Lingua Ebraica e sue Affini* (Venezia: Antonio Zatta, 1756): 14, Bonifazio Finetti says he has taken his translation of the Lord's Prayer from the 1658 *Dottrina Cristiana tradotta in lingua Ebraica da Giovanni Bat(t)ista Jona* (see text 38), but he adds, "abbiamo stimato bene di sostituire ad alcune voci Rabbiniche, di cui senza necessità si ha quegli servito, le pure ebraiche o Bibliche.'' In two notes he justifies the changes he has made to stichs 6 and 7:

> As Hebrew does not have a word that gives the precise meaning of 'daily,' the author (Jona) has made use of *temidi,* though strictly speaking that means 'perpetual' or 'sempiternal'. . . . Other writers have tried to give the precise meaning of 'daily' by making use of the biblical paraphrase *debar jom bijomo,* literally 'something of day in its day,' that is, 'of every day.' In this translation I have simply repeated the word *lehhem* ('bread'), as that seems to me the best solution to using only pure Hebrew and making its meaning absolutely clear. . . . The word *mahhal* used by Jona is rabbinic, not biblical Hebrew, and is an altered form of *hhamal* which is biblical and has the same meaning of 'forgive.' How the change came about is not clear, but perhaps the most appropriate word would be *heniahh* which is the term we have adopted here.[111]

אבינו שבשמים
יתקדש שמך
תבוא מלכותך
יעשה רצונך
כאשר בשמים כן בארץ
לחמנו לחם כל יום תן לנו היום
וניח לנו חובותינו
כאשר אנו מניחים לחיבינו
ואל תביאנו לנסיון
והצילנו מהרע אמן

50. Date unknown

Cambridge, Trinity College, F. 12.128 (= Loewe 87), p. 17

As this is a collection of well-known Christian prayers, the MS of course contains the Lord's Prayer. The first stanza is taken as it stands from either Francesco Donati (1618; see text 35) or from one of the versions of G. B. Jona (1639, 1651 or 1658; see text 38). From the fifth petition to the end (including the doxology) the text is taken from Tremellius (1554; see text 22). The fourth petition, however, presents us, as far as can be seen, with a fresh translation, unless of course it is taken from an as yet unknown source. With omission of the preposition *'t,* this petition occurs also in one of the texts of the Lord's Prayer given by Franz Xaver Stoeger, 1839 (N 75).

אבינו שבשמים
יתקדש שמך
תבוא מלכותך
יעשה רצונך
כאשר בשמים כן בארץ
תן לנו היום את־לחם חקנו
וסלח לנו את־חובותינו
כאשר אנחנו סולחים לחובינו

ואל תביאנו ביד מסה
כי־אם הצילנו מהרע
כי לך הממלכה והגבורה וההוד לעולמי־עד אמן

51. 1805

Thomas Yeates: London, British Museum, Add 11.659, folio 9vo

On 7 June 1805 Thomas Yeates (1768–1839) began this translation and called it, "A Hebrew Version of the Four Gospels attempted in the Bible Hebrew, and diligently executed on the basis of the Greek Text, and the English authorised Version." He continues with, "This work took up three years, aided by an extensive apparatus. . . . The Translator wished to have prosecuted so desiderable a work to the whole of the New Testament but did not meet with the aid so arduous a work required, but suffice it to say that it has been the ground of several Editions, which have laboured hard to supercede it, at the cost of many thousands of pounds, and yet may be found a valuable document towards setting the Hebrew Version for the Jews throughout the World."[112]

אבינו אשר בשמים
יתקדש שמך
תבוא מלכותך
יהי רצונך
כאשר בשמים כן בארץ
לחמנו על חק יום תן לנו היום
וסלח לנו חובותינו
כאשר אנחנו סולחים לחובינו
ואל תביאנו לידי מסה
כי אם הצילנו מרע
כי לך הממלכה והגבורה והכבוד לעולם ועד אמן

52. 1814

London Society for Promoting Christianity amongst the Jews, p. 6vo

The Society[113] was founded in 1809, and from its inception conceived the idea of producing a translation of the New Testament for distribution to Jews. Matthew came out in 1814, Mark in 1815, and the entire New Testament was published in 1817 with the title *bryt ḥdšh ʿl py mšyḥ, nʿtq mlšwn ywn llšwn ʿbry* (London: A. Macintosh, 1817).[114] To quote W. T. Gidney, "the work (was) accomplished by two men, one of whom was a learned Jew, Mr. Judah d'Allemand, from Germany."[115]

A revised edition of the London Society Hebrew New Testament which appeared in 1833 introduced three changes in the original translation of the Lord's Prayer—in place of *'sr bšmym* it has *šbšmym;* in place of *lmsh* it has *lydy nsywn;* the last stich is replaced by the W. Greenfield translation (see text 53).[116]

אבינו אשר בשמים
יתקדש שמך
תבא מלכותך

יהי רצונך
כבשמים כבארץ
תן לנו היום לחם חקנו
וסלח לנו את־חבתינו
כאשר אנחנו סולחים לחובינו
ואל תביאנו למסה
אך הצילנו מרע
כי לך הממלכה והגבורה והתפארת לעולמים אמן

53. 1831

William Greenfield

Copies of the Polyglot edited by Brian Walton having become extremely rare, Samuel Bagster, the London publisher, decided to supply the want and, in order to include a Hebrew translation of the New Testament, he approached William Greenfield (1799–1831).[117] The main work, in two heavy folios, came out with the title *Biblia Sacra Polyglotta . . . accedunt Prolegomena . . . auctore Samuel Lee* (London: Bagster, 1831). Bagster also made extracts from the main work available in small volumes, and frequently published the Greenfield translation with another version *en face* in English or some other European language.

In the Lord's Prayer Greenfield uses the London Society 1814 translation (text 52) unchanged in stichs 1,3,4,6,8,11; in 2,5,7,9,10 he makes various changes. With one further change (*ytqdš* in place of *yqdš*) this Greenfield translation was also used by C. H. F. Bialloblotzky (*Liturgiae Ecclesiae Anglicanae partes praecipuae, scilicet preces matutinae et vespertinae, nunc primum*[118] *in Hebraicam linguam traductae* [London, 1833]); S. Apostolides (*L'Oraison Dominicale en Cent Langues Différentes* [London: W. M. Watts, 1869]); and Reinhold Rost (*The Lord's Prayer in Five Hundred Languages* [N 75]).

אבינו אשר בשמים
יקדש שמך
תבא מלכותך
יהי רצונך
כאשר בשמים כן גם בארץ
לחם חקנו תן לנו היום
וסלח לנו את חבתינו
כאשר אנחנו סלחים לבעלי חובינו
ואל תביאנו למסה
כי אם הצילנו מן הרע
כי לך הממלכה והגבורה והתפארת לעולמים אמן

54. Pre-1839

Anonymous

In 1839 Léonard Richard brought out in Paris a *Manuel des Langues Mortes et Vivantes* (N 69). In this he includes no less than five Hebrew translations of the Lord's Prayer: (1) Bibliander (1548; text 19): 38, no. 75; (2) G. B. Jona (1651; see text 38): 67, no. 133; 84, no. 168; (3) Elias Hutter (1593; text 29): 70, no.

139; 95, no. 185; (4) Abraham ben Isaac de Troki (1593; text 28): 77, no. 155; (5) this anonymous version: 73, no. 146.

In this last case he does not say who the translator is..The version is unlike the other four in that it is a composite effort drawing on several earlier versions, though relying mostly on that of David Wolder, 1591 (text 27).

אבינו שבשמים
יתקדש שמך
תבוא מלכותך
יעשה רצונך
כבשמים ובארץ
את־לחמנו תמיד תן לנו היום
וסלח לנו את־חיבינו
כאשר אנחנו סולחים לחובו
ואל תביאנו למסה
כי־אם הצילנו מרע אמן

55. 1844

Paul-Louis-Bernard Drach

Paul-Louis-Bernard Drach (1791–1865) was a rabbi who, after becoming a Catholic,[119] was keen on getting Catholics to say their prayers in Hebrew. With this end in view he published *Pius Philohebraeus. Le Pieux Hébraïsant. Contenant les principales prières chrétiennes . . .* (Paris: Gaume, 1853). Various delays prevented the work from being published for nine years, though it had been ready for press in the summer of 1844.[120] It was republished in 1855, and used again by Courdavault, *L'Hébreu appris facilement sans maître* (Lille [*sic*]: Desclée–De Brouwer, 1903). All three editions contain the same printer's errors.

אבינו שבשמים
יתקדש שמך
תבא מלכותך
יעשה רצונך
כאשר בשמים כן בארץ
הטריפנו היום את־לחם חקנו
וסלח לחובותנו
כאשר אנחנו סלחים לבעלי חובנו (*sic*)
ואל־נא תביאנו לידי נסיון
כי־אם הצילנ (*sic*) מרע אמן

56. Pre-1849

L. Spire

In Vienna in 1849 Alois Auer published *Sprachenhalle:* 1 *Das Vater Unser in 608 Sprachen und Mundarten;* 2 *Das Vater Unser in 206 Sprachen und Mundarten*. Under the name of L. Spire he included a Hebrew translation of some originality. Protracted investigations have so far failed to unearth any details about this L. Spire, or even, indeed, the period when he might have lived.

As stich 6 corresponds to the version by the London Society (1814; text 52) and stich 10 to the version by Greenfield (1831; text 53), the probability is, therefore, that he was a contemporary of Auer.

אבינו שבשמים
יתקדש שמך
תבוא מלכותך
יעשה רצונך
כמו בשמים כן בארץ
תן לנו היום לחם חקינו
וסלח לחטאתינו
כאשר אנחנו סולחים לחוטאים כנגדנו
ואל תוליכנו לידי נסיון
כי אם הצילנו מן הרע אמן

57. 1851

Joachim Heinrich Raphael Biesenthal

J. H. R. Biesenthal (1800–86)[121] edited a newly revised and completed edition of H. C. J. Frommann's Hebrew version of Luke (text 46). There are so many changes in the Lord's Prayer that to all intents and purposes it is a new translation, even though each change has been selected from the various existing versions. This Frommann/Biesenthal Luke came out in 1851 and was republished in 1855 and again in 1869.

אבינו שבשמים
יתקדש שמך
תבא מלכותך
יהי רצונך
כבשמים כבארץ
תן לנו דבר יום ביומו לחם חקנו
וסלח לנו את חטאותינו
כי גם אנחנו סלחים לכל חיבינו
ואל תביאנו לידי נסיון
כי־אם הצילנו מן הרע

58. 1854

Robert Young

Robert Young (1822–88) was an Edinburgh publisher with a personal interest in and knowledge of Hebrew.[122] Among the many and important publications for which he was responsible, he decided to include his own translation of the Westminster Shorter Catechism,[123] which came out in 1854 with the title *spr ḥnwk lyldym qṭnym*. His most original touch in the form of the Lord's Prayer as given here comes in the fourth petition. The same year also saw his new translation of Matthew (which for some unknown reason stops at 7:29) in which he gives what is substantially the 1831 Greenfield translation (text 53) of the Lord's Prayer, modified in three places by the 1833 London Society translation (see text

52), though of these changes the only notable one is the substitution of *lydy msh* for either *lmsh* or *lydy nsywn*.

אבינו אשר בשמים
יקדש שמך
תבוא ממלכתך
יעשה רצונך
בארץ כאשר בשמים
תן לנו היום את לחמנו אשר יום ביום
וסלח לנו את חובינו
כאשר גם סולחים אנחנו לחיבינו
ואל תביאנו לידי נסיון
כי אם הצילנו מן הרע
כי לך הממלכה והגבורה והכבוד לעולם עולמים אמן

59. 1863

London Society for Promoting Christianity amongst the Jews

In 1863 the London Society decided to make yet another revision of its 1817 translation which had already been revised in 1833 and 1838. Matthew came out the same year, the four gospels in 1864 and the entire New Testament in 1865; this was reprinted without further changes in 1867 and 1886. The translation of the Lord's Prayer was revised to such an extent that it must count as a new version. Who was responsible for it is not certain, but it might well have been J. C. Reichardt.

אבינו אשר בשמים
יתקדש שמך
תבא מלכותך
יעשה רצונך
כמו בשמים כן גם בארץ
תן לנו היום לחם צרכנו
וסלח לנו את חובתינו
כאשר אנחנו סולחים לחיבינו
ואל תביאנו למסה
כי אם הצילנו מן הרע
כי לך הממלכה והגבורה והתפארת לעולמים אמן

60. 1877

Franz Delitzsch

The Hebrew translation of the New Testament by Franz Delitzsch (1813–90) is so well known that it requires little comment.[124] However, it should perhaps be stressed that in the course of the ten editions of it which appeared during Delitzsch's lifetime, a few changes were made by Delitzsch himself. It might well be worthwhile having a critical edition in which, considering his eminence as a scholar, the successive improvements could be followed through.

As far as the Lord's Prayer is concerned, however, Delitzsch found it necessary to make only a single correction. The translation, entitled *spry hbryt hḥdšh n'tqym mlšwn ywn llšwn 'bryt,* appeared in 1877, and in the last stich of the Lord's Prayer used *hṣylnw;* in the third and all subsequent[125] editions this was altered to *ḥlṣnw.* That the importance of this Delitzsch translation is widely recognized may be seen from the fact that S. P. Re'emi recently found it worthwhile to compile an *Analytical Concordance to the Delitzsch Hebrew Translation of the New Testament* (Jerusalem: Nur Press, 1973–74).

Since 1948 Père Jean-Marie-Paul Bauchet,[126] a French priest, has been heavily involved in the work of providing Israeli Christians with their *lectio divina* in Hebrew and so inevitably had a number of occasions to publish translations of the Lord's Prayer. In at least three cases he has made use of the Delitzsch version, minus the doxology and with the following corrections: (1) *Evangelium secundum Matthaeum, Versio delitzschiana emendata* (Jerusalem: Saint-Pierre de Sion, 1948); here in stich 5 he changes *kmw* to *k'šr* and in stich 6 emends *lḥm ḥqnw* to *lḥm hywm;* (2) *Liber Precum in honorem Sancti Ignatii* (Jerusalem: Saint-Pierre de Sion, 1948); here, as well as the two changes mentioned above, in stich 7 he omits initial *w* and reads *slḥ lnw 'l ḥwbwtnw;* (3) his translation of the whole New Testament: *hbryt hḥdšh b'bryt* (Rome: Tipografia [della] P[ontificia] U[niversitas] G[regoriana], 1975); here he introduces a new correction to stich 5 which now reads *kbšmyym kn b'rṣ;* for stichs 6 and 7, however, he has reverted to the original text of Delitzsch.[127]

אבינו שבשמים
יתקדש שמך
תבא מלכותך
יעשה רצונך
כמו בשמים כן בארץ
את־לחם חקנו תן לנו היום
וסלח לנו את־חבותינו
כאשר סלחנו גם אנחנו לחיבינו
ואל תביאנו לידי נסיון
כי־אם חלצנו מן הרע
((כי לך הממלכה והגבורה והתפארת לעולמי עולמים אמן))

61. 1883

Isaac Salkinson

In 1885, two years after Salkinson's death, the first edition of the New Testament in Hebrew was published with the title *hbryt hḥdšh bh'tqh ḥdšh mlšwn ywn llšwn 'br.* The second edition with corrections by Christian David Ginsburg (who had helped in preparing the first edition for the press) appeared the following year in 1886, and there were many subsequent editions. Salkinson (1820–83), born at Wilna, was a Jew who became a Christian in London in 1849, and eventually became a Presbyterian minister.[128]

The Salkinson version of the Lord's Prayer (which was not subject to any changes by Ginsburg) was used by Judah David Eisenstein in the chapter entitled "mqwrym l'wnglywn bsprwt yśr'l" (= The Sources of the Gospels in the Literature of Israel), which is part of a work he compiled and published in 1928 as *'wṣr wykwḥym* (= A Collection of Polemics and Disputations). It was republished in 1969, and in this edition the Lord's Prayer is on p. 334, col. 2.

אבינו שבשמים
יתקדש שמך
תבא מלכותך
יעשה רצונך בארץ
כאשר נעשה בשמים
תן לנו היום לחם חקנו
וסלח לנו את אשמתנו
כאשר סלחים אנחנו לאשר אשמו לנו
ואל תביאנו לידי מסה
כי אם הצילנו מן הרע

62. 1892

Gustaf Dalman and Isaac Cohn

Gustaf Marx (1855–1941), better known under his pseudonym Dalman, was the disciple of Franz Delitzsch who, helped by Isaac Cohn, brought out the eleventh edition of the Delitzsch New Testament in 1892. Some of the revisions they made affect the translation of the Lord's Prayer.

אבינו שבשמים
יתקדש שמך
תבא מלכותך
יעשה רצונך
כאשר בשמים גם בארץ
את לחם חקנו תן לנו היום
ומחל לנו על חבותינו
כאשר מחלנו גם אנחנו לחיבינו
ואל תביאנו לידי נסיון
כי אם תחלצנו מן הרע
((כי לך הממלכה והגבורה והתפארת לעולמי עולמים אמן))

63. 1898

Alfred Resch

The chances are that one day Alfred Resch will be considered the German scholar who shed more light than anyone else on the problem of how the gospels were formed. His ideas were so much ahead of his time that he remains unrecognized, and I have been unable to discover any published biographical details. In 1898 he published *Die Logia Jesu nach dem griechischen und hebräischen Text wiederhergestellt. Ein Versuch* (Leipzig: J. C. Hinrichs). On p. 73 he gives his reconstruction of the Lord's Prayer in Hebrew, which amalgamates Matthew and Luke and is clearly inspired by Salkinson's translation (text 61).

אבינו שבשמים
יתקדש שמך
תבא מלכותך
יעשה רצונך
כאשר בשמים כן גם בארץ
את לחם חקנו תן לנו היום
וסלח לנו את אשמתנו
כאשר גם אנחנו סלחים לכל אשר אשם לנו
ואל תביאנו לידי מסה
כי אם הצילנו מן הרע

64. 1915

James W. Thirtle

James W. Thirtle wrote what is still the best commentary on the Lord's Prayer in English: *The Lord's Prayer: An Interpretation Critical and Expository* (London: Morgan and Scott, 1915). In his preface the author says he has "been careful throughout this work to exhibit the Prayer as related to circumstances and conditions that cannot justly be overlooked. . . . Jewish history and customs have been surveyed with care." As a result, he has examined the Hebrew substratum of each phrase and so is able to give a "Hebrew Rendering" (Appendix, pp. 212–13) that does not lack for originality.

אבינו שבשמים
יתקדש שמך
תבא מלכותך
יעשה רצונך
כבשמים כבארץ
את־לחם מחיתנו תן לנו היום
ושמט־נא את־חבותינו
כאשר גם אנחנו היינו עשים שמטה לאשר היו חיבים לנו
ובמסה אל תביאנו
כי־אם הצילנו מן הרע

65. 1922

Joseph Gedaliah Klausner

J. G. Klausner (1874–1958) was a Jewish writer whose life of Jesus was published in Jerusalem in 1922 under the title *yšw hnṣry wzmnw ḥyym wtwrtw*. It was translated into English by Herbert Danby, *Jesus of Nazareth: His Life, Times and Teaching* (London: Allen and Unwin, 1925) and into French by Isaac Friedmann and M. R. Laville, *Jésus de Nazareth: son temps, sa vie, sa doctrine* (Paris: Payot, 1933). Naturally the Lord's Prayer is included in this work.[129]

אבינו שבשמים
יתקדש שמך
תבוא מלכותך
ייעשה רצונך

כמו בשמים כן גם בארץ
את לחם חוקנו תן לנו היום
ומחל לנו על חובותינו
כמו שמחלנו גם אנו לחייבינו
ואל תביאנו לידי ניסיון
אלא תחלצנו מן הרע

66. 1964

The Catholic Liturgy in Modern Israeli Hebrew

Many interesting details about the interim translations of Christian liturgical texts into Hebrew are given by Pinchas Lapide (*Hebräisch in den Kirchen* [N 7]). Particularly relevant here is chap. 6, ''Christiana Neo-Hebraica im Staate Israel'' (pp. 113-215). As far as Israeli Catholics are concerned, the text of the Lord's Prayer would seem more or less fixed in the form found in: (a) the Tridentine Ritual, translated as *sdr hqrbn hqdwš kmnhg rwm'* (duplicator production: no place of issue, n.d., imprimatur 3 March 1964); (b) *sdr s'wdt h'dwn lpy mnhg rwm'* (= the *Missale Romanum*), published (but no publisher named) in Jerusalem, 1975.

It is doubtful if all the several eastern rites[130] and the many Protestant denominations have any sort of agreed text; yet obviously an investigation must sometime be made into the current situation.[131]

אבינו שבשמים
יתקדש שמך
תבוא מלכותך
יעשה רצונך
כבשמים כן בארץ
את לחם חקנו תן לנו היום
וסלח לנו על חטאינו
כפי שסולחים גם אנחנו לחוטאים לנו
ואל תביאנו לידי נסיון
כי־אם חלצנו מן הרע אמן

67. 1969

Jean Carmignac

In my own research I have made use of the help that the documents from Qumran are able to give us for a fuller understanding of the Lord's Prayer. The results of my work were published in *Recherches sur le Notre Père* (N 5), where (p. 396) I put forward the first Hebrew translation to take into account the valuable information provided by these documents. The various arguments that support my rendering occupy the bulk of the book,[132] particularly pp. 70–333.

אבינו אשר בשמים
יקדש שמכה
תבוא מלכותכה
יעשה רצונכה

כאשר בשמים ועל ארץ
לחמנו למחר תן לנו יום יום
ושא לנו נשינו
כאשר גם[133] אנו נשאנו למשינו
ואל תביאנו במססה
כי (אם) הצילנו מן הרשע

68. 1976

Ludwig M. Faust

Ludwig M. Faust, S.J., has been professor of Greek and Hebrew for a long time. In 1964 he produced (by duplicator and for private circulation) a sheet entitled *Text und Struktur des Psalmes Vaterunser nach einer Rückübersetzung aus dem Griechischen und Sahidischen,* which he revised in 1976. I must thank him for allowing me to quote his translation, even though it has not proved possible to reproduce the typography essential for his presentation of it to the scholarly world. Its particular interest lies in the way he has been able to use details of the Sahidic version in order to throw light on the Hebrew.

אבינו אשר בשמים
יתקדש שמכה
תבוא מלכותכה
יהי רצונכה
כבשמים כן גם בארץ
לחמנו אשר בא תן לנו יום הזה
וסלח לנו את אשר יש עלינו
כמו גם אנחנו סולחים לאלה אשר יש לנו עליהם
ואל תביאנו אל מסה
כי־אם הושיענו מיד הרע

III. Analysis

Before criticizing any of these translations we must consider the purpose for which the translation was made so that our assessment can be made in the light of that purpose. For instance, a translation into the language of the Mishnah for the benefit of Jews accustomed to that form of Hebrew and a version in modern Hebrew for the benefit of Jewish Christians living in Israel today will differ because they have different aims and yet each translation will be perfectly legitimate.

Mostly, however, Christians look to a Hebrew version of the Lord's Prayer in order to have access to the most likely form in which it was originally composed by Jesus for his disciples (Matt 6:9–13; Luke 11:2–4). That it was in fact composed in Hebrew is not unlikely since prayers at that time were normally said in Hebrew and an *official* prayer (and that is what the Lord's Prayer was expressly intended to be) could hardly have been in any other language.[134] Apart from that consideration we are now in a position where serious arguments can be put forward to support the hypothesis that the whole primitive text of Matthew was not (as suggested by Widmanstadt in 1555) Aramaic, but really was what over thirty patristic texts (the earliest of which is Papias c. A.D. 120) assert it to have been, namely, Hebrew.[135]

The task of reconstructing the original wording of the Lord's Prayer acquired an unexpected tool with the discovery of the Dead Sea Scrolls which provide us with firsthand information on the sort of Hebrew that was being used in Palestine about the time of Christ. More than that, they introduce us to the poetics of that period, to the literary procedures available to Jesus when he decided to cast his prayer in the form of a poem.[136] By making use of this tool we should now be able to reconstruct the original Lord's Prayer with a far higher degree of accuracy than has hitherto been possible.

Stich 1: *Our Father who art in heaven.*
This stich hardly presents any difficulty; the Hebrew of it must be in the form *'bynw . . . bšmym*. The one problem is whether the relative pronoun should be the usual biblical form *'šr,* or whether it should be *š* which, though it became the rabbinic usage, is nevertheless already attested in the later works of the Old Testament canon. The vast majority of translators make use of *š,* but quite a respectable minority has opted for *'šr:* Bodleian Or 62 (texts 1 and 2), Nigri, Pfefferkorn, Leib (marginal variant), Bibliander, Hutter (1599, but not 1593), Félicien de Pont-Saint-Esprit, Lydyat, Kemper, Yeates, London Society (1814 and 1863, not 1833 nor 1838), Greenfield, Young, Carmignac and Faust.

Qumran documents use the form *'šr* almost exclusively, and the actual phrase *'šr bšmym* (used in Exod 20:4 and Deut 5:8) recurs at Qumran in 1QH (frg. 1, line 1) and in 11QBer (frg. 1, line 7). The alternative form, *šbšmym,* is so far attested only in rabbinic writings after the beginning of the Christian era.

Stich 2: *Hallowed be thy name.*
Versions of the Lord's Prayer in Spanish or Italian have proved stumbling blocks to some translators who, under their influence, intrude the verb 'to be' in the Hebrew translation. Examples include the ninth-century translator, Vaticano Ebraico 100, Alliance Israélite 442. In each case, however, the Hebrew sounds so false that this particular suggestion can be safely eliminated.

Most other translators have realized that Jesus must have used a jussive[137] of either the passive or reflexive form of the root *qdš*. The only real choice is between the N-stem *yqdš* and the HtD-stem *ytqdš*. Of the authors studied, nineteen use the former and forty-three the latter. The arguments in favor of HtD are fairly persuasive; it was adopted by the two old Christo-palestinian translations (Syriac and Galilean Aramaic); it is used in Jewish prayers, notably the Qaddish;[138] and it is used in the following Qumran texts: 1QS 3.4,9; 1QM 11.15, 17.2; 1QH 11.10. In the face of this evidence I feel a strong inclination to alter my 1969 translation, except that the N-stem which I decided to use then still has the advantage of parallelism with *y'śh* in stich 4. Not that the two forms mean exactly the same thing—if Jesus used the HtD, then what he said was, "may your name sanctify itself," that is, "may it manifest its own sanctity"; if he used the N, then his meaning would have been "may your name be endowed with sanctity." Not having these distinctions the Greek is no help in deciding between them, and theology can prefer one way or the other.

It will be noticed that the pronominal suffix *kā* concludes each of stichs 2, 3 and 4. The usual practice at Qumran is to write this with a final *hê,*[139] so that here we would have *šmkh.* This is a refinement that Faust has already adopted in his translation.

Stich 3: *Thy kingdom come.*

It would scarcely seem possible to avoid translating this into *tb(w)' mlkwtk(h),* that is, with both subject and verb in the feminine, yet the following seventeen all write *yb(w)',* with the verb in the masculine: Psalterium Cusanum, Bodleian Or 62 (texts 1 and 2), Bodleian Hebr. f 15, Georges de Rahyn, Vaticano Ebraico 100, Petrus Nigri, Munich Clm 28.233, Aldo Manuzio, Matthäus Adrianus, Kilian Leib, Alfonso de Zamora, Isaac Levita, Alliance Israélite 442, Roccha a Camerino, Isaac de Troki, and Cesare Mainardi. So many instances can hardly be due to all the translators nodding at their task, and the presence of two hebraists in the list of the caliber of Isaac Levita and Isaac de Troki precludes the possibility. The fact that the verb comes before the subject might possibly account for it, or it may simply be due to the influence of similarity with the verbs *y(t)qdš* and *y'śh.* It is interesting to note that from the beginning of the 17th century the translators are unanimous in having the verb in the feminine.

A more serious problem attaches to the noun *mlkwt.* Lydyat and Young are the only two who prefer the alternative *mmlkh* as a translation of the Greek *basileia,* which in fact can stand for yet a third word in Hebrew.[140] The three words are: *mlwkh* (royalty): this is used twenty-four times in the Hebrew Bible, always in the singular and most frequently with the meaning of 'royalty', that is, kingliness, or kingly power; *mlkwt* (reign): used ninety-one times in the singular and once in the plural, it is most frequent in the later books (Esther, Daniel, Ecclesiasticus) and generally with the meaning of 'reign,' that is, the act of reigning; *mmlkh* (realm, kingdom): used sixty-six times in the singular, fifty-eight in the plural, and most frequently with the meaning of 'realm' or 'kingdom.' All three terms are attested in Qumran documents where they are used with a clear conception of these distinctions: *mlwkh* means the power possessed by a ruler in 1QM 6.6; *mlkwt* is used nine times with the meaning of 'royalty' or 'reign'; *mmlkh* is used twice in the singular and twice in the plural. Where the context allows the precise meaning to be determined, the meaning is 'realm' (1QH 6.7; 4Q176 frgs. 1–2, col. 1, line 2).

In the Lord's Prayer it is neither the royalty nor the realm of God that we ask for, since neither of these can normally be said to come or to arrive; what we ask for is quite evidently that God's reign should come, that it should be established in us, in our hearts.[141] In other words, it is the *mlkwt* that we ask for, and the translators who adopted this term from rabbinic literature (where its meaning is always 'reign' and never 'realm') displayed a sound intuition in doing so. The two English translators, Lydyat and Young, would seem to have been influenced by the usual wrong translation 'kingdom.'[142]

Stich 4: *Thy will be done.*
When they deal with the subject here (the Father's will) the translators are almost unanimous; there are only six who do not use *rṣ(w)nk(h)*. These six are: Raḥabi, who uses a paraphrase, and five who use *ḥpṣk* (Psalterium Cusanum, Bodleian Or 62 [texts 1 and 2], Lydyat and Félicien de Pont-Saint-Esprit), though strictly speaking *ḥpṣk* indicates 'desire' rather than 'will.'

Over the verb ('to do'), however, the translators are divided. Shem Tob and Alliance 442 have clearly allowed themselves to be influenced by vernaculars—the first by Italian (*sia fatta*) and the other by Spanish (*sea hecha*), and thus they give, respectively, *yhyh 'śwy* and *yhyh n'śh*. Of the others, twenty-five use *yhy* or *yhyh* (or even *hyh*), and of these two (ninth-century missal and Bibliander) have it in the feminine (*thyh*), while thirty-eight use *y'śh* (one, Lydyat, has the apocopated from *y'ś;* two, Bodleian Or 62 [text 2] and Vaticano Ebraico 100, have the feminine: *t'śh*) and some, like Pfeiffer, admit both as possible.

Now in Greek, the verb *genēthētō* can mean either 'to become' or 'to be accomplished.' This can be seen in the New Testament where the passive of 'become' is used in preference of 'do' or 'accomplish.'[143] In theory either meaning could be correct here. But Qumran provides a clue as to what choice we should make since there are six instances where the noun *rṣwn* (the 'will') is paired with the verb *'śh* ('to do'): 1QS 9.13,23; 11.17; CD 2.20–21; 3.12; 4QpPs^a 1.5. On this basis we must decide in favor of *y'śh rṣ(w)nk(h)*.

Stich 5: *On earth as it is in heaven.*
Though the meaning of the phrase is clear,[144] we are faced with twenty-five different translations in Hebrew. The reason is that the first part of the expression ('as' or 'like') can be equally well expressed three ways: *k, k'šr, kmw;* and the second part ('so') can be expressed in four ways: *w, k, gm, kn*. Of these *kmw* is so rarely used at Qumran that it can be safely eliminated, while *w* as the obvious equivalent for the Greek *kai* can be given a decided preference.[145] In effect, our choice is limited to only two possibilities: *k . . . w* as in the ninth-century missal, Psalterium Cusanum, Munich Clm 28.233, Pfefferkorn, Adrianus, Boeschenstein, Münster (1520), the Italian Jew of 1520–30, the 1554 Anonymous, Marini, Petri, Mayr (1623), Caignon and the pre-1839 Anonymous; or *k'šr . . . w* as in Bodleian Or 62 (texts 1 and 2), Mainardi and Carmignac.[146] I prefer the second alternative because *k'šr* provides a parallelism with the use of *'šr* in stich 1.

The majority of translators prefix *b* to *'rṣ* ('earth'), probably to imitate the Latin "in terra." As the Greek makes a distinction between *en ouranō* ('in heaven') and *epi tēs gēs* ('on the earth'), it would seem reasonable to suppose a similar distinction in the Hebrew. Only two of the translations do this, that of

Raḥabi and my own; but I am prepared to have second thoughts about it, especially since the original of *epi tēs gēs* in 1 Chr 29:11 is simply *b'rṣ*.

Stich 6: *Give us this day our daily bread.*
Here, owing to the word *epiousion,* the number of translators in disagreement goes up to forty-four. Out of all the translators we are considering, forty-two take the word to mean 'daily,' but to translate this into Hebrew they resort to one or another of fifteen possibilities: four translate it by *tmyd* (ninth-century missal, Psalterium Cusanum, Bibliander, Sisti), two by *htmyd* (Mainardi, Félicien de Pont-Saint-Esprit), sixteen by *tmydy* (Georges de Rahyn, Adrianus, Boeschenstein, Münster [1520], the Italian Jew of 1520–30, Alfonso de Zamora, Marini, Petri, Roccha a Camerino, Wolder, Jona [1651, 1658], Bernhard, Abraham ben Jacob [3 out of 9 times], Rosenbaum, the pre-1839 Anonymous, the Carmel of the Pater), four by *htmydy* (Bodleian Hebr. f 15, Munich Clm 28.233 [assuming *r* is in error for *t*], Manuzio, Donati), one by *tmydyt* (Shem Tob [2 MSS]), one by *htmydym* (Pfefferkorn), one by *tmydynw* (Epstein), one by *hymm* (Bauchet [1948]), three by *ywm ywm* (Bodleian Or 62 [texts 1, 2], Nigri, Leib), one by *ywm bywm* (Réal), one by *kl ywm* (Finetti), one by *dy lywm* (Lydyat), one by *dbr ywm* (Hutter [1599]), four by *dbr ywm bywmw* (Hutter [1593], Frommann, Abraham ben Jacob [6 out of 9 times], Raḥabi), and one by *'šr ywm bywmw* (Young).

Some translators take a hint from Prov 30:8 and construe *epiousion* as our 'ration' or 'dole' of bread. To translate this they resort to one of three possibilities: fifteen translate by *ḥqnw* (Isaac Levita, the 1554 Anonymous, Tremellius, Isaac de Troki, Pfeiffer, Kemper, Cambridge [Trinity College, Loewe 86], London Society [1814], Drach, Biesenthal, Delitzsch, Dalman, Resch, Klausner, the Israeli Liturgy), one by *'l ḥq ywm* (Yeates) and two by *ṣwrknw* (Domenico, London Society [1863]). Three other translators prefer Jerome's suggestion that the word means 'supersubstantial,' but each of these translates it differently: *htwšyh* (Caignon), *'l hqywm* (Jona [1639]) and *šhw' ṭwb mkl hmzwnnw* (Alliance Israélite 442). Of the remaining two solutions, one takes the word to mean bread as the 'support' or 'staff' of our life: *ms'd ḥyynw* (Vaticano Ebraico 100). The other, following the Sahidic, takes it to mean 'that which comes': *'šr b'* (Faust).

Yet surely the most obvious solution to the problem must seem to lie in the fact which is twice mentioned by Jerome (*Commentariorum in Evangelium Matthaei Libri Quatuor,* book 1 on Matt 6:11; *Tractus in Librum Psalmorum* on Ps 135:25), namely, that the Gospel according to the Hebrews used the word *māḥār* ('tomorrow') which exactly agrees with *epiousion*. But if this solution is so obvious why has none of the translators made use of it? The probability is that for one of three reasons they felt the clue to be suspect—some deny that a Matthew in Hebrew ever existed; some deny that a Matthew in Hebrew, even if it did exist, could have any bearing on the problem; some merely feel the absurdity of stipulating in prayer that today's delivery must be of tomorrow's bread.

There is, however, one consideration that has so far not been taken into account by this third group: if the word *māḥār* were preceded by the preposition *l,*[147] all trace of absurdity would be removed and the whole problem would disappear. In Num 11:18 and Josh 7:13, and possibly also in Exod 8:6,[148] *lmḥr* has the meaning of 'until the next day' or 'until tomorrow.' That this possibility should not have occurred to any of the translators we have so far considered is all the more curious since it has been suggested by at least fifteen commentators on Matthew.[149] Before 1969 there was a solitary translator who did take account of Jerome's clue, viz. J. W. Thirtle (*The Lord's Prayer: an Interpretation Critical and Expository* [text 64]: 232–35), but even he failed to understand how Jerome's *mḥr* ('tomorrow') might be a clue to an original *lmḥr* ('until tomorrow') and so he fell back on correcting the quotation in Jerome and reading *mḥytnw* ('our sustenance'). To accept the proposed solution is to see that the whole problem has been a false one; if the proposal is accepted then future translators will all be happy to render the phrase *lḥmnw lmḥr,* "(Give us today) our bread until tomorrow."[150]

Turning now to the rest of the petition, for the verb 'give,' despite Tremellius and his followers, who look to Prov 30:8 in support of the translation *hṭrypnw,* there is only one possible word in Hebrew that this imperative can represent, whether we spell it *tn* or, as at Qumran, *tnh.*

For the word 'today' we may either follow Luke's *to kath' hēmeran* and translate *ywm ywm* (with Petri), *ywm bywm* (with Réal) or *dbr ywm bywmw* (with Frommann and Biesenthal), or we can follow Matthew's *sēmeron* and translate *hywm.* One argument in favor of *ywm ywm* and Luke is that it is easier to drop the repetition and add the article than it would have been to drop the article and duplicate *hywm* into *ywm ywm.* But in favor of *hywm* is the fact that generally Matthew represents the original better than Luke.[151]

The translation of 'bread' by *lḥm* is not in dispute, but twenty-one translations give it the particle *'t.* Grammatically there is nothing against this, but as it is not essential, and since the stich already threatens to be too long, the balance of probability would seem to be against including *'t.*

Finally, we need to consider the order of the words. Seventeen have the verb at the beginning, but the Greek order, with the complement at the front, is perfectly natural in Hebrew, and so the sentence flows melodiously, whether we read *laḥmenû lᵉmāḥār tēn lānû yôm yôm,* or *laḥmenû lᵉmāḥār tēn lānû hayyôm.*

Stich 7: *And forgive us our debts.*

For the verb some translators adopt the second person jussive. As there is no obvious reason for this, the imperative (which the Greek uses both here and in stich 6) should certainly be preferred. The real problem is to decide which verb should be employed. Here the renderings show a great variety, and between them make use of eight different roots to convey the ideas of 'remit, pardon, forgive, cancel': (1) *šlḥ* (Caignon) means 'to send away'; only a very forced usage could make it fit this context. (2) *rṣh* (Domenico) means 'to delight in, take pleasure in,' and so it hardly fits the context of the Lord's Prayer. (3) *kpr* (Mainardi) means 'to cover (a sin) by making atonement,' and its liturgical use for the sacrifices in the temple suggests an idea which is not likely in a Christian prayer. (4) *šmṭ* (Thirtle), as in Deut 15:2, is used of debts being remitted in sabbatical years; in the Lord's Prayer it might give the overtone that we are asking God to treat us as though we were already living in the unending Sabbath. (5) *nwḥ* (Psalterium Cusanum, Bodleian Or 62 [text 1], Vaticano Ebraico 100, Adrianus, Finetti) in the G means 'to rest,' in the H 'to leave'; however, it is used in Eccl 10:4 with the sense of 'pacifying' ("Yielding allays the anger of a king") and in 4QFlor 1.7 (quoting 2 Sam 7:11) it is used in the sense of 'relief' (from enemies). (6) *mḥl* (fifteen translations) in rabbinic literature certainly means 'to forgive,' but, as it is never used in the Bible and has not been found in Qumran documents, it seems unlikely that it could have been either a familiar word to the apostles or the word used by Jesus in the Lord's Prayer. (7) *slḥ* (forty-one translations) is a word meaning 'to forgive' which is perfectly normal and used both in the Bible and at Qumran; it merits serious consideration. (8) *nś'* (Bibliander, an alternative reading of Pfeiffer, and Carmignac) opens a new perspective. This word is used with the sense of 'remit' or 'pardon' at least twenty times in the Bible and is so used at Qumran in 1QH 16.16 (quoting Exod 34:7) and in CD 3.18. Apart from that, however, it has a particular claim on our attention because, as we shall see, the roots of two other words likely to have been used in its immediate context are *nš'* (or *nšh*) 'to lend' and *nsh* 'to tempt,' and the resulting play of sound between *nś'*, *nš'* and *nsh* produces the well-known alliteration of Hebrew poetry. To say that of itself this is sufficient to exclude *slḥ* would certainly be going too far, but at least Bibliander's solution has that sort of appeal which I find adequate to justify its adoption.

The first question to be decided with respect to the verbal complement concerns what it is that we want to be remitted. The plain meaning of the Greek in Matthew is 'our debts' and yet an astonishing number of translators feel obliged to translate Matthew as though he really meant 'trespasses.' This false solution, whatever the Hebrew chosen for it, may be summarily rejected: 'our offences' (*'šm[w]tynw* eight times, *'šmtnw* twice, *'šmynw* once), 'our sins' (*ḥṭ'[w]tynw* thrice, *ḥṭ'ynw* thrice), 'our iniquities' (*'w[w]n[w]tynw* four times, *'wnynw* once), 'our transgressions' (*pš'ynw* once). A larger number prefer using the root *ḥwb: ḥ(w)b(w)tynw* (thirty-three times), or *ḥwbynw* (two or three times). This at least has the advantage that, though it is found only in Ezek 18:7, it does possess the double meaning of both 'fault' and 'debt.'

If, however, we want to take up the suggestion of Bibliander, we must look for some word from the root *nš'* or *nšh* which means 'to lend on interest': *n^{e}šî* (2 Kgs 4:7), *maššê^{h}* (Deut 15:2), *maššā'* (Neh 5:7; 10:32) or *maššā'ā^{h}* (Deut 24:10; Prov 22:26). The first one, in the form *n^{e}šê(y)nû,* has the advantage of possessing the maximum assonance with the rest of the group, though Bibliander himself (as well as the Anonymous of 1554 and Félicien de Pont-Saint-Esprit) prefers to translate *mašš$^{e'}$ôtênû* (this plural being attested in Prov 22:26). The four remaining translators (Petri, Réal, Frommann, Biesenthal) translate the Lucan text which has 'our sins' and not 'our debts.' Three of them adopt *ḥṭ'wtynw* as the translation, while Réal chooses *'wnnw*.

Stich 8: *as (indeed) we forgive/forgave our debtors.*
Here we reach the maximum disagreement with fifty-eight divergent opinions. Taking the words in the same order they occur in the Greek: *hōs:* sixteen translate *kmw(+š)*—this can be eliminated at once as being purely rabbinic and unknown either to the Bible or at Qumran; forty-four translate *k'šr*—this can be accepted without qualms as the ordinary usage both of the Bible and at Qumran. *kai:* though the *kai* of *hōs kai hēmeis* can refer either to the word before or to the one after, in Hebrew it could refer only to the pronoun that follows. Hence, twelve translate *gm*—these are perfectly justified, but so also would any future translator who preferred *'p;* five translate *w,* which is without justification in Hebrew. *hēmeis:* for the pronoun 'us' the two forms available were adopted as follows: forty-three translate *'nḥnw,* and twenty use *'nw*. Both forms are correct, but the second can be preferred for two reasons—it is shorter (and the line will be on the long side anyway) and it sounds in greater harmony with the following verb.

Aphēkamen: the Greek *textus receptus,* which has the verb in the present, is followed by the Vulgate, by many of the translations currently in use, as well as by fifty-two of the Hebrew versions, all of which agree in using the participle. As critical texts have restored the aorist,[152] the Hebrew will require the perfect and this, in fact, has been used by nine of these translations (Bodleian Or 62 [text 1], Hutter [1593], Lydyat, Félicien de Pont-Saint-Esprit, Carmel, Delitzsch, Thirtle, Klausner, Carmignac). The actual verb used must of course be the same as that in stich 7 and so it will be either *slḥnw* or, better, *nś'nw*.

Tois opheiletais hēmōn: the last three words echo the *ta opheilēmata hēmōn* of stich 7: 'our debts . . . our debtors' and so the thirty-three translations that previously had *ḥ(w)b(w)tynw* now have *ḥy(y)bynw;* among these the Italian Jew of 1520–30, followed by S. Münster, amplifies his translation with the support of Deut 15:2 and writes *b'ly ḥ(w)b(w)tynw* 'the masters of our debts,' but the mere length of this phrase makes his suggestion hardly possible. If we turn instead to Bibliander's hypothesis, one possibility would be to use the causative participle from *nšh* or *nš'* *(mš[']]ynw),* on the assumption that the causative here would mean 'debtor,' by analogy with *lwh* and *'bṭ* ('to borrow') whose causatives mean 'to lend.' Against this is the fact that so far the form remains unattested. The versions proposed by Petri, Réal, Frommann and Biesenthal, the four translators of the Lucan text, have, of course, no bearing on the problem of translating this particular clause in Matthew.

Stich 9: *and lead us not into temptation.*
Hebrew does not admit a negative before an imperative; rather, it requires the negation (normally *'l*) with the second person jussive, exactly as the Greek has here: *mē eisenenkēs hēmas*. The controversy over what exactly the Greek means has been long, and the solutions proposed have been many. Thanks to Johannes

Heller a solution has been proposed which has every appearance of being definitive:[153] in Hebrew, if a verb in the causative is preceded by a negative, the negation can be referred either to the cause or to the effect; a parallel in English might be the difference between 'not cause us to do it' and 'cause us not to do it': in the first case we would be presumed to have done it freely, in the second that we had been forced to abstain. Applying this to the Lord's Prayer, the difference is between asking God not to cause us to enter temptation and asking him to cause us not to enter (that is not to consent to) temptation. This grammatical rule is illustrated in Qumran documents,[154] but it need not detain us here, as the present inquiry is into the wording of the original Hebrew, not into its interpretation.

For the negative, four translations (Nigri, Alliance 442, Réal, Rahabi) employ *l'* instead of *'l* and thus make the petition into a positive demand: "Thou shalt do that we shall not consent to temptation." There is nothing against this, except that it makes this petition the only one that does not have the force of an imperative, an imbalance that is highly improbable.

Of all the translations fifty-eight have the verbal form *tby'nw* ("grant it that we enter not"), and four others use the same root, but in a different form. This impressive majority would by itself seem sufficient to rule out the five alternatives adopted by the others: *hlk* ('to go'), used in the causative by Isaac Levita, Epstein, Réal and Spire, is not as close to the Greek as *bw'*; *nhg* ('to conduct'), used in Vaticano Ebraico 100 and Lydyat; and *nhl* ('to lead'), used by Pfefferkorn, are both theoretically possible, unlike either of the following: *nś'* ('to bear, to carry') and *ntn ršwt* ('to give power')—the first of these is an alternative in Lydyat's text, while the second (even more impossible as a translation) comes from Alliance Israélite 442. The pronoun 'us' can be rendered either by a suffix or by a separate word *'(w)tnw,* but the first solution is shorter and sounder. Manuzio imitates the Latin "nos inducas" by placing *'wtnw* before *tby'*.

There are three possibilities for expressing the concept of temptation. Forty-eight translators use *nsywn,* twenty-two use *msh* and none uses *nswy*. The first is a late biblical term found only in Ecclesiasticus (4:17; 6:6; 13:12) and is never employed at Qumran. Jesus is far more likely to have used either *msh* which is frequent in the Bible, or *nswy* of which there are three instances at Qumran (1QS 1.18; DibHam 5.18; 6.7) as well as two in Ecclesiasticus (33:1 = 36:1; 44:20). As all three terms mean more or less the same thing, the choice of one or another would make little difference.[155]

Under the influence of formulae used in rabbinic literature, twenty-four translators add *lydy* ('in the hands of [temptation]'), and three others add *lyd* or *byd* in the singular ('in the hand of [temptation]'). But if such a formula had existed in Hebrew, the Greek translator would not have failed to render woodenly, *eis (tas) cheiras*,which he has not done (cf. Mark 9:31; 14:41; Matt 17:22; 26:45; Luke 9:44; 24:7).

Stich 10: *but deliver us from evil.*

The word *alla* which begins this stich in Greek has the force of sharpening an opposition. The translators cope with this in seven ways: eight use *w* (a simple *wāw*); nine, *'l'*; thirteen, *'bl;* two, *rq;* four, *'k;* one, *ky;* thirty-one, *ky-'m*. The second of these *('l')* can be eliminated immediately as it is mishnaic and post-biblical. Two others (*'k* and *rq*) can probably be eliminated as well, since they seem rather to mean 'only.' On the other hand, *'bl,* which in fact is not used at Qumran, does have a strong adversative meaning in six of its instances in the Old Testament, and so it must be allowed as a possible candidate. A stronger candidate is the simple *wāw,* but strongest of all is *ky-'m* because it has not only that extra emphasis but also the precise meaning required. The effect of using the simple *wāw* would be to combine stichs 9 and 10 into a single unified petition,[156] as was proposed by Calvin; he, however, can hardly have influenced any of the eight who employ it here since two are pre-Calvin (Psalterium Cusanum, Shem Tob); two are Jews (Alliance 442 (?), Isaac de Troki); three are Catholic (Félicien de Pont-Saint-Esprit, Jona [1651], Finetti); and one is Lutheran (Kemper).

A total of seven ways are proposed for translating the Greek *rusai hēmas* ('deliver us'): forty-nine assume it represents *nṣl*. This is a hefty majority, most of them have it in the form *hṣylnw,* and their decision is far from unlikely; but at least four of the other options remain real possibilities. Six use *ḥlṣ* ('to withdraw': Georges de Rahyn, Lydyat, Delitzsch [3rd ed. onwards], Dalman, Klausner, Catholic Liturgy [1964]); two employ *šmr* ('to preserve': Shem Tob, Vaticano Ebraico 100); one chooses *nṣr* ('to guard': Nigri); two use *pdh* ('to ransom': Isaac Levita, Kemper); two have *g'l* ('to redeem': Pfefferkorn and an alternative in Lydyat); and one adopts *hwšy'* ('to save': Faust). Of all these, the last is the least probable, as a Greek translator would certainly have chosen *sōzō* rather than *ruomai*.

The problem with the following prepositional phrase is whether the meaning of *apo tou ponērou* is 'from (the) evil' or 'from the Evil One,' that is, from the devil. To mean the former (evil in general), the Greek would use the neuter; to mean the latter, it would use the masculine, which in fact it does, since every Greek MS has the definite article, which means the reference is to a particular and identifiable being. It is almost certainly the Latin *a malo,* which lacks the definite article, which has misled so many translators. Twenty-three have *mr',* seven have *mr'h* (all thirty of these omit the article) and fourteen have *mkl r'* where the extra *kl* ('all') is an addition suggested not by the Greek text but by the idea of 'evil in general.' Only seventeen translations insert the article, and they fall into three groups—six have *mhr'* (Tremellius, Wolder, Neander, Donati, Jona [1658], Finetti); ten have *mn hr'* (Bibliander, Greenfield, London [1833], Spire, Biesenthal, Young, Delitzsch, Salkinson, Resch, Thirtle); one has *mn hr'h* (Domenico). The last two proposals with *min* before the article rather than an assimilated *mē* are supported by Qumran, where it was the exclusive usage. Even so it would appear that none of these solutions is in fact the correct one, and neither is that of Faust who adds *yd* ('from the hand of'), since Qumran shows that at the time of Christ the word *r'* ('evil' with the sense of 'wicked person') had been largely supplanted by *rš'* ('wicked, perverse'), though it was retained for the more abstract sense of wickedness in general.[157] The preferred translation here therefore should be *mn hrš'* vocalized *min hārāšā'* "from the wicked one." Such was exactly the translation given in 1630 by Lydyat, the only one of all the translators to do so.

The Doxology

The unanimous agreement of critics that this is a late appendix to the Lord's Prayer obviates any necessity to discuss it in detail, but it may still be useful to point out how the form of the poem, that is, two stanzas of five strophes each, is completely ruined by tacking on any sort of doxology as a sort of eleventh stich, particularly one like this, written in prose.[158] Therefore both Delitzsch and Dalman, though including a translation of it, enclose it in parentheses. But an earlier pre-critical period naturally assumed the addition was an integral part of the original text. Consequently it does remain of some interest to see what in fact they made of it.

With only a few exceptions (the Corrector of Bodleian Hebr. f 15, Domenico and Ṙaḥabi) the majority render 'for thine' by *ky lk* which, we may add, at Qumran probably would have been spelled *ky' lkh*. As in stich 3, four translations are offered here for 'the kingdom': eleven propose *hmmlkh;* nine, *hmlkwt;* two, *mlkwtk;* and three, *hmlwkh*. From what has been said in the discussion of stich 3, *hmmlkh* should have been avoided since this sense of 'kingdom' does not form a class with 'power' and 'glory.' *Hmlkwt* would have been better, but better still would be *hmlwkh,* since it conveys the desired sense of 'reign' or 'royalty.' Furthermore, this distinction is supported by 1 Chr 29:11, the probable source of the doxology: "To you, Lord, greatness, power, magnificence, splendor and majesty; for everything in heaven and on earth is for you, Lord, the kingdom *(hmmlkh),*" with distinction between subjective attributes and objective reality.

For 'the power' there are six proposals: sixteen translate by *whgbwrh;* three by *wgbwrh;* one with *hgbwrh;* three with *wḣkḥ;* one by *whšlṭwn;* and one with *wḥylk*. Of these, the first would have been the most likely, as it not only reflects the literary styles both of the Bible and of Qumran usage, but it also happens to be the actual term used in 1 Chr 29:11.

In translating 'the glory' we are faced with seven proposals: seven translators use *whkbwd;* four adopt *wkbwd;* seven employ *whhwd;* one opts for *whwd;* four choose *whtp'rt;* one uses *whšbḥ;* and one employs *wtwšbḥtk*. Eliminating those translations which omit the article or add a suffix, since neither can be right, two of these proposals have a superior claim: *whhwd* and *whtp'rt,* since each is listed in the source text.

It would be most unusual if *eis tous aiōnas* had been used to represent anything other than *l'wlmym*. Some of the translators, nevertheless, have selected one or another of the various alternative biblical formulae.

IV. Conclusions

The overall impression left after studying all these translations is that only eight of them stand out above all the rest—Manuzio, Münster, Tremellius, Isaac de Troki, Hutter, Jona, the London Society and Delitzsch. This is not to suggest that the others are best forgotten; some of them indeed, and notably Bibliander and Lydyat, evince very penetrating intuitions that prove to be of the greatest value in reconstructing the original prayer.

Comparing so many translations made over such a long period does bring home to one how even the most scholarly of the translators have probably been quite unaware of the degree to which they were following a current fashion: all the sixteenth-century translators (i.e., 1508–1600) have, with very few exceptions, a German background; with the exception of Lydyat, Réal and Pfeiffer, the background for all those of the seventeenth century is Italian (since even the German Mayr not only died in Rome, but had gone there precisely to get his Hebrew translation published); in the century from 1639 to 1730 every translation (except Réal and Pfeiffer) is due to a Jewish Christian, while in the nineteenth century England produced four translations in rapid succession and that of the London Society went through several revisions. In this connection it may also be noted that as yet I have been unable to discover a single translation made in Spain since that of Shem Tob ben Shafrut in 1380, nor for that matter have I yet discovered a single one made in America.

Another point that is relevant here is how certain translations, after a run of popularity, suffer an abrupt fall into oblivion, only to be replaced by others which are not always better. The value to any research project of having access to collections of previous efforts is precisely the help they afford in avoiding what is specious and ephemeral.

What Qumran has done for New Testament scholarship in general, it has done for research into the Lord's Prayer. Surprising numbers of forgotten suggestions take on a fresh look of respectability when they can be supported by the type of Hebrew now known to have been in use at the time of Christ. It is possible that we have only just begun to appreciate the value of this aspect of the discoveries.

Lastly, and most importantly, this present survey has brought into focus just how much effort has gone into the quest by so many writers (and readers) for an exact recovery of the prayer Jesus taught his disciples. Where this sort of fidelity is the goal, the urge for truthfulness is itself a part of how the three first petitions are being fulfilled: May your name be sanctified, your reign come, your will be done, on earth as in heaven, and in the twentieth century as in the first.[159]

NOTES

1. So various collections of the epistles and gospels for Sundays and festivals have been translated into Hebrew; however, the Lord's Prayer does not occur in any of these.

2. Neither does P. Levertoff give the Lord's Prayer in his *Missale Judaeorum Fidei Christianae;* see "Dr. Levertoff's Liturgy in Latin" in *Judaism and Christianity, Essays Presented to the Rev. Paul P. Levertoff, D.D.* (Ed. Fr. Lev Gillet; London: J B. Shears, n.d., but Preface dated August 1939): 57–70.
3. See Samuel Berger, *Quam noticiam linguae hebraicae habuerint christiani medii aevi temporibus in Gallia* (Nancy: Berger-Levrault, 1893) and Matthias Thiel, *Grundlagen und Gestalt der hebräischkenntnisse des frühen Mittelalters* (Spoleto: Centro Italiano di Studi sull'alto Medioevo, n.d., but *Vorwort* dated October 1972).
4. Listed chronologically, they include the following: *Oratio Dominica* Πολύγλωττος, πολύμορφος, *Nimirum Plus Centum Linguis, Versionibus aut Characteribus Reddita & Expressa* (Editio Novissima; Londini: Dan. Brown & W. Keblewhite, 1700): verso of the title page; Benj. Schultze, *Orationis Dominicae Versiones Plurium Linguarum* (Leipzig: Rumpf, 1748): I 4 r° and v°; Johann Friedrich Fritz, *Orientalisch- und Occidentalischer Sprachmeister . . . Sondern auch das Gebet des Herrn in 200 Sprachen und Mund-Arten* (Leipzig: C. F. Gessnern, 1758): 135–36; *Bibliotheca Sacra, post . . . Jacobi Le Long & C. F. Boerneri iteratas curas . . . continuata ab Andrea Gottlieb Masch,* Pars I (Halae: J. J. Gebaverus, 1778): 416–22; Gabriel Peignot, *Mélanges littéraires, philologiques et bibliographiques* (Paris: A. A. Renouard, 1818): 93–97; Francois Pérennès, *Dictionnaire de Bibliographie Catholique* 1 (= vol. 39 of the *Encyclopédie Théologique de Migne* [Paris: J. P. Migne, 1858]): col. 15; C. W. Russel, *The Life of Cardinal Mezzofanti; with an Introductory Memoir of Eminent Linguists, Ancient and Modern* (London: Longman and Brown, 1858): 39–47; Andreas Borel, *L'Oraison Dominicale Quammultilingue ou le Pater Noster Polyglotte en plus de douze cents langues, idiomes et dialectes, patois et jargons* 1 (apud Leonem Philiponam, Taturigi ad Ornaenum = Bar-le-Duc, 1878): 7–8, 13; *British Museum: General Catalogue of Printed Books* 144 (London: Trustees of the British Museum, 1962): cols. 499–501; *The National Union Catalog, Pre-1956 Imprints. A Cumulative Author List Representing Library of Congress . . .* 341 (Chicago: Mansell or American Library Association, 1974): 285–88.
5. I have deliberately limited myself to Hebrew, but a parallel investigation could well be devoted to translations in Aramaic, if anyone felt Jesus had taught the prayer in that language or if he thought the Gospel of Matthew had been composed in it. The first to imagine Matthew had originally been written in Aramaic was Johann Albert Widmanstadt (or Widmanstetter; *Liber Sacrosancti Evangelii De Jesu Christo Domino & Deo Nostro . . . characteribus & lingua Syra, Jesu Christo vernacula, Divino ipsius ore consecrata & a Joh. Evangelista Hebraica dicta, Scriptorio Prelo diligenter Expressa* [Wien: M. Cymbermann, 1555]).

Against this opinion is the explicit testimony of Papias that Matthew was written in Hebrew, and the testimony of several Fathers that the Judeo-Christian sects boasted of having preserved the Hebrew of Matthew (see a recent study by A. F. J. Klijn and G. J. Reinink, *Patristic Evidence for Jewish-Christian Sects* [Leiden: Brill, 1973]). The basis for assuming that Matthew wrote in Aramaic is the assumption that Hebrew was (more or less) unknown in Palestine at the time of Christ. The documents from Qumran and Murabba'at prove this was not so and provide us with evidence that Hebrew was in fact in general use (see Pinchas Lapide, "Insights from Qumran into the Languages of Jesus," *RevQ* 8 [1975]: 483–501). With regard to the language in which Jesus composed the Pater Noster, see Jean Carmignac, *Recherches sur le Notre Père* (Paris: Letouzey & Ané, 1969): 30–33 and 33–52. For the Pater Noster in Aramaic, see either Gustaf Dalman, *Die Worte Jesu . . . mit Anhang: A) Das Vaterunser . . .* (2nd ed.; Leipzig: Hinrichs, 1930): 283–365; or Karl Georg Kuhn, *Achtzehngebet und Vaterunser und der Reim* (Tübingen: J. C. B. Mohr, 1950): 32–38.
6. Hugo Dausend, *Das älteste Sakramentar der Münsterkirche zu Essen literar-historisch untersucht* (Liturgische Texte und Studien 1; Missionskolleg St. Ludwig, 1920).
7. Pinchas E. Lapide, *Hebräisch in den Kirchen* (Forschungen zum jüdisch-christlichen Dialog 1; Neukirchen: Neukirchener Verlag, 1976): 21.
8. For the letter of Agobard to Louis the Pious, see *De Insolentia Iudaeorum* (Migne: PL 104, cols. 69–76).
9. For Bodo see Allen Cabaniss, "Bodo-Eleazar: A Famous Jewish Convert," *JQR* 43 (1953): 313–28 and Bernard Blumenkranz, "Du nouveau sur Bodo-Eleazar?" *REJ* 112 (1953): 35–42.
10. Readers will, I hope, appreciate that in omitting the (sometimes imaginative) vowel points from all transcriptions of Hebrew texts my aim is to avoid the side issues in which they would involve the discussion.
11. Fr. Xav. Kraus, "Die Handschriften-Sammlung des Cardinal Nicolaus v. Cusa," *Serapeum, Zeitschrift für Bibliothekwissenschaft, Handschriftenkunde und ältere Litteratur* 25 (1864): 353–65, 368–83; 26 (1865): 24–31, 33–42, 49–59, 65–76, 81–89, 97–100.

12. J. Marx, *Verzeichnis der Handschriften-Sammlung des Hospitals zu Cues bei Bernkastel a. Mosel* (Trier: Schaar und Dathe, 1905).
13. C. Hamann, "De Psalterio Triplici Cusano" in *Realgymnasium des Johanneums zu Hamburg. Bericht über das 57 Schuljahr, Ostern 1890 bis Oster 1891* (Hamburg: Lütcke und Wulff, 1891).
14. I am glad to thank Mr. R. A. May, Assistant to the Keeper of Oriental Books at the Bodleian, for having communicated to me this precision.
15. The pagination is western and begins at the end.
16. This doxology was added by a later hand.
17. A list of the MSS is given in Alexander Marx, "The Different Versions of Ibn Shaprut's Eben Boḥan" in *Studies in Jewish Bibliography and Related Subjects in Memory of Abraham Solomon Freidus* (New York: Alexander Kohut Memorial Foundation, 1929): 265–70; see also D. S. Loewinger and B. D. Weinryb, *Catalogue of the Hebrew Manuscripts in the Library of the Juedisch-Theologisches Seminar in Breslau* (Wiesbaden: Otto Harrassowitz, 1965): no. 233 (here, however, Paris 831 is included by error, as it contains a different work by Shem Tob ben Shafrut).
18. Several authors have confused the translation of Matthew made by Shem Tob ben Shafrut with the translation edited by Sebastian Münster and Jehan du Tillet; the earliest to do so was Richard Simon in the *Histoire Critique des Versions du Nouveau Testament* (Rotterdam: R. Leers, 1690): 231. This particular error is the basis of a study by Adolf Herbst (*Des Schemtob ben Schaphrut hebräische Übersetzung des Evangeliums Matthäi nach den Drucken des S. Münster und J. du Tillet-Mercier neu herausgegeben* [Göttingen: Dieterich, 1879]). That the identification is false was proven by Alexander Marx ("Jewish Translations of Matthew into Hebrew" in the Freidus Festschrift [N 17]: 270–73).
19. Omitted in O and M.
20. O and M give this as a feminine *tmydyt*.
21. O adds *wttn* before *lḥmnw* and omits *tn hywm lnw*.
22. O inserts *lnw*.
23. There are two studies on Georges de Rahyn: (1) Louis Léger, "Georges d'Esclavonie Chanoine pénitencier de la cathédrale de Tours au 14e–15e siècles" in *Zbornik u slavu Vatroslava Jagića* (Berlin: Weidmann, 1908): 112–19, reprinted in *La Revue des Bibliothèques* 19 (1909): 145–53; (2) Guy Oury, "Un directeur de Moniales au début du XVe siècle: Georges de Rain, dit Georges d'Esclavonie," *Le Bulletin Trimestriel de la Société Archéologique de Touraine* 34 (1964): 223–41.
24. Written in the margin, by the same hand.
25. The MS has been studied by: (1) S. E. and J. S. Assemanus in *Bibliothecae Apostolicae Vaticanae Codicum Manuscriptorum Catalogus . . .* 1/1, *complectens Codices Ebraicos & Samaritanos* (Roma: Typographia Linguarum Orientalium, 1756): 70–71; (2) Umberto Cassuto, *I manoscritti Palatini Ebraici della Bibliotheca Apostolica Vaticana e la loro Storia* (Studi e Testi 66; Vaticano, 1935): 29–44; (3) Umberto Cassuto, *Bybliothecae (sic) Apostolicae Vaticanae Codices Manu Scripti . . . Codices Vaticani Ebraici: codices 1–115* (Vaticano, 1956): 144–45; (4) P. Lapide, *Hebräisch in den Kirchen* (N 7): 64–68.
26. For Petrus Nigri see Jacobus Quetif and Jacobus Echard, *Scriptores Ordinis Praedicatorum . . .* 1 (Paris: Ballard or Simart, 1719): 861–63; Bernhard Walde (*Christliche Hebraisten Deutschlands am Ausgang des Mittelalters* [ATAbh 6/2–3; Münster i.W.: Aschendorff, 1916]), who gives the New Testament texts in Latin transcription with a retranscription into Hebrew; Thomas Willi, "Christliche Hebraisten der Renaissance und Reformation," *Judaica* 30 (1974): 78–85, 100–25, esp. 78–85 and 100–03.
27. Alternative reading in the margin: *hazbechenu* (= *hśbqnw*).
28. The four last letters of *mikkol* seem to be crossed out.
29. The copyist has mistakenly written *r* instead of *t* (= *htmydy*).
30. There are several biographies of Aldo Manuzio; one of the best is still Ant. Aug. Renouard, *Annales de l'imprimerie des Alde, ou Histoire des trois Manuce et de leurs Editions* (3 vols.; Paris: Antoine-Augustin Renouard, 1803–12).
31. See Henri Omont, "Essai sur les débuts de la typographie grecque à Paris (1507–1516)," *Mémoires de la Société de l'Histoire de Paris et de l'Ile-de-France* 18 (1891): 2–6.
32. Joseph Prijs and Bernhard Prijs, *Die Basler Hebräischen Drucke, 1492–1866* (Olten und Freiburg i. Br.: Urs Graf Verlag, 1964): 16–17.
33. Joh. Bernardus De-Rossi, *Annales Hebraeo-Typographici ab An. 1501 ad 1540* (Parma: Ex Regio Typographeo, 1799): 8, no. 35.
34. For M. Adrianus see: (1) Ludwig Geiger, *Das Studium der Hebräischen Sprache in Deutschland*

vom Ende des XV. bis zur Mitte des XVI. Jahrhunderts (Breslau: Schletter, 1870): 41–48; (2) *Allgemeine Deutsche Biographie* 1 (Leipzig: Duncker und Humblot, 1875): 124–25; (3) H. de Vocht, *History of the Foundation and the Rise of the Collegium Trilingue Lovaniense* 1 (Louvain: Publications Universitaires, 1951): 241–42; (4) François Secret, "Notes sur les hébraïsants chrétiens," *REJ* 124 (1965): 157–77, esp. 160–61.

35. For details on J. Boeschenstein see Ludwig Geiger, *Studium* (N 34): 48–55, 135; a bibliography is given in Moritz Steinschneider, *Christliche Hebräisten* (1896–1901; rpt. Hildesheim: H. A. Gerstenberg, 1973): 53–54 [=19].

36. These three letters have no meaning in such a context; they seem to be included merely to fill out the line.

37. For a description, see Moritz Steinschneider, *Die Handschriften-Verzeichnisse der Königlichen Bibliothek zu Berlin* 2, *Verzeichniss der Hebräischen Handschriften* (Berlin: G.Vogt, 1878): 53, no. 77.

38. For an excellent study of Leib, see Joseph Deutsch, *Kilian Leib, Prior von Rebdorf. Ein Lebensbild aus dem Zeitalter der deutschen Reformation* (Reformationsgeschichtliche Studien und Texte 15–16; Münster i. W.: Aschendorff, 1910).

39. Deutsch (N 38): 41–42.

40. The years 1502–23 were edited by J. C. von Aretin, and the years 1524–46 by I. J. J. von Döllinger.

41. Edited by J. C. Schlecht.

42. For details see Ludwig Geiger, *Studium* (N 34): 74–88; V. Hantzsch, *Sebastian Münster: Leben, Werk, wissenschaftliche Bedeutung* (Abhandlungen der philologisch-historischen Classe der Königlich-Sächsischen Gesellschaft der Wissenschaften 18; Leipzig: Hinrichs, 1898); Erwin I. J. Rosenthal, "Sebastian Muenster's Knowledge and Use of Jewish Exegesis" in *Essays in Honour of Dr. J. H. Hertz* ([London: Edward Goldston, 1943]: 351–69; rpt. in *Studia Semitica* 1, *Jewish Themes* [Cambridge: Cambridge University, 1971]: 127–45); K. H. Burmeister, "Johannes Campensis und Sebastian Münster. Ihre Stellung in der Geschichte der hebräischen Sprachstudien," *ETL* 46 (1970): 441–60.

43. At first glance the date would appear to be 1528, and some bibliographies actually give this. However, through a magnifying glass it becomes quite clear that 1538 is correct.

44. With a slight change in the title, Martin Le Jeune published another edition of this work dated Paris 1554, but for the Lord's Prayer in this he chose the Hebrew version given in no. 21 below.

45. In 1557 it was republished (again in Basel) by Henricus Petri; in 1582 by Sebastianus Henricpetri (*sic*); earlier, in 1551, it had been pirated by Jean Cinqarbres (= Quinquarboreus) in an edition published by Martin Le Jeune (= Juvenis) in Paris, and was twice copied out by hand: once by whoever wrote MS Harl. 7634 in the British Museum, and again c. 1680 by Rupert Re(g)nauld (= Reginaldus), a monk of the abbey of Hautvillers, in what is now MS 45 of the municipal library of Epernay.

46. Herbst (N 18).

47. The S. Münster text (including his own personal corrections) was the one to which Conrad Gesner turned for *Mithridates. De Differentiis Linguarum . . . Observationes* (Zürich: Froschover, 1555) in which he gives, on a foldout, versions of the Lord's Prayer in twenty-two languages, including Hebrew. Later this was published again by Caspar Waserus (Zürich, 1610) and still later used by Joh. Reuter for his *Oratio Dominica XL Linguarum* (Riga, 1662; this first ed. cannot now be traced; 2nd ed. Rostock, 1675; rpt. ed. B. Jegers [Copenhagen: Imanta, 1954]). It has probably been used by other and later collectors of the Lord's Prayer. The Münster text also occurs in Johannes Claius (= Klaj), *Catechesis Minor D. Martini Lutheri Germanice, Latine, Graece et Ebraice Edita studio et opere Iohannis Claii Hertzbergensis, Witebergae Anno 1572,* but Claius leaves out the doxology, since it does not occur in the Luther text (see J. Carmignac, *Recherches* [N 5]: 323), and in the sixth petition he has altered *bnsywn* to *lnsywn*.

The S. Münster text is also used, with a few misprints, in (1) the Hebrew grammar of Casp. Melissander, *Prima Hebraicae Linguae Elementa in Usum Scholasticae Iuventutis brevissime conscripta* (Antverpiae: Christophorus Plantin, 1586); (2) Hieronymus Megiserus, *Specimen Quadraginta Diversarum Atque inter se differentium linguarum et dialectorus; videlicet, Oratio Dominica, Totidem linguis expressa* (Francoforti: Ioannes Spiessius, 1593; new ed. 1603), where the doxology is omitted; (3) John Wilkins (*An Essay Towards a Real Character and a Philosophical Language* [London: Gellibrand, 1668]: 435–39), into whose text a few errors have crept; (4) Januarius Xystus (= Gennaro Sisti), *Officium Pentaglotton B. Mariae Virginis* (Napoli: F. C. Mosca, 1741): 3. In stich

5 a different translation has been substituted, either that of Roccha a Camerino (text 26) or the 1620 version of Georg Mayr (text 36); in stich 10 he has substituted that of Elias Hutter (1593 and 1599; texts 29, 30); in stich 6 he prints *lḥmnw tmyd*—this could be a misprint for *lḥmnw tmydy,* but it could also be a substitution from Bibliander (text 19). The same translation of the Lord's Prayer (and also Benedictus, Magnificat, Nunc Dimittis) occurs in *Officium Parvum Beatae Mariae Virginis Hebraicè, Graecè, Latinè, Hispanicè, Anglicè, Gallicè, Germanicè, Italicè* (Mexici: ex typographia Joseph M. Lara, 1870): 232.

48. Münster: *yqdš.*

49. Münster: *swlḥym.*

50. Münster: *bnsywn.*

51. Münster: *mr'.*

52. Münster: *hmlkwt.*

53. Münster: *wgbwrh.*

54. Münster omits *wl'wlmy.*

55. For biographical details see the brief notice in the *Dictionnaire de la Bible* 1 (Paris: Letouzey & Ané, 1926): col. 420, and Joseph Rodriguez de Castro, *Biblioteca Española* 1 (Madrid: Imprenta Real de la Gazeta, 1781): 399–400.

56. For details see: Melchior Adam, *Vitae Germanorum Theologorum* (Heidelberg: Jonas Rosa, 1620): 402–03; the short notice by Emil Egli ("Bibliander" in *Realencyclopädie für protestantische Theologie und Kirche* [3d ed.; Leipzig: J. C. Hinrichs, 1897]: 185–87); and Egli's more detailed study in the *Analecta Reformatoria* 2, *Biographien: Bibliander, Ceporin, Johannes Bulliger* (Zürich: Zürcher und Furrer, 1901): 1–144.

57. On these MSS see my "Une ancienne traduction allemande du Notre Père en Hébreu," *Mitteilungen des Instituts für Orientforschung* 15 (1969): 207–16. So the mysterious author of that good Hebrew translation of the Lord's Prayer has now been identified as Theodor Bibliander.

58. For details see *The Jewish Encyclopedia* 6 (1904): 623; and *LTK* 5 (1960): col. 775.

59. There are two biographies of I. Tremellius: (1) A. Friedrich Butters (Zweibrücken, 1859); (2) Wilhelm Becker (Breslau: Dülfer, 1887; rev. *Schriften des Institutum Judaicum in Berlin* 8 [Leipzig: J. C. Hinrichs, 1890]).

60. Catechisms: (1) Carolus a Roorda, *Hinnuk, hoc est Catechesis sive Prima Institutio aut Rudimenta Religionis Christianae Ebraice, Graece, et Latine explicata* (Leiden, 1591); (2) Thomas Ingmethorpe, *A Short Catechisme, by law authorised in the Church of England for young children to learne: Translated into Hebrew* (London: R. Milbourne, 1633); (3) Anonymous (Preface signed G. S.), *Catecheticae Versiones Variae sive Catechismus communis Quadrilinguis, tam Prosâ quam Carmine: Hebraice, Graece, Latine et Anglice. In Tyronum gratiam descriptus. The Common Catechisme in foure Languages* (London: Company of Stationers, 1638). Grammar: Anonymous, *Alphabetum Hebraicum. In quo literae Hebraicae describuntur, punctorum vocalium, accentuum forma et vis: cum appellatione syllabarum et dictionum Hebraicarum,* published by Iacobus Stoer, 1596. MSS: (1) London, British Museum, Sloane 5242: *Janua angusta ducens ad terram promissam, sive Elementa Religionis Polyglotta;* this was written at Oxford in 1664 by the Dean of Christchurch, Henry Adrich; (2) Oxford, Bodleian Or. 19 (olim 68); this contains the Tremellius version no less than three times: in square, rabbinic and Samaritan characters.

61. There is a short description of the MS by Giuliano Tamani, *Catalogo dei manoscritti ebraici della Biblioteca Marciana di Venezia* (Firenze: Leo S. Olschki, 1972): 279.

62. A fairly complete account of his life is given by Mingarelli, *Marci Marini Brixiani . . . Annotationes Literales in Psalmos . . . nunc primum editae opera et studio D. Joannis Aloysii Mingarelli . . . qui etiam Auctoris vitam . . . addidit* (Bologna: Thomas Colli, 1748): ix–xxii.

63. On Marco Marini as Censor see Gustavo Sacerdote, "Deux index expurgatoires de livres hébreux," *REJ* 30 (1895): 257–83.

64. For biographical details see *Allgemeine Deutsche Biographie . . .* 25 (Leipzig: Duncker und Humblot, 1887): 487–88.

65. The title is repeated in Hebrew.

66. Fridericus Petri was thought by his contemporaries to have achieved perfect mastery of biblical Hebrew. In 1573 he published *Evangelia anniversaria, quae dominicis diebus et in Sanctorum festis leguntur, Hebraice conversa,* which went into a second edition (Antwerp: Plantin, 1581); this does not contain the Lord's Prayer.

67. For biographical details see E. Amann in *Dictionnaire de Théologie Catholique* 13 (Paris: Letouzey & Ané, 1937): cols. 2757–58; and O. Pfeuffer in *LTK* 8, cols. 1345–46.

68. A rather neglected author: some details may be found in *Joannis Molleri Flensburgensis Cimbria Literata* 1 (Copenhagen: Orphanotrophium Regium, 1744): 739–41.
69. In 1680 the Troki version of the Lord's Prayer was cited by Jonah Rapa in his *plpwl 'l zmn zmnym zmnyhm* (ed. G. Belasco; London: J. Jacobs, 1908): 24. Sometimes labeled the "rabbinic" translation, and printed with occasional variants, it can also be found collected in the following: 1715 Joannes Chamberlayne (*Oratio Dominica in diversas omnium fere gentium linguas versa* [Amsterdam: Goereus]): 2; 1748 Benjamin Schultze (N 4) and Johann Friedrich Fritz (N 4): 63; 1787 Lorenzo Hervas (*Saggio Pratico delle Lingue con Prolegomeni, e una raccolta di orazioni dominicali in più di trecento lingue, e dialetti* [Cesena: Gregorio Biasini]): no. 4; 1805 J. J. Marcel (*Oratio Dominica CL Linguis versa et propriis cujusque linguae characteribus plerumque expressa* [Paris: Typis Imperialibus]): 4; 1806 Giambatista (*sic*) Bodoni (*Oratio Dominica in CLV linguas versa*... [Parma: Bodoni]); 1839 Léonard Richard (*Manuel des Langues Mortes et Vivantes, Contenant... l'Oraison Dominicale en 190 Langues* [Paris: Mansut]): 77, no. 155; 1870 Pietro Marietti (*Oratio Dominica in CCL linguas versa et CCXXX characterum formis vel nostratibus vel peregrinis expressa* [Rome: S. Congregatio de Propaganda Fide]): 8 (in three typefaces).
70. A photoprint of this edition of Wagenseil is now available (Farnborough, Hampshire, England: Gregg, 1970).
71. A photoprint edition is now available with introduction by Trude Weiss-Rosmarin (New York: Ktav, 1970).
72. See his *Lettres à S. A. Mgr le Prince de*... (in fact, Brunswick-Lunebourg), Lettre IX: Sur les Juifs. These letters were published November 1767 and may be consulted in *Oeuvres Complètes de Voltaire* 26 (Paris: Garnier, 1879): 518. See also Joshua Szechtman, "Voltaire on Isaac of Trocki's Hizzuk Emunah," *JQR* 48 (1957): 53–57.
73. Wagenseil writes *whṣlynw* and Deutsch *wtṣylnw*.
74. For details see (1) a short autobiography published as an appendix to *Oeffentliches Aussschreiben (sic) an alle Obrigkeiten, welcher massen der ietzigen Welt und Posterität... könne geholfen* (Nürnberg, 1602); this is reprinted in the *Unschuldige Nachrichten von Alten und Neuen Theologischen Sachen* (Leipzig, 1716): 392–400; (2) *Johannis Molleri Flensburgensis Cimbria Literata* 2 (Copenhagen: Orphanotrophium Regium, 1744): 392–96; (3) Christian Gottlieb Jöcher, *Allgemeines Gelehrten - Lexicon,* Part 2 (Leipzig: Gleditschens, 1750): cols. 1789–90; (4) Redslob in *Allgemeine Deutsche Biographie* 13 (Berlin: Duncker und Humblot, 1881): 475–76; (5) G. Müller in *Realenzyklopädie für protestantische Theologie und Kirche* 8 (Leipzig: Hinrichs, 1900): 496–97.
75. See, e.g., the following: (1) Andreas Müller von Greiffenhagen (under pseudonyms Thomas Ludeckenius or Barnimus Hagius), *Oratio orationum s. orationis dominicae versiones praeter authenticam fere centum* (1680, republished later under his real name); (2) Anonymous (= Benjamin Motte?), *Oratio Dominica* (N 4; I have not yet discovered anything about editions earlier than this one). This also gives a transcript in Samaritan characters which has misled the following collectors to consider it a "Samaritan version": 1748 Schultze and Fritz (N 4); 1787 Lorenzo Hervas (N 69); 1805 J. J. Marcel (N 69); 1896 Giambatista (*sic*) Bodoni (N 69): *bis,* viii and ix; 1839 Léonard Richard (N 69): *bis,* 70 no. 139, and 95 no. 185; 1839 Franz Xaver Stoeger, *Oratio Dominica Polyglotta... Delineationibus Alberti Düreri cincta* (München): *bis;* 1870 Pietro Marietti (N 69): *bis,* 9 and 10; and 1905 Reinhold Rost, *The Lord's Prayer in Five Hundred Languages* (London: Gilbert and Rivington); (3) Joannes Chamberlayne (N 69): 1; several collectors have followed this slavishly, not realizing they quote elsewhere the identical Hebrew text written in Samaritan characters. Catholic editors often suppress the doxology and by so doing unconsciously return to the original text of Elias Hutter.
76. Previously there had been at least two other translations of the entire New Testament into Hebrew—one by Simon Atumanos (fourteenth century) and another by Erasmus Oswald Schreckenfuchs (sixteenth century). Neither was ever published and both MSS are lost.
77. One or another of the Hutter editions is the source from which the following drew their Hebrew versions of the Lord's Prayer: M. Christoph Crinesius, *Babel Sive Discursus De Confusione Linguarum* (Nürnberg: Halbmayer, 1629): 39–40; Johann Christoph Adelung, *Mithridates oder allgemeine Sprachenkunde mit dem Vater Unser als Sprachprobe in bey nahe fünfhundert Sprachen und Mundarten* 1 (Berlin: Voss, 1806): 367; Giambatista (*sic*) Bodoni (N 69): ii and vi; Anonymous, MS 703 in the Cecil Roth Collection of Leeds University, pp. 1 and 3 (it omits both the doxology and the word *mr'*); Wilhelm Haas, *Das Gebet des Herrn in 100 Sprachen und Mundarten* (Basel, 1830): the Lord's Prayer is given three times: no. 18; no. 19 (in German transcription); no. 22 *bis* (in rabbinic characters).

78. For the role of Frederic III in the publication of the Heidelberger Katechismus in 1563 and the role of Frederic IV in its diffusion, see W. Volkert, "Kurpfalz zwischen Luthertum und Calvinismus" in *Handbuch der Bayerischen Geschichte* 3, *Franken, Schwaben, Oberpfalz* (Munich: Max Spindler, 1971): 1306-17. I am much obliged to Dr. Isolde Burr for bringing this article to my attention and for having supplied me with its text.
79. An unsigned article in a work by Placido Lugano (*Italia Benedittina* [Rome: Francesco Ferrari, 1929]) mentions (pp. 347-48) that at the beginning of the seventeenth century a number of monks at Vallombrosa spoke Greek and Hebrew well enough to be capable of conducting philosophical and theological debates (*disputazioni*) in those languages. The author of this article lists seventeen Vallombrosian orientalists (356 n. 18), but he nowhere refers to or names the seventeenth-century figures of Cesare Mainardi and Amerigo de Gualterottis, nor the eighteenth-century Lotario Bucetti.
80. For details see: Paolo Sebastiano Medici, *Catalogo de' Neofiti Illustri usciti per misericordia di Dio dall' Ebraismo e poi rendutisi gloriosi nel Cristianesimo* (Firenze: Vincenzio Vangelisti, 1701): 13-15; W. Faber, "Zwei Übersetzer des Neuen Testaments" (Domenico Gerosolimitano and Giovanni Battista Jona), *Saat auf Hoffnung* 15 (1888): 33-38; Gustavo Sacerdote, *I codici ebraici della Pia Casa de' Neofiti in Roma* (Atti della R. Accademia dei Lincei, Anno 289 [= 1892]. Serie Quarta. Classe di Scienze morali, storiche e filologiche 10/1ª): 158-94 ("Memorie"; esp. 178-80); Paul Rieger, *Geschichte der Juden in Rom* 2 (1420-1870) (Berlin: Mayer und Müller, 1895): 173; William Popper, *The Censorship of Hebrew Books* (New York: Knickerbocker Press, 1899).
81. Bibliographical details may be found in J. Quetif and J. Echard, *Scriptores Ordinis Praedicatorum*... 2 (Paris: A. Picard, 1910): 482. A life of Donati was written by Maria-Giuseppe Sebastiani, Bishop of Bisignano, and published at Rome in 1669, but I have so far not been able to locate a copy of it.
82. For biographical details see Ignatius Agricola, *Historia Provinciae Societatis Jesu Germanicae Superioris: Pars Secunda, ab anno 1591 ad 1600* (Augsburg: Happach und Schlüter, 1729): 262-63; Franciscus Antonius Veith, *Bibliotheca Augustana* 6 (Augsburg: Veith, 1790): 134-47.
83. For his extraordinary industry as a translator see Carlos Sommervogel, *Bibliothèque de la Compagnie de Jésus* 5 (new ed.; Paris: Picard, 1894): cols. 809-18.
84. This is his invariable spelling; others, however, refer to him sometimes as Lydiat and sometimes as Lydiatt.
85. On this fascinating personality the following may be consulted: (1) His personal correspondence (Oxford, Bodleian, 313); (2) *Pauli Freheri* . . . *Theatrum Virorum Eruditione Clarorum* (Nürnberg: Johann Hofmann, 1688): 523-25; (3) Antony a Wood, *Athenae Oxonienses* . . . 2 (London: Bennet, 1692): cols. 46-48; (4) A. F. Pollard, in *Dictionary of National Biography* 16 (ed. Sidney Lee; London: Smith and Elder, 1893): 316-18.
86. Alternative reading: *tṣb.*
87. Alternative reading: *ykl.*
88. Alternative reading: *tn.*
89. *Sic;* probably for *slḥnw.*
90. Alternative reading: *tś' nw.*
91. Alternative reading: *g' lnw.*
92. For details see (1) Julius Bartoloccius de Celleno, *Bibliotheca Magna Rabbinica,* Pars Tertia (Roma: S. C. Propaganda Fidei, 1683): 48-52; (2) P. S. Medici, *Catalogo de' Neofiti Illustri* (N 80): 24-29; (3) W. Faber, "Zwei Übersetzer" (N 80); (4) François Secret, "Notes sur les hébraïsants chrétiens et les Juifs en France . . . Une anecdote sur Giovan Battista Jona," *REJ* 129 (1970): 235-36.
93. The same 1651 *Alphabetum* version also occurs elsewhere: (1) 1771, in a new Alphabetum by the Propaganda press: *Alphabetum Hebraicum, addito Samaritano et Rabbinico, cum Oratione Dominicali, Salutatione Angelica et Symbolo Apostolico* (p. 14); (2) 1806, in Bodoni (N 69), who gives it seven times, each time with a single alteration in stich 10, which now reads *wtṣylnw* instead of *whṣylnw;* he lists it as "Hebraice" (pp. i, iii, iv, v, vii), "Palmirene hebraica dialecto" (p. xxviii) and "Judaeo-Teutonice hebraica" (p. clxxvii); (3) 1839, in Léonard Richard (N 69) who gives it twice (p. 67 no. 133 and p. 84 no. 168), labeled "judeo-Teutonice dial. hebraica"; (4) 1870, in Pietro Marietti (N 69) who gives it five times (pp. 4-6); however, he also gives (p. 3) the original 1639 Jona version as it had been published in 1668.
94. Details may be found in two works by Pierre Dubois, *Notes Biographiques des Capucins de Provence avant la Révolution* and *Annales Générales des Capucins de la Province de saint Louis de Provence, 2ᵉ partie 1651-1720,* p. 319. Typewritten copies of these two works may be found in the library of the Capuchins in Paris, at 32 rue Boissonade.

95. André Réal was a Minim friar, but even the fullest history of his order devotes only a few lines to him; see Giuseppe Maria Roberti, *Disegno Storico dell' Ordine de' Minimi* 2 (1600–1700) (Rome: Tipografia Poliglotta, 1908): 637.
96. Schimmelpfennig provides some details about August Pfeiffer in *Allgemeine Deutsche Biographie* 16 (Berlin: Duncker und Humblot, 1887; rpt., 1970): 621–24.
97. There is an excellent study of Kemper by Hans Joachim Schoeps, *Philosemitismus in Barock* (Tübingen: J. C. B. Mohr, 1952): 92–133.
98. There are details about Abraham ben Jacob (including the story of his conversion) written by himself, in Louis Hymann, *The Jews in Ireland. From the Earliest Times to the Year 1910* (Shannon: Irish University Press, 1972): 27–29. See also Joshua Block, "An Early Hebrew Translation of the Book of Common Prayer" in *Festschrift für Aron Freimann* (ed. Alexander Marx and Hermann Meyer; Berlin: Soncino Gesellschaft, 1935): 145–48.
99. The author prefaces this work with an interesting testimonial: "I certify that during the time I was translating and transcribing this Prayer Book for the use of the Christian Israelites that, lest they should deem it an offence to use a book of prayer written by a Gentile, I abstained from eating any thing forbidden by the Law of Moses, nor did I use any Pens but new ones, that had not been used in any other writing." It is signed Marianne Nevill, Dublin, Oct. 25, 1829.
100. On one occasion the text reads *'šr bšmym*.
101. In one case the variant is *b'rṣ k'šr bšmym;* in another, *k'šr bšmym kn b'rṣ*.
102. In one instance the variant is *tn lnw hywm hzh lḥmnw tmydy;* in a second, *tn lnw hywm 't lḥmnw tmydy;* and in a third, *tn lnw lḥmnw tmydy hywm*.
103. On two occasions *kl* is omitted.
104. Twice the reading is *wmḥwl lnw 't kl 'wnwtynw*.
105. In two cases the text reads *mkl r'*.
106. Six times out of nine the doxology is omitted.
107. On H. C. I. Frommann see the short account (perhaps by J. H. R. Biesenthal) in *Jewish Intelligence* 18 (1852): 132–37; and Biesenthal's more comprehensive biographies in *Dibre Emeth oder Stimmen der Wahrheit* 11 (1855); rpt. in *Saat auf Hoffnung* 6 (1868–69): 217–42; and *Leben von den Todten. Eine Sammlung von Lebensbildern gläubiger Christen aus dem Volke Israel* (ed. Carl Axenfeld; Barmen: I. F. Steinhaus, 1874): 1–31.
108. There is a short study by Franz Delitzsch, "Ezechiel Rakibi," *Saat auf Hoffnung* 14 (1876): 186–90. A longer study is S. Schechter, "Notes on Hebrew MSS. in the University Library at Cambridge," *JQR* 6 (1893): 136–45. This includes an appreciation of Ezekiel Raḥabi written in Hebrew by one of his friends (pp. 141–42).
109. S. Schechter, "Notes" (N 108): 145.
110. Reading uncertain.
111. This Finetti translation is borrowed by Lorenzo Hervas (1787) as his no. 2.
112. There is an entry on Thomas Yeates signed D(avid) S(amuel) M(argoliouth) in the *Dictionary of National Biography* 63 (1900): 311–12; 21 (1937–38): 1226–27.
113. See W. T. Gidney, *The History of the London Society for Promoting Christianity amongst the Jews, From 1809 to 1908* (London: London Society . . . , 1908). Unfortunately, this work, substantial though it is (672 pp.), does not always help one to state who translated what.
114. From this translation the Lord's Prayer was taken by Wilhelm Haas into his *Das Gebet des Herrn* (N 77), where he gives it four times: no. 17 (Samaritan characters), no. 20 (Hebrew characters), no. 21 (in German transcription), no. 22 (in rabbinic characters). Nine years later it was incorporated by Franz Xaver Stoeger into his *Oratio Dominica Polyglotta* (N 75).
115. Gidney, *History* (N 114): 55.
116. Including these three alternations, the London Society translation of the Lord's Prayer is given in at least three other works: (1) Christian Czerskier, *The Book of Common Prayer . . . Translated into Hebrew* (London: London Society . . . , 1836), where the doxology of the Lord's Prayer is often omitted; slight changes were made in the new edition of 1842; (2) Elias Sołoweyczyk, *qwl qwr' 'w htlmwd whbryt hḥdšh. spr mty'* (Paris: Charles Blot, 1869); (3) Moses Margoliouth, *The Lord's Prayer No Adaptation of Existing Jewish Petitions, Explained by the Light of "the Day of the Lord"* (London: S. Bagster, 1876). In this one change is made: stich 8 is corrected so that it agrees with Yeates 1805 (text 51) and with the London Society 1863 (text 59).
117. See the following for details: "A funeral sermon. On the Death of the late Mr. William Greenfield, who departed this life Nov. 5 1831. Preached . . . by Thomas Wood," *The British Preacher* 3 (London: F. Westley and A. H. Davis, 1832); Samuel Bagster, "Memoir of William

Greenfield M.R.A.S.," *The Imperial Magazine and Monthly Record* 4 (1834): 9–16, 63–72; and an article by G(ordon) G(oodwin) in the *Dictionary of National Biography* 23 (London: Smith and Elder, 1890): 76–77.
118. This is not strictly accurate, as the Abraham ben Jacob translation had been written in 1717 and had been made available by Marianne Nevill in 1829.
119. See: (1) the autobiographical account of his conversion, *Lettre d'un Rabbin converti aux Israélites ses frères* (Paris: Beaucé-Russand, 1825); (2) P. Klein (= M. Catane), "Mauvais juif, mauvais chrétien," *Revue de la Pensée Juive* 7 (1951): 87–103; (3) André Raye, in *Dictionnaire de Spiritualité* 3 (Paris: Beauchesne, 1957): col. 1706.
120. Interesting details will be found in the author's lengthy Preface.
121. See the notice on him in *Saat auf Hoffnung* 23 (1886): 236–40. A more detailed biography was written by William Thomas Gidney. His library is preserved in the Biesenthal Collection of the University of Aberdeen.
122. For details see *Encyclopedia of Living Divines and Christian Workers of all Denominations in Europe and America. Being a supplement to Schaff-Herzog Encyclopedia of Religious Knowledge* (ed. Philip Schaff and S. M. Jackson; Edinburgh: T. & T. Clark, 1887).
123. In 1864 another translation into Hebrew of the Westminster Shorter Catechism was published in Dublin, Edinburgh, London and Belfast by Henry Sheil McKee under the title: *spr hḥnwk hqṭwn.* This, however, merely reproduces the 1838 London Society translation of the Lord's Prayer (text 52).
124. The reader may, however, be urged to consult what Delitzsch himself has to say about it in "Eine Übersetzungsarbeit von 52 Jahren" in *Schriften des Institutum Judaicum in Leipzig* 27 (Leipzig: W. Faber, 1891).
125. I have not yet had an opportunity to inspect the previous (2nd) edition of 1878.
126. On Père Bauchet see Pinchas E. Lapide, *Hebräisch in den Kirchen* (N 7): 119–36.
127. In 1962 a Hebrew rendering of the St. John Chrysostom Liturgy was published in Nazareth, *Hē Theia Leitourgia tou Ioannou tou Chrusostomou eis tēn ebräikēn phōnēn.* The translator makes use of Delitzsch, with some of Bauchet's alterations: stich 5: *k'šr;* stich 7: *wslḥ lnw 'l ḥwbwtynw;* doxology: *h'z* instead of *whgbwrh.*
128. See John Dunlop, *Memories of Gospel Triumphs among the Jews During the Victorian Era* (London: S. W. Partridge, 1894): 373–87.
129. One might have imagined that the Lord's Prayer would also have been included in the life of Jesus by Paul Levertoff, *bn h'dm: ḥyy yšw' hmšyḥ wp'lyw* (London: עדות לישראל, 1905), particularly as the author was a Christian Jew.
130. See, however, n. 127 regarding the St. John Chrysostom Liturgy and its translation of the Lord's Prayer according to Delitzsch and Bauchet.
131. *byt hlḥmy* (a Catholic catechism in modern Hebrew: n.d., no place of issue) gives an adaptation of the Lord's Prayer on p. 18. The text is so expanded that it can scarcely be counted as a translation.
132. The English translation of this book (and, where necessary, its adaptation) has been done by dom Aelred Baker. A publisher for it, however, has still to be found.
133. *gm* or *'p.*
134. See J. Carmignac, *Recherches sur le Notre Père* (N 5): 30–33. As far back as 1876 Moses Margoliouth had said, "It would be arrant hardihood to maintain that that prayer, or indeed any part of the Sermon on the Mount, was first uttered in any other language but in that of Hebrew" (*The Lord's Prayer* [N 116]: 95 n. 2).
135. Carmignac, *Recherches* (N 5): 33–51.
136. Carmignac, *Recherches* (N 5): 383–86.
137. It would be interesting to know what led to the use of *hqdš* (N-stem imperative) in the Psalterium Cusanum, and what induced both Nigri and Leib to use *nqdš* (N-stem perfect).
138. For references see Dalman, *Die Worte Jesu* (N 5): 304–06.
139. For statistical details see Malachi Martin, *The Scribal Character of the Dead Sea Scrolls* 1 (Louvain: Publications Universitaires, 1958): 51*–52*, list 34.
140. It is worth trying to fix the difference between these three terms with some precision: (a) *mlwkh* designates the royal dignity and power of a king or ruler; (b) *mlkwt* designates the exercise of that power—kingship as craft; (c) *mmlkh* designates the territory or domain over which, and the inhabitants over whom, the king reigns (or rules) by exercising his royal powers. In other words 'royalty' (*mlwkh*) is a quality subjectively inherent in the person of the king; when this person acts as king, this is the activity of 'reigning' (*mlkwt*); the entire sphere affected by these acts, that is, the country and people over which these acts are effective, constitutes the 'realm' or the 'kingdom' (*mmlkh*).

The reason it is worthwhile making these distinctions is that without them we never quite grasp the meaning of the phrase *basileia tou theou* as it is used in the gospels. The problem is felt most acutely by people accustomed to German and English, where the translations "Reich Gottes" and "the kingdom of God" are so traditional that they mislead even exegetes and theologians, with the result that any theology of the New Testament based on these wrong expressions becomes at least partly deformed and mutilated. For further clarifications see J. Carmignac, "Règne de Dieu ou Royaume de Dieu?" *Foi et Langage* 1 (1976): 38–41.

141. See J. Carmignac, *Recherches* (N 5): 91–102. In German the usual translation is "Dein Reich komme"; this is unfortunate. Dalman has worded the relevant chapter title with particular care, "Die Königsherrschaft Gottes" (*Die Worte Jesu* [N 5]: 310), thus establishing a point which he amplifies on p. 312 by saying, "Dass... 'Malkhut' nicht mit 'Reich,' sondern mit 'Königsherrschaft' wiederzugeben ist." English is equally unfortunate since the meaning of the word 'kingdom' has become narrowed in ordinary usage to such an extent that even scholars can be misled by its restricted sense.

142. On this see Joseph Bonsirven, *Le Règne de Dieu* (Paris: Aubier, 1957) and Rudolf Schnackenburg, *Gottes Herrschaft und Reich* (Freiburg im Briesgau: Herder, 1963). There is a very thoughtful appendix in Schnackenburg: "Note on the Need for Theology to Acquire a Fixed Terminology."

143. See J. Carmignac, *Recherches* (N 5): 107.

144. There is the vexed question of whether this stich refers only to the preceding one or whether it refers *in globo* to the whole group formed by stichs 2, 3, 4. In this latter case we would be asking for these three things (the name sanctified, the reign established, the will done) to be perfected on earth as they are in heaven. This, however, is not a problem that affects the translation into Hebrew. For further details see Carmignac, *Recherches* (N 5): 112–17.

145. See Carmignac, *Recherches* (N 5): 110–11.

146. See Carmignac (*Recherches* [N 5]: 336), where an oversight has led to *kn* being printed, though from p. 111 of the same work it is plain that this should have been *k'šr*.

147. The preposition *l* before *mḥr* is in fact used by the translation into Galilean Aramaic: *pittan delimehar* (see Dalman, *Die Worte Jesu* [N 5]: 322, 325).

148. The adjective *epiousion* can also convey the same nuance; see G. Kroening, "Was bedeutet *artos epiousios*?" *Gymnasium* 22 (1904): cols. 165–68.

149. They are listed in Carmignac, *Recherches* (N 5): 137–38.

150. For a fuller discussion of the problem see Carmignac, *Recherches* (N 5): 127, 137–38, 214–21.

151. See Carmignac, *Recherches* (N 5): 118–20.

152. See Carmignac, *Recherches* (N 5): 230–31.

153. J. Heller, "Die sechste Bitte des Vaterunser," *ZKT* (1901): 85–93; a translation in French is found in Carmignac, *Recherches* (N 5): 437–45.

154. For further details see Carmignac, *Recherches* (N 5): 236–304.

155. See Carmignac, *Recherches* (N 5): 255–68.

156. See Carmignac, *Recherches* (N 5): 312–17.

157. The distinction made at Qumran between *r'* and *rš'* is also observed in the Hebrew text of Ecclesiasticus 33:14 published by Joseph Marcus in *JQR* 21 (1930–31): 223–40: "Wickedness (*r'*) is opposed to goodness... the good person is opposed to the wicked (*rš'*) one."

158. For further details see Carmignac, *Recherches* (N 5): 320–33.

159. It would be impossible to list all the many people who have helped me in preparing this survey, but I owe a particular debt of gratitude to the following: M. Francis Peyraube of the Bibliothèque Nationale in Paris, Dr. Hubert Klein of the Staatsbibliothek in Berlin, the Rev. Roger Le Déaut, the Rev. Martin McNamara, the Rev. Brian Daley, and Fr. Jacques Robert, and indeed also to Dom Sylvester Houédard of Prinknash Abbey who made the translation from French to English.

3

JEWS AND JUDAISM IN *THE LIVING NEW TESTAMENT*

ELDON JAY EPP

The first of William Sanford LaSor's writings that came to my attention (apart from his inductive *Hebrew Handbook,* 1951) was a small pamphlet, privately printed, on "Isaiah 7:14—'Young Woman' or 'Virgin'?" (n.d., but c. 1953). This treatise issued from the heat of controversy in some circles over the adequacy and accuracy of the then new *Revised Standard Version* of the Old Testament, and in this particular case the issue was its accuracy in translating the well-known Isaiah passage. It is Professor LaSor's insistence on accuracy—in this and other instances—as the exclusive alternative to the inadmissible practice of translating a biblical text to suit one's own theology that prompts the present essay. Just as it was unpopular in some circles to defend the *RSV* in the early 1950's (as Professor LaSor quickly discovered), so in some—perhaps the same—circles today a criticism of the popular, best-selling *Living Bible* may be equally unwelcome. Yet, welcome or not, simple honesty, objectivity, and a facing of the facts, as exemplified so admirably by Professor LaSor in my every experience with him over the years, are the prerequisites to all scholarship worth the name, and I shall not shrink now from fulfilling, as best I can, those scholarly obligations.

I. Theological Impoverishment in *The Living New Testament*

Normally a paraphrastic translation, such as *The Living New Testament, Paraphrased*[1] (hereafter *LNT*), would require little scholarly comment, for such a work ordinarily is recognized and used for what it is—a paraphrase (as, e.g., in the case of Clarence Jordan's *The Cotton Patch Version* or even *Letters to Young Churches* by J. B. Phillips). The *LNT,* however, demands attention because of its extraordinarily wide distribution and extensive use, but particularly because of its clear theological slant, easily recognizable both by those in sympathy with its evangelical stance and by those outside. Naturally, every biblical translation will reveal something of the views and biases of its translators, but the *LNT* is noteworthy for its obtrusion of a simplistic revivalism, as evidenced by the frequent importation of evangelical terms and revivalist clichés into the text when there is no direct textual (and sometimes no inferential or contextual) warrant for such terms or phraseology. The following random examples (using the *RSV* for convenient comparison, though always the Greek New Testament is the final basis for comparison) may seem trivial when viewed in isolation, but together they show something of the theological complexion and religious level of the *LNT:* Three times in 1 Cor 14:22–24 the *LNT* uses "unsaved" for "unbelievers"; it has the "way to heaven" or "way to be saved" for "gospel" (Gal 1:6,8,11) or for "righteousness of God" (Rom 3:21); it has "be saved" for "justified" (Rom 3:28–31; Gal 2:16–17; 3:8; James 2:24–25) or for "righteousness" (Gal 2:21; Phil 3:9), or "get right with God" for "righteousness" (Rom 9:31), and reads "declared him fit for heaven" in place of "reckoned as righteousness" (Gal 3:6; cf. Rom 4:4; contrast James 2:21,23), or "take away sins" for "justify" (Rom 3:26, cf. 25), or "glorious life" for "justification" (Rom 5:16).

There are, moreover, numerous passages that are vastly amplified by modern evangelical jargon as they are recast for the paraphrase, such as the diffusive rendition of Rom 1:17, which in the *RSV* reads, "For in it [= the gospel] the righteousness of God is revealed through faith for faith," but which in the *LNT* becomes, "This Good News tells us that God makes us ready for heaven—makes us right in God's sight—when we put our faith and trust in Christ to save us. This is accomplished from start to finish by faith." Or hear the modern altar-call appeal in the prolix version of Rom 3:22 (*RSV:* "[Now has been manifested] the righteousness of God through faith in Jesus Christ for all who believe. For there is no distinction") as it appears in the *LNT:* "Now God says He will accept and acquit us—declare us 'not guilty'—if we trust Jesus Christ to take away our sins. And we all can be saved in this same way, by coming to Christ, no matter who we are or what we have been like." Nearly as expansive is the *LNT*'s "We . . . are counting on Christ's death to clear away our sins and make us right with God" (Gal 5:5) for what the *RSV* renders, "By faith we wait for the hope of righteousness" (cf. Rom 4:3; 9:31 in the *LNT*).

The *LNT* also has worked into the text of the New Testament a host of additional references to being "saved,"[2] at least one to being "born again" (1 John 3:9), and a few additional references to being "lost" (Luke 15:7; 19:9; Col 2:18; cf. Gal 5:4). The reader of the *LNT* will observe also that the editorial page headings frequently are in the same vein. Finally, the *LNT* contains at least two anachronistic mentions of "the Bible" (2 Tim 3:16; 4:4) and one to the Old and New Testaments (Matt 13:52, where a footnote acknowledges the anachronism).

Some of these alterations and additions in the text may be justifiable on hermeneutical grounds, particularly when it is remembered that the *Living Bible* paraphrases were designed originally for children; yet for the innumerable mature readers, many of whom will not even be aware of the paraphrastic nature of the work—to say nothing of their failure to recognize its liberties with the text—the *LNT* will be an unperceived but significant means for depriving them of the depth and richness of much in New Testament theology.

This deprivation of theological riches by the *LNT* is worth a further, brief examination because much of the affected material is related, at least indirectly, to the central subject of this essay. To begin with the obvious (and admittedly incidental), "to get to heaven" hardly touches the surface of the rich meaning of "eternal life" (Mark 10:17) or of "salvation" (Rom 1:16), nor does "I am a Christian; I am on my way to heaven" adequately comprehend "I know him [i.e., Christ]" in the Johannine sense of the term (1 John 2:4), nor are "wonderful story" (Mark 1:1) or "way to heaven" (Gal 1:6,11) sufficient explications of "gospel" as early Christianity employed the term. Moreover "put aside your own pleasures" (Mark 8:34; cf. Luke 9:23) is hardly more than the most superficial aspect of "let him deny himself."

Among the larger issues, the treatment of eschatology is a matter for concern inasmuch as the Jewish apocalyptic background of New Testament thought many times is obscured or even removed by the translation or paraphrase of the *LNT,* thereby impoverishing our understanding of those portions of the New Testament. For example, the dualistic two-age structure of apocalyptic, which certainly lies behind 1 Cor 2:6–7 and perhaps also 2:8, disappears completely when "not a wisdom of this age or of the rulers of this age, who are doomed to pass away" (2:6 *RSV*) becomes, in the *LNT,* "wisdom, but not the kind that comes from here on earth, and not the kind that appeals to the great men of this world, who are doomed to fall," and there are similar transformations in 2:7–8. Later, 1 Cor 10:11, where Paul speaks of Christians as those "upon whom the ends of the ages have come" (with both nouns plural, as in the Greek text and contrary to most English translations, though here the *ASV* happens to be correct), is an important statement of Paul's understanding of the human situation as "between the times" or as existence in the overlap of "this age" and the "age to come." To be sure, the eschatological context is retained in the *LNT* when the passage is rendered as "in these last days as the world nears its end," but the modern revivalist flavor and the recasting of the language remove completely Paul's subtle but technically precise reference to the two ages of apocalyptic thinking that form the critical background of his thought in this crucial passage—crucial not only for understanding Paul's Jewish apocalyptic orientation but particularly for demonstrating the essential similarity of Paul's message to that of Jesus with respect to the Kingdom of God. Similarly, the contrasting "this age" and "that age" of apocalyptic are obscured in Luke 20:34–35 by the *LNT*'s use of "here on earth" and "get to heaven," respectively, for the apocalyptic terms. As a matter of fact, the rather consistent translation of "this age" and of "the age to come" by "this world" or "this life" and by "the world to come," respectively,[3] while perhaps technically justifiable, will appear to most biblical theologians to reduce materially the proper apocalyptic flavor of these passages and to clothe them much more with the simplistic notions of this life and the afterlife, or even of time and eternity. Yet, as all will recognize, the aforementioned apocalyptic conceptions cannot be equated so facilely with these everyday terms for mortal life and immortality; however, when these identifications are made, as in the *LNT,* the clear result is a toning down of the Jewish apocalyptic background of New Testament thought—a background long recognized as essential for its full and proper interpretation and understanding.

On another aspect of New Testament eschatology, and one much debated in recent and current scholarship, the enigmatic term "Son of man" loses all of its ambiguity in the *LNT,* where it is translated, variously, as "I [= Jesus], the Son of Mankind";[4] or "I, the Man of Glory";[5] or "I, the Man from Heaven";[6] or simply as "I" (i.e., Jesus) or by an equivalent pronoun.[7] Naturally, there are innumerable views as to how and even whether Jesus used the term "Son of man"; some will hold that Jesus used the term of himself in all three of its categories, namely, the earthly, the suffering, and the apocalyptic Son of man sayings, and that this use constitutes a clear messianic claim for himself; others will take the position that Jesus used only two, one, or none of these categories of sayings as self-messianic claims. This, however, is not the place even for a review of the problem, though the *LNT*'s handling of the term "Son of man" at least requires illustration.

Those, on the one hand, who think that the so-called present or earthly Son of man sayings constitute no messianic claim on the part of Jesus (because in these Jesus was using the Semitic idiom, "Son of man," for "one" or "I") will applaud the *LNT*'s translation of "Son of man" as "I" at Luke 7:34: "But I eat My food and drink My wine, and you say, 'What a glutton Jesus is! And He drinks!'" rather than "The Son of man has come eating and drinking; and you say, 'Behold a glutton and a drunkard. . . .'" (*RSV*). In most of these earthly sayings, however, the *LNT* employs "I, the Son of Mankind" or "I, the Man from Heaven," and, moreover, it maintains no consistency even in parallel passages (e.g., "I" in Luke 7:34, as above, but "I, the Son of Mankind" in Matt 11:19; or "I, the Son of Mankind, have no home of My own . . ." in Matt 8:20, but "I, the Man from Heaven, have no earthly home at all" in Luke 9:58). Hence, it is obvious that no careful analysis of these sayings lies behind the varying translations. Even those, on the other hand, who are inclined to take all of the Son of man sayings as authentic to Jesus doubtless will find the *LNT*'s treatment of the so-called future or apocalyptic Son of man sayings disconcerting, for the eschatological dimension often is diminished and sometimes obscured by the unambiguous identification of the present, earthly Jesus with the future, heavenly Son of man. A striking example of this is Matt 10:23, where the words (in the *RSV*), "When they persecute you in one city, flee to the next; for truly, I say to you, you will not have gone through all the towns of Israel before the Son of man comes," become (in the *LNT*) "When you are persecuted in one city, flee to the next! I will return before you have reached them all!" Almost no one will deny that the original context here is an eschatological one, yet this aspect of the passage is obliterated by the *LNT*, for the word "return," without the apocalyptic connotations provided by the term "Son of man"—connotations that disappeared from the *LNT* with the removal of "Son of man"—assumes its ordinary, everyday meaning of "come back, rejoin." Naturally, the difficulty of this notoriously vexing passage is thereby alleviated in the *LNT*, but this is accomplished by an arbitrary removal from the passage of the problematic element itself.

Further, more typical examples of the unambiguous identification of the earthly Jesus and the future Son of man occur several times in Matthew 24 and 25, where, e.g., 24:27 in the *RSV* reads, "For as the lightning comes from the east and shines as far as the west, so will be the coming of the Son of man," but the *LNT* has, "For as the lightning flashes across the sky from east to west, so shall My coming be, when I, the Son of all Mankind, return." The *LNT* goes on, then, to replace "Son of man" with the personal pronoun referring to Jesus, as follows (24:30–31): "And then at last the signal of My coming will appear in the heavens. . . . And the nations of the world will see Me arrive in the clouds of heaven, with power and great glory. And I shall send My angels. . . ." Other examples of future Son of man sayings so treated in the *LNT* are numerous.[8] Now, if Jesus did use the term "Son of man" in these so-called future Son of man sayings (which seems clear on source-critical and form-critical grounds) and if it were to be allowed that he did identify himself with that Son of man, thereby making messianic claims for himself (which is more difficult to demonstrate), then certainly he did so in far more subtle and indirect ways and in a less personal and egotistic fashion than the *LNT* suggests, for the *LNT* efficiently obscures all of the third-person indirectness, the intriguing ambiguity, and the enigmatic nature of any messianic claims of Jesus that might be inherent in his use of the term "Son of man." This, at the very least, represents a failure to appreciate the richness—to say nothing of the mystery—with which the synoptic gospels portray the messianic self-understanding of Jesus; regrettably, the serious reader of the *LNT* will be impoverished and all readers will be misled by this approach.

It is to be expected, I suppose, that biblical translations into everyday language—but more so paraphrases—will tend to obscure the historical background of the biblical text, partly because everyday language tends to shun unfamiliar, technical terminology and partly because such translations or paraphrases often are designed for current usefulness and direct edification. That the *LNT* shows to a marked extent this tendency to cloud the historical and ideological milieu of the New Testament is evident from the preceding paragraphs. A further illustration, from another thought-world that shaped Paul's theological conceptions, concerns Paul's references (and those in Ephesians and Colossians) to the cosmic spirit-forces of the universe. Though the subject entails much controversy, most would agree that this background is reflected at least in Rom 8:38–39; 1 Cor 15:24; Gal 4:3,8–9; Eph 1:21; 3:10; 6:12; and Col 1:16; 2:8,10,15,20. It is striking that in the *LNT*, with but two exceptions, the cosmic spirit-world virtually disappears from these passages. The familiar passage in Rom 8:38–39 becomes, in the *LNT:*

> For I am convinced that nothing can ever separate us from His love. Death can't, and life can't. The angels won't, and all the powers of hell itself cannot keep God's love away. Our fears for today, our worries about tomorrow, or where we are—high above the sky, or in the deepest ocean—nothing will ever be able to separate us from the love of God demonstrated by our Lord Jesus Christ when he died for us.

Here there is no mention or even a remnant of the technical terminology of "principalities and powers." These terms disappear also from 1 Cor 15:24, where the *RSV* reads, ". . . after destroying every rule and every authority and power," but where the *LNT* has ". . . having put down all enemies of every kind." They are removed also from Eph 1:21, where ". . . far above all rule and authority and power and dominion" (*RSV*) becomes ". . . far, far above any other king or ruler or dictator or leader" (*LNT*); and "principalities and powers in the heavenly places" (*RSV*) in Eph 3:10 is rendered "all the powers of heaven" (*LNT*). Colossians 2, with a major passage on the cosmic spirit-forces, is similarly transformed so as to remove—in radical fashion—all references to this Hellenistic background, for "the elemental spirits of the universe" in 2:8 are submerged in the *LNT*'s phrase, "wrong and shallow answers built on men's thoughts and ideas"; in 2:10 Christ as "the head of all rule and authority" (*RSV*) becomes "He is the highest ruler, with authority over every other power"; the famous *Christus victor* passage in 2:15, "He disarmed the principalities and powers and made a public example of them, triumphing over them in it [the cross]" is transformed by the *LNT* to read, "In this way God took away Satan's power to accuse you of sin, and God openly displayed to the whole world Christ's triumph at the cross where your sins were all taken away"; and in 2:20 the reference to Christians having died with Christ "to the elemental spirits of the universe" (*RSV*) becomes, in the *LNT,* "Since you died, as it were, with Christ and this has set you free from following the world's ideas of how to be saved—by doing good and obeying certain rules . . . , "which is a paraphrase that eradicates completely the cosmic motif of the passage. The Galatians 4 passage, also referring to "elemental spirits of the universe" (4:3) and "weak and beggarly elemental spirits" (4:9), is treated in an unexpected fashion by the *LNT,* which interprets "elemental spirits" as "Jewish laws" (see further below). The two passages retaining something of the spirit-forces motif in the *LNT* are Col 1:16 and Eph 6:12, the former clearly so by mention of Christ creating "the spirit world with its kings and kingdoms, its rulers and authorities," but the latter is slanted toward the Jewish thought-world by the insertion of the word "satanic," which is not found in the Ephesians text: "For we are not fighting against people made of flesh and blood, but against persons without bodies—the evil rulers of the unseen world, those mighty satanic beings and great evil princes of darkness who rule this world; and against huge numbers of wicked spirits in the spirit world" (Eph 6:12, *LNT*). Though little of this will be seriously misleading, the obscuring of an underlying thought-world and orientation is still very much a loss.

This impoverishment of New Testament thought, somewhat randomly illustrated in these several ways, will have to be endured by the readers of the *LNT;* unfortunately, most will be unaware that they have been thus deprived. Regrettable as this may be, much more worrisome is the prospect of clergy or laymen exegeting the New Testament text on the basis of the *LNT;* if that were to happen, what chance is there, for instance, that Paul's doctrine of righteousness would be properly discerned from this paraphrase, or that the teaching of the Epistle of James would be properly understood from it, when, for example, the same phrase in the same Old Testament quotation, "reckoned to him as righteousness" (*RSV*), is rendered in the *LNT* as "declared him fit for heaven" at Gal 3:6, or as "cancelled his sins and declared him not guilty" at Rom 4:3 (cf. 4:22 *LNT*), but is phrased as "declared him good" in James 2:23 (cf. 2:21 *LNT*). Moreover, Christological studies based on the *LNT* will founder, not only because of the various transformations of "Son of man," but also on the *LNT*'s rather loose and indiscriminate use of "Messiah" for "Son of David" (Matt 12:23), for "Lord" (Luke 1:76), for "Consolation of Israel" (Luke 2:25), for "Kingdom of God" (Luke 23:51), and for "Son of man" (Mark 9:12; Luke 24:7; John 9:35; 12:34), and because of the free sprinkling of the text, especially in the Fourth Gospel, with additional mentions of "Messiah" (John 2:11,23; 3:26; 4:39,53; 6:30; 8:31; 10:42; and 12:37,42).

All of this (and what follows) is not to say that a reader can learn nothing from the *LNT;* certainly this reader has learned much, for any fresh rendition of the New Testament text time and again forces the reader back to the original text to see whether the new version has aptly captured the flavor of the text or has missed it—inevitably a fruitful exercise. Nevertheless, many of the most serious dangers of a paraphrase seem to have found a concentration here in the *LNT,* such as a lack of consistency in the treatment of parallel passages, of identical terms or ideas, and of related contexts; the tendency not only to insert theological preference and bias, but to elaborate them in paraphrastic digression; and the strong inclination to turn ancient technical terms and concepts into contemporary religious jargon congenial to the paraphraser's theological point of view. It is incumbent, therefore, upon all who are concerned with the study and propagation of the New Testament to inform themselves or to be informed about the exact character of the *LNT*.

II. Castigation of Judaism in *The Living New Testament*

The theological impoverishment illustrated above often is due to the *LNT*'s failure to appreciate—or even to recognize—the Jewish background of the biblical theology of the gospels or of Paul. Attention is directed now, however, to the more direct and specific treatment of Jews and Judaism by the *LNT,* and in this respect anyone sensitive to Jewish-Christian dialogue readily will discern that the *LNT* seems not only to misunderstand and thereby denigrate Pharisaic Judaism (by reducing it to a mere legalism), but the *LNT* appears almost to take pleasure in castigating and chastening the Jews and Judaism—to punish them by tongue-lashing and to reprimand them for failing to accept "their Messiah" (see below)—while all along wishing also, it would seem, to preach the gospel to any Jewish readers.

First, however, let it be acknowledged that in one respect at least the *LNT* removes an unfortunate impression of the Jews produced on the surface of the Fourth Gospel due to that gospel's peculiar and extensive *negative* use of the term "the Jews." Whether legitimate or not as a translation or justifiable hermeneutically, the *LNT* (not often noted for consistency) has quite consistently substituted "Jewish leaders" for "the Jews" in contexts where the Fourth Gospel portrays hostility between Jesus and "the Jews."[9] Doubtless this is correct historically, both on the basis of comparison with the synoptic gospels and on other grounds, for certainly all "the Jews" were not opponents of Jesus during his ministry (What other audience did he have?), nor were "the Jews" as a whole his accusers and murderers, as at least a superficial reading of the Fourth Gospel in other versions quite clearly suggests.[10] Yet, this particular "correction" of John's gospel by the *LNT* is widely countermanded by its portrayal elsewhere of the Jews and Judaism.

The castigation of the Jews and the denigration of Judaism by the *LNT* come in several ways, and they are bound to be offensive to Jewish readers, are sure to mislead Christians in their understanding of Judaism—ancient and modern, and are likely to have a deleterious effect on contemporary Jewish-Christian relations. In this connection, one of the more curious alterations by the *LNT* is the philologically plausible though inappropriate and quite unnecessary use of "nation" rather than "generation" in Matt 11:16; 12:39–45; 16:4; and Luke 17:25 (cf. Luke 11:32); and Acts 2:40. *Genea* in all of these passages clearly means "generation" in the sense of "contemporaries" and does not refer to the "nation" of Israel either in its historical perspective or in its then contemporary status. Accordingly, when the *LNT* reports that Jesus referred to Israel as "an evil, faithless nation," "this evil nation," or "this evil, unbelieving nation" (Matt 12:39,45; 16:4); that Jesus predicted his rejection "by this whole nation" (Luke 17:25; *RSV* reads "by this generation"); that Jesus referred to the condemnation of "this nation" in the last judgment and said that "this nation won't listen" (Luke 11:32, even though this latter clause is not in the Lucan text); and that "Peter preached a long sermon, telling about Jesus and strongly urging all his listeners [who were all Jews] to save themselves from the evils of their nation" (Acts 2:40, where *RSV* properly translates ". . . Save yourselves from this crooked generation"), the net effect is to defame—in the eyes of the reader—the whole nation of Israel, past and present, though this by no means was the original intention in any of these passages.

In these passages and elsewhere, the *LNT* seems almost to be scolding the (ancient and modern) Jews for not accepting "Jesus, your Messiah" (*LNT* at Matt 27:17,22, rather than "Jesus who is called Christ") or "the Jews' Messiah" (the *LNT*'s rendering of "the King of the Jews" at Matt 27:11; cf. "our Messiah," "their [the Jews'] Messiah" at Luke 23:2-3; John 12:11). Observe also that in the *LNT* Jesus' response to the inquiry as to whether he is "the Jews' Messiah" is a straightforward "Yes" (Matt 27:11) or "Yes, it is as you say" (Mark 15:2; Luke 23:3), rather than the amgibuous "You say so" of the Greek text. All of this is set in bold relief, as we have seen, by the added editorial comment of the *LNT* that "this nation won't listen" (Luke 11:32)! Something of a Jewish evangelization theme appears also in the *LNT*'s curious combining of vv 9 and 10 of Luke 19: "This man [Zacchaeus] is one of the lost sons of Abraham, and I, the Son of Mankind, have come to search for and to save such souls as his" (though the Lucan text has neither "lost" in v 9 nor "such as his" in v 10). A similar motivation would appear to lie behind the frequent transformation of passages in the Fourth Gospel, including several instances where Jews or Jewish leaders are mentioned specifically in the context, in which phrases like "believe in him/Jesus" are turned into specific statements of belief that Jesus is Messiah (John 6:30; 8:31; 10:42; 12:37,42; cf. 2:11,23; 4:39,53) or even that "Jewish leaders . . . believed in Jesus as their Messiah" (12:11); in none of these passages does the word "Messiah (Christ)" actually appear in the Johannine text. This heightening of the Messiahship of Jesus is evident in other ways in the *LNT*, including alterations resulting in Jesus making more direct divine claims for himself (e.g., Matt 21:13 and Luke 19:46; Matt 26:64 and Luke 22:70; Matt 12:6; and transformations of the term "Son of man"); rewriting parables of Jesus so that they speak specifically of or apply directly to Jesus himself with respect to his death and resurrection (John 12:23-24) or his Second Coming (Matt 24:44-51; 25:1-13,31-46; Mark 13:34-37); numerous additional insertions into the text of the word "Messiah";[11] and in incidental ways, such as substituting "God's Son" for "a son of God" in Matt 27:54 (but not in Mark 15:39), and the frequent replacement of "Holy One of God" by "Holy Son of God" (Mark 1:24; Luke 4:34; John 6:69; also "Holy Son" for "Holy One" in the Psalm quotation in Acts 2:27, but not in 13:35).

Along the same line, the substitution of "nation" for "generation" by the *LNT* in the Matt 12:38-45 pericope (discussed earlier) is accompanied by other improper changes, namely, the use of "miracle" and "proof" for "sign" in 12:38-39 (which is appropriate for the Fourth Gospel, but not for the synoptics, where "sign" regularly means an indication of apocalyptic fulfillment) and the addition of the phrase, "to prove that He was really the Messiah" in 12:38. These changes effectively remove all of the eschatological background and flavor from the pericope, with the result that the pericope in the *LNT* now focuses entirely upon proof that Jesus is Messiah and upon belief in him as Messiah.

Pursuing further this heightened theme of Jesus as Messiah, there is in the *LNT* a disturbing consistency in exonerating Jesus from seemingly mistaken notions about the appearance of the eschaton in his very own generation. This exoneration can be observed in connection with some instances of *genea* ('generation') in the gospels that were not relevant to the earlier discussion of that term. Already this tendency to exempt Jesus from any appearance of miscalculation was observed at Matt 10:23, where the *LNT* eliminates the immediacy of the apocalyptic event by removing the eschatological character of the passage entirely, leaving Jesus with nothing that might be construed as a misconception about the eschaton and attributing to him only the most innocuous comment about his rejoining the disciples before they have finished their preaching mission among "the cities of Israel." A more striking example is found in the *LNT*'s version of Mark 13:30 (and parallels), which occurs in the so-called "Little Apocalypse" (Mark 13). It is obvious that the *LNT* interprets this entire section wholly and unambiguously in terms of Jesus' own Second Coming (see *LNT,* Mark 13:29-37, where "My coming" and "My return" occur four times without warrant from the Marcan text; cf. also Matt 24:27,30,33,39,44; Luke 21:34). The *LNT* also retains the famous statement of ignorance in Mark 13:32 (*LNT:* "no one. . . , nor I Myself, knows the day or the hour when these things will happen; only the Father knows"; *RSV:* "of that day or that hour no one knows. . . , nor the Son, but only the Father"), but—perhaps to maintain consistency with this acknowledgment of ignorance—the *LNT* removes completely Jesus' indication that the end (which, however, can still be calculated from signs; Mark 13:7-29) will come in his own generation; instead, the *LNT* makes it easy to interpret the Second Coming as imminent in *our* own time rather than as imminent in *Jesus*' own time: Mark 13:29-30:

> *RSV:* So also, when you see these things taking place, you know that he [= the Son of man] is near, at the very gates. Truly, I say to you, this generation will not pass away before all these things take place.
>
> *LNT:* And when you see these things happening that I've described, you can be sure that My return is very near, that I am right at the door. Yes, these are the events that will signal the end of the age.

Thus, the clear indication of the Marcan text that Jesus predicted the appearance of the eschaton in his own generation is thoroughly obliterated, and the synoptic parallels to these Marcan passages are similarly treated in the *LNT:* "Truly, I say to you, this generation will not pass away till all these things take place" (*RSV,* Matt 24:34; ". . . till all has taken place," Luke 21:32) becomes "Then at last this age will come to its close" in the *LNT* of Matt 24:34, and "I solemnly declare to you that when these things happen, the end of the age has come" in the *LNT*'s version of Luke 21:32. The imminence and yet the indefiniteness of modern revivalist eschatology has been imposed upon the synoptic narrative at these points in the *LNT,* and this imposition has been carried through with a rigid consistency, even though such consistency is rarely noticeable elsewhere in the *LNT* when parallel passages are in question.

Heightening the Messiahship of Jesus will appear to be at best a highly indirect castigation of the Jews, though many modern Jews will feel its sting if it is tied in with a Jewish evangelization theme—as it quite clearly is in the *LNT*. A further and more pointed illustration of the *LNT*'s excoriation of the Jews comes in Paul's characterization of the Israel of his time in Rom 11:28: "As regards the gospel they are enemies of God, for your sake; but as regards his election they are beloved for the sake of their forefathers" (*RSV*). This, in the *LNT*, becomes "Now many of the Jews are enemies of the Gospel. They hate it. But this has been a benefit to you, for it has resulted in God's giving His gifts to you Gentiles. Yet the Jews are still beloved of God because of his promises to Abraham, Isaac, and Jacob." The *LNT*'s added invective seems as unnecessary as permitting Caiaphas to characterize his fellow "chief priests and Pharisees" as "You stupid idiots" (*LNT*, John 11:49) and as unwarranted as the *LNT*'s transfer of Judas' guilt for betraying Jesus to the Jewish leaders by altering a pronoun, a participle, and a verb from singular to plural in John 19:11: "So those [= Jewish leaders, see v 12] who brought Me to you have the greater sin" (*LNT*), rather than "Therefore he who delivered me to you has the greater sin" (*RSV*). A further curiosity is the change by the *LNT* in Matt 18:17, where an uncomplimentary use of the term "Gentile" is eliminated from Jesus' words: If a brother sins against another and rejects the judgment of the church in the matter, "let him be to you as a Gentile and a tax collector," says the *RSV*, but the *LNT* reads, "then the church should excommunicate him." Likewise, "Gentiles" disappears in similar circumstances from the *LNT* at Matt 5:47; 6:7; and 3 John 7 (but not at Gal 2:15, where the word also has negative connotations).

The chief denigration of Judaism by the *LNT* occurs, however, in its treatment of Torah or Mosaic law and its understanding (or, rather, misunderstanding) of Judaism as mere legalism, a theme not only frequent in the *LNT*, but seemingly belabored at every opportunity. The most obvious opportunities come, naturally, in Paul's discussion of the law in Romans and Galatians, but the reader of the *LNT* who begins with Matthew will discover the theme very quickly from the footnote at the first mention of "Pharisees" in the New Testament text (Matt 3:7), where "Pharisees" are defined as "Jewish religious leaders who strictly followed the letter of the law but often violated its intent." Another footnote in a similar vein has been attached to the pericope on the rich man and Lazarus at Luke 16:31: "Even Christ's resurrection failed to convince the Pharisees, to whom he gave this illustration."

These comments on Pharisees introduce a most difficult and delicate problem. Certainly the gospels, quite apart from the *LNT*, already display a distinctly negative attitude toward the Pharisees and toward their development of oral Torah, and certainly also Jesus is portrayed frequently as critical of the Pharisees. Yet the term "Pharisee" must not be taken—as it too often is—as a synonym for "hypocrite"; obviously there were hypocrites among the Pharisees, as there are in all human groups. As a matter of fact, however, Jesus himself not only was conversant with the Pharisees in legal matters but shows a highly positive attitude toward Torah (see Matt 5:17–19; Luke 16:17). Shocking as the thought may be to most Christians, where within the Judaism of his day does Jesus the Jew fit except somewhere within Pharisaic Judaism? Despite recent attempts to place him among the Essenes or the Zealots, he does not fit in either group, and most assuredly he cannot be placed with the Sadducees. It is one thing, therefore, for the gospels to portray for us a Jesus who is critical of certain legalistic maneuvers by other Jewish teachers (Dare I say fellow-Pharisees?), but it is quite another thing to generalize from these several instances to a general characterization of all of Judaism—past and present—as a mere legalistic system, devoid of religious substance or feeling and unworthy of respect. The *LNT* appears to fall into this latter trap, as evidenced, for instance, by its paraphrase of John 1:17, "the law was given through Moses" (*RSV*), which in the *LNT* reads, "Moses gave us only the Law with its rigid demands and merciless justice." Furthermore, the not incorrect though unnecessary addition of "wrong" before "teaching of the Pharisees and Sadducees" in Matt 16:12 and of "proud, self-righteous" before "Pharisee" in Luke 18:10–11; the similar insertion of "evil" before the "hearts" of the Pharisees at Luke 16:15; and the several references in Hebrews to "the old system of Jewish laws," or the like (Heb 10:1; 8:4; cf. 7:18,28; 9:8–10,13) are additional evidences of a negative stance toward Judaism by the *LNT*. The same theme appears in the *LNT*'s rendition of Matt 23:2–3, where the original text has Jesus speak positively of the scribes and Pharisees as legitimate successors of Moses, though he censures their hypocrisy: "The scribes and the Pharisees sit on Moses' seat; so practice and observe whatever they tell you, but not what they do; for they preach, but they do not practice" (*RSV*); here the *LNT* gives a strikingly different complexion and emphasis to Jesus' words, including harsh sarcasm: "You would think these Jewish leaders and these Pharisees were Moses, the way they keep making up so many laws! And of course you should obey their every whim! It may be all right to do what they say, but above anything else, *don't follow their example!* For they don't do what they tell you to do."

Our problem with Pharisaic Judaism—the only kind of Judaism there was after A.D. 70—is compounded by St. Paul's attitude toward it, for it is well recognized that Paul the Pharisee held (or rather developed) a view of Torah that was untypical of Pharisees generally; not all Pharisees—probably, in fact, very few—felt oppressed by the law, enslaved by it, and in bondage to it as Paul did. Rather, the normal attitude of the average Pharisee no doubt was that of joyful and willing obedience so as to fulfill very precisely the whole will of God. Paul's psychological make-up prevented him, apparently, from sharing this common, positive view; hence, his own negative judgment on the Pharisaic regulations and his tendency to emphasize the legalistic character of the Judaism of his day are not unexpected and indeed are obvious enough in his writings, but it is unfair to Judaism, then and now, further to heighten these peculiarities of Paul or to extend and expand upon them so that they become the exclusive terms in which Judaism is defined and by which it is characterized and apprehended. Paul, after all, also has a fundamentally positive attitude toward law as something "holy" (Rom 7:12 [*LNT* omits "holy"]; cf. 3:31 [*LNT* so transforms the clause, "We uphold the law,'' as to eliminate it]; Gal 3:21) and as that which leads to Christ (Rom 10:4 [*telos* as ''goal''; the *LNT* treats it as ''termination'']; Gal 3:19,23–24).

With all this in mind, we need to examine Paul's discussion of law in Romans and Galatians as these letters are paraphrased in the *LNT*. First, there are a number of incidental, yet quite pointed expansions that heighten the legalistic aspect of Judaism and do so in a disparaging fashion. For example, in Rom 7:6, ''not under the old written code'' (*RSV*) becomes in the *LNT* ''not in the old way, mechanically obeying a set of rules''; in Rom 10:1–3 the third-person reference by Paul to ''Israel'' acquires, in the *LNT*, the second-person directness of a sermon to ''the Jewish people,'' and Paul's terse statement of v 3, ''For, being ignorant of the righteousness that comes from God, and seeking to establish their own, they did not submit to God's righteousness'' (*RSV*), is rendered ''For you don't understand that Christ died to make you right with God. Instead you are trying to make yourselves good enough to gain God's favor by keeping the Jewish laws and customs, but that is not God's way of salvation'' (*LNT*).

Galatians in the *LNT* heightens the legalistic depiction of Judaism in a marked fashion. Gal 2:4, which refers to ''false brethren . . . who slipped in . . . that they might bring us into bondage'' (*RSV*), becomes, in the *LNT*, ''so-called 'Christians' there—false ones, really—who came to spy on us and see . . . whether we obeyed Jewish laws or not. They tried to get us all tied up in their rules, like slaves in chains''; and v 5, where Paul reports that he and his companions did not yield to them ''that the truth of the gospel might be preserved for you'' (*RSV*), becomes, as the *LNT* has it, ''for we did not want to confuse you into thinking that salvation can be earned by being circumcised and by obeying Jewish laws.'' Similar expansions, with varying degrees of intensity, occur in the *LNT* also at Gal 2:12,17,18,19; 3:3; 4:21,24–25,29,31; 5:2,6,11,18. Particularly notable, however, are the following expressions employed by the *LNT* in Galatians to describe Judaism: ''that impossible system'' (3:13); ''slaves to Jewish laws and rituals'' (for *RSV*'s ''slaves to the elemental spirits of the universe'' at 4:3); ''another poor, weak, useless religion of trying to get to heaven by obeying God's laws'' (4:9, for *RSV*'s ''weak and beggarly elemental spirits''); ''slaves to the law'' (4:5, for ''under the law''); ''free from these chains'' (4:12); ''. . . Jerusalem, the mother-city of the Jews, the center of that system of trying to please God by trying to obey the Commandments,'' with the further statement that ''the Jews, who try to follow that system, are her [Hagar's] slave children. But our mother-city is the heavenly Jerusalem, and she is not a slave to Jewish laws'' (4:25–26); and ''Don't get all tied up again in the chains of slavery to Jewish laws and ceremonies'' (5:1).

Finally, the editorializing page headings in the *LNT* are not immune from the defamation theme illustrated above: ''The Pharisees blaspheme Jesus'' (at Matthew 12); ''Jewish leaders try to kill Him'' (John 8; cf. John 7); ''Most Jews have searched in vain'' (Romans 11); and ''Jewish laws can't save'' (Galatians 3).

One major area of concern remains, and that is the *LNT*'s misuse of the Old Testament—the Jewish Bible—by twisting a number of Old Testament quotations that occur in the New Testament into *explicit,* and thereby often anachronistic, statements about Jesus Christ, or by turning them into pronouncements by Jesus (and once by Paul) rather than oracles of God, with some startling results. Some of these transformations yield pointed jibes at the Jews, though obviously not all involve straightforward castigation of the Jews or active denigration of Judaism; rather, many show a lack of respect for the "Sacred Writ" of Judaism; an absence of historical accuracy; or an overriding imposition of Christian elements upon Jewish literature, thereby compromising the integrity of that literature; and, regrettably, a certain stealthiness at times in making the alterations.

A peculiarity of earliest Christianity (and one that has persisted in most conservative Christian circles) is the tendency to interpret numerous aspects of the Christ-event as fulfillments of specific Old Testament passages that thereby are understood as divine prophecies (in the predictive sense of that term). The earliest church obviously found a rationale for its own history and a justification for its beliefs in these fulfillments of prophecy. As is well recognized, an Old Testament passage had to be neither oracular nor taken strictly in its context to be "prophetic" for the earliest church (as is illustrated, among other places, by the use in Matt 2:15 of Hos 11:1), and consequently (though not alone for this reason) ancient and modern Judaism has been both mystified by and resentful of such usage by Christians of passages from the Jewish Bible.

In this connection, the *LNT* is certain to dismay contemporary Jewish readers even further, for it reinforces and in some ways expands the role of predictive Old Testament "prophecies" in the gospel narratives and in the theological discussions of Paul. This clear tendency is first illustrated in Matt 11:10, quoting Mal 3:1. In place of the *RSV*'s simple, "This is he of whom it is written, 'Behold I send my messenger before thy face, who shall prepare thy way before thee,' " the *LNT* has "For John is the man mentioned in the Scriptures—a messenger to precede Me, to announce My coming, and prepare people to receive Me." The lack of secondary quotation marks in the *LNT* makes the "Me" and "My" refer explicitly to Jesus, whereas any such reference to Jesus is at best implied in Matthew. A further illustration occurs in Matt 21:13 and Luke 19:46, where the *LNT,* by omitting the secondary quotation marks, has Jesus call the Temple his house rather than God's: "The Scriptures say My Temple is a place of prayer." Also, Jesus' response to the arresting soldiers in Mark 14:49 is of interest: "Day after day I was with you in the temple teaching, and you did not seize me. But let the scriptures be fulfilled" (*RSV*); the *LNT* makes more explicit this prophetic reference to Jesus: "Why didn't you arrest Me in the Temple? I was there teaching every day. But these things are happening to fulfill the prophecies about Me."

Unusual liberties with an Old Testament quotation are taken by the *LNT* in Rom 9:33, where Paul quotes Isa 28:16 as follows: "Behold, I am laying in Zion a stone that will make men stumble, a rock that will make them fall; and he who believes in him will not be put to shame'' (*RSV*); the *LNT* transforms this into ''I have put a Rock in the path of the Jews, and many will stumble over Him (Jesus). Those who believe in Him will never be disappointed.'' The *LNT* has quotation marks around this text, exactly as quoted above, which will lead any unthinking reader to suppose that the name ''Jesus'' is part of the Old Testament scriptural text; moreover, in place of the introductory phrase, ''as it is written,'' in *RSV*, the *LNT* announces: ''God warned them [= the Jews, see v 31] of this in the Scriptures when he said. . . .'' Or consider Rom 10:21, where a quotation from Isaiah disappears completely from the *LNT* and is transformed into a didactic jibe at the (contemporary?) Jews: *RSV* reads, ''But of Israel he [God] says, 'All day long I have held out my hands to a disobedient and contrary people.' '' The *LNT* has, ''In the meantime, He keeps on reaching out His hands to the Jews, but they keep arguing and refusing to come.'' It is important to notice that no quotation marks enclose this passage in the *LNT*, nor is it in any way made clear that it is an Isaiah quotation (as is v 20 that precedes). Something similar has happened in Rom 11:8, where another quotation (Deut 29:4; Isa 29:10) is given an explicitly Christian interpretation by the *LNT* and where the last part of the quotation looks as if it is a direct comment of Paul—*RSV:* ''As it is written, 'God gave them a spirit of stupor, eyes that should not see and ears that should not hear, down to this very day' ''; this becomes, in the *LNT*, ''This is what our Scriptures refer to when they say that God has put them [= the Jews, see v 7] to sleep, shutting their eyes and ears so that they do not understand what we are talking about when we tell them of Christ. So it is to this very day.'' Incidentally, the phrase, ''our Scriptures,'' in juxtaposition with ''them'' [the Jews] suggests that Paul is claiming the Old Testament exclusively for Christians, as does the Epistle of Barnabas in the early second century—a quite un-Pauline claim!

Again, in Rom 15:21 an Isaiah quotation (52:15) referring to the Servant of God [Israel] is made explicitly Christian: *RSV* reads, ''As it is written, 'They shall see who have never been told of him, and they shall understand who have never heard of him,' '' which, in the *LNT*, is ''I have been following the plan spoken of in the Scriptures where Isaiah says that those who have never heard the name of Christ before will see and understand.'' Admittedly, Paul did mean to refer to ''Christ,'' that is, to Jesus Christ, when he employed this Old Testament passage, but it is misleading to imply that Isaiah spoke of ''the name of Christ''; perhaps Old Testament quotations are better left in their exact phraseology, both out of fairness and in the interest of leaving them their integrity as texts. A further case is Rom 11:26, where ''Jews'' has been substituted for ''Jacob''—a justifiable interchange of terms, but a dangerous practice as we have seen. It is worth mention, finally, that the *LNT* has erased all indication that two Old Testament quotations constitute Rom 11:34-35—a phenomenon already observed elsewhere—thereby obscuring the scriptural background and richness of Paul's thought. The Old Testament quotations that remain in the *LNT* are ample evidence, however, that it has as a major theme that ''The Old Testament tells about Jesus,'' as the page heading at John 5 puts it.

III. Conclusion

This summary of the ways in which the *LNT* treats passages that relate directly or indirectly to the Jews and Judaism may seem most uncharitable toward a literary endeavor that obviously was both serious and well intentioned and that—even more obviously—has been extraordinarily successful in terms of distribution, use, and acclaim. Uncharitable or not, however, the conclusion that emerges concerning the *LNT,* at least from the angle of its treatment of the Jews (but quite certainly of wider application also) is unmistakable: In whatever ways and for whatever purposes the *LNT* is used, it must not be used for the exegesis of a New Testament text and it must not become the final authority for the exposition of a New Testament passage. To be fair to those responsible for the *LNT,* however, it should be added that the "Preface" of the edition used for this study commends the *LNT* only as "a companion to the favored translation" used by any reader; unfortunately, only the more serious readers of the *LNT* will employ it in this supplementary fashion.

It is encouraging to observe (also from the "Preface") that the Paraphrase Revision Committee for the *LNT* intends continually to revise the work "as desirable changes become evident, with a general revision every five years"; their generous invitation to general readers and scholars for suggestions toward such revisions is a further source of encouragement. Perhaps the present essay will be taken as a response to that invitation, even though it is by one who happened upon the *LNT* only recently and whose late responses are very largely negative. Moreover, if the observations furnished here are rather sharply phrased, this pointedness—tempered at times by irritation—is due to the conviction alluded to at the outset (a conviction instilled by Professor LaSor and others) that every treatment of biblical literature must be objective and in accordance with proper historical method.

NOTES

1. A Meridian Book (New York: World, 1972) which incorporates the previously published *Living Gospels, Living Letters,* and *Living Prophecies*.
2. Rom 3:31; 4:2,4–5,11–12; 9:32; 11:5; 15:9; 1 Cor 15:17; Gal 2:18; 3:12; 4:3,21; 5:2; Phil 3:3–4,12; Col 1:23; 2:20; 1 Tim 1:9; Heb 4:2; 6:1,19; 7:18; 2 Pet 2:19.
3. E.g., Matt 12:32; Mark 4:19; 10:30; Luke 16:8; 18:30; Rom 12:2; 1 Cor 2:6; Eph 1:21; Heb 6:5; "this evil world," 2 Cor 4:4; Gal 1:4; cf. also "end of the world" for "end of the age" in Matt 13:39,40,49; 24:3; 28:20; or the occasional rendering of "this age" as "this life" (Matt 13:22; 2 Tim 4:10) or as "here on earth" (Mark 10:30; Luke 20:34; 1 Cor 2:6) or "now" (Luke 18:30) or "day after day" (Titus 2:12); in 1 Tim 6:17 the reference to "this age" disappears altogether.
4. Matt 12:8,40; 16:27; 17:12; 18:11; 19:28; 20:28; 24:27; 25:31; 26:64; Mark 9:31; 10:33–34; 13:26; Luke 9:44; 18:8; 19:10; John 6:62.
5. Mark 8:38; Luke 9:26; 12:40; 22:69; John 1:51; 6:53.
6. Mark 2:10,28; 10:45; Luke 9:58; 12:8; 21:27; John 3:13; 6:27.
7. Matt 12:31; 13:37,41; 16:13,28; 17:22–23; 20:18–19; 24:30–31,33,39,44; 26:2,24,45; Mark 8:31; 9:9; 13:27; 14:21,41,62; Luke 5:24; 6:5; 9:22; 11:30; 12:10; 17:22–26,30; 18:31–33; 21:36; 22:22; John 12:23; 13:31.

8. Matt 16:27–28; 19:28; 24:33,39,44; 25:31–33; 26:64; Mark 13:26; 14:62; Luke 9:26; 12:8,40; 17:22,24,26,30; 18:8; 21:27,36; 22:69.
9. "Jewish leaders" for "the Jews" occurs in the *LNT* in the following passages: John 1:19; 2:18; 5:10,15,16,18; 7:1,11,13,15,35; 8:31,48,52,57,59; 9:18,22; 10:19,24;31; 11:8,19,31,33,36,45; 12:11; 13:33; 18:14,20,36; 19:12,31,38; 20:19. It is doubtful, however, that Jewish leaders are meant in 11:19,31,33,36,45; 12:11; 18:20; and 8:31 is also doubtful. Why the substitution of terminology has not been carried through in 6:41 and 8:22 (where "the Jews" is retained by the *LNT*) is not clear.
10. See my article, "Anti-Semitism and the Popularity of the Fourth Gospel in Christianity," *CCAR Journal* (Central Conference of American Rabbis) 22 (1975): 35–57.
11. See, e.g., Matt 12:38 and Luke 11:16,29; Matt 16:1; 16:16 and Luke 9:20; Matt 17:10 and Mark 9:11; Luke 2:38; 20:41–44; 21:8,13; 24:21; John 3:26.

4

THE LIFE-SETTING OF THE EPISTLE OF JAMES IN THE LIGHT OF JEWISH HISTORY

RALPH P. MARTIN

Writing in reference to Acts 21:17–26 in his popular commentary on the Acts of the Apostles, William LaSor comments:

> There are several indications that the church at Jerusalem at that time was largely Jewish and maintained good relations with the non-Christian Jewish community. James, we know, stood in high regard among the Jews.[1]

The purpose of this short essay is to look once more at the enigmatic character called James the Just, the Lord's brother, with particular reference to the *Zeitgeschichte* of the period in which his death is set. From that discussion we may venture a tentative hypothesis regarding the life-setting of the document known as the "epistle of James."

I

The diversity of traditions that cluster around James as the head of the Jerusalem church is not easily explained. He is abruptly introduced into the narrative in Acts at the time of the Council in A.D. 49, having assumed the leadership-role after Peter's disappearance from the city following his release from prison (Acts 12:17). But it seems that, already while Peter was in confinement and under sentence (Acts 12:4), James had taken command, since the message of Peter's release is to be taken directly to "James and the brethren" (Acts 12:17).[2]

The puzzle is that he is suddenly brought on to the scene without explanation and is accorded a unique status. He was in a position of authority at the Council meeting, and he gave a decisive ruling on the issue of what conditions were required for the admission of the Gentiles (Acts 15:13–21).[3] His third appearance in Acts is again set in Jerusalem when he received Paul (Acts 21:18–26) and directed him to attest his true and loyal Jewishness by accepting the responsibility for the four men who had taken a Nazirite vow—a suggestion which Paul accepted without demur (21:26). Again, James spoke and acted with authority and as the titular head of the *Urgemeinde* surrounded by a collegium of elders.[4]

There is a suggestion offered by S. G. F. Brandon[5] that Luke has quickly passed over the question of how James came to this office because he was somewhat embarrassed by these episodes, and since he was out of sympathy with what James stood for. Moreover, when the book of Acts was published, the Jerusalem church had perished from the scene. More likely Luke has not diverted the reader's attention to James because he wished to focus attention on Paul and the Pauline mission by keeping the Jerusalem community in low profile.

II

But that the Jerusalem *Urgemeinde* did represent a significant factor in early Jewish-Christian history is clear from what we learn from Josephus about James' fate.[6] The clearest and most historically reliable version is in *Ant.* 20.197–203.[7] In the three or four months' interval between the decease of Festus in A.D. 62 and the arrival of his successor L. Lucceius Albinus in the office of procurator, the high priest Ananus II took action and had "James the brother of Jesus" put to death, along with certain other men. There was a Sanhedrin trial and a formal indictment of James for offenses against the law.[8] A verdict of guilty led to his execution carried out by stoning, i.e., on a religious charge, but there is a tantalizing obscurity as to the real nature of these charges brought against him. However, the execution was unpopular with those "citizens who were reputed to be most fair-minded and to be devoted to the law" (i.e., the Pharisees), and this fact suggests that James was not known for any religious iconoclasm, nor put to death for a violation of the Torah. They secretly petitioned Herod Agrippa II, who had appointed Ananus, to have him reproved. Others went in private delegation to meet Albinus on his journey from Alexandria to Caesarea and complained that Ananus had called the Sanhedrin together without the procurator's consent. Ananus was rebuked and deposed from the high priesthood by Agrippa.

In an account of the deaths of the priestly leaders in *J.W.* 4.314–25, Josephus reveals an open sympathy for Ananus, thereby betraying his kinship with Ananus' Sadducean spirit.[9] He alleges that Ananus' death and shameful exposure at the hands of the Zealots was a disaster for the Jews, since it took away "the captain of their salvation" and gave an opportunity to the Zealots who conspired to bring about that death to start the train of events that led to the catastrophe of A.D. 70 in the fall of Jerusalem. From a Christian perspective, the episode involving James and Ananus is also credited with the fateful onset of the end of the Jewish war. Hegesippus (in Eusebius, *Hist. eccl.* 2.23.18) notes that, immediately (*euthus*) following the death of James, the siege of Jerusalem was put in hand by Vespasian.

The bias of Josephus is well known. One of his clearest motives is to explain how it came about that the Jewish war and the destruction of Jerusalem in A.D. 70 were directly attributable to Jewish nationalist hotheads and revolutionaries called the Zealots. It is therefore to be expected that he would cast Ananus in a good light and indicate that the sacerdotal aristocracy, represented by the Sadducean group around him, was anxious to repress the Zealots. The question is naturally posed at this point: Was that the real reason Ananus moved against James? Was it because of James' involvement in Zealotic activity? And did Ananus feel little compunction about his action in calling a *synedrion* on his own authority because he believed that he could justify the putting down of a Zealot movement to his Roman overlords?[10]

In *Ant.* 20.180–81, Josephus informs us that from A.D. 59 on, there was internecine strife between the different strata of the Temple clergy.[11] The lower hierarchy (*hoi hiereis*) was in tension with the aristocratic high priesthood (*hoi archiereis*). The latter retaliated when the priests committed acts of violence by depriving them of their sole source of income, their tithes. We gather that the issue was socio-economic more than concerned with religious matters. The aristocratic hierarchy was wealthy and, out of concern for the *status quo* which brought it its prosperity, preferred Roman rule. The lower order had no such preference and sided with the Zealots, at least in their ideals for freedom and equality. It was the refusal of this lower clergy to continue the daily sacrifice for the Emperor's well-being, in A.D. 66, that was the immediate occasion of the Jewish war, though this simply brought matters to a head.[12] Once the battle lines were drawn, the Sadducean aristocracy and Agrippa tried to suppress the priests, who in turn were aided by the Zealot nationalists and *sicarii.*

III

We come back to the question of James' supposed involvement in the events that swirled around the Jerusalem *Urgemeinde* in these tumultuous years. His sympathies would certainly have lain with the priestly orders, and the evidence both of Acts 6:7; 21:20 (which remark on the considerable number of priests who were messianists)[13] and the datum in Eusebius, *Hist. eccl.* 2.23.5,6 (which makes James a Nazirite and a member of the priesthood who was "permitted to enter the sanctuary")[14] points in that direction. He is known as a person of commanding stature and leadership, so that it is not difficult to conceive of him as playing a significant role in opposing injustice and defending the poor. His desire to exhibit his true nationalism in the center of Judaism would explain his concern to have Paul show his Jewish orthodoxy and loyalty.[15] And it shows that the animosity of Ananus could well have been directed at securing his removal and at encompassing his death.

IV

But what of the "letter" that traditionally bears the name of James? In seeking to place it in a suitable *Sitz im Leben der alten Kirche* the main problem is that it reflects a double line of teaching. On the one hand, it professes deep concern for and sympathy with the poor and persecuted (2:1–9; 5:1–6); on the other side, it deplores violence, anger and killing, and counsels against impatience and taking action in a precipitate way (1:20; 2:11–13; 3:13–18; 4:1–4).[16] May we propose that in James we meet a leader caught in a very delicate position and trying to effect a *modus vivendi* between opposing factions? He was in declared sympathy with the needy priests, whether Jewish or messianic, and championed their cause. On the other side, he opposed the Zealot manifesto of violent law-breaking, murder and hatred. He has learned from the Christian elements in his Jewish piety the need to be tolerant and restrained (the very virtues commended in 3:17)[17] and to live together in mutual respect, without recrimination (3:9,10; 4:11: verses that condemn the divisive name-calling at a time of patriotic and nationalist fervor).[18] At the same time, he knew the hollowness of mere religious profession without practical application (2:14–26);[19] and the poor and the oppressed who were the very people whom the rich Sadducean priests despised and exploited (1:10,11; 5:1–6) were most to be encouraged and supported.[20]

His main message, however, is an overt call to have done with revolutionary method as a way of accomplishing the divine purpose. His counsel is to be "slow to speak, slow to anger, for the anger of man does not promote the righteousness of God" (1:19,20). The better path is that of patient waiting for God to act (5:7–11),[21] even if it entails an acceptance of prevailing injustice and hardship (1:2–4). Oaths of allegiance to the Zealot cause are an invitation to divine disapproval (5:12) as well as to national suicide. The "humble" who wait for their vindication from God will be rewarded (4:6; cf. 4:10); and there is need, above all else, for wisdom from God (1:5–8) that is meek (1:21; 3:13) and peace-seeking (3:17,18).[22]

But James is not rightly to be classed as quietist and fatalistic. He issues a call to action, in terms of a renouncing of all bitterness and rancor within the Jewish fold (3:1–12), and his teaching is informed by the prospect that when the Judge comes he will save the afflicted and destroy the proud and the oppressor (4:6,12).

James, on this hypothesis, is himself mirrored in the "righteous man" who prayed to God to avenge the cause of the poor as he sought to reconcile opposing factions within the Jerusalem priesthood (5:6). The tragedy was that his call was misunderstood, and even willfully ignored, by Ananus who reacted violently to James' eschatological denunciations of the rich and influential (4:6–12; 5:1–9), perhaps more so than to James' messianic pietism and unpatriotic sentiment;[23] and he had him killed.[24] Yet James exemplified in his martyrdom the same spirit he lived by and sought to inculcate in his "letter" to his persecuted and errant jingoistic brethren of the messianic faith.[25]

NOTES

1. William Sanford LaSor, *Church Alive!* (Glendale, CA: Regal Books, 1972): 318.
2. Cf. O. Cullmann, *Peter: Disciple, Apostle, Martyr* (London: SCM, ET 1953): 37ff

3. The status given to James is further seen in Gal 2:9 where his name ranks first in the list of the "pillar" apostles, and in 1 Cor 15:7 where a resurrection appearance to him is mentioned explicitly.

To these sparse details later literature added its quota of embellishment. In a part of the second-century *Gospel according to the Hebrews* (found in Jerome, *De viris illustribus* 2) James is skeptical about the resurrection of his earthly brother (cf. John 7:5), but his doubts are dispelled as Jesus appears to him and tells him to end his self-imposed fast, "My brother, eat your bread, for the Son of man has risen from those who sleep."

The resurrection appearance is invested with solemn significance in the *Gospel of Thomas* logion 12 (which may be dependent on the *Gospel of the Hebrews*). To the disciples' query concerning who will be the leader when Jesus has left them, Jesus replied: "In the place to which you have come, you will go to James the Just, for whose sake heaven and earth came into existence." Further traditions which accord James a preeminence and a caliphate-like status are mentioned in B. Gärtner (*The Theology of the Gospel of Thomas* [London: Collins, ET 1961]: 56–57), who thinks that the importance of James may well be evidence of the way in which Jewish-Christian ideas became fitted into a gnostic system.

The Clementine literature (e.g., *Clem. Recogn.* 4.35) and Hegesippus, whose memoirs are preserved in Eusebius (*Hist. eccl.* 2.23.4–18), give him an even more exalted position as teacher and leader. Epiphanius (*Pan.* 29.4) adds to the tribute of his priestly rank the precise detail that he was permitted to function as high priest once a year as he entered the most holy place on Yom Kippur (Lev 16).

The purpose underlying these traditions is certainly to bolster the importance of the church at Jerusalem as the Mother Church, a trend visible in Eusebius' statements (*Hist. eccl.* 2.1.2; 3.5.2; 7.19.1) that James occupied the bishop's seat in Jerusalem after the Lord's ascension. What is at work here is a conscious bid to establish a succession-list, with the primacy accorded to James, on the analogy of the succession-lists of Jewish high priests after the exile. The primacy of James is appealed to as a counterblast to the claim registered at Rome and Antioch that Peter was the prince of the apostles and the *fons et origo* of apostolic authority. The interesting suggestion is made by F. F. Bruce (*New Testament History* [London: Thomas Nelson, 1969]: 352) that a lot of these idealized pronouncements about James' priestly and high-priestly station stem from the desire to see him as a second Aaron, in tandem relationship with Jesus, "the prophet like unto Moses."

4. See H. Conzelmann, *History of Primitive Christianity* (Nashville: Abingdon, ET 1973): 55,110.

5. S. G. F. Brandon, "The Death of James the Just: A New Interpretation" in *Studies in Mysticism and Religion Presented to Gershom G. Scholem* (Jerusalem: Magnes, 1967): 60. This essay has not had the influence it deserves, even if part of its thesis is disputable. I am glad to pay tribute to the stimulus it has provided in the writing of this contribution.

6. "This is one of the rare cases in which the writing of the church's history can lean for support on non-Christian sources," comments H. Conzelmann (N 4): 111.

7. The historical details are commented on by B. Reicke, *The New Testament Era* (London: A. & C. Black, ET 1969): 209, 212–17.

8. "He accused them of having broken the law" (*paranomēsantōn*) in Josephus' text (*Ant.* 20.200) is ambiguous; it may refer to a transgression of the Torah (but there is objection to this, see p. 98 above), or to a violating of the Roman law. Just possibly it reflects on the situation in which Paul had allegedly introduced Trophimus into the Temple area (Acts 21:27–29). Perhaps, therefore, James' friendly attitude to Paul was interpreted as an act of disloyalty to the patriotism for which Ananus stood.

The memoirs of Hegesippus (in Eusebius, *Hist. eccl.* 2.23.4–18) and Clement of Alexandria's acceptance of the tradition (in *Hypotyposeis* 7, cited in Eusebius, *Hist. eccl.* 2.1.4,5) fill in the details of a public debate between the Jewish leaders and James. As part of the *mise en scène* James is hurled from the Temple pinnacle and clubbed to death for his audacity in proclaiming, "Why are you asking me about the Son of man? He is seated in heaven at the right hand of great power, and he will come on the clouds of heaven." This allusion to a parousia is interesting, since it may refer back to the occasion of the debate (*Hist. eccl.* 2.23.10): "there was an uproar among the Jews, the scribes, and the Pharisees who said that the whole people was in danger of *looking for Jesus as the Messiah*."

9. See E. Mary Smallwood, "High Priests and Politics in Roman Palestine," *JTS* N.S. 13 (1962): 14–34 (esp. 25ff.).

10. See Bruce (N 3): 354.

11. Further comment on this situation is given in Brandon, "The Death of James" (N 5): 66; cf. his *Jesus and the Zealots* (Manchester: The University Press, 1967): 113ff. See too Michael Grant, *The Jews in the Roman World* (New York: Scribner, 1973): 175.

12. The conflict over *isopoliteia*—equal civic rights—at Caesarea is a leading historical cause of the

outbreak of the Jewish war (Josephus, *Ant.* 20.184). But in fact the ground of the conflict was prepared over the period of the second procuratorship, from A.D. 44 to 66, as Reicke (N 7): 202ff. and E. Schürer (*The History of the Jewish People in the Age of Jesus Christ* 1 [rev. Geza Vermes and Fergus Millar; Edinburgh: T. & T. Clark, 1973]: 455–70) observe.

13. They are also described as "all zealous for the law" (*pantes zēlōtai tou nomou*) in 21:20.

14. Most scholars dismiss Hegesippus' testimony at this point, probably rightly so (see above, nn. 3,8). Reicke (N 7): 215 is willing to concede "some value" to these biographical data.

15. Especially since the Zealots were exerting pressure through terrorist campaigns (Josephus, *Ant.* 20.185–86) to root out all traces of alien influence from Jewish life.

16. On 4:1–4 which accuses its readers of murder, strife and illicit desire see now M. J. Townsend, "James 4.1–4: A Warning against Zealotry?" *ExpTim* 87 (1976): 211–13. The most troublesome part of this section is v 2 which uses the verb "to kill" (*phoneuete*). J. Cantinat (*Les épîtres de saint Jacques et de saint Jude* [Paris: J. Gabalda, 1973]: 198–99) wants to give a metaphorical sense to the verb on the ground that (1) "you kill" stands parallel with "you fight and wage war"—assumed to be metaphorical—and is equivalent to these verbs, and (2) the nonliteral usage is found elsewhere in the Bible (Matt 5:21–26; 1 John 3:15). However, as he grants, in the other two places where James has the verb (2:11; 5:6) the literal sense is clearly intended, and this is a strong argument for the same meaning at 4:2.

17. The links between James and the Q version of Jesus' teaching, especially in Matthew 5–7 and Luke 6, have often been noted. Cf. Cantinat (N 16): 27–28.

18. Josephus (*Ant.* 20.180) writes of the enmity between the priestly group and the people in Jerusalem on the one side, and the high priests on the other: "And when they clashed, they used abusive language (lit. "spoke evil of one another"—*kakologousin allēlous*) and threw stones." The similarity in wording with James 4:11 (*mē katalaleite allēlōn*; cf. 3:8) is noteworthy.

19. Granted that these verses read very much like a polemic against Paul's teaching of *sola gratia, sola fide,* especially when 2:24 with the adverb *monon* is read as a counterthrust to Rom 3:28 (W. G. Kümmel, *Introduction to the New Testament* [Nashville: Abingdon, ET 1975]: 410 n. 29), may there also be a historical cause for this connection between James and Paul? If James or the editor of his teaching was faced with the problem of clearing up the ill-reputation Paul and his disciples had fastened on themselves—echoes of which are heard in Acts 21:21–24—one of the surest ways to do this would have been to stress the importance of "works" as an evidence of true faith.

20. James' diatribe on "showing favoritism" (2:1) finds a striking coincidence in the tribute paid to him by Hegesippus (in Eusebius, *Hist. eccl.* 2.23.10, the Jewish leaders say: "you respect no man's person"). Cf. Brandon, *Jesus and the Zealots* (N 11): 125 n. 1, and the references there given.

21. The eschatological tone of these verses may be observed, with the prospect of a parousia (see above, n. 8).

22. The "piety of the poor," characteristic of the *'ănāwîm,* the "quiet in the land," is built on the Jewish teaching in the canonical Psalms and Job as well as the wisdom school (e.g., *Wisdom of Solomon*). See G. von Rad, *Wisdom in Israel* (Nashville: Abingdon, ET 1972): 198ff.

Such a submissive disposition is the opposite of "jealousy/zeal" (*zēlos*) reprobated in 3:14,16; cf. 4:5 which may be translated: "Do you suppose that it is to no purpose that scripture speaks, 'The spirit that dwells in us *opposes envy?*' " But the text is a *crux interpretum*. See C. L. Mitton, *The Epistle of James* (London: Marshall, Morgan and Scott, 1966): 153–56.

23. See earlier, p. 99.

24. The death of "the righteous man" in 5:6 may be compared with the fate of the "righteous man" in Wis 2:12–13.

25. In our view it is a more important question to try to place the epistle in some historical and cultural context than to inquire about its authorship and provenance. The theory given out above does not require that James, the brother of Jesus, should be the author—a position hard to defend in view of the literary style and the presence of allusions drawn from Hellenism and hellenistic Judaism (cf. Kümmel [N 19]: 411) as well as its slow reception into the canon. On the other side, there are signs that its genre is more that of a literary mosaic, containing a series of separate parenetic tracts loosely connected, rather than of a letter. But cf. F. O. Francis, "The Form and Function of the Opening and Closing Paragraphs of James and 1 John," *ZNW* 61 (1970): 110–26.

Nor is it an insuperable objection to a proposed Palestinian origin of the epistle that in 1:1 the prescript addresses "the twelve tribes in the Dispersion." The term *diaspora* may refer to the Jewish-Christian readers as those who formed the true Israel who live on earth but whose real home is in a heavenly land, the Zion of God's presence (as in Heb 12:22). F. F. Bruce ([N 3]: 353 n.7) suggests that the term speaks of "the sum-total of Jewish believers in Jesus, considered as the new Israel."

The lack of structure and the precise detail of the exordium may point in the direction of the view that the teaching on James was assembled and promulgated by an editor, a hellenistic Jew, conversant with the LXX and the wisdom literature whose features are prominent in the treatise. It is to this man that we owe the final shape of the "letter"—and perhaps the tribute paid to his master as the "righteous man" in 5:6,16.

On James "the righteous"—a common designation found in most strata of the evidence to do with the man—see H. J. Schoeps, "Jacobus Ο ΔΙΚΑΙΟΣ ΚΑΙ ΩΒΛΙΑΣ," *Biblica* 24 (1943): 398–403.

II. Old Testament Studies

5

THE STRUCTURAL ANALYSIS OF DIDACTIC TEXTS

GLENDON E. BRYCE*

The appearance of three journals within the past decade, each of them devoted to the structural analysis of the Bible, signal the increasing impact of structuralism upon biblical studies.[1] This new development in the field of hermeneutics comes precisely at a time when biblical scholars are reassessing the role of traditional scholarship. From its commencement, represented by the first attempts to discover the original sources of the Pentateuch, biblical scholarship has imposed upon itself a twofold task. First, scholars have sought to understand and interpret the text of the Bible as it has been received, a *textus receptus* that represented not only the conflation of specific recensions but also the long series of decisions about its canon and form that have affected its final configuration. Second, scholarship has sought to reconstruct the historical, cultural and religious setting of the Bible, a *tâche difficile,* which could not be denied if its books were to be considered products of human thought, and for some a *tâche nécessaire,* because it is the claim of some Jewish and Christian theologians that the unique message of the Old and New Testament is a *Heilsgeschichte,* a holy history. Now, however, after more than a century of this reconstructive enterprise, some scholars are beginning to look with greater interest upon the first task, that of interpreting the Bible in its final form, whether by an analysis of its rhetorical features or by an understanding of how the process of canonization shaped the whole.[2] Biblical scholarship has arrived at a new intersection, where temporarily all of the manifold results of its research converge, an *embouteillage,* where the different perspectives deriving from these two approaches find themselves in direct confrontation. It is at this point that a new direction has been opened for biblical interpretation by structuralism.

I. Structural Analysis and Semiotics

If the central interpretative problem has always been a question of methodology,

*Completed during a year of study at the Sorbonne at the Ecole Pratique des Hautes Etudes.

to choose from among the several possible hermeneutical perspectives the one that will reveal the meaning of the text, structural analysis selects as its point of entrée that which is most fundamental to signification, without which communication would be impossible.[3] It seeks to discover what a text signifies, its message, by focusing upon those elements that are constitutive of discourse itself and by interpreting these in logical terms. In order to do this, of course, it must employ a *metalangue,* a consistent set of axioms, definitions and symbols by means of which it can describe the linguistic object under consideration and clearly show what aspects of it are under scrutiny. Since by nature language is polysemous, lending itself to more than one interpretative perspective, not all aspects of a text can have the same status with regard to signification, even though all of them in one way or another contribute toward the formation of its message. Structuralism selects from among the manifold elements that are involved in communication those features that are most relevant to the message that the text embodies and seeks to convey. With respect to biblical interpretation it mediates between the two approaches just mentioned.[4] It takes that which is manifest in the text as its object of study, whether it be at a point where the tradition has clearly demarcated a discursive unit or at some earlier, more hypothetical stage. At the same time relevant historical and cultural factors are allowed to play their role in the process of interpretation. The hermeneutical task, then, as envisaged by structuralism, is to discover the isotopy of the text, the common axis of signification where all the various linguistic phenomena interlock and where they manifest the communicative intention of the text itself.[5]

Unlike traditional approaches that select some aspect of content as the key to unlock meaning, structural hermeneutics is based upon the medium of communication itself.[6] To be more specific in delineating what is meant by structural hermeneutics, as a distinct branch of semiology, the study of systems of signs, semiotics assigns a privileged place to language. For both disciplines communication and signification occupy the central place. But for semiotics it is language that is the indispensable tool without which knowledge would be impossible. It is the place where society meets and where individuals demonstrate their competence. It is also the medium by means of which the power of thought, its abstraction and symbolization, are realized *ad infinitum.* Therefore, the structures of language may be abstracted as an algorithm by which communication and signification can be understood.

Utilizing the recent discoveries about the nature of language, semiotics replaces the traditional distinction between form and content with a more pertinent differentiation, that of form and substance.[7] Substance is the amorphous continuum which delineates the boundaries of a language, whether a specific alphabet or phonetic system, or a dictionary listing all of the recorded meanings of the entries. Form is the structuring system, the organizing principles that produce meaning, what is, with respect to the lexical entries, the grammar of the language. Just as the form or structuring principles that comprise the syntax of a language are an immanent system that is articulated in the act of speaking or writing, so the structures that organize language at its narrative and discursive levels, where meaning is realized, are a system immanent within signification. In contrast to the traditional definition utilized in biblical studies, form is not a specific configuration of content determined by a variety of variable historical and cultural factors, i.e., the *Sitz im Leben* as Gunkel defined it. Rather, it is the ensemble of structures found within the content, the system that organizes and shapes the substance. The form, which is articulated in the act of communication, is the system that exists before it and that makes signification possible.

With respect to the structure of the narrative, the initial task, the determination of the constant elements, was first broached by the Russian folklorist, Vladimir Propp, in his foundational study, *Morphology of the Folktale.*[8] By an analysis of the variant and invariant elements in the folktale, Propp determined what the fundamental constituents of the narrative were. What had traditionally been regarded as the constant factor in a story was the dramatis personae, the actors who were allegedly endowed with fixed roles and rather permanent attributes. Propp demonstrated that the dramatis personae were in reality an unstable element, varying from one story to another, with different actors playing the same roles. It was the functions or actions that formed the stable constituents of the narrative. Therefore, Propp defined the dramatis personae functionally; as "actants" the actors are determined by the spheres of action in which they participate.[9] An "actant," then, whether a person or an object, may be defined as a sphere determined by a function, as the following two symbols indicate:

$$A(f).$$

The functions themselves, which may be called the *morphologues* or narrative components, form the substance of the narrative, equivalent to what Lévi-Strauss, in his analysis of the Oedipus myth, called the mythemes.[10] However, whereas Lévi-Strauss was content merely to pose the mythemes and determine their relations primarily on the semantic level, Propp analyzed the *morphologues* on the syntagmatic plane. He discovered that it was the investment of the thirty-one functions or narrative components with a specific order that produced the story as it unfolded from beginning to end. The form of the story, then, is the narrative syntax, that which is found within a narrative but which is presupposed by it. Stories consist of substance and form, but it is the form that produces the narrative and determines its signification.

Focusing upon an aspect that Propp had neglected, A. Julien Greimas proceeded to refine his analysis, providing a more adequate description of the "actants" and the states within the narrative. In his preliminary study Propp had concentrated upon the functions and left aside the question of the attribution of states or qualities to the "actants."[11] Taking up this feature of the narrative, Greimas drew attention to the change of states that occurs in a story. Since an "actant" can receive an attribution, whether this be a subjective quality or an item possessed, a story involves an oriented relation between a subject and an object, what defines the nature of the quest. This factor, of course, adds a third element to the narrative, the transformational function, that which changes the ''actant'' from one state to another. The states of the ''actants'' are determined by the transformational function. However, when one ''actant'' moves from one state to another, from a state of lack or need to a state of possession or plenitude, immediately another narrative program with another ''actant'' is implied. In order for one ''actant'' to possess something, another ''actant'' must be deprived of something. A simple story is by nature polemical because even in its simplest form it implies two narrative programs, one for the hero and another for the anti-hero or villain. At the end of the story the places where the attributions or objects come to rest, and the ''actants'' to whom they are assigned, determine the nature of the story and which ''actant'' is the hero.

In his analysis of the narrative structure, Greimas not only reduced the number of functions and redistributed the ''actants'' according to a more logical scheme but also introduced the modal values, which at a superior level control the narrative.[12] Accepting as a preliminary definition the statement of Bernard Pottier, that a modality is the modification of a predicate by a subject, Greimas demonstrated that the modalities in reality embody the competence of the ''actants'' and thus determine their functions. At the level of the syntax of the sentence, of course, the modal verbs, such as ''wish'' or ''know,'' are those that govern the state or function embodied in the following infinitive or noun clause. Similarly, in the narrative the modalities rule the functions of the ''actants'' and represent their competence. This competence may be virtual, involving obligation and volition, or actual, consisting of cognition and power. These four modalities, which make the performance possible, orient the various ''actants'' on their respective modal axes, as the following diagram shows.[13]

Axis of Cognition	Sender → Object → Recipient
Axis of Volition (and Obligation)	↑
Axis of Power	Helper → Subject ← Opponent

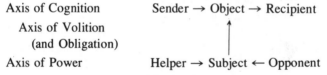

Beginning with the modalities that lie on the vertical axis, one may assert that a story involves a relationship between a Subject and an Object, a positive relation that determines the orientation of the hero or heroine. The Subject desires the Object (Axis of Volition). This also involves the relationship between the volition and obligation of the Subject, which may also include the Sender, determining the nature of his contract—whether prescriptive (obligation determining volition) or permissive (volition determining obligation). In order to enter into possession of the Object, however, the Subject must obtain the assistance of agents who will help him overcome the Anti-Subject or villain and the Opponent. The Anti-Subject is in reality the principal ''actant'' in the other narrative program, having the same scheme but with the roles reversed. Defined ''actantially,'' the Opponent is the agent, whether personal or impersonal, that hinders the Subject in his quest, and the Helper represents those agencies that help the Subject achieve his goal (Axis of Power). The third axis, which lies on the plane of communication, sets in place the Sender, who as a separate ''actant'' may establish a contract with the Subject, but whose main function is to give the Object that is desired to the Recipient (Axis of Cognition). Both the Sender and the Recipient may be identified with the Subject, who in this case would commission himself to seek and possess the Object that he would eventually apprehend. In order to understand the performance of the Subject, however, it is important to realize that it is the acquisition of the modal values that enables the Subject to begin his actual performance and become the hero of the story. Therefore, a narrative may be interpreted as a group of "actants" among which the various modalities circulate as objects, and ultimately the realization of the functions of the "actants" is determined by the possession and attribution of these modal values.

What now becomes evident is that a narrative consists of a series of interlocking levels composed of the states, the functions and the modalities, and it is the superior levels that determine the inferior ones. Syntagmatically, the initial and final states of a story, the situation of lack described at the beginning, which Greimas calls the inversed content, and the restoration or liquidation of lack at the end, the posed content, are correlated by inversion.[14] It is the series of functions that form the main body of the story, the topical content, that effects the change of states that takes place within the correlated content. The Subject of the topical content of the story, where the main action occurs, has as his first task the acquisition of the competence, represented by the modalities, in order to succeed in his performance. In the narrative, as interpreted syntagmatically by Propp, the acquisition of these modal values, particularly those of cognition and power, occurs in the qualifying test as the result of which the Subject receives a Helper. It is at this point that the potential sphere of action represented by the "actant" becomes dynamic by its investment with a modality. Through the Helper, the Subject receives the knowledge and power that he needs. Thus, in the principal test, which follows, the power represented by the modalities is actualized, manifested in those narrative components that describe the victorious performance of the Subject over the Anti-Subject. However, not until the power released radiates, establishing its own sphere of influence, are the old polarities realigned in a new configuration determined by the Subject. Thus, not until the Subject is recognized as the hero, a function that takes place at the cognitive level, does he realize the effects of his performance. Even though the subject has overcome the Anti-Subject and restored the situation of lack, he must undergo a final glorifying test before he is given the Object of his quest. These three narrative components on the syntagmatic plane, the qualifying test, the principal test and the glorifying test, form a narrative isotopy, the common axis of meaning being the struggle of the Subject.

In summary, in the narrative structure the states are subject to the functions represented by the "actants," and the "actants" in turn realize the power of action embodied in the modalities. It is in the interplay between the "actants" and the modalities, then, that one important aspect of the deep structure of the narrative may be recovered.

This model, which has been effectively utilized to recover those relations that represent the deep structure of the narrative, can also be applied to didactic texts.[15] The link between these two different literary genres already exists at the level of communication represented by the Sender, the Object and the Recipient of the "actantial" model. Just as the axis of cognition involves the communication of an Object by a Sender to a Recipient in a narrative structure, so the communication of a cognitive object by a teacher to a student involves the same "actantial" roles. In a narrative, behind every act of enunciation, no matter how obtrusive or hidden, whether in an autobiography, where the pronoun of the first person announces the omnipresence of the author, or in a story that unfolds in the third person, reflecting the omniscience of the story-teller, is an enunciator. Thus, as in the narrative, all aspects of the instruction in a discourse are controlled by the knowledge and the perspective of the teacher. In both types of texts the enunciator may be represented by an actor or element installed in the text as the speaker, whether an individual or a figure in a thematic role. Thus, the axis of communication may involve two levels, that of the author himself who, on the axis of cognition, controls the discourse, and that of the delegated enunciator who, as an "actant" in the story, brings into play all of the elements of the narrative model. In a didactic text, of course, all these are set in place by the teacher who wishes to communicate the object that he possesses, his knowledge, to the student. Consequently, both the narrative and the didactic text, involving the various states, the different functions of the "actants," and the several modal values that circulate, are controlled by the author or teacher at the highest level, that of the enunciation.

The difference between a didactic text and a narrative, however, is that in an instructional discourse the teacher installs the disciple as the virtual Subject of a quest oriented by his desire to acquire the Object, in this case the knowledge that the instructor possesses.[16] At the beginning of the instruction the disciple, who will become the eventual Subject of the action envisaged, is assumed to be in a state of ignorance. Like the hero in a story, the student must first acquire the competence, the cognition necessary for his eventual performance. Only by his acquisition of the cognition offered to him can the student be equipped with the *savoir-faire* to become the actual Subject of the quest that the instruction describes and for which it prepares him. By the conclusion, however, the student is endowed with the competence. What effects the transformation between what may be called, by analogy to the narrative, the inversed and posed content, the situation of lack and the state of plenitude of knowledge, is the series of functions that the disciple, as the virtual Subject of the quest, has accomplished. Of course, in order to succeed in this virtual quest, the disciple must be endowed with the modalities commensurate with the virtual performance in view. Therefore, a didactic text, as it communicates the *savoir-faire* proper to its eventual objective, the transmission of cognition to the disciple, installs him as the Subject of a performance that, though virtual, brings into play all of the elements of the narrative structure including the various "actants" and the different modalities. This also involves the viewpoint of the enunciator, who, on the axis of cognition, controls the various elements as well as the knowledge that is communicated and also the investment of the various figures who represent the "actants" with thematic roles.

II. The Structural Analysis of a Didactic Text

Having completed this brief sketch of a few of the more important aspects of the theory of structural analysis as represented by semiotics, the incumbent task is now one of analysis, to show how a didactic text can be analyzed and in what ways this analysis differs from traditional methods. As an example the small wisdom-"book" in Proverbs 25, which may be designated "The Book of the Men of Hezekiah," has been selected. It provides a brief exemplar that has already been analyzed from the perspective of rhetorical criticism.[17] For this reason it offers a good model for comparison, showing the difference between the two approaches. Focusing upon a few of the more important structural features of "The Book of the Men of Hezekiah," the following study will seek to show in what way they represent the deep structure of the text under consideration.

The first task of a structural analysis is to determine the precise limits of the discursive unit under scrutiny.[18] Ultimately, this is confirmed, not by the configuration manifested on the surface of the text, but by the relationships of the "actants" and the modalities that recover a coherent structure at deeper levels. Initially, the establishment of a discursive unity by the rubrics marking the beginning, the middle and the end of the instruction is an important preliminary indication, for it is precisely those elements that appear, disappear and reappear that mark the conjunctions and disjunctions, which in a narrative may be temporal or geographical, indicating the introduction and conclusion of a discourse. Proverbs 25 commences with a statement containing an attribution and a function. "The glory of kings is to search out a matter" (v 2). The instruction concludes in the same way. "To search out difficult things is glorious" (v 27).[19] The second element that forms a rubric is a figuration qualifying the function of the courtier. "To eat much honey is not good" (v 27 = v 16). These four rubrics, which form a chiasmic pattern, represent important aspects of the correlated content that mark the inversion or change of states described in the instruction. Thus, the reappearance of the rubrics at the end of the instruction in a slightly modified form represent important features that must subsequently be analyzed in detail.

Having introduced the king as the Subject of a quest for which he is qualified by his unsearchable mind (v 3), "The Book of the Men of Hezekiah" in extremely condensed form describes the situation of lack, the inversed content, in an injunction that employs imagery derived from the craft of metallurgy. The royal court is likened to silver that contains dross, and the auditor is commanded to become a refiner, purging the court of those of base mettle so that the throne of the king will be established in purity:

> Take away the dross from silver, and a vessel emerges to the smith;
> Take away the wicked from the presence of the king, and his throne
> will be established in righteousness.[20]

The isotopy of the first imperative, which is metaphorical, is one of production. It involves two functions, the refining of the ore itself and the casting of the vessel. The second function, however, is dependent upon the first, and this explains the direct causal connection between the two parts that omits mention of the actual casting of the vessel. To this command a second one is adjoined by the use of the same verb, thus linking the figurative element to a literal imperative that provides the basic signification. When placed in juxtaposition, however, the actual isotopy of the first command becomes the figurative isotopy of the second. As the figurative elements, the dross and the silver, give way to the literal ones, the wicked and what is in "the presence of the king," and as the impersonal axis of meaning is replaced by a personal one, paradigmatically, the literal command receives its evaluation from the figurative one. The sphere around the king is thus marked positively. When read syntagmatically, however, the sphere representing "the presence of the king" is unmarked and ambiguous. Is it a sphere marked positively by the king, or is it neutral, simply referring to what is around him?

This ambiguity concerning the nature of the sphere around the king, which is clarified in the second command, is important because it defines the nature of the quest of both the king and the hero who will be introduced in the next admonition. In the very last element of the second imperative the climax of the two commands is achieved by the positive marking of this sphere. The object in view in the two injunctions is the substance of which the product is composed, whether the vessel or the throne. In the first command the isotopy is impersonal but the substance, the silver, is positive. The first part of the second imperative, the actual command, replaces the impersonal isotopy with a personal one, the wicked and the king, but also leaves the sphere designated by the phrase "from the presence of the king" ambiguous and unmarked. The last element, however, while it returns to the impersonal isotopy, the throne, marks the sphere positively. The throne will be established in righteousness. Rendered in terms of the personal isotopy of the preceding command, it asserts that when the wicked are removed from the presence of the king, it is the righteous who will remain in his presence. If the situation of lack is that the king is surrounded by the wicked, the task enjoined by "The Book of the Men of Hezekiah" is to remove the wicked from the presence of the king so that he can be united with the righteous in a long and just rule. This task, of course, implies the double narrative program that has been described earlier and that may now be represented by the following formula.

$$\text{(1) F trans.} \quad [S \rightarrow (S_3 \cup S_1 \cap S_2)]$$ [21]

The first admonition of "The Book of the Men of Hezekiah" marks the transition from the inversed to the topical content. It introduces the virtual Subject of the quest who, on the axis of cognition, is the Recipient of the instruction at the level of communication. Within the instruction itself he is the courtier whom the enunciator endows with the volition that will subsequently orient the teaching. The courtier desires to receive an appointment to the royal court so that he can have a place among the great men who are in the presence of the king. Of course, if he possessed the power, he could seize a position at court, dispossessing another of it. The volition expressed in such an action would then be actualized by the power of the courtier.

$$(2)\ \text{F ref.}\quad [S_p \rightarrow (S_v \cap S_1 \cup S_2)]$$[22]

But not only does the courtier lack the power that would enable him to succeed in this act of theft, the very action itself would reveal an improper volition. Thus, the instructor warns him,

> Do not put yourself forward in the presence of the king,
> or stand in the place of the great.

If he did this, the king would be compelled to make him yield to another who already possessed the place by right or by power, and he would be put lower in the presence of the prince (v 6). Actually, the instructor is seeking to communicate to the disciple the proper volition. The contract that he offers to him is a prescriptive one, not a permissive one; the modality of volition is to be determined by that of obligation.

$$(3)\ \text{F trans.}\quad Se \rightarrow (S_v \cap O_o)$$[23]

The admonition also implies that the function of the courtier is to be a persuasive one. When he has manifested his righteousness by his proper volition, the king, who possesses the power, will offer him the object that he seeks, a position in his presence in the royal court. Paradoxically, the success of both the Subject, the courtier, and the Sender, the king who wishes to see the righteous restored to his presence (1), is dependent upon this critical virtual modality (3).[24]

If the transformational modality is one of proper volition, the first part of the instruction (vv 7–15) shows how this modal value is critical for the performance of the Subject. The first test of the courtier occurs when he has an altercation with a colleague, a serious incident that provokes him to consider legal action (vv 7–8). But this is a mistake, for a precipitous action at court could precipitate his own defeat and cost him a valuable ally, as represented in the following formula that includes the restorative function given in the counsel.

$$(4)\ \text{F ref.}\quad S_2 \rightarrow [(S_2 \cup S) \rightarrow (S_2 \cap S)]$$[25]

By rejecting a decision made in haste and by seeking to persuade his colleague privately, the Subject may change his potential Opponent into an actual Helper. Moreover, the counsel against acting in too much haste manifests the modal qualification that characterizes the whole discourse. In this section it appears in that counsel that stresses the fact that the courtier is not to talk too much. He should not disclose the secret of another, nor boast nor seek to persuade too strongly (vv 9,14,15). The pertinent differential traits or *sèmes* that are inherent within the language of the text in this part are those that involve the private as against the public, the hidden in contrast to the revealed, and the individual rather than the many.[26] On a comparative scale the critical contrast is that of "less" rather than "more," clearly demarcated at the end of the section by the transitional rubric (v 16) that counsels "enough" as it warns against "too much." This scale, marked at one end "sufficient" and at the other end "too much," is determined initially with respect to volition. It is by the application of this virtual modality, the proper volition, that the courtier is able to discriminate what is sufficient for his performance as it is actualized by his knowledge and his power. Thus, the acquisition of the competence embodied in the modalities, what in the narrative syntax of Propp is the qualifying test, is dependent upon the transformational modality of volition.

Between the two parts of the instruction the transitional rubric that summarizes the content of the teaching intervenes (v 16). The counsel to eat only sufficient honey is a figuration that, at the level of the narrative syntax, is embodied in the orientation of the Subject toward the Object. Just as the object of the figure determines and fixes the desire of the subject who wishes to consume it, so the "actantial" Subject is defined in terms of the Object.[27] What determines whether the Subject will succeed in possessing the Object, that which invests him with his specific definition, is in this text the qualification of his volition. This volition, of course, has two aspects, the volition-to-be and the volition-to-do.[28] If the volition of the Subject to be, to enter into possession of the Object, is determined by the obligation-to-do, to act according to the terms of the contract, the reverse is also true. It is the obligation-to-be that determines the volition-to-do. At the level of the textual manifestation the one attribute that represents this obligation and volition is "righteousness" (v 5). Although this term, when invested with its full range of semantic content, is richer than the modal values that it represents here, what is pertinent to the determination of its meaning in this instruction pertains primarily to volition. The pertinent differential trait that characterizes it is its marking when it passes from the realm of the virtual to the actual functional sphere. It is this factor that makes the specific modality of volition transformational, determining the various actors.

Utilizing the taxonomic categories of contraries and contradictories, represented on the classical square of oppositions, respectively, by the horizontal and diagonal axes,[29] the positions of the various actors invested with their semantic content may be represented as follows:

		Volition		
Axis of Sender	Righteous	. . . .	Wicked	
	Sufficient Volition			Excessive Volition
Axis of Subject	Non-Wicked	. . . .	Unrighteous	
		Non-Volition		

The vertical axis of the wicked on the right side of the square is characterized by too much volition. On the axis of the Sender, the evil men in the royal court seek to overthrow the king and seize the throne. On the axis of the Subject, the unrighteous courtier, who is the Anti-Subject or villain, plots with the wicked to dispossess the righteous of his position at the court. Thus, the righteous man may be deceived by the wicked and fall before him; in this case the righteous Sender would become an unrighteous Subject. On the vertical axis of the righteous, the ambiguous position of the non-wicked represents that of the Subject to whom the instruction is primarily addressed. This is the courtier who is oriented toward the righteous but who is still in search of a position at the royal court. He may be tempted to join the unrighteous and try to gain a place at court by force (2). Thus, the instructor seeks to install in him the proper volition, that which is determined by the obligation posed by the contract. This is stated succinctly in the figure concerning the honey whose importance is underscored by its use as a transitional and a concluding rubric. If the courtier finds honey and eats too much, in the end he will lose the object of his desire in a most unpleasant way.

The second part of the topical content, which follows the rubric (vv 17–26), also unfolds on the axis of power. Having acquired a Helper in the first part, the Subject is now equipped to confront the Opponent. Thus, the pertinent categories of meaning or *sèmes* that orient this section are those of opposition and duress, represented in the content of those instructions and proverbs that speak of hatred, cruelty, anger and contention, and employ the imagery of the war club, vinegar poured on a wound, and the north wind. Before entering the arena of combat, the contestant is given the tactical advice enabling him to identify his opponent and assess his strength. A false witness is armed with powerful weapons—a war club, a sword or a sharp arrow—and an untrustworthy man can unexpectedly bring severe injury as a foot when it slips (vv 18–19). Whereas the task enjoined in the first part of the instruction is one of persuasion, the role of the courtier has now changed. His task is one of interpretation, to scout the enemies' positions, to identify potential sources of conflict, and to be prepared to confront the enemy in strength.[30] In direct contrast to the first instruction in the preceding section (4), this part begins by warning the courtier not to seek too much support from his allies, lest he make potential enemies out of his friends, as represented in the formula that follows.

$$(5)\ \text{F ref.}\quad S_2 \rightarrow [(S_2 \cap S) \rightarrow (S_2 \cup S)]$$

It is also of interest that the principal test, which this section contains, is also qualified by the limitation placed on the volition of the Subject. The contrast between the categories of "enough" and "too much" also runs throughout this part. Seeking too large a place may also create for the courtier new sources of conflict; thus, a place in the corner of a roof-top is better than living in a large place in conflict with a contentious woman (v 24)! The enemy is characterized by his excess in cruelty (v 20). In contrast, the desire of the courtier for moderation, even in the moment of victory when his enemy comes to him in need, his rejection of total war and his sustenance of his enemy even in the flush of victory, demonstrate his righteousness. It is at this point that the topical content climaxes with the victory of the Subject. Having confronted the Anti-Subject in the principal test, and not only having defeated him but also having shown mercy to him, the courtier will be rewarded by Yahweh (v 22).[31] What is this reward? Apart from the context of the instruction it is unspecified, but within this specific wisdom-"book" it cannot be other than the reward envisaged by the quest itself, a position in the presence of the king and a place with the great.

The conclusion of "The Book of the Men of Hezekiah" attests the transformation that has taken place between the inversed and posed content and also, by implication, the recognition of the Subject, what in the syntagmatic scheme of Propp is the glorifying test. The first element of the posed content, which mentions the fall of the righteous man before the wicked (v 26), marks the shift from the potential state of the courtier to the actual state of the great man. The courtier is now addressed as the righteous man; by his acquisition of righteousness he has now joined those who are in the presence of the king. This also represents the change in "actantial" roles from that of Subject to that of Sender. From the perspective of the enunciator, the change of "actantial" roles signifies the change of the virtual Subject to that of the actual Subject. On the plane of communication the Recipient has now received the Object from the Sender. Having apprehended the Object, the cognitive message, the Recipient has now been endowed with the cognition to commence his own actual performance. The modality commensurate with the performance has now been put in place, and the student can now begin his own actual quest. This will, of course, involve the same task as the instruction envisages, the persuasive and interpretative functions that will ultimately enable the aspiring courtier to succeed and gain a place at the royal court.

If the first element of the posed content involves the reappearance of the quality of righteousness, marking the completion of the task assigned in the inversed content, the two closing rubrics that end the instruction confirm this shift from the potential to the actual state. Careful consideration of the first of the two closing rubrics shows that the previous prescription to eat only sufficient honey (v 16) appears here as a statement without a conditional clause (v 27a). Whereas previously the courtier was reminded to eat only sufficient honey if he had found some, here the righteous man is cautioned not to eat too much of the honey that, by implication, he has found. That this omission of the conditional element is not just the abbreviation of the earlier prescription but marks a deliberate change is corroborated by the last element in the instruction. The final rubric (v 27b) manifests the transformation of the content of the instruction in two ways. First, the attribution of glory, ascribed in the first rubric (v 2b) to the king, has now given way in favor of the integrating function, the quest. Since the rubric that immediately precedes and also the first element of the posed content are addressed to the righteous man, the dropping of the name of the king from the last rubric must be deliberate or at least represent a generalizing tendency. Thus, the righteous who are members of the royal court have now been designated participants in the quest.

The second significant change in the last rubric concerns the object of the quest. The search of the king for meaning (*dbr*) that God has hidden has now become a quest for glorious things (*kbdm*). It is to be noted that the first part of the first rubric at the beginning of the instruction remains unchanged as a fundamental presupposition. It represents the essence of reality that God has hidden. The second part, which concerns the quest of the king, is changed at the end. This change has already been prepared for by the discovery of honey, that which concretizes in a figure the result of the quest as it manifests itself. Thus, that which God has hidden, the essence, is now manifest as a glorious thing in its appearance. This transformation is one that combines essence with manifestation, a veridiction that is realized on the cognitive plane.[32] Now that the situation of lack has been overcome and the king has been joined with the righteous, together they can embark on a quest to reveal the essence of reality in a glorious manifestation. Together the two closing rubrics combine the two modalities that effect the transformation from essence to manifestation, the modalities of volition and cognition.

Far from merely providing a procedure for the verification of the existence of a discursive unit entitled "The Book of the Men of Hezekiah," the structural analysis just pursued, although extremely abbreviated, has considerably deepened our understanding of the dynamics of the text operating within the wisdom-"book." Besides showing the specific transformations that have occurred in the instruction, it has brought into sharp focus the transformational elements that do not appear on the surface of the text but that play a significant role in determining the way in which meaning is realized in the text. What the text signifies has not been determined by speculation concerning its origin or alleged setting, nor has it been achieved by what James Barr has referred to as the "illegitimate totality transfer," the importation of general meanings of terms derived from studies of other passages into this specific text.[33] Rather, meaning grows out of the specific semantic investment of the terms within the discursive unit under consideration. This meaning, which in its totality forms the message, is not made up of a group of fixed entities independent of one another. Indeed, signification cannot exist in isolation from the dynamics of the text in which it appears. Thus, it can only be accounted for by what the text aims at and what it achieves as it realizes those structures that are fundamental to signification itself. For this reason the isotopy of a discourse can only be discovered by an investigation that searches out the deep structures and that reveals what the positions and the relations within these ensembles signify with respect to the communicative intention of the text itself. Structuralism, then, beckons biblical scholarship to return to the reality of the text but also to a reality that can only be grasped at its profoundest levels. For the task of interpretation itself is a quest, one that begins with that which is hidden and hopefully ends with that which is gloriously revealed.

NOTES

1. *Sémiotique et bible* (1975); *Semeia* (1974); *Linguistica Biblica* (1969).
2. J. Muilenberg, "Form Criticism and Beyond," *JBL* 88 (1969): 1–18; J. Jackson and M. Kessler, eds., *Rhetorical Criticism* (Pittsburgh: Pickwick, 1974); J. A. Sanders, *Torah and Canon* (Philadel-

phia: Fortress, 1972); B. S. Childs, "The Old Testament as Scripture of the Church," *CTM* 43 (1972): 709–22; "A Call to Canonical Criticism," *Int* 27 (1973): 88–91.

3. A. J. Greimas, *Sémantique structurale* (Paris: Librairie Larousse, 1966): 5–17; *Du Sens* (Paris: Editions du Seuil, 1970): 7–56; R. Barthes, "Elements de Sémiologie," *Communications* 4 (1964): 91–144; J. Culler, *Structuralist Poetics* (Ithaca: Cornell University, 1974): 3–31.

4. Jacques Escande, "Un discours évangélique, Matthieu chap. V à VII—Essai d'analyse structurale" (Mémoire de diplôme, Ecole Pratique des Hautes Etudes, VI Section: Sciences Economiques et Sociales, 1975): 16–17; A. J. Greimas, "Les actants, les acteurs et les figures" in *Sémiotique narrative et textuelle* (Paris: Librairie Larousse, 1973): 168–75; *Du Sens* (N 3): 249–57.

5. For the meaning of "isotopy" see Greimas, *Sémantique* (N 3): 96; *Du Sens* (N 3): 188–89; M. Teţuscu, *Précis de sémantique française* (Paris: Librairie Klincksieck, 1975): 90–98. Culler's description and critique contain some misconceptions ([N 3]: 77–95).

6. N. Moloud, *Langage et structure* (Paris: Petite Bibliothèque Payot, 1969): 59–68. For the distinction between semiology, semiotics and semantics see Teţuscu (N 5): 10–11; O. Ducrot and T. Todorov, eds., *Dictionnaire encyclopédique des sciences du langages* (Paris: Editions du Seuil, 1972): 113–22.

7. L. Hjelmslev, *Prolégomènes à une théorie du langage* (Paris: Editions du Minuit, 1971): 70–85 (*Prolegomena to a Theory of Language* [Madison: University of Wisconsin, 1963]). See also Ducrot and Todorov (N 6): 36–41; Teţuscu (N 5): 18–22.

8. Vladimir Propp, *Morphology of the Folktale* (2d ed.; Austin: University of Texas, 1968); Greimas, *Sémantique* (N 3): 172–220; C. Lévi-Strauss, *Anthropologie structurale deux* (Paris: Plon, 1973): 139–73.

9. Propp (N 8): 20–21, 79–80; Greimas, *Sémantique* (N 3): 155.

10. C. Lévi-Strauss, *Structural Anthropology* (Garden City, NY: Doubleday, 1967): 207. Application of the theories of Lévi-Strauss to the Bible may be found in E. Leach, *Genesis as Myth. And Other Essays* (London: Jonathan and Cape, 1969) and D. Patte, "Structural Network in Narrative: The Good Samaritan," *Soundings* 58 (1975): 241–42; *What is Structural Exegesis?* (Philadelphia: Fortress, 1976): 53–83.

11. A. J. Greimas, "Un problème de sémiotique narrative: les objets de valeur," *Langages* 31 (1973): 13–35; *Du Sens* (N 3): 167–73.

12. Greimas, *Sémantique* (N 3): 192–221; "Les Actants" (N 4): 161–65; *Du Sens* (N 3): 175–83; "Pour une théorie des modalités," *Langages* 43 (1976): 90–107. Descriptions of the method of Greimas may be found in E. Mélétinski, "L'étude structurale et typologie du conte" in *Morphologie du Conte* (Paris: Seuil, 1965): 222–30; C. Galland, "Introduction à la méthode de A.- J. Greimas," *Foi et Vie* 13 (1974): 13–27. The "actantial" model is presented in R. Scholes, *Structuralism in Literature* (New Haven: Yale University, 1974): 104–09 and by Culler (N 3): 233–34. An English translation of Greimas' analysis of the Bororo myth may be found in "The Interpretation of Myth: Theory and Practice" in *Structural Analysis of Oral Tradition* (ed. P. Maranda and E. Maranda; Philadelphia: University of Pennsylvania, 1971): 81–121.

13. Translations of the French terms are largely uniform except for Sender (*Destinateur*), which is also rendered "Dispatcher" (Culler [N 3]: 233) or "Ordainer" (J. D. Crossan, "Structuralist Analysis and the Parables of Jesus," *Linguistica Biblica* 29–30 [1973]: 42).

14. Greimas, *Du Sens* (N 3): 187–88 (translated as "The Interpretation" [N 12]: 82–83).

15. Greimas, "Un problème" (N 11): 26; Escande (N 4): 32–105.

16. Escande (N 4): 42–49.

17. G. E. Bryce, "Another Wisdom-'Book' in Proverbs," *JBL* 91 (1972): 145–57.

18. Escande (N 4): 16–17, 37–40; L. Marin, "Essai d'analyse structurale d'un récit-parabole: Matthieu 13/1–23," *ETR* 46 (1971): 38–41.

19. For a discussion of the interpretational difficulties attendant on this verse, see Bryce (N 17): 148–50.

20. For discussion see W. McKane, *Proverbs* (Philadelphia: Westminster, 1970): 590–91.

21. The symbols are F trans. (transitive function), S (Subject), $\rightarrow$ (transformation), S_3 (Subject: the wicked), $\cup$ (state of disjunction), S_1 (Subject: the king), $\cap$ (state of junction), S_2 (Subject: the righteous). The significance of these symbols for structural analysis is discussed by Greimas, "Un problème" (N 11): 19–34.

22. Symbols not previously used are ref. (reflexive), p (power) and v (volition).

23. I.e., the Sender (Se) causes that the virtual Subject endowed with volition (S_v) comes into possession of the Object, which is obligation (O_o).

24. The numbers refer to the preceding numbered formulae.

25. Placing S_2 outside the bracket indicates that he causes both states.
26. For the meaning of *sème* see Teţuscu (N 5): 46–51; Greimas, *Sémantique* (N 3): 22–29.
27. J.-C. Coquet, "La relation sémantique sujet-objet," *Langages* 31 (1973): 80–81; Greimas, "Un problème" (N 11): 16; *Sémantique* (N 3): 176–77.
28. Greimas, "Pour une théorie" (N 12); *Du Sens* (N 3): 169–71; Coquet (N 27): 81–89.
29. A. J. Greimas and F. Rastier, "The Interaction of Semiotic Constraints," *Yale French Studies* 41 (1969): 86–105 (also in *Du Sens* [N 3]: 135–55). A volume of essays devoted to this subject has been edited by F. Nef, *Structures élémentaires de la signification* (Paris: Presses Universitaires de France, 1976): 9–172.
30. For a discussion of the *faire persuasif* and the *faire interprétatif* see A. J. Greimas, *Maupassant* (Paris: Editions du Seuil, 1976): 81.
31. Greimas, "Un problème" (N 11): 22–23.
32. For an explication of the Aristotelian square of veridiction see Greimas, "Les actants" (N 4): 165–66; *Maupassant* (N 30): 81–82.
33. James Barr, *The Semantics of Biblical Language* (London: Oxford University, 1961): 218–19.

6

THE CANONICAL SHAPE OF THE BOOK OF JONAH

BREVARD S. CHILDS

I. Historical-Critical Problems

The history of the interpretation of the book of Jonah has been reviewed many times and need not be rehearsed in detail.[1] The attempt to interpret the book as a straightforward historical report met with resistance at a very early date. The search for alternate theories of interpretation led, on the one hand, to various allegorical and typological moves, and, on the other hand, to innumerable rationalistic ploys, e.g., that Jonah had dreamed the story, or that the ship which rescued him was named "the great fish"! During the last century research has focused on the study of extra-biblical parallels from folklore,[2] and on determining the literary genre of the story.[3]

A rather wide consensus has developed on assigning a postexilic dating to the composition of the book chiefly because of the language and vagueness in the historical references to Nineveh. The apparent knowledge of the book by Sirach (49:10) and Tobit (14:4,8) sets a definite *terminus ad quem* for its composition.

During the latter part of the nineteenth century various attempts were offered which questioned the literary integrity of the book,[4] and a variety of sources were posited to account for the tensions within the book. From this endeavor only two observations have received much support. The secondary nature of the psalm in chap. 2 has been widely accepted and a possible dislocation of 4:5 has been defended. But even here a minority opinion has continued to resist even these moves.[5] In sum, the basic unity of the book has been strongly maintained by modern critical scholarship.

The effort to specify the literary genre of the book of Jonah has met with less agreement. It has been characterized as a fable, didactic novel, prophetic legend, and parable. Others have described the book as a midrash,[6] or even as an allegory.[7] More recently, Keller has sought to demonstrate the book's affinity to the so-called "Confessions of Jeremiah."[8] In the end, many commentators opt for a mixed genre with the presence of many eclectic features.

The most crucial and perplexing problem of the book turns on the interpretation of its major purpose. Broadly speaking, in the history of interpretation two major interpretations have emerged with, of course, innumerable variations within each group. The first alternative interprets the book of Jonah as focusing on some aspect of unfulfilled prophecy. The main issue is described either as Jonah's effort not to be a false prophet, or in analyzing the relation of conditional to unconditional prophecy, or in the failure of the prophecy against the nations to have been fulfilled. This position has generally been defended by Jewish interpreters,[9] but also by an impressive number of non-Jewish exegetes (Calvin, Hitzig). The recent interpretations of Keller[10] and Clements[11] fit generally into this category.

The second major pattern of interpretation sees the point of the book to lie in the attempt to extend the message of salvation to the Gentiles against the resistance of the Jews. This interpretation has been defended mainly by Christian scholars,[12] although a variation of the approach is reflected in the early Jewish defense of Jonah who is pictured as fleeing lest he bring indirect judgment on Israel by converting the heathen.[13]

The impasse has arisen because both exegetical positions find warrants in the text to use as support, but then, again, both positions reflect serious weaknesses as well. The first theory of interpretation points out the connection of the Jonah story with the prophetic figure of 2 Kings 14. In this role reference to Jonah the prophet is remembered because his word had been fulfilled. Again, the reason for Jonah's flight, explicitly stated in 4:2, focuses on his knowledge that the judgment against Nineveh would not be carried out. Finally, Jonah's call in chap. 1 also relates to the larger problem of the role of prophecy in Israel.

However, there are persistent difficulties with this approach which have not been adequately resolved. The office of prophet does not ever seem to be at stake in such a way as might have been expected in this interpretation. Again, the message that all prophecy is ultimately conditional was already a truism within Israel (cf. Jeremiah 18), and hardly needed an elaborate defense. The lesson that God was both just and merciful was also already obvious to every Hebrew. Even the theme of God's right to repentance does not seem to be the point of the book, but an implicit assumption.

The second interpretation which focuses the book on the conversion of the Gentiles seeks to support its theory by pointing out Jonah's use of the ancient Hebrew formula in 4:2, which provided the grounds for Israel's election (Exod 34:6–7). Again, the contrast between Jonah the Hebrew, and the heathen of chap. 1 seems to have a parallel in chap. 3. Finally, the lesson from the plant in chap. 4 turns on God's concern for his whole creation rather than with the issue of prophecy *per se*. Nevertheless, serious obstacles also emerge in relation to this interpretation. The book does not reflect any antagonism between Jew and Gentile nor does the role of Nineveh as the enemy of Israel play any role. The descriptive formulae are all bland and stereotypical.

In sum, neither of the major interpretations has been able to achieve a clear consensus nor to do justice to the full range of exegetical problems in the biblical text.

II. The Canonical Shape of the Book

In an effort to describe how the book of Jonah functions in its canonical context, it seems wise to begin with the form-critical problem. What is the form and function of the Jonah story? It has long been noticed that the book climaxes in chap. 4 with a didactic point. Once this point has been made, the book comes to an abrupt end. Moreover, the retrospective explanation of 4:2 succeeds in closely tying the preceding scenes to the didactic point of the final chapter. It is crucial to observe how the point is made. It emerges from the dialogue between God and Jonah and is self-contained. It does not need to be explained by the author of the story. The form-critical implication to be drawn from this observation is that the story now functions as a parable. In spite of the probability that the elements of the story may have once functioned independently of its present form, the story now functions as a parable. The audience receives the word in unmediated form from the story itself.

The significance of the parabolic form can be further elucidated by contrasting its form and function with other suggested genres. The story is different from a prophetic legend whose meaning is supplied by means of a redactor's framework imposed upon the story (e.g., 1 Kgs 16:29ff.). Again, the story of Jonah is not symbolic action which points to another dimension of reality by means of carefully contrived adumbration. Moreover, the story does not belong to the genre of midrash, even though there are elements of midrashic technique involved, because the major concern of the narrative does not turn on explaining a difficulty in a biblical text. Finally, the story does not function as an allegory which requires the proper key in order for its hearers to perceive its meaning. However, even though this form-critical analysis of how the story functions does rule out certain interpretations, it does not offer in itself a criterion for adjudicating between the two conflicting interpretations which were discussed above. To resolve this problem, we shall have to seek evidence of canonical shaping of the final form of the book.

The majority of critical scholars are convinced that the prayer in chap. 2 is a later interpolation into the original story. Among the various reasons brought forward against the originality of the prayer, two stand out. It is argued that the prayer has not only disturbed the structure of the story, but also has introduced a confusing note into the one clear message of the book. In terms of the original structure the first and second commissions to Nineveh are clearly parallel (1:1 and 3:1). Then in each of these two chapters the focus of the story falls on the heathen reaction, the threat of judgment, the prayer for deliverance and the ensuing rescue. Chap. 4 shifts the perspective to Jonah. His reaction to Nineveh's repentance is described, which in turn evokes the lesson in a divine response.

In this reconstruction of the original story Jonah never changes in voicing his opposition to his mission. He first flees, but is compelled to return by God's direct intervention. He then carries out his commission, but is angry at its success. His explanation (4:2) indicates his consistent resistance from the beginning. He knows in advance that God will not carry through with his threat. The issue turns on the fulfillment of the prophet's word. Jonah resisted because he did not want to be a false prophet. In his response God defends his right as creator to let his mercy to his creation override the prophetic word. By removing chap. 2 the sharp lines of the original story emerge, thus confirming the interpretation which related the purpose of the book to the issue of unfulfilled prophecy.

But what is the effect on the story when in its final form the lengthy prayer of Jonah is introduced in chap. 2? This move appears to be a crucial one in the canonical shaping. First of all, the structure of the book is substantially altered by the introduction of the prayer of chap. 2. As has been convincingly demonstrated by Landes,[14] chap. 2 now functions as a parallel to chap. 4. The similar introductory formulae as well as the consistent structure would serve as literary evidence for an intentional structural paralleling of the chapters. The effect of the parallel is that the meaning of chap. 4 is now strongly influenced by chap. 2.

In chap. 2 Jonah prays to God from the belly of the fish. It has long been noticed that the prayer is not a cry for help, but is a prayer of thanksgiving for deliverance already experienced. The Hebrew text is unequivocal in its use of verbs of completed action in striking contrast to the Septuagint's attempt to remove this problem. In its present narrative context the threat to Jonah's life lay in his being drowned in the sea. The large fish was the divine means of deliverance! The prayer of Jonah is a veritable catena of traditional phrases from the Psalter.[15] Jonah prays in the stereotyped language of the psalms which every faithful Jew had always used. He first describes the threat to his life in the fixed language of the complaint psalm, which, however, because of the context of the ongoing narrative, works to provide a new and remarkable dimension of historical specificity. Jonah is thankful for his rescue and ascribes praise to his God: "Deliverance belongs to Yahweh!" (v 10 [v 9E]).

In chap. 4 Jonah again prays to his God and once again he makes use of traditional language. The formula of v 2 appears first in Exod 34:6 in the giving of the covenant to Israel at Sinai, but has become an integral part of the liturgical language of the Psalter as well (Pss 86:15; 103:8; 111:4; 112:4; 116:5; 145:8). But this time the appeal to the same divine attribute of mercy evokes a negative response in the prophet. He is angry because God has "repented of the evil" intended for Nineveh.[16] If his anger had once stemmed from concern over the fulfillment of the prophetic word, there has been a noticeable shift in the expanded narrative. The structural parallelism of chaps. 2 and 4 which contrasts the two prayers of Jonah refocuses the narrative. The issue now turns on the scope of divine mercy. Jonah is thankful for his own deliverance, but resentful of Nineveh's inclusion within the mercy which had always been restricted to Israel. This interpretation is further supported by the prayer of the king. His response, "Who knows, God may yet repent and turn from his fierce anger," is a citation from Joel 2:14, and a continuation of the same covenant formula which Jonah uses in 4:2. Clearly the issue is now on the recipient of the divine mercy.

The inclusion of the prayer of Jonah in chap. 2 has had another effect on the interpretation of the story. The prayer affords the reader an avenue into the faith of the prophet. Obviously, Jonah's personality is not the issue, but rather Jonah is portrayed as a typical Jew who shares Israel's traditional faith. In his trouble he renders thanksgiving to God and is confident of divine rescue. In sum, the effect of the prayer from a canonical perspective is to typify Jonah! The lesson which was directed to Jonah now also serves a larger audience. The book addresses those other faithful Jews who have been set apart from the nations by the Mosaic covenant, and who were sustained by the sacred traditions of their Psalter.

There are several other observations which can be made in regard to the effect of the prayer in chap. 2 on the interpretation of the book as a whole. The initial characterization of the book as a parable which directly communicates its message to its audience still holds. Nevertheless, the inclusion of the prayer has had the effect of complicating the simple parabolic form. The story has been given a different literary structure and another internal dynamic has been set in motion. Jonah no longer serves simply as the reluctant messenger of God to whom the message in chap. 4 is directed. Rather, his role has been expanded by fashioning him into a representative figure and thus establishing a link between Israel and the heathen. Of course, it is the complexity of the form within the final shape of the book which has caused the difficulty of interpretation and has afforded genuine warrants for the various critical analyses.

The crucial question now arises as to how one is to relate these two different interpretations found in the book. If the above analysis is at all correct, the final form of the story does seek to address the issue of God's salvation being extended to the nations as well as to Israel. But this final redactional stamp has not obliterated the earlier form of the story, but refocused it. In my judgment, the final reworking of the story simply extended the original point. In the "first edition" the theological point turned on God's rule as creator to override his prophetic word for the sake of his entire creation. The "second edition" merely amplified the point respecting the whole creation in terms of the nations, but it did not alter the basic creation theology by substituting one of election.

Is it possible to make any further observations as to the historical process lying behind the development of the canonical shape of the story? There is no evidence to suggest that the two levels of the story were separated by a long historical development. Not only is the language of one piece, but the midrashic method of handling the tradition is represented just as much by the reconstructed first stage as by the final form. It seems more likely to suggest that the force which effected a shift in the function of the book derived from the canonical process itself. When the book was collected within a corpus of other sacred literature, the need arose to specify the addressee as the covenant community. Thus the original inner prophetic problem of unfulfilled prophecy against the nations was expanded. Again, the effect of ordering the book in a larger collection can be seen on the new reading of the significance of Nineveh. To be sure the idiom within the biblical text is neutral and lacks any specific reference to

Israel's historical relationship to the Assyrians. But this historical dimension is now supplied by the role of the larger canon. Thus the reader brings to the story a common memory respecting the Ninevites to whom Jonah was sent with a message of repentance, and he has in his canon the book of Nahum.

Finally, the canonical setting of the story in the period of Jeroboam II (2 Kings 14), rather than placing it in the postexilic period, assures seeing the issue raised by the book as constitutive to the theological relation between Israel and the nations. The issue is not to be historicized and derived from an alleged postexilic narrowness of Judaism, but serves as a critical prophetic judgment on Israel in line with the rest of the prophetic witnesses of the Old Testament.

III. Theological and Hermeneutical Implications

1. By determining that the book of Jonah functions in its canonical context as a parable, the older impasse regarding the historicity of the story is bypassed as a theological issue. Because the book serves canonically in the role of a parable, it is as theologically irrelevant to know its historicity as in the case of the Parable of the Good Samaritan. In both instances historical features are incorporated within the narrative, but this determination does not affect the canonical role which the book plays.[17]

2. The canonical shape of the book of Jonah offers an example of an editorial process which retained intact elements of an earlier interpretation. A subsequent editing of the book shifted the focus, but did not eliminate the earlier level. To the extent to which the earlier interpretation has been retained in the final shape of the book, it continues to offer a genuine canonical witness. In the case of the book of Jonah, the final form did subordinate one interpretation to another and offered a clear guideline as to the primary message. Thus the two interpretations reflect an inner relationship within the canon and are not to be played against each other.

3. The form of the book of Jonah is unique in the Book of the Twelve. The book does not contain the oracles of Jonah, nor is the material biographical in the strict sense. Rather, the authority of the book rests on the prophetic function of the book as bearer of a message. All attempts, therefore, to defend the prophet's reputation—he fled out of love of Israel (Rashi), or he resisted the divine decision from concern over God's glory—miss the purpose of the book within the canon. Such apologetics serve to weaken rather than enhance the truth of the book.

4. The canonical shape of the book of Jonah resists the attempts of both Jew and Christian to politicize the biblical message. On the one hand, the divine attack on Jonah's resistance is not to be derived from postexilic narrowness, but is theologically grounded in the nature of God as creator. On the other hand, the case for seeing Jonah's resistance as directed toward the inclusion of the nations is not to be dismissed as a later Christian bias, but is a genuine Old Testament witness directed against a misunderstanding of the election of Israel.

NOTES

1. E. Bickerman, *Four Strange Books of the Bible* (New York: Schocken, 1967): 3–49.
2. Hans Schmidt, *Jona, eine Untersuchung zur vergleichenden Religionsgeschichte* (Göttingen: Vandenhoeck & Ruprecht, 1907).
3. H. W. Wolff, *Studien zum Jonabuch* (Neukirchen-Vluyn: Neukirchener Verlag, 1965).
4. Cf. the careful review in G. A. Smith, *The Book of the Twelve Prophets* 2 (New York: Armstrong, 1899): 509ff.
5. Cf. esp. G. Landes, "The Kerygma of the Book of Jonah," *Int* 21 (1967): 3–31; and N. Lohfink, "Jona ging zur Stadt hinaus (Jona 4,5)," *BZ* NF 5 (1961): 185ff.
6. K. Budde, "Midrasch des Buches der Könige," *ZAW* 12 (1892): 40ff.; A. Feuillet, "Les sources spéciales du Cantique de Jonas," *RB* 54 (1947): 181–83.
7. P. R. Ackroyd, *Exile and Restoration* (London: SCM, 1968): 244–45.
8. C. A. Keller, "Jonas. Le portrait d'un prophète," *TZ* 21 (1965): 329–40.
9. S. D. Goitein, "Some Observations on Jonah," *JPOS* 17 (1937): 63–77; Bickerman (N 1); A. Rofé, "Classes in the Prophetical Stories: Didactic Legends and Parables" in *Studies on Prophecy* (VTSup 26 [1974]): 141–64, esp. 153ff.; cf. also F. Weinreb, *Das Buch Jonah. Der Sinn des Buches Jonah nach der ältesten jüdischen Überlieferung* (Zürich: Origo, 1970).
10. Keller (N 8).
11. R. E. Clements, "The Purpose of the Book of Jonah" in *Congress Volume* (VTSup 28 [1976]): 16–28.
12. E. Haller, *Die Erzählung von dem Propheten Jona* (Munich: C. Kaiser, 1958): 50ff.; Wolff (N 3); W. Rudolph, *Joel-Amos-Obadja-Jona* (Gütersloh: G. Mohn, 1971): 323ff.; O. Kaiser, "Wirklichkeit, Möglichkeit und Vorurteil. Ein Beitrag zur Verständnis des Buches Jona," *EvT* 33 (1973): 91–103.
13. Cf. Bickerman's careful survey of the history of this interpretation (N 1): 16–19.
14. Landes (N 5): 6.
15. Cf. the standard commentaries for a list of seven or more references.
16. Cf. the discussion by J. Jeremias, *Die Reue Gottes. Aspekte alttestamentlicher Gottesvorstellung* (Neukirchen-Vluyn: Neukirchener Verlag, 1975): 98ff.
17. The canonical dimension of the problem is lacking in G. Ch. Aalders' *The Problem of the Book of Jonah* (London: Tyndale, 1948) which falls back into a rationalistic apologetic.

7

HISTORY OF RELIGION IN PSALM 82

CYRUS H. GORDON

It is not uncommon to be invited to write for a volume in honor of one of our teachers. But now I have the rarer pleasure of contributing an article to the *Festschrift* of a student. William S. LaSor was one of my first doctoral candidates soon after the Second World War. Those were good years, when teachers and students had ample opportunity to exchange and discuss each other's ideas in small classes. (Those small classes, alas, are becoming distant memories in this age of cost-accounting.) Dr. LaSor's academic career has given me much satisfaction. May his writings continue to enrich biblical scholarship for many years to come!

The main factor responsible for the current phase of Old Testament studies is Ugaritic. This holds for linguistic, literary and intellectual aspects of the subject. During all of Old Testament history, the Hebrews were exposed to their pagan neighbors, and adopted some facets of Canaanite culture[1] while reacting against others.[2]

Psalm 82 shows that the composer knew about the Old Order, when the pantheon (*'dt 'l,* in v 1, = *'dt ilm* in Ugaritic) was presided over by God (Elohim, in v 8). The psalmist attributes the doom of the Old Order to its corruption in terms of social injustice, when the powerful wicked were allowed to oppress the helpless poor. The psalmist tells the gods that they must therefore die like mortals. Prophetically the psalmist concludes by calling on God to rule the entire world. When Psalm 82 was written, Canaanite paganism had centuries of vigorous survival in store. The victory of the God of Israel, and the demise of the Canaanite pantheon, are thus proclaimed long before the birth of Christianity and Islam. Psalm 82 thus reflects an awareness of the history of religion, marking a transition from the stage reflected in the Ugaritic tablets, to the monotheistic ideal of classical Israel. The author also knows that El/Elohim, who once presided over the old pantheon, now reigns as the one and only God of the whole world. For this to take place, the pagan deities had to die, and the biblical author states this in terms now familiar also from Ugaritic literature.

Transliteration:

1) *mizmôr l^{e}'āsāp*
'ĕlôhîm niṣṣāb ba'ădat-'ēl
b^{e}qereb 'ĕlôhîm yišpōṭ
2) *'ad-mātay tišp^{e}ṭû-'āwel*
ûp^{e}nê r^{e}šā'îm tiś'û-selā^{h}
3) *šipṭû-dal w^{e}yātôm*
'ānî wārāš haṣdîqû
4) *pall^{e}ṭû-dal w^{e}'ebyôn*
miyyad r^{e}šā'îm haṣṣîlû
5) *lô' yād^{e}'û w^{e}lô' yābînû*
baḥăšēkā^{h} yithallākû
yimmôṭû kol-môs^{e}dê 'āreṣ
6) *'ănî-'āmartî 'ĕlôhîm 'attem*
ûb^{e}nê 'elyôn kull^{e}kem
7) *'ākēn k^{e}'ādām t^{e}mûtûn*
ûk^{e}'aḥad haśśârîm tippōlû
8) *qûmā^{h} 'ĕlôhîm šopṭā^{h} hā'āreṣ*
kî-'attā^{h} tinḥal b^{e}kol-haggôyîm

Translation:

A psalm of Asaph.
God presides over the pantheon;
In the midst of the gods He rules:
"How long will ye judge iniquitously
And favor the wicked? Selah.
Judge the poor and the fatherless;
Vindicate the needy and indigent!
Rescue the poor and the pauper;
Save (them) from the hand of the wicked!"
They neither know nor understand,
(But) walk about in darkness,
So that all the foundations of the earth totter.
I say: "Ye are gods,
And all of you are deities.
But ye shall die like mankind,
And fall like any of the princes.
Arise, O God, rule the earth;
For thou shalt take over all the nations!"

Commentary

1) The meaning of *niṣṣāb* 'presides' is fixed by the context; God is ruling the pantheon and laying down the law.

In Ugaritic, El is the president of the pantheon. El (= Elohim) becomes the one God when all the rest of the pantheon are eliminated. Gods can die according to the ancient religions of the Near East. In the Babylonian Creation Epic, the god Kingu is put to death so that his body may provide materials for creating man. In Ugaritic mythology gods can kill each other; the death of Baal is particularly important in the fertility cult.

For *'dt ilm* 'the pantheon' see *UT* § 19.1816.

4) The duty of rulers (gods and kings alike) is to protect the weak from the strong. Social justice may be defined as the upholding of the principle that in any conflict of interest, the weak must be rescued from the strong. To clarify this with an illustration: If a widow defaults on her mortgage payments, legally her creditor can foreclose, but according to "social justice" she is in the "right," and he is "wrong." In the prophetic writings, *mišpāṭ* (translated 'justice') means 'social justice,' not 'legal justice.'

5) Our world collapses when it is ruled by the forces of social injustice. The rottenness of the Old Order is described as bringing on its own destruction.

6) God tells the deities that they are up to that point divine. Note that in this Psalm *'ĕlôhîm* is treated both as the singular 'God' and as the plural 'gods.' The

grammatical number of the words in agreement with *'ĕlôhîm* tells whether it is singular or plural. The context never leaves any doubt.

"Sons of the most high" is parallel to, and synonymous with, "gods" and is therefore translated "deities."

7) "Ye shall die like mankind" is to be compared with the following passage in the Ugaritic Epic of *Krt* (16.1[125].17–23). *Krt,* who was regarded as a divine king, is confronted with the prospect of dying. His children say to him: "Wilt thou die like mortals?. . . How can it be said, '*Krt* is a son of El, the scion of *Lṭpn* (= El) and *Qdš* (= Asherah)?' Or can gods die, nor the scion of *Lṭpn* live?"

8) The New Order is hailed by calling on God to rule the world and take possession of all the peoples. There are to be no more local or ethnic gods, but only one Lord of the Universe. The root *nḥl* generally means 'to inherit.' God has indeed inherited the jurisdictions of all the deities that have perished, but the preposition *b- (tinḥal bᵉkol-haggôyîm)* suggests '(ruling) over' as in *mšl b-* 'to rule over'; see M. Dahood, *Psalms II* (AB 17; Garden City, NY: Doubleday, 1968): 271.

The psalmist thus indicates not only a spiritual awareness, but also a knowledge of the history of religion in Canaan. We need not moralize, but we should be able to answer the question: "What did the gods of Canaan do that was so wicked?" We will limit ourselves to one striking example: The goddess Anat hired an assassin to kill the hero Aqhat so that she could confiscate the bow that Aqhat had refused to sell her. This is not Hebrew propaganda; it is recorded in the sacred literature of Ugarit. The Hebrews consciously reacted against Canaanite values, and Psalm 82 tells why, albeit without the specific examples with which Ugarit now provides us.

NOTES

1. For example, the Hebrew language and Old Testament prosody were borrowed from the Canaanites.

2. E.g., the idolatry, polytheism and moral values of Canaan were rejected by the religious leaders of ancient Israel. When Leviticus 18 forbids bestiality (v 23) because the older population practiced it (vv 24–30), we can take the text at its face value. In the fertility cult of Canaan, bestiality had an honored place, for in the sacred texts of Ugarit, Baal copulates with heifers (5[67].5.17–22 and 10[76].3.20–38). This kind of sexual activity among his devotees, far from being sinful, was *imitatio dei*.

8

ORACULAR ORIGIN OF THE STATE

MEREDITH G. KLINE

Because of an overall misreading of Gen 4:15 and a misleading fascination with the supposed "mark of Cain" in particular, the import of this verse as an inceptive divine disclosure concerning the institution of the state has escaped attention. It is set in a judicial context. Form-critical analysis has led to the observation that Genesis 4 exhibits a legal-court pattern closely paralleling the judgment pattern in Genesis 3.[1] Within the judicial process, Gen 4:15 is a response of the judge to a complaint against his judgment. Direction in the quest for the meaning of the response may be expected from a study of the appeal (Gen 4:13,14).

I. Cain's Appeal

Cain's complaint-appeal is expressed in the quantitative terms common in negotiations of various kinds:[2] "My punishment is greater than I can bear" (4:13). The alternative interpretation of v 13 as an acknowledgment by Cain that his sin was beyond forgiveness is not favored by the active form of the infinitive or by Cain's concern, as he continues his complaint (4:14), with the severity of the punishment—not with the enormity of his sin.

Banishment from the face of the ground (v 14a) and from the face of God (v 14b)—so Cain saw his punishment. In the second half of v 14 the significance of each aspect of the punishment mentioned in the first half of the verse is traced in turn, so that the verse as a whole assumes an A:B::A′:B′ form. To be driven from the death-defiled ground, forced to leave by its refusal to yield him its life, was to be doomed to an unsettled, wandering exile existence (v 14c). To be denied access to the face of God was to be abandoned to the mortal perils of a lawless world (v 14d). Cain laments that the ground will not respond to his labor and, far more intolerable, God will not respond to his cry.

It is this second (or B) element in Cain's description of his fate to which God's response (v 15) is addressed, and what needs to be perceived if we are to understand v 15 is the juridical nature of the situation referred to in v 14b and d.

"I will be hidden from your face" (v 14b). The point of Cain's complaint is that he will be denied God's judicial oversight. The N-stem of the verb is not to be taken here as reflexive, but passive.[3] Cain does not bemoan the fact that he must henceforth ever be trying to conceal himself from God's judicial scrutiny. Quite the contrary, it is the absence of such scrutiny that worries him—not, to be sure, the absence of scrutiny of his own actions but of the violence that threatens him.

The judicial connotation is regularly present when it is said that God hides his face.[4] The expression is common in the lament genre in the Psalms, which is a form of legal (covenantal) appeal. In Psalm 27, for example, where the writer describes himself as seeking God's face (v 8)[5] and pleads with God not to hide his face (v 9a), the judicial significance of that plea becomes evident as the psalmist goes on to request that he not be abandoned to the hostility of false witnesses who are testifying against him (v 12). Constantly, where the image is found in the Psalter, the concern is for divine judicial intervention. How long will God hide his face? Let God hear the cry of the psalmist and see the evil done against him; let God speedily exercise judgment, delivering the afflicted and requiting his enemy (Pss 10:11; 13:2; 22:25; 30:8; 44:25; 69:18; 88:15; 102:3; 143:7). Job asks why God hides his face as he pleads—in vain it seems—for a legal hearing for his mysterious case (Job 13:24; cf. 18ff.). In the covenant administration defined in Deuteronomy, the hiding of God's face from Israel means his absence from their midst (Deut 31:17,18), not entering into judgment in their behalf to avenge their blood (Deut 32:20; cf. 35–36,41ff.). A similar usage is found in the prophets (Isa 8:17; Mic 3:4).

The passive formulation, which is used in Gen 4:14b (Cain will be hidden from God's face), has the same judicial connotation as the active.[6] Thus, in Isa 40:27, Israel's complaint that its way is hidden from God has as its parallel the thought that God disregards Israel's plea for vindicating judgment. In Jer 16:17, the fact that the offenders' ways are not hidden from God's face means that his eyes are upon their iniquity to recompense it (cf. Ps 10:11).[7] See also Ps 38:10; Job 3:23; and Isa 65:16.

In view of Gen 4:16a (lit. "Cain went away from the face of Yahweh"), it may be that the similar terminology of Cain's complaint intends to suggest that his hiddenness from God will be attributable to the distance that will be put between him in his exile east of Eden and the presence of God in the garden. Of course, that would be to misconstrue the significance of the Creator's special theophanic identification with his garden-sanctuary. But one need not expect Cain to be orthodox. In fact, for Cain to suggest that his problem was a matter of geography is precisely the kind of obscurantism that is to be expected here. The theme of the obscuration of man's ethical responsibility by metaphysical theories of existential predicament begins with the Satanic version of man's probationary decision. Ignoring the issue of sovereign, divine command and human obedience, Satan reduced the matter to a question of metaphysical evolution towards godhood (Gen 3:5). Subsequently, Adam explained his hiding from God's presence as due to his nakedness, a physical problem for which it had seemed reasonable to seek a geographical solution—behind the trees (Gen 3:8–10).[8] That is the theological tradition in which Cain stood. Moreover, avoidance of confession of blame and guilt would be consistent with Cain's own previous behavior. But though Cain's statement would thus involve the idea of physical separation from God, that idea would still figure only as the (false) rationale for the problem of judicial hiddenness which constitutes the essential point of the complaint: in his accursed exile from Eden he will be beyond the range of God's judicial oversight.

Apparently, Cain once again feels aggrieved by the difference in God's treatment of him and his brother. God's rejection of Cain's offering had prompted the jealous hatred that led to the murder of the favored Abel (Gen 4:4ff.). Now Cain sees another instance of discrimination in the fact that God hears and heeds the legal plea[9] of Abel's blood calling for vengeance (Gen 4:10ff.),[10] whereas, as Cain supposes, his own cry for judicial assistance will not reach the ears of God over the distance put between them.

The consequences of the judicial dereliction Cain anticipates (Gen 4:14b) will be, he laments, that everyone in the family of mankind, kinsmen all of his innocent victim, Abel, will be let loose in a mindless blood feud to take vengeance on him (v 14d): "Everyone who finds me will kill me."[11] Hidden from God's face, he will have no judge to appeal to. Society east of Eden will be devoid of God's judicial ordering. Cain will be exposed to lawless men bent on vengeance. He will be *ex lex* on a God-forsaken earth.

What Cain dreaded as his fate was that unbearable forsakenness depicted as overtaking the one who speaks in the lament of Psalm 22. In his suffering he complains that he is abandoned to the malice of the encompassing wicked: "Everyone that sees me laughs me to scorn (v 8).... My God, why have you forsaken me.... I cry... you do not hear" (vv 2,3; cf. Matt 27:46; Mark 15:34). Thus he suffers until God heeds his cry and ceases to hide his face from him (v 25).

II. God's Response

That Cain's world was not now totally severed from God's judicial interest, as he complained, was made at once evident by the fact that this complaint received a hearing and a response (Gen 4:15). Agreeably, the content of the response was to the effect that there would be a divinely sanctioned law structure in man's fallen exile-world. The response contains no direct reflection on the first element in this complaint; man was indeed to be an outcast, a creature driven across the face of the cursed earth. But the second element of the complaint is dealt with explicitly in the response. God does not mitigate his announced judgment, but he does clarify it, correcting Cain's misconception.[12] God's face will not be hidden; there will be an exercise of the divine *imperium* among men (v 15a; cf. v 14b). Hence, the situation will not be such that Cain will be a prey to anarchical terrorism (v 15b; cf. v 14d).

The introductory *lākēn* gives the response the formal character of a solemn affirmation. This word, usually mistranslated "therefore," signalizes a vow, binding asseveration or oath.[13] It is often found introducing divine declarations, either by itself or with formulae of oracular pronouncement like "thus says Yahweh," "utterance of Yahweh," and the oath formula "as I live."[14] It is used in statements sealing agreements or providing guarantees of commitments (cf. Gen 30:15; Exod 6:6; Num 25:12; Judg 11:8; 1 Sam 28:2; 2 Kgs 19:32; 22:20; Isa 7:14; 61:7). Of particular interest for the interpretation of Gen 4:15 is the usage of *lākēn* in conjunction with *'ôt* (Isa 7:14; cf. Isa 37:30,33; 2 Kgs 19:29,32).

"If anyone kills Cain, he shall be avenged sevenfold." This asseveration of Gen 4:15a is in the form of a law, the formulation being of an infrequent type in which the offense is expressed by a participle[15] and the penalty by a third-person imperfect (usually preceded by an infinitive absolute).[16] God's response to Cain is then to be seen as the promulgation of a law—a law that envisaged the establishment of an entire law-order.

In the laws with participial protasis the subject of the verb in the penalty clause (usually *môt yûmat,* "he shall be put to death") is the offender denoted by the participle. But in the apodosis in Gen 4:15a a different verb (*yuqqām*) is used, and the reference made by Lamech to this divine pronouncement later in the same chapter (v 24) indicates that the object, not the subject, of the participial action is the subject in this penalty clause. However, even though the law says that Cain is to be avenged rather than that vengeance is to be taken on the one who kills him, the avenging of Cain is to be accomplished through the punishment of his slayer. Either way, therefore, this divine legal provision calls for the punishment of the murderer and thereby institutes a structure for the administration of justice—a structure that was to be more precisely defined by subsequent revelation.[17]

This judicial order is characterized by the prescription in Gen 4:15 as an administration of *divine* justice. For the adverbial *šib'ātayim* 'sevenfold,' which serves instead of the infinitive absolute usually used in laws of this type to strengthen the verb in the penalty clause, describes the stipulated vindication as divine in its ultimate authority. In support of that, it will suffice here to mention only some of the more pertinent data. The brief selection does, however, represent a variety of literary traditions and the passages individually are reflective of Gen 4:15 in various ways.

From the revelatory form of the divine work of creation (Gen 1:1–2:3) seven emerges as a sign of divine action in its perfection. This sabbath-seven sign in the heightened form of the Jubilee symbol is connected with divine vindication when the final Jubilee, the messianic *mīšarum* act, finds exposition as "the day of vindication (*nāqām*) of our God" (Isa 61:2b). In Leviticus 26, the curse with which God threatens Israel for breach of his covenant, the covenant whose sign is the sabbath, is called a "vindication of the covenant" (v 25), and it consists in his punishing them sevenfold for their sin (v 24).[18] From the historical records of the monarchy comes the account of the sevenfold avenging of the Gibeonites for Saul's blood-guilt with reference to them (2 Sam 21:1ff.). That it is a matter of divine vindication is evident from several factors: the episode unfolds from a judicial response of the Lord to David, who has sought God's face; the offense was a violation of an oath in God's name; and the punishment takes place "before Yahweh." Turning to the Psalms, the lament of Psalm 79 appeals to God to avenge the blood of his people and vindicate his name (vv 9,10) by returning the taunts of the enemy sevenfold into their bosom (v 12). The same motif appears in the New Testament apocalyptic tradition in the judicial appeal of the martyrs to the Lord to avenge their blood (Rev 6:10). This appeal is set within the framework of the book with the seven seals, and, more significantly, the sevenfold judgment series of the seven trumpets and the seven vials of divine wrath are both presented as responses to these appeals of God's people for vindication (Rev 8:3,4 and 15:7; cf. 5:8).[19] It is then a common conception throughout biblical literature that sevenfold vindication is divine vindication.[20]

Mendenhall, in his illuminating study of the root *nqm,* shows that in its biblical usage, as elsewhere, the taking of vengeance into one's own hands in blood feud in a situation devoid of orderly legal procedure is not what is in view. "Instead of representing merely a primitive custom incompatible with any stable peaceful society, the root *NQM* has to do with the very foundations of political legitimacy and authority long before the time of Moses."[21] The "vengeance of Yahweh" is an exercise of the legitimate divine sovereignty, or *imperium,* whether for defensive or punitive vindication. As for Genesis 4, Mendenhall feels the two occurrences of *nqm* there are probably survivals of an old usage in which it had associations with the blood feud, but he qualifies that with the observation that the custom is attributed in Genesis 4 to the intervention and authority of Yahweh.[22] And that, he suggests, strongly implies that God is to be understood as the logical subject of the action denoted there by *nqm.*

It would appear that the Genesis 4 usage of *nqm* is actually quite consistent with the normal usage as Mendenhall has analyzed it. In the case of Gen 4:15, what is authorized by Yahweh is not the custom of blood feud, but precisely the kind of political-judicial order whose legitimate acts of vindication are normally denoted by the root *nqm,* and, indeed, one that is ultimately an administration of God's own *imperium.* Quite apart from the presence of the root *nqm* in this verse, we have seen that the divine response is a correction of Cain's false assumption that he was being driven into a situation of lawless vengeance. The fact that *nqm* is used in the penalty clause of this divine prescription is, in the light of Mendenhall's study, highly significant as a further confirmation that Gen 4:15 contemplates the establishment of an institutional structure for a legitimate judicial office in man's fallen world.

Understood as a foundational revelation of the judicial order of the state, Gen 4:15 fits coherently into the thematic development of the early chapters of Genesis. The Lord's earlier judicial pronouncements concerning fallen mankind (Gen 3:16ff.) revealed that history was to be informed by the principle of common grace–common curse, with the institution of the family continuing as a societal framework for man's cultural occupation. The Gen 4:15 disclosure supplemented that with its intimation of the emergence of the authority-structure of the state as a further provision of the common grace of God. It is with precisely this theme of the city of man that the narrative continues in Gen 4:17ff.,[23] and the second occurrence of *nqm* in Genesis 4 is in the declaration of one who stands in the dynastic succession of the city. Lamech's boast (Gen 4:23,24) cites the tradition about the divine avenging of Cain, but Lamech repudiates the divine authorization of his office. Absolutizing the judicial authority in himself, he regards himself incomparably more competent for vengeance than any deity who might have promised Cain sevenfold vengeance. The seventy-sevenfold vengeance Lamech threatens is not an escalation of the blood feud but an idolatrous perverting of the divine institution of the state.[24] When the city of man theme resumes in Gen 6:1ff., this ideology of divine kingship becomes explicit in the self-identification of the royal tyrants as sons of the gods.[25] The judgment of God overtook the world of Genesis 6, but immediately after the record of the deluge the narrative returns to the theme of the city of man. And in the postdiluvian covenant by which God renewed the earth-order of common grace, the stipulation concerning the state's avenging function is presented in terms drawn from Genesis 4. The murder to be avenged is a Cain-like act of fratricide (Gen 9:5). The authorization of blood-vindication is formulated in the participial style of Gen 4:15 (Gen 9:6), and this interrelationship furnishes additional support of the present thesis.[26]

God's legally formulated response to Cain's complaint (Gen 4:15a) gave solemn assurance that his face would not be hidden (cf. v 14b), for he would establish in his common grace the political order of the state as an authority ordained of God, a minister of God to execute his vengeance in this world. Cain was not provided with a divine guarantee that he would never be a murderer's victim. Verse 15a assumes the possibility of Cain's being killed and simply tells him that in that event there will be divine vindication.[27] Cain had not complained that he had no guarantee of absolute inviolability but that he would be exposed to absolute anarchy. The divine response announces that, on the contrary, controls will be instituted. Just as the curse addressed to Adam and Eve (Gen 3:16ff.)—the curse with the implicit disclosure of common-grace provisions—had in view all men and women, so this supplementary disclosure of the common-grace order, though directed to Cain, had to do with all mankind. After all, why should Cain have been singled out for a unique individual protection from lawless violence?[28] Cain would participate in the benefit that would be afforded by the promised law-order, but that was just incidental to the common provision for all.

Gen 4:15a answers to v 14b, and v 15b corresponds to v 14d. Thus, in Gen 4:15b the language of Cain's complaint in v 14d is repeated in order to negate its point: since the world would not be a lawless chaos, but judicially structured, it would not really be the case that anyone and everyone who came upon Cain would be bent on killing him.

The present interpretation differs from the usual views as to the general structure of Gen 4:15. According to most interpreters the first part of the verse quotes God's response and the second part relates an additional action. But on the view taken here, v 15b does not refer to some distinct divine act but is rather a recapitulation of God's response.[29] Grammatically, this clause with *wāw*-consecutive plus imperfect is of the narrative summation type where the *wāw* may be translated "thus."[30] The word *'ôt,* on this view, refers to the divine response quoted in v 15a. We must return to the question of the meaning of *'ôt,* but may first observe that the infinitive clause following *'ôt* is not a negative final clause but a restatement of the substance of God's response. A similar use of the infinitive after *'ôt* to express the substance of the "sign" is found in Ezekiel 20: "[the sabbath] will be a sign between me and you, an acknowledgment that I, Yahweh, am your God" (v 20; cf. v 12). Gen 19:21 offers an interesting grammatical and situational parallel to Gen 4:15. Here too it is a matter of response to an appeal in the midst of judgment. Lot bargains with the Lord of the angels for a small concession (vv 19,20). The response assures him that his request is granted and the content of that grant (which is one with the content of the appeal[31]) is expressed, as in Gen 4:15b, by *l^ebiltî* and the infinitive: "I grant you this request that I should not overthrow the city." Translating Gen 4:15b accordingly, it reads (freely): "Thus Yahweh gave Cain an *'ôt* to the effect that everyone who came upon him would not be out to kill him."

As for the word *'ôt,* it is first to be noted that it may have a verbal rather than visual character.[32] It is used for prophecies delivered without any visual accompaniment then and there (cf. Isa 7:14; 37:30; Deut 13:2). In the encounter of Isaiah with Ahaz the verbal *'ôt* that God gives is in definite contrast to the visible kind of sign that Ahaz had refused. A prediction embodied in a name is designated an *'ôt*. Isaiah and his children are "signs" (Isa 8:18) by virtue of their prophetic names (cf. Isa 7:3; 8:3; 12:2); in effect, it is their names that constitute the sign.[33] In Exod 3:12, God gives as an *'ôt* that he has sent Moses a verbal assurance that after the exodus Israel will serve God on this mountain where he was now speaking to Moses. A similar usage is found in Josh 2:12. The *'ôt* Rahab requests is usually identified as the scarlet cord (cf. vv 18,21), but it seems rather to be a reference to the oath that has just been mentioned. Rahab asks the spies to swear by Yahweh (v 12a) and specifies that their oath be one of fidelity (*ḥesed*) to her father's house (v 12b). Then, repeating her request, she asks that they give an *'ôt* of truth or faithfulness (*'emet*) to her (v 12c), again specifying that they show mercy to her family (v 13). In complying, the spies unite the doubled request, committing themselves to deal with her in both *ḥesed* and *'emet* (v 14). Apparently, commentators have missed what seems to be the obvious identification of this *'ôt* with the oath[34] precisely because they have been under the domination of the notion that an *'ôt* must be something visible.

An *'ôt* may then consist simply of words. We must, however, try to identify the special characteristics of statements that may be so designated. It would appear from the above examples that within the sphere of religious relationship at least, *'ôt* is applicable to affirmations of intention, assurances of commitment, prophetic guarantees. Moreover, all these instances involve divine authentication of the trustworthiness of what is affirmed. The *'ôt*-statement is directly spoken by God, inspired by God or sanctioned by his name.[35]

It is in the light of this usage that *'ôt* is to be understood in Gen 4:15b. Verse 15a, the referent of *'ôt,* is a direct divine revelation, a self-authenticating divine word, prophetically decretive, affirming God's intention to institute a judicial order. Enhancing the *'ôt*-character of this oracular pronouncement and affording it an oath quality[36] is the inclusion in it of the symbolic seven, sign of divine presence and sanction.

There is then no reference in Gen 4:15 to an unspecified wonder-sign that God performed for Cain's personal assurance, with the reader left to speculate about what it might have been. And certainly the language does not suggest a "mark of Cain" imprinted on his body. Such interpretations assume that Cain was being given a special individual guarantee, but that, as we have seen, is not the point of the passage. It is rather concerned with a general world-order that would condition the life of all men. The meaning of the passage will therefore be brought out if we translate, not "And Yahweh gave a sign to Cain," but "Thus Yahweh signified to Cain that . . . ."

The author's concern with the subject of God's judicial relation to men is attested once again in Genesis 4 when he turns from the Cainite succession to the line of Seth (vv 25,26). For he capsulates the nature of this community in their act of confessing (naming) Yahweh as covenant Lord to whom their judicial appeal was directed. There is, of course, a radical difference between the exercise of God's *imperium* that is in view in Gen 4:15, and his vindication of the blood of Abel and the martyr-seed of the woman restored in the line of Seth and continuing to the last judgment (cf. Rev 6:10,11). To Cain, God signified that for mankind in general he would provide in his common grace an institutional agent to bear the sword of his wrath in the temporal course of world history (cf. Rom 13:4). For the people of his covenant, God's judicial vindication is an act of his saving grace, a coming in personal immediacy as their eschatological, redemptive Avenger.

NOTES

1. In a recent reexamination of the matter, W. M. Clark finds nine elements in this pattern, covering the entire episode from the initial imposition of divine obligation to the execution of judgment ("The Flood and the Structure of the Pre-patriarchal History," *ZAW* 83 [1971]: 195–203). Narrative development, style and specific vocabulary all come under the influence of the judicial form.
2. Cf. expressions like "is it too small," "it is enough," "too much," "how long," "speedily." This is a point of contact between Cain's lament and Psalter laments. On this, see further, p. 133.
3. In other instances of the phrase with the verb in the N-stem (see below), the reflexive meaning is not suitable because of the impersonal nature of the subject of the action. If, with M. Dahood (*Psalms I* [AB 16; New York: Doubleday, 1965]: 64), we regard the verb as an infixed-t formation of *sûr* ('turn aside'), the reflexive meaning would be awkward even in Gen 4:14.
4. If Dahood's parsing of the verb is correct (see n. 3), an adjustment in the translation is necessary, but this would not affect our discussion of the judicial force of the idiom.

5. The use of this idiom by the vassals of the Pharaoh (EA 165:5ff.) shows that it has been adopted from the secular judicial field to express the religious-covenantal relationship.
6. On Dahood's parsing (see n. 3 above), the passive form would mean that something had been turned aside or removed from God's presence or attention. In Gen 4:14b, an excellent parallelism with the image of being driven away in v 14a then results.
7. Relevant here is the evidence, biblical and extra-biblical, for the use of this eye-terminology in connection with the royal office of surveillance and investigation.
8. This hiding in Genesis 3 is a case of the offenders hiding themselves from judicial exposure and punishment. The verb (N and HtD of *ḥābā'*) is not the one used in Gen 4:14. But this close parallel to our Genesis 4 passage does lead us to expect that the hiding from the face of God in the latter will also have a judicial orientation.
9. Cf. Gen 18:20; Deut 22:24,27; 2 Kgs 8:3; Job 16:18.
10. See Ps 18:7 for an expansion of the idea of the "voice" coming before the divine judge.
11. In a discussion of this passage commendable for its perception of what some of the real issues are, R. Rushdoony (*The Institutes of Biblical Law* [Nutley, NJ: Craig, 1973]: 358ff.) presents an interpretation of Cain's fear quite the reverse of that offered above. He suggests that Cain fears not the absence of a judicial authority structure but the existence of one, namely, the already existing law-order of the family. Then, according to Rushdoony, God acts to protect Cain from execution by the family because God's design for the family's role in law enforcement excludes the execution of the death penalty, that being reserved for the state when it should emerge.
12. W. M. Clark ([N 1]: 197) interprets Gen 4:15 as a mitigation of the sentence and sees it as corresponding in this respect to v 21 in the parallel Genesis 3 pattern.
13. Cf. F. C. Goldbaum, "Two Hebrew Quasi-Adverbs: לכן and אכן," *JNES* 23 (1964): 132–34. Is it composed of emphatic *lamed* and *kēn*, 'yes,' a compact 'verily, verily'? "Agreed!" would be a suitable translation in many cases; it is an equivalent of *'āmēn*.
14. See Ezek 5:11; 35:6,11; Zeph 2:9; cf. Jer 5:2 (where the *lākēn* is possibly to be taken as a quotation of the false swearers); 1 Kgs 22:16,19; Isa 5:13,14,24 (where *lākēn* is an alternate for *'im lô'*).
15. The reinforcing of the participle of the protasis by *kol* is found elsewhere in legal, decretive and imprecatory genres. See J. G. Williams, "Concerning One of the Apodictic Formulas," *VT* 14 (1964): 486–88. Cf. Exod 22:18.
16. See Exod 21:15,17; 22:17,19; 31:14; Lev 24:16; cf. Lev 20:2,9–13,15,16,27. Alt's classification of the participial formulation as apodictic does not commend itself. The participial protasis is simply a variation of the usual "if" clause in casuistic law. Cf. G. J. Wenham, "Legal Forms in the Book of the Covenant," *Tyndale Bulletin* 22 (1971): 102; M. Weinfeld, *Deuteronomy and the Deuteronomic School* (Oxford: Clarendon, 1972): 239.
17. In Exod 21:20, a law dealing with the killing of a slave, *nāqôm yinnāqēm* appears in the penalty clause. G. E. Mendenhall, commenting on the ambiguity of the subject, whether master or slave, observes that neither one is the logical subject of the passive verb. "Rather, it is a command that the sovereign authority of Yahweh should be placed in action in order to punish/redress an action that is incompatible with the sovereignty of that same ultimate authority" (*The Tenth Generation* [Baltimore: Johns Hopkins University, 1973]: 91).
18. The sevenfold covenant curse appears in the extra-biblical treaties too. See, e.g., *Sefîre* I.A.27ff. and II.A.6ff. (*KAI* 222, 223).
19. Judicial appeal, constituting, as it thus does, the setting for the major structural heptads of the book, emerges as a fundamental perspective in the Apocalypse. The book revolves around the appeal of the martyr-church for covenantal vindication—"Come, Lord Jesus"—and his response as Lord of the covenant and Judge of the nations, giving assurance of timely judicial intervention—"I come quickly." Such is the closing summation in Rev 22:20.
20. Cf. also Gen 7:2,3; 21:28ff.; Lev 4:6,17; 8:11; Isa 30:26; Ps 12:7; Prov 6:31. The association of seven with oaths is to be noted in view of the combination of the seven motif and *lākēn,* itself an introduction to oaths, in Gen 4:15.
21. Mendenhall (N 17): 75.
22. Mendenhall (N 17): 74, 88.
23. As this narrative shows, the curse of exile was tempered by a measure of stability and community. And it was this city community that was invested with the judicial function referred to in God's response to Cain. Gen 4:15 does then speak indirectly to Cain's complaint about his exile-existence (Gen 4:14a and c) but without having to correct his understanding of this aspect of his judgment.

24. Lamech's conjoined claims of seventy-sevenfold vengeance and divine status are another indication of the significance of seven as a divine emblem in the sevenfold avenging of Gen 4:15.
25. Cf. my "Divine Kingship and Genesis 6:1–4," *WTJ* 24 (1962): 187–204.
26. Clark ([N 1]: 196) sees in this stylistic comparison evidence of a possible "legal background" for Gen 4:15.
27. For posthumous vindication compare the case of the slain slave in Exod 21:20.
28. God's judgment on Cain's act of murder was, indeed, distinctive in its sentence of exile rather than the death penalty subsequently prescribed for that crime; but that is another matter.
29. B. Jacob (*Das erste Buch der Tora—Genesis* [Berlin: Schocken, 1934]: 146) adopts a similar view of the structure, but in other respects his exegesis differs widely from that given here. According to Jacob, Cain is told that he will be punished (not avenged) and yet he himself will not be killed because the punishment will descend only after a sevenfold delay. Jacob's handling of the participial phrase in v 15a is particularly awkward; taking it as a broken quotation of v 14d, he detaches it from the following clause.
30. Cf., e.g., Gen 21:32a and Josh 24:25.
31. In the responses to both Cain and Lot, their positive statements are recast in negative form.
32. The discussion of *'ôt* by K. H. Rengstorf ("σημεῖον," *TDNT* 7 [1971]: 209 ff., esp. 211f.) does not do justice to the evidence for the nonvisual usage. The argument drawn from the association of *'ôt* with *rā'āʰ* is pressed too far, particularly in view of the range of meaning of *rā'āʰ* (cf., e.g., Isa 13:1).
33. Note the contrast between the *'ôt* function of Isaiah and his sons (Isa 8:18) and the hiding of Yahweh's face from the house of Jacob (v 17).
34. In Isa 19:20 *'ôt* is a synonym of *'ēd*, 'witness,' in a context of judicial appeal and response.
35. Foundational to the general semantic development of *'ôt* is its formal function of pointing or identifying. It is used as a synonym for the identifying name (Isa 55:13; Exod 13:9; cf. 3:15) and as a designation of the name-bearing standard (Num 2:2; cf. Isa 19:19,20). Also, "signs" are given so that people might know God's name, Yahweh. It was natural then that in theological usage *'ôt* should designate what identified or named God as author, whether the self-authenticating word spoken or inspired by God, or the event—supernatural happening or fulfillment of prediction—that pointed in attestation to the divine identity of such a word.

It is beyond the scope of this article to attempt a broad lexical survey of *'ôt*, but it should be observed that the relation of *'ôt* to Akkadian *ittu* ('sign') has been dismissed too lightly in the treatments of *'ôt* in the theological dictionaries (cf. K. H. Rengstorf [N 32]: 209 and F. J. Helfmeyer, *TDOT* 1 [1974]: 167). The semantic range of the two is remarkably similar and this makes it difficult not to accept an etymological relationship (cf. especially the *idat-* base of *ittu*). The common duplication of *ittu* written Á.MEŠ GISKIM.MEŠ, "signs and wonders," is an interesting parallel to the frequent biblical combination of *'ôtôt* and *môpᵉtîm*. Of particular importance among the meanings of *ittu* are: 'characteristic, nature (as in the divine name written *ᵈMan-nu-i-da-at-su-i-di*, "Who-understands-his-nature"; cf. Judg 13:18), signal, password, inside (i.e., authentic) information, (due advance) notice (used with *riksu* 'contract'), acknowledgment, proof, omen.' The aspects of verbal, legal confirmation and oracular disclosure are especially significant for the meaning of *'ôt* in Gen 4:15.
36. See n. 20 above.

9

THE TOWER OF BABEL REVISITED

ROBERT B. LAURIN*

The story of the Tower of Babel in Gen 11:1–9 is generally recognized to be the climax of a series of accounts dealing with man's rebellion against God. From the Garden of Eden incident onward the Priestly writers have collected and adapted various traditions which depict the root cause of man's troubles in the world, namely, his rebellion against the creator God and his refusal to accept his creaturely status with its limitations. All this is in part a preparation for Gen 12:1–3 and Yahweh's call of Abram to effect a reconciliation with "all the families of the earth." But though the general structure is clear, the explicit significance of the account of the Tower of Babel is not. One can see in the Cain and Abel story the problem of destroyed family relationships, or in Lamech's boast the tragedy of the blood feud, or in the Flood account the curse of society-wide violence and corruption (6:11–12). But what is the evil in the Tower of Babel tradition? The view of most commentators is epitomized in Von Rad's words: "The city arises as a sign of their valiant self-reliance, the tower as a sign of their will to fame."[1] The people's sin was thus their desire to be great apart from God. They wished to determine their life independently of God, since (it is usually pointed out) the name of God is not mentioned.

The interpretation of the pericope is made difficult by the subtlety of the narrative. Nothing is stated directly as to the reason for divine judgment, except the laconic "this is only the beginning of what they will do" (11:6). But what were they doing? Were they being condemned for desiring security and fame, as is usually said? This does not seem a fit reason for judgment. Were they displaying an overweening pride? This is possibly the implication of v 6, but it is not stated. Perhaps in the search for an answer we have not taken sufficient account of the tower and its purposes. It has been noticed for a long time that the narrative probably refers to the building of a "ziggurat."[2] This was a multi-leveled structure with a temple on top, designed to provide a dwelling for the god of the area, and a means for approaching him through sacrifices and offerings. The details of the ziggurat are well known, and need not be discussed here.[3] The important

*Dr. Laurin, Dean and Professor of Old Testament, American Baptist Seminary of the West, died on July 20, 1977. [G. A. T.]

point is that the tower had cultic significance; it was a means for worshiping a Mesopotamian deity. Thus it is clear that the Tower of Babel story does not deal with the people's attempt to build a secular society in their "valiant self-reliance" and "will to fame." Such a procedure would have been strange in the ancient world where the gods, though sometimes questioned, were not denied reality. Worship of the gods lay at the heart of Babel's life, as the tower attests. Neither, therefore, does the story give us an "example of human pride vaunting itself in the presence of the Almighty."[4] There is no prophetic oracle of reproach here like one finds in Amos 1–2, nor is there a picture of men seeking to storm heaven by means of the tower. The phrase: "Come, let us build ourselves a city, and a tower with its top in the heavens" (11:4) is only Old Testament hyperbole for special height (cf. Deut 1:28). And, of course, whatever aetiological backgrounds the story originally had—the explanation of tower ruins, the existence of different languages, the reason for the name Babel—these have receded into a secondary place in the overall theological scheme of the author or collectors. What, then, was the tale meant to teach?

I would suggest that the story, which is not just about a tower but about "a city, and a tower" (11:4; cf. 11:5,8,9), is an artful parable about the failure of pagan idolatry to provide the necessary foundation for a continuing culture. The story does not condemn the building of culture which is clearly seen in 4:17–26 as part of the blessing of 1:26–28. It was quite natural for the people who gathered after the Flood to look for security lest they "be scattered abroad upon the face of the whole earth" (11:4). Old Testament theology never espouses asceticism or withdrawal from the world. The story also does not really condemn the construction of an idolatrous culture. The author's technique is far more subtle than this. His method is not so much condemnation as illustration, and in this he follows the wisdom approach. Idolatry does not work; instead of unity it brings disunity, instead of cohesion it brings dispersion. It is true that he describes this as the active judgment of God, but this is simply the familiar Old Testament approach of ignoring secondary causes.

How do we understand this? What is the fundamental theology that is being expressed? It is simply that a person can only become a person and function positively in this world by accepting the limitation of being a creature in a world where God is sovereign. One must see the stories in Genesis 4–11 as integrally linked with Genesis 3. Man's basic sin is to attempt to be "like God" (3:5), that is, to refuse limitations and to function as sovereign. Each of the incidents in chapters 4–11 illustrates some transgression of limits, either individually or corporately, and the inevitable destructive results. The self-sufficient boast of individual power in Lamech's song (4:23–24) and the corporate boast of technological power in the Tower of Babel story (11:4) are complementary examples.

Idolatry does not work, therefore, because it forgets limitations and perverts the understanding of God's sovereignty. An idol, in the long run, is the servant of man. The idol is worshiped only in order to obtain what man wishes. Man is the one who determines what is right and good. Man, in this sense, functions as sovereign, though he needs the power of the gods. And man left to himself, as these stories illustrate, inevitably destroys. He is limited, incomplete, needing the sovereign presence of God for direction just as surely as he needs God for life.

It is this that the story of the city and the tower seeks to illustrate. The authors—J traditionist and P circle—were both claiming that the attempt to build the imperishable city or to establish the indestructible name was doomed if it was founded on that which the tower symbolized—an idolatrous view of reality. This would have had peculiar significance for the audiences to which the account was addressed. For those who heard it in the days of the J traditionist (tenth century B.C.), when the Israelites were seeking to build a unified society in the midst of Canaanite Baalism, the story warned that such an attempt was ill-formed if it was not based solidly on the worship of Yahweh. The events of subsequent days showed graphically the validity of this judgment when the increasing idolatry of the Solomonic monarchy, with its concomitant devaluation of human life, brought about the division of the kingdom. And the narrative also had particular significance for the Priestly collectors. They were seeking to provide guidance for the exiles in the establishment of another new society in Palestine, this time in the sixth century B.C. Once again the old tale warned that the reconstituted nation could not hope to survive if pagan worship and theology—now clearly with Babylonia in mind—provided the basis of its life. It was in this spirit that Ezra sought so vehemently to purge the syncretistic worship that had developed among the returned exiles in Jerusalem.

The theology that underlies this warning about idolatry is not made explicit here, but we can read it out of the mass of literary materials that have survived from this ancient period. Idolatry, by and large, based its life on cultic routine, not on personal morality or relationship. The gods were worshiped because of fear of the loss of fertile power or in an attempt to manipulate their forces. To sin was not to break relationship, but to break the cultic routines. Thus the emphasis on responsibility in interpersonal affairs because of the worth of the other, so dominant in Old Testament instruction, was usually lacking in idolatrous theology. If the gods did not care for relationship, but looked on people as slaves created to do the menial tasks of earth (as, e.g., in the Atraḫasis epic), then this was bound to have its effect on one's view of other people. Others were of utilitarian value, not personal value. It was this attitude that pervaded the latter days of Solomon's reign, and that was the basis for the strong prophetic denunciation of the leadership in the eighth and seventh centuries B.C. All this was fatal to unity within a society, and thus to its continuing stability, as Israel's history demonstrated. And in a world of many "towers" or ziggurats, and thus of many gods, competing loyalties inevitably tended to disintegrate the strength of a larger culture.

The ancient tale of the city and its tower, therefore, concludes with judgment. The language of the people is confused by the Lord, communication is made impossible, and so they drift apart into separate societies and nations, leaving their building project unfinished. And the comment is made: "Therefore its name was called Babel, because there the Lord confused the language of all the earth" (11:9). So this story, born from an aetiological background, seeks to show that man's independence from the true God is the cause of disunity and division among peoples. The different languages are symbolic of this. Misunderstandings, hate, confusion are the actual effects. Men cannot speak to each other because of self-interest. Thus the narrative warns any culture that the attempt to build the "great society" on human achievements and inventions alone without the true divine dimension is doomed to confusion and failure. Men working only with themselves and idolatrous loyalties inevitably tend to misunderstanding and confusion. This is why the divine grace expressed in the promise to Abraham (Gen 12:1–3) is so important.

NOTES

1. G. von Rad, *Genesis: A Commentary* (2d ed.; Philadelphia: Westminster, 1972): 148.
2. E. A. Speiser warns that identification with the ziggurat Etemenanki at Babylon is ruled out by chronology, since this was the achievement of Nabopolassar and Nebuchadnezzar in the seventh/sixth centuries B.C. Thus "it could not have been known in that very form to J, whose work dates to the tenth century, let alone to J's sources which have to be older still. What inspired the present biblical theme in the first instance was not monumental architecture but literary tradition. We need look no farther than the account of the building of Babylon and its temple that is given in Enūma eliš VI, lines 60–62" (*Genesis* [AB 1; Garden City, NY: Doubleday, 1964]: 75). In any case, Speiser sees the background in "the religious architecture of Mesopotamia" (p. 76), and certainly the P writers would have associated the building particularly with the tower at Babylon.
3. Cf. A. Parrot, *The Tower of Babel* (London: SCM, 1955) for a helpful survey of the literary and archaeological evidence.
4. B. Vawter, *A Path Through Genesis* (New York: Sheed & Ward, 1956): 107.

10

MID ROCK AND SCRUB, A UGARITIC PARALLEL TO EXODUS 7:19

MARVIN H. POPE

In the first of the ten plagues visited on the king of Egypt to induce him to let the Israelites go, the water of the Nile was turned to blood so that the fish died and the water stank and became undrinkable (Exod 7:17–24). "YHWH said to Moses, 'Say to Aaron, "Take your rod and stretch your hand over the waters of Egypt, over their rivers, over their canals, and their ponds, and over all their water pools, that they may become blood; and there shall be blood through all the land of Egypt, both in the trees and in the stones (*ûbā'ēṣîm ûbā'ăbānîm*)." ' " The LXX translators apparently had no trouble with the last phrase and rendered literally *en te tois xulois kai en tois lithois*. The Vulgate, however, assumed that the wood and stone meant vessels or receptacles of those materials and added an explanatory term: *tam in ligneis vasis quam in saxeis,* and likewise the Targum: *ûbᵉmānê 'ā'ā' ûbᵉmānê 'abnā'*. Rashi explained the phrase as designating "water which is in vessels of wood and in vessels of stone (*mym šbkly 'ṣ wbkly 'bn*)." Similarly Ibn Ezra opined that the meaning of *wb'ṣym wb'bnym* is the water which was in the houses in wooden vessels or in basins made of stone (*wṭ'm wb'ṣym wb'bnym hmym šhyw bbtym bkly 'ṣ 'w bkywr hn'śym m'bn*). Modern versions have regularly followed this line, with slight variation in wording. Luther rendered, "beide in holzernen und steinernen Gefässen." *KJV* and *RSV* render, "both in *vessels* of wood, and in *vessels* of stone," with *KJV* italicizing the addition. Moffatt rendered, "even in bowls of wood and stone jars," while *AT* has, "in both pails and stone jars." The English version of *JB* has "even down to the contents of every tub or jar"; *NEB*, "even in their wooden bowls and jars of stone"; *NAB*, "even in the wooden pails and stone jars." *JPSV* and *NJV* likewise perpetuate the conjecture of the Targum, Vulgate and medieval commentaries, the latter with "even in vessels of wood and stone." *TEV* carries on the tradition with "even in the wooden tubs and stone jars," while *LBP* has the expansive, "and even the water stored in bowls and pots in the homes."

Now it is certainly conceivable that "trees" and "stones" might designate vessels made of wood and stone, as it has indeed been assumed for two millennia in the case of Exod 7:19, despite the lack of other attestations of this usage in Hebrew, either biblical or post-biblical. In Akkadian *abnu* 'stone' is actually used for containers made of that material. *CAD* cites "57/183 stone (bowls) for oil" (57/183 *ab-nim* Ì.GIŠ) and "one stone (bowl) for honey" (1 *ab-nu* LÀL).[1] There is apparently no attestation in Akkadian of the parallel use of *iṣu* 'wood' for a container made of that material. This could very well be explained by the fact that wood was scarce in ancient Mesopotamia and more in demand for uses other than for common containers.

Few critics have questioned the assumption that wood(s) and stone(s) in Exod 7:19 designate vessels made of those materials, and lexicons list this special meaning under each word *'ăbānîm* 'stone vessels' and *'ēṣîm* 'wooden vessels.'[2] B. D. Eerdmans, however, suggested that the trees and stones refer to the water contained therein, i.e., the sap of trees and the springs which flow from the rocks: "Sogar das Wasser in den Steinen, die Quellen und der Saft der Bäume wird zu Blut."[3] In 1947 J. Coppens[4] called attention to what he termed a "curious Ugaritic parallel" to the puzzling phrase of Exod 7:19 in 23[52].66, the Poem of the Gracious and Beautiful Gods, which reads *ṯm tgrgr labnm wl'ṣm šb' šnt*. Under the influence of Eerdmans' suggestion concerning the trees and stones of Exod 7:19, which he cited and rendered in French "jusque à la sève des arbres et l'eau des sources," Coppens translated the Ugaritic line "Là, ils séjourneront près des sources et des arbres durant sept années." Coppens regarded the context of the Ugaritic passage as obscure, but took it as containing the description of the *mdbr qdš* mentioned in the preceding line. It is there in the wilderness of Qadesh that the divinities with whom the latter part of the poem is concerned will sojourn. The meaning "springs" (*sources*), ascribed to *abnm* 'stones' on the basis of Eerdmans' suggestion with regard to Exod 7:19, presented no problem or gave no pause to Coppens, who concluded: "Quoi de plus naturel que de songer aux sources et aux arbres les deux élements qui constitutent l'oasis sacrée et qui doivent en rendre le séjour agréable?"[5]

The assumption that the gracious gods' sojourn in the desert was meant to be agreeable to them is one of the factors contributing to the obscurity which Coppens and others have found in this provocative poem. Without going into detail on the numerous items on which obscurity, confusion and dissent persist, a brief summary of the larger context of the "curious parallel" may dispel some of the misapprehension. The gracious gods (*ilm n'mm*) who are begotten by El (not without protracted difficulty on the part of the senescent sire of gods and men in achieving or maintaining erection of his prodigiously elongated "hand"[6]) do not appear particularly benign. It seems likely, therefore, that the epithets 'gracious' (*n'm*) and 'beautiful' (*ysm*) are antiphrastic euphemisms. When at length El managed to impregnate the eager and patient females, the nature and action of the resultant progeny appear detrimental to the environment. The mouths of the newborn gods stretch from earth to heaven, and they devour the denizens of sky and sea (23[52].61–64):

Lip to earth, lip to heaven,	*špt larṣ špt lšmm*
and there entered their mouths	*wlʿrb bphm*
birds of sky and fish of sea.	*ʿṣr šmm wdg bym*
They rose [ ]	*wndd* [ ]
They bolted right and left	*yʿdb uymn ušmal*
with their mouths, but were not sated.	*bphm wltšbʿn*

The gods were generally conceived as supernatural in size, power and action, but the mouths and appetites of these voracious infants seem exceptional even for gods. The lips stretching from earth to sky, or from hell to heaven, and taking in their sweep both birds and fish, presumably also gathered in terrestrial fauna and flora in between.[7] Apparently El regarded their ravening as ecologically intolerable, and decided to banish the predators and their mothers to the desert or steppe-land, presumably to reduce the drain on the food supply of the fertile area on which mankind depends for survival (23[52].64–68):

O wives whom I espoused,	*y aṯt itrḫ*
O children whom I sired,	*y bn ašld*
Up, grub mid the desert Qdš,	*šu ʿdb tk mdbr qdš*
There forage	*ṯm tgrgr*
mid stones and shrubs	*labnm wlʿṣm*
seven full years,	*šbʿ šnt tmt*
eight cycles of time.	*ṯmn nqpt ʿd*
The gracious gods walked the steppe,	*ilm nʿmm ttlkn šd*
Roamed the desert edges.	*tṣdn pat mdbr*

Details need not distract us here. The point of interest in the passage just cited is the phrase *labnm wlʿṣm* which, in spite of the reverse order of the words and the use of the all-purpose preposition *l* rather than *b,* is manifestly a variant of the enigmatic expression of Exod 7:19.

Though nothing is said to indicate that the gracious gods' roaming in the desert was a pleasant experience, we may reasonably assume that it was not. There is nothing to suggest that they were in an oasis. On the edge of the desert they encountered a personage called Guardian of the Sown (*nǵr mdrʿ*) to whom they gave the command, "Open!" The Guardian of the Sown did open a breach for them and they entered (*wptḥ hw prṣ bʿdhm wʿrb hm;* 23[52].70–71) and asked for food and drink. Presumably their fare during the desert sojourn had been spare and not at all agreeable, given their robust appetites. The text breaks off as the long-deprived deities are assured that there is food and drink.

S. E. Loewenstamm allotted a brief note in his commentary to the troublesome phrase *ʿṣym wʾbnym* of Exod 7:19, in which he called attention to the remote Ugaritic parallel 3[ʿNT].3.19–22; 1[ʿNT.IX].3.12–14, but ignored the closer and more relevant parallel already cited above.[8] It is expedient to cite the more remote parallel in order to show its misapplication to the closer parallel. The context is

Baal's message to his sister Anat regarding a cosmic secret he wishes to share with her:

I have something I would tell you,	*dm rgm iṯ ly wargm(n)k*
a word I would spell you,	*hwt waṯnyk*
a word about wood, a whisper about stone,	*rgm 'ṣ wlḫšt abn*
the sighing of heaven toward earth,	*tant šmm 'm arṣ*
the deep toward the stars.	*thmt 'mn kbkbm*

Loewenstamm quite properly pointed to the parallelism here of wood and stone, with heaven and earth and with deep(s) and stars, and to the cosmic implications of the combination. Z. Zevit[9] adduced the closer Ugaritic parallel which Loewenstamm had overlooked, and carried over the cosmic connotations of earth, deep and stars both to the other Ugaritic passage and to Exod 7:19.

The latter passages, however, do not appear to have the cosmic sweep of the passages relating to Baal's secret plan to build a splendiferous palace of molten gold, silver and lapis lazuli on Mount Ṣapān.[10] The lips of the glutton babes indeed reach from earth to heaven and take in everything between, birds of heaven and fish in the sea, but when they are banished to the wilderness, desert or steppe-land to forage for seven years, there is no further mention of the prodigious reach of their mouths. The parallel to *'ṣm wabnm* in this instance is *mdbr qdš,* and the reason for the exile to the relatively barren region was presumably to save the cultivated area from being ravaged. With reference to Egypt in Exod 7:19, the interest is in the total water supply of the country, the rivers, canals, pools or reservoirs, including any water that might be found beyond the fertile, irrigated area, even the precious little that might exist in the desert. Both in Exod 7:19 and in the Ugaritic parallel in 23[52].66, the phrase "woods and stones," or the reverse, aptly characterizes the arid and barren desert area beyond the sown where both food and water are scarce, though not entirely lacking. In both instances *'ṣ(y)m* appears to correspond to our colloquial usage, "the sticks," to designate outlying, rustic backwoods areas remote from the centers of habitation. Rocks and stones too are associated with desert aridity and sterility. The vegetation that survives among the dry rocks is generally stunted growth which we designate as scrub or shrub (Old English *scrybb*). Thus we may translate the phrase in both instances as "scrub and rock," with no particular cosmic implication either in the Ugaritic passage 23[52].66 or in Exod 7:19.

NOTES

1. *CAD* A/1,61a.
2. BDB 6b (2), 78lb (2b); KB² 1, 8b (8).
3. B. D. Eerdmans, *Das Buch Exodus* (Alttestamentliche Studien 3; Giessen: A. Töpelmann, 1910): 23 n. 1.
4. J. Coppens, "Miscellanées Bibliques XII: Un parallèle ougaritien curieux, Ras Shamra, SS, 1. 66, et Exod., VII, 19," *ETL* 23 (1947): 177–78.
5. Coppens (N 4): 178.

6. Cf. M. Pope, *El in the Ugaritic Texts* (Leiden: Brill, 1955): 35–42.
7. The lip to earth, lip to heaven motif also describes the hungry mouth of Môt, Death (5[67].2.2–6):

[Lip to ea]rth, lip to heaven	*[špt la]rṣ špt lšmm*
[t]ongue to the stars	[*l]šn lkbkbm*
[Baa]l will enter his inwards	*y'rb [b']l bkbdh*
In his mouth will descend like an olive fritter	*bph yrd kḫrr zt*
produce of earth and fruit of trees.	*ybl arṣ wpr 'ṣm*

The great dragon *tnn* is similarly described as spanning sea and sky in text 1003.3-10:

[ ] to/from the earth	[ ] *un barṣ*
Snout nuzzled sea,	*mḫnm ṯrp ym*
Twin-tongue licked sky,	*lšnm tlḥk šmm*
Whisked sea twin-tail.	*ṯṯrp ym ḏnbtm*
Dragon to muzzle she put,	*tnn lšbm tšt*
Bound him to the peak of Leb[anon].	*trks lmrym lb[nn]*

The *hapax legomenon mḫnm* is not a "nouveau toponym biblique," "the land of Mahanaim," as Virolleaud supposed (*PRU* 2,12), but rather a common noun in the dual designating the twin-nostriled proboscis of the dragon, parallel to two other nouns in the dual, *lšnm* and *ḏnbtm,* designating the bifurcated tongue and tail of the monster. The two extremities, snout (cf. Ar. *maḫann-at)* and tail, brush (cf. Syr. *ṯrp)* the sea, while the tongue licks the sky. A garbled echo of this motif of mouth spanning heaven and earth and tongue licking the sky is preserved in Ps 73:9:

They put in the sky their mouth	*štw bšmym pyhm*
And their tongue walks the earth	*wlšnm thlk b'rṣ.*

RSV rendered the latter colon, "and their tongue struts through the earth." A walking tongue is a difficult metaphor which *TEV* tells us, without hint of doubt, means, "give arrogant orders." Now the verbal form *tihălak* is unusual, attested elsewhere only in Exod 9:23 where the subject is 'fire' = 'lightning.' It seems likely that *thlk* is a corruption of an original *tlḥk* in both instances. Note the striking similarity of the Ugaritic *lšnm tlḥk šmm* and the biblical *wlšnm thlk b'rṣ*. The switching of heaven and earth is explained by the confusion of *lḥk* 'lick' and *hlk* 'go.' M. Dahood (*Psalms II* [2d ed., AB 17; Garden City, NY: Doubleday, 1973]: 190) has made the verbal parallel between Ps 73:9b and the Ugaritic 23[52].61–62 appear more striking than it really is by putting one Ugaritic word in the wrong line, dividing thus: *št špt larṣ* etc., thus making Ugaritic *št* correspond to the Hebrew *šātû* 'they set.' The error of this arrangement is manifest simply by noting that *št* in the Ugaritic passage is the last word of the cliche *ynqm bap ḏd št/aṯrt,* "suckers at the teats of the breasts of the Lady (cf. Ar. *sitt*)/Asherah," which recurs in 23[52].24,59,61. Thus *št* cannot be construed with the following line, even to enhance the parallel.
8. S. E. Loewenstamm, *The Tradition of the Exodus in its Development* (in Hebrew) (Jerusalem: Magnes, 1965): 36-37 n. 37.
9. Z. Zevit, "The Priestly Redaction and Interpretation of the Plague Narrative in Exodus," *JQR* NS 66 (1975-76): 193-211; on the blood plague in particular, see 199-200.
10. Cf. Pope, *El in the Ugaritic Texts* (N 6): 99-102.

11

THE DATE OF NEHEMIAH RECONSIDERED

RICHARD J. SALEY

Whereas there was debate among earlier scholars as to the patron of Nehemiah, it has been held virtually indisputable since the publication of the Elephantine papyri (1906 on) that the king under whom Nehemiah labored was Artaxerxes I. The basis for this identification is the occurrence of the names of Johanan, Sanballat, and his sons, Delaiah and Shelemiah, in a papyrus dated to 407 B.C.[1] The first is said to be high priest in Jerusalem at the time, the second governor of Samaria, while the latter two appear to be carrying on the affairs of state for their aged father. In addition, Bagoas is mentioned as the governor of Judah. Since Johanan was the second successor of Eliashib (Neh 12:10–11 [emended],22), a contemporary of Nehemiah,[2] as was Sanballat,[3] the synchronisms would seem to leave no doubt. The Artaxerxes mentioned by Nehemiah can be none other than Artaxerxes I (465–424), while the date formulas within the Memoirs themselves fix Nehemiah's first mission between 445 and 433 (Neh 2:1; 5:14; 13:6) and his second sometime thereafter (Neh 13:6–7).[4]

If it must be recognized, then, that the Elephantine papyri bear the responsibility for this generally accepted view of Nehemiah's dating, it must also be admitted that the testimony offered therein is indirect—Nehemiah is not mentioned—and that the use of this by scholars to fix Nehemiah's dates derives from inference. Neither epigraphic material bearing the name of Nehemiah nor non-epigraphic finds definitely attributable to his period and capable of secure dating within relatively narrow confines have yet been discovered. Until such is forthcoming, all attempts to date Nehemiah must be by way of his contemporaries for whom data from antiquity are available. Hence, as just noted, the assignment to the reign of Artaxerxes I rests on securing the *floruit* of Sanballat and of Eliashib (by means of Johanan).

I. The Account of Josephus

It should not be presumed, however, that all source materials relevant to this problem point unequivocally in the same direction. Of particular moment is the scheme of events recorded by Josephus in *Ant.* 11.297–328. In 11.297–303 it is stated that upon the death of Eliashib, Joiada assumed the office of high priest, and upon his demise, Johanan. This Johanan, states Josephus, murdered his brother Jesus in the temple during a quarrel that centered about Jesus' friendship with Bagoas and the latter's promise to obtain the high priesthood for him. The result was that Bagoas, the general of Artaxerxes, defiled the temple and levied a seven-year tribute upon the Jews. Upon the death of Johanan, Jaddua became high priest, and it was to his brother, Manasseh, that Sanballat, whose appointment as governor was due to Darius [III], gave his daughter Nikaso in a political marriage. Thereupon in 11.304–12, after a brief note on the murder of Philip of Macedonia and the accession of Alexander, Josephus relates the refusal of the Jerusalem elders to allow Manasseh access to the altar unless he divorce his wife. Torn by his loyalties, Manasseh consulted his father-in-law on the matter, and was informed that he could retain both wife and high priesthood, if he were willing to serve at a new temple to be erected on Mt. Gerizim with the consent of Darius. Manasseh, we are told, gratefully accepted the offer and, indeed, acquired quite a following "as many priests and Israelites were involved in such marriages." 11.313–28 proceeds to treat the events surrounding Alexander's defeat of Darius and his subsequent campaign in Syria-Palestine. Sanballat, who initially backed Darius, switched his allegiance to Alexander during the latter's siege of Tyre, supplying him with his own troops, and in the exchange, receiving Alexander's permission for the proposed temple which was summarily erected. Shortly after this encounter with Alexander, Sanballat is said to have died. The remainder of book 11 (329–47) is of little concern to us here.

The welter of secondary literature which had arisen prior to the mid-1950's concerning this account of Josephus happily has been summarized by H. H. Rowley.[5] He notes that apart from C. C. Torrey most modern writers regard the account as unhistorical. Some do feel that an incident from the time of Nehemiah has been transferred to the following century. Generally speaking these scholars fall into two camps: those who transfer the whole, insofar as they find any reliable kernel of fact in it, to the time of Nehemiah; and those who accept the fourth century date for the building of the Gerizim temple, but transfer all else to the fifth century. In short, then, those who do not dismiss the recorded events in 11.297–328 out of hand differ in the main only on the date of the Samaritan temple. Otherwise it has usually been argued that Josephus is guilty of constructing a series of totally untrustworthy episodes from a tortured understanding of the book of Nehemiah.[6] He has placed Sanballat a century too late and under the wrong monarch(s). The biblical account of the marriage of Sanballat's daughter to one of the sons of Joiada (Neh 13:28) has been misconstrued as to one of the sons of Johanan. Bagoas, the governor of Judah whose activity is firmly fixed in the late fifth century, has been moved to a point more than half a century later. Finally, the high priestly succession—Eliashib, Joiada, Johanan, Jaddua (Neh 12:22)—has been pushed into the fourth century, when at least the first two, and the beginning of Johanan's term, and perhaps even its end and the beginning of that of Jaddua, belong to the fifth century.[7]

II. The Validity of Josephus' Account

If, however, Josephus has based his work upon the book of Nehemiah, he has concealed it well. It is far removed from his account of Nehemiah's times and comes only after his final treatment (Esther) of the biblical text. Indeed, it would be more than passing strange if Josephus had removed the accounts of 11.297ff. from the book of Nehemiah, only to put them later under different kings than that under whom he placed Nehemiah. Elsewhere in book 11 he is bent on taking the biblical records as they are and making them fit into his chronology of the Persian kings: Cyrus, Cambyses, Darius, Xerxes, Artaxerxes, which is, incidentally, correct as far as it goes. Because of the confused nature, chronologically speaking, of the narrative in Ezra-Nehemiah, he has felt free in places to emend the text to the name of the next appropriate king. Hence after the initial decree of Cyrus, the letters of Ezra 4 are attributed to the time of Cambyses. (These letters occur in 1 Esdras 2 immediately before the interpolated section dealing with Darius and the three bodyguards, and immediately after the decree of Cyrus.) He then proceeds to relate the story of the rebuilding of the temple under Zerubbabel in the time of Darius, while placing Ezra and Nehemiah in that order in the reign of Xerxes.[8] Finally, the story of Esther, queen to Artaxerxes,[9] is added to make the chronology complete. But when it comes to the events found in 11.297ff., Josephus does not place them under Xerxes, where he has put Nehemiah, but under Artaxerxes and Darius. However, he is careful to qualify both names to make it clear that these are not to be understood as the same Artaxerxes and the same Darius who were present in his previous chronological restructuring of the biblical text. It would appear, then, to be highly inconsistent with his methodology to suppose that Josephus at this point had transposed material from the book of Nehemiah to the reigns of two later kings. In short, this section has all the earmarks of coming from a source completely independent of the biblical records.

A. Büchler has analyzed the narrative from the completion of the Esther story to the end of book 11 and has concluded that Josephus used three different sources.[10] The first of these (302–c. 325) relates events from the marriage of Manasseh and Nikaso to the erection of the Gerizim temple and the death of Sanballat. Büchler has posited 11.302 as the beginning of this source, which he labels Samaritan in origin, but it seems to us arbitrary to exclude 11.297–301 (the account of Johanan, Jesus and Bagoas).[11] It is possible that the terse account of 11.297–301 was contained in an independent source, but there appears to be no valid reason for separating it from 11.302ff.[12]

It could be argued that if this is a Samaritan source, it would be unlikely to contain the account of a struggle for control within the Jerusalem priesthood that occurred several years prior to the main interest of the source, i.e., the events directly leading up to the building of the Gerizim temple. But such need not be the case at all. The narrative of 11.297–301 is at pains to describe the heinous nature of Johanan's act of fratricide within the Jerusalem temple; indeed when Bagoas enters the temple, defiling it, he is heard to say that he (i.e., a Gentile) is purer than the dead corpse lying within the sanctuary. For this action, and the resultant seven-year tribute imposed upon the Jews, Bagoas receives no rebuff. Rather he is labeled as the instrument used by the Deity to punish the Jews for the outrage perpetrated in the temple by the legitimate high priest. What could have been more appropriate than for the author of a Samaritan source to have exploited this incident by making it the introduction to his account of the building of the Gerizim temple? The implications are transparent; the erection of the temple was occasioned by the expulsion of Manasseh because of his marriage, though he had every right to the priesthood. In sharp contrast is the despicable deed of a recent Jerusalem high priest, which apparently had not resulted in his removal from office, though he had caused the defilement of the temple and placed Judah under divine judgment. Who could doubt the propriety and legitimacy of both the new temple and of Manasseh's role as high priest?

We would therefore hypothesize that Josephus came upon this first source (which included 11.297–301), added to it the names of Eliashib and Joiada at the beginning to bring his high-priestly chronology up to date, and then used it for the first part of his history of this period. But what can be said of the accuracy of this source?

Earlier we saw that five points of controversy have arisen regarding the story in *Ant.* 11.297–c. 325(328): (1) the dating of the Samaritan temple; (2) the dating of Sanballat; (3) the account of the marriage of Sanballat's daughter to Manasseh; (4) the dating of Bagoas; and (5) the dating of the high-priestly succession: Eliashib, Joiada, Johanan, Jaddua. Each of these must be handled in order.

1. Dating of the Samaritan Temple

The era of the building of the Samaritan temple, formerly the object of considerable scholarly debate, has now been decisively settled. The archaeological evidence from the excavation of Tell Balâṭah (Shechem) indicates a sudden and elaborate reconstruction of the city during the last third of the fourth century, involving the whole tell, after some two centuries of abandonment. Piecing this archaeological data together with the classical sources for this era (Josephus, Quintus Curtius, Eusebius and Syncellus), G. E. Wright, director of the excavation, has reconstructed the course of events surrounding the advent of Alexander, and involving the destruction of Samaria and the rebuilding of Shechem. While we need not enter into a full discussion of his argumentation here, his conclusions relative to *Ant.* 11.302–c. 325 are of major significance; viz., "That we may accept . . . as fairly certain . . . the substantial reliability of Josephus' first source about the Samaritans: namely, the story about the founding of the temple on Mt. Gerizim by permission of Alexander the Great, and about the 8,000 Samaritan soldiers given to aid Alexander's campaign, whom he settled in Egypt as a provincial guard.''[13]

2. *Dating of Sanballat*

This, then, brings us to the second consideration. If the erection of the temple at the time of Alexander has been substantiated, what of the purported connection of Sanballat with that event?

With the discovery of the Wâdī Dâliyeh papyri, the presence of a Sanballat II as governor of Samaria under Artaxerxes II has been substantiated and, of equal importance, the principle of papponymy for the ruling house of Samaria.[14] With the existence established of a Sanballat I under Darius II (and most likely under Artaxerxes I and Xerxes II), and of a Sanballat II under Artaxerxes II, there would seem to be no valid objection to accepting a Sanballat III under Darius III. On the basis then of the data from the Elephantine papyri, Josephus, and the Wâdī Dâliyeh papyri, Frank Cross has been able to proffer the following reconstruction for the rulers of Samaria during the latter half of the fifth century and the first two-thirds of the fourth century.

Table 1

RULERS OF THE HOUSE OF SANBALLAT[15]

Sanballat I
Delaiah
Sanballat II
(Yeshua?)
Ḥananiah
Sanballat III

The acceptance of the Sanballat of Josephus' account as Sanballat III has consequently been forthcoming from a number of other scholars concerned with this era of Israelite history.[16]

3. *The Marriage of Sanballat's Daughter*

We are brought then to the matter of the purported marriage of Manasseh to Nikaso (*Ant.* 11.302–03). The majority of scholars have supposed that Josephus has transferred the incident of Neh 13:28 to the following century, and at that, confused the participants. Some have gone further and suggested that the priest expelled by Nehemiah was Manasseh, or through combination with the Johanan-Jesus incident, Jesus or Johanan.

But if the existence of a Sanballat III now appears likely, there would seem to be no reason to deny that there could have been two such diplomatic marriages—one between the daughter of the Sanballat contemporary with Nehemiah and one of the sons of Joiada, and the other between the daughter of Sanballat III and one of the sons of Johanan. The picture that we glean from the book of Nehemiah is that this was a time of friendly relations and intermarriage between the leading families of Jerusalem and those of Ammon and Samaria. There is no reason to believe that such policies ceased after the time of Nehemiah. Indeed, given the political uncertainties of that era, one might expect the policies to have proliferated. If the parties named in the two accounts were identical, the situation would be different, but such is not the case.[17] In short, one must agree with those scholars who now feel that there is no impediment to accepting both episodes as authentic.[18]

4. Dating of Bagoas

Thus far we have seen that new data lends credence to certain items found in Josephus' first source: the Gerizim temple, the presence of Sanballat, and the marriage of Sanballat's daughter to Manasseh. But concerning the matter of Bagoas there are no new data; the opinion continues to prevail that Josephus (or his source) has here confused the notorious Persian eunuch of the fourth century, Bagoas, with the Persian governor of Judah of the same name who was contemporary with Johanan in the late fifth century. Even scholars who are now convinced of the basic accuracy of Josephus on the points just mentioned, still hold him at fault here.[19] But it must be asked whether the episode portrayed by Josephus (*Ant.* 11.297–301) is not really plausible as it stands in its historically given context.

The cunning and ruthless exploits of the Bagoas under whose influence the last three kings of Persia ruled (and in the case of two, ceased to rule) are well attested in Persian history.[20] Driven by an insatiable lust for power, he sought control of the Persian government. The extent to which he was successful in achieving this is depicted by Diodorus:

> As for Bagoas, after he had administered all the King's affairs in the upper satrapies, he rose to such power because of his partnership with Mentor that he was master of the kingdom, and Artaxerxes [III] did nothing without his advice. And after Artaxerxes' death he designated in every case the successor to the throne and enjoyed all the functions of kingship save the title.[21]

Unable to reconcile his position with that of Ochus, Bagoas had him poisoned. In his stead, the eunuch appointed as ruler Arses, the son of Ochus, after having slain all other heirs to the throne. When Arses, after less than two years of reign, attempted to free himself from the tyranny of Bagoas' dominion, he in turn was murdered along with all his children. The throne was then granted to a member of the court, Darius III. "That he was only a son of Arsames, son of Ostanes, the brother of Artaxerxes II, shows how completely the main line of the royal house had been wiped out by Ochus and Bagoas."[22] Darius, however, failed to be the submissive ruler Bagoas had envisioned and Bagoas attempted to poison him also. The plan, however, backfired, with the king, in a deed of sheer irony, forcing Bagoas to drink the deadly cup instead.

With this sketch of the cunning and sway of the infamous eunuch as background, we must concern ourselves with one of the major episodes in his career. Before Bagoas assassinated Artaxerxes III, he played a key role in his military machine. When a huge army of predominantly Persian troops and Greek mercenaries was amassed by Artaxerxes for his second attempt to retake rebellious Egypt (344/3), it was Bagoas who was appointed commander-in-chief. With the successful completion of the campaign, ending almost sixty years of Egyptian independence, Bagoas was named vizier. At this time the political situation in Syria-Palestine was less than secure from a Persian point of view. The revolt of the satraps (c. 368–360) in the western part of the empire was in the not too distant past, and its memory no doubt lingered. Much more immediate were the conditions occasioned by the hard-fought initial attempt of Ochus to retake Egypt in 351/50, which ended in Persian defeat. Large-scale revolt had broken out in Phoenicia led by Tennes, king of Sidon; parts of Cilicia also had joined in, while the nine kings of Cyprus declared their independence. An initial attempt to squelch the uprising by Belesys, satrap of "Beyond the River," and Mazaios, satrap of Cilicia, was unsuccessful. In 345 Ochus himself appeared on the scene and through a bit of treachery retook Sidon. Tennes was executed, while the inhabitants burned the city over their own heads to avoid capture. Heading toward Egypt, Ochus swept through Palestine, apparently destroying such sites as 'Athlît, Makmish, Tell el-Qasîleh, Hazor, Megiddo, Jericho and Lachish.[23] The implication of several Palestinian states in the rebellion, including Judah, seems evident. In light of the extent of the conspiracy, it is quite conceivable that Bagoas, a short time later, would have had a vital interest in securing southern Palestine, particularly as it lay on the eastern flank of the newly retaken Egypt. In fact, knowing Bagoas' temperament, one would have expected him to go further and to meddle in the affairs of Judah to the extent of gaining assurance that the ruling high priest would be loyal to him and to Persia.[24] This is precisely the picture that Josephus paints. He refers to Bagoas as the *stratēgos* of Artaxerxes—not as the governor (*satrapēs*) which would have been appropriate for the fifth-century Bagoas—and portrays him as conspiring with Jesus, his friend, to obtain the high priesthood for him.

One obstacle remains, however, to the designation of the Bagoas of Josephus as the eunuch of Artaxerxes III, rather than the governor of Judah under Artaxerxes II. It has been maintained that Josephus means to fix the latter as the monarch in question. The discussion revolves around the genuineness of the adjective *allou* modifying Artaxerxes (*Ant.* 11.297), and its interpretation. Marcus indicates that the word is textually uncertain and has been designated a gloss by several scholars. After a brief discussion of the matter, he rules in favor of the retention of the word, but translates the phrase "of the second Artaxerxes," i.e., Artaxerxes II.[25] This designation seems to us to be unwarranted. From Josephus' handling of the Persian kings in the biblical records, it is obvious that he was not aware of the number of kings that bore the name Artaxerxes, and it is too much to assume that by calling Artaxerxes *allos,* he meant to designate him as Artaxerxes II, as opposed to Artaxerxes III. In fact, since he mentions only two kings by that name, he probably thought that this one was the second Artaxerxes; however, this is not at all to say that his second Artaxerxes could not have been Artaxerxes III.

Conversely, if one wishes to regard *allou* as spurious, it would make little difference. Josephus could have confused the Artaxerxes of his source with the Artaxerxes of Esther, but even if he did—which we doubt—it would hardly pass any historical judgment on which monarch was referred to in his source. In short, then, we find no evidence to support the notion that the king of this account need be considered other than Artaxerxes III;[26] the Bagoas in question should not be confused with the fifth-century governor of Judah.

In summary, the actions of Bagoas, the *stratēgos* of Ochus, as depicted by Josephus, are exactly what one would have expected from him under the circumstances. It seems to us very probable that Josephus is correctly relating events that actually transpired in the first decade of the second half of the fourth century.

5. *High-Priestly Succession*

The implications of this for the fifth and final matter to be considered, that of the high-priestly succession, are profound. Since the publication of the Elephantine papyri, it has generally been contended that Josephus is not to be trusted at this point. If, however, a Johanan and a Jaddua appear fixed in that office in the third quarter of the fourth century, a fresh examination of the biblical basis for understanding that succession, viz. the list of Neh 12:1–26, is clearly in order.

With many others, we take the list of Neh 12:1–26 to be a secondary addition to the Chronicler's work.[27] The compiler is obviously attempting to update the priestly chronology of 1 Chr 5:27–41 (6:1–15E), which runs from Levi to Jozadak, father of Jeshua, so as to bring it down into the postexilic period. The high-priestly line which he offers in order of direct descent is, as presently preserved: Jeshua, Joiakim, Eliashib, Joiada, Jonathan, Jaddua (vv 10–11). The structure of the list is worth noting. Vv 1–7 deal with the priests in the days of Jeshua and vv 8–9 with the Levites of the same time. Following this, in vv 10–11, is the succession of high priests noted above. The text then resumes with the mention of the heads of the priestly families in the days of Joiakim (vv 12–21), and of their contemporary Levites (vv 24–25).

Tucked away in vv 22–23 is a notice telling where information may be found regarding the priests and Levites who served under the succeeding high priests; of these v 22 names Eliashib, Joiada, Johanan, Jaddua; v 23, Johanan, son of Eliashib. The list ends in v 26 with the statement that "these [the Levites of vv 24–25] were in the days of Joiakim, son of Jeshua, son of Jozadak, and in the days of Nehemiah the governor, and of Ezra the priest the scribe."

The following series of relationships, taken at face value, form the crux of the passage: Jonathan, son of Joiada (v 11); Johanan, successor of Joiada (v 22); Johanan, son of Eliashib (v 23). With regard to the first, the most plausible solution, it seems to us, is to agree with most scholars that the name of Jonathan in v 11 is a scribal error for the very similar, though admittedly not identical, Johanan.[28]

However, the problem is by no means entirely settled by this emendation. Still remaining are the apparently contradictory assertions that Johanan was the son of Joiada (v 11 and presumably v 22, though the relationship is not spelled out in the latter instance), and also the son of Eliashib (v 23). One or the other of two proposed solutions is espoused by most scholars—either *ben* in v 23 means 'grandson,' or 'descendant,' not 'son'; or Johanan was the son of Eliashib and brother of Joiada.[29] Both, as a matter of fact, are plausible. The usage of *ben* in this sense is well attested at Elephantine,[30] while one cannot discount the possibility that the compiler erroneously translated a succession order (v 22) into a genealogical order (v 11). Be that as it may, what is important here is that both views have in common the endorsement of the high-priestly succession: Eliashib, Joiada, Johanan, Jaddua.

Integral to the dating of the latter part of this succession is the understanding of the enigmatic phrase *'al-malkût dāryāweš happārsî* in v 22, literally "concerning the reign of Darius the Persian." While there has been more than one attempt to correct what is obviously a corrupt reading, the most felicitous is that of Rudolph who has posited that an original *sēper dibrê hayyāmîm 'ad* has been lost by haplography (cf. v 23). Making only this single emendation, the text reads: "The Levites in the days of Eliashib, Joiada, and Johanan, and Jaddua, the heads of fathers' houses and the priests, were written in the Book of the Chronicles until the reign of Darius the Persian."[31]

It is important to note, however, that the syntactical structure of v 22—whether taken with Rudolph or as received—allows for no historical judgment as to the Darius involved. That matter has to be settled on other grounds. If Darius I may be summarily discounted, then Darius II and Darius III must remain lively candidates for the title of "Darius the Persian."[32]

We must turn now to our primary concern, that of correlating Josephus' handling of the high-priestly chronology with that of the biblical text. Of primary importance at the outset is the recognition that whereas a Johanan and a Jaddua are firmly fixed in the fourth century by Josephus' narrative, the same is not true of an Eliashib and a Joiada. His only information regarding the former seems to have been limited to Eliashib's connection with Nehemiah, and Josephus was apparently as ignorant of the activities of Joiada as we are. The appearance of both in *Ant.* 11.297 is brief, just long enough for them to die. Moreover, it is highly improbable that this terse notice of their demise formed the introduction to Josephus' Samaritan source. Much more likely, if not indeed certain, is the addition of this by the historian in accordance with his desire to account for the whole high-priestly succession as he knew it. In short, then, there is no authenticated historical information in Josephus which would fix Eliashib and his son Joiada to the fourth century—granted this is probably where he thought they belonged—or for that matter to the fifth. The same amount of ambiguity is present in the biblical text, where Eliashib and Joiada are contemporary with an unspecified Artaxerxes, and the priestly succession ends in the reign of an equally unspecified Darius.

At the outset it was noted that the traditional dating of Nehemiah depends in the last analysis on securing the *floruit* of Sanballat and of Eliashib (by means of Johanan). But since the discovery of the Wâdī Dâliyeh papyri the evidence regarding the former may be regarded as ambiguous. In addition, we must now think in terms of at least two high priests named Johanan during the Persian period, one in the late fifth century (Elephantine) and the other in the mid-fourth (Josephus).[33] The matter, simply put, revolves around which of these two Johanans was the successor of Joiada son of Eliashib. Or to put it differently, *whether Nehemiah properly belongs to the fifth century or to the fourth century depends upon which Johanan, Eliashib and Joiada preceded!*

If one wishes to argue that the Johanan in question is that attested by the Elephantine papyri, then the succession: Eliashib, Joiada, Johanan, Jaddua, would belong to the fifth century, and a Johanan II and a Jaddua II would have functioned in the third quarter of the fourth century. In such a case Josephus would be guilty of telescoping his materials by identifying the Johanan and Jaddua of the high-priestly list at his disposal (reflecting Neh 12:1–26) with the Johanan and Jaddua of his Samaritan source. "Darius the Persian" would be reckoned as Darius II. The matter of Johanan son of Joiada, as opposed to Johanan son of Eliashib, could be handled in either of the two manners in vogue—either by claiming that *ben* means 'grandson,' or by positing that Johanan was the brother of Joiada. The patron of Nehemiah would of course then be Artaxerxes I and his *floruit,* the traditional 445 to sometime after 433. The synchronisms of this position are outlined in *Table 2*.

The obvious alternative would be to argue that the Johanan of the list in Nehemiah and that of the Bagoas-Jesus incident are one and the same person. If

Table 2
CHRONOLOGICAL SCHEME FOR NEHEMIAH UNDER ARTAXERXES I

Persian Kings	*High Priests*	*Governors of Samaria*
Artaxerxes I (465–424)		
Nehemiah (445–after 433)	Eliashib	Sanballat I
	Joiada	
Xerxes II (423)		
Darius II (423–404)		
	Johanan I	Delaiah
	Jaddua I	
Artaxerxes II (404–358)		
		Sanballat II
		(Yeshua?)
Artaxerxes III (358–338)		
		Ḥananiah (in 354)
Bagoas (c. 343)	Johanan II	
Arses (338–336)		
Darius III (336–331)	Jaddua II	Sanballat III

this be the case, there would be no need to posit a second Jaddua. The succession: Eliashib, Joiada, Johanan, Jaddua, would belong to the fourth century, and "Darius the Persian" would be Darius III. Josephus in this instance would have correctly identified—most likely by chance—the Johanans and Jadduas of his two sources. (It could not be held to his discredit that he was ignorant of the Johanan of the fifth century [Elephantine].) The patron of Nehemiah would be Artaxerxes II, and his dates would be 384 to sometime after 372. *Table 3* reflects this understanding of the data.

Table 3

CHRONOLOGICAL SCHEME FOR NEHEMIAH UNDER ARTAXERXES II

Persian Kings	*High Priests*	*Governors of Samaria*
	Johanan I	
Artaxerxes II (404–358)		
Nehemiah (384–after 372)	Eliashib	Sanballat II
	Joiada	
		(Yeshua?)
Artaxerxes III (358–338)		
		Ḥananiah (in 354)
Bagoas (c. 343)	Johanan II	
Arses (338–336)		
Darius III (336–331)	Jaddua	Sanballat III

The question as to whether Johanan was the son of Eliashib or of Joiada could again be handled in either of the manners described above, or still a third option could be entertained. As was noted above, the compiler who inserted the list of Neh 12:1–26 into the Chronicler's history (assuming this is all from one hand) was attempting to update the priestly chronology of 1 Chr 5:27–41 (6:1–15E) to include the postexilic period. He knew of Jeshua and Joiakim and had a document (or documents) before him that contained the names of priests and Levites relative to at least one of these. Moreover, he knew of two other registrations that had been made, one in the days of Eliashib, Joiada, Johanan and Jaddua until the reign of "Darius the Persian," and another that extended until the days of Johanan son of Eliashib. This information he noted in an attempt to give a semblance of completeness to his list (vv 22–23). It is hypothetically possible that what he then did was to identify the Johanan son of Eliashib of the one registration with the Johanan son of Joiada son of Eliashib of the other, knowing that in the era in question it was not unknown for one to be called the son of his grandfather. By thus coalescing the two lists—if this is what happened—he would have created the standard chronology of postexilic high priests used by later generations (including Josephus), i.e., Jeshua, Joiakim, Eliashib, Joiada, Johanan, Jaddua (vv 10–11). The process is schematized in *Table 4*.

With such an arrangement Johanan son of Eliashib would be the Johanan (I)

Table 4

HYPOTHETICAL UNDERSTANDING OF THE DEVELOPMENT OF THE POSTEXILIC HIGH-PRIESTLY CHRONOLOGY BY THE COMPILER OF NEH 12:1–26

The Compiler's Sources			*The Compiler's Reconstruction of the Chronology*
Jeshua	Eliashib	Eliashib	Jeshua
Joiakim	Joiada	Johanan	Joiakim
	Johanan		Eliashib
	Jaddua		Joiada
			Johanan
			Jaddua

The Actual Chronology
Jeshua
Joiakim
Eliashib I
Johanan I
Eliashib II
Joiada
Johanan II
Jaddua

of Elephantine, and Johanan the son of Joiada, the Johanan (II) of Josephus. That it would not be totally unexpected to find another Eliashib may be supported both by the practice of papponymy and the prevalence of the name in this era. If two Jadduas and one Eliashib may be posited for the initial option (*Table 2*), there would appear to be no reason a priori against having two Eliashibs and one Jaddua.

Of course, what is sketched in *Table 4* represents only conjecture; there is no way that it can be proven (or one supposes for that matter, disproven). It must be emphatically stressed that *the possibility of a fourth-century dating for Nehemiah in no way rests upon acceptance of this scheme!*

Other options for reconstructing the high-priestly chronology are possible, of course.[34] In addition, none of those offered here need necessarily be considered complete. To acknowledge gaps or possible gaps in the seams of any of the reconstructions would mean no more than a paucity of source material, whether to the compiler of Neh 12:1–26, to Josephus or to us. Completeness in this case has no bearing on probability. One might be prone to accept the first scheme (*Table 2*) because we are accustomed to thinking of the fifth-century chronology as basically fixed and the determination of the fourth as a problem. But it must be asked why a very late redactor—most scholars so identify the compiler of Neh 12:1–26—should be better informed about the fifth-century priesthood than the fourth.

III. Conclusions

We are brought then to the matter of deciding which of the proposed chronological orderings is most likely. Given the paucity of additional data relative to the fifth and fourth centuries, we must admit that convincing grounds for final judgment are lacking. Within the present confines of our knowledge the solution to the problem is best left open. The Johanan which Eliashib and his son Joiada preceded could have been either Johanan I or Johanan II, i.e., *the patron of Nehemiah could have been either Artaxerxes I or Artaxerxes II!*

Finally, of several other items which bear on the date of Nehemiah, only one can be touched on here and that ever so briefly—the inscribed vessel found at Tell el-Maskhūṭa bearing the name of Qainū, son of Gashmu. The various avenues of approach for dating this are: (1) the typology of the silverware; (2) the dating of the Athena-tetradrachms associated with the find; (3) archaeological and historical considerations relative to the Qedarites; (4) the paleography of the inscription.

None of these we feel is able to fix the bowl precisely in the late fifth century as opposed to the early fourth.[35] In short, we must reopen an issue that was considered closed in the first decade of this century and make allowance for the possibility that the patron of Nehemiah could have been either Artaxerxes I or Artaxerxes II. The implications of this for the vexing question of the date of Ezra are profound, but that is a study which shall have to await another time.

NOTES

1. A. Cowley, *Aramaic Papyri of the Fifth Century B.C.* (Oxford: Clarendon, 1923): 108–19 no. 30.
2. Neh 3:1,20–21; 13:4,7,28.
3. Neh 2:10,19; 3:33; 4:1; 6:1–2,5,12,14; 13:28.
4. A second mission has been denied by some, but this would seem to us to rely upon a hypercritical interpretation of Neh 13:6. For a recent defense of this view see U. Kellermann, *Nehemia-Quellen Überlieferung und Geschichte* (BZAW 102; Berlin: Alfred Töpelmann, 1967): 49ff.
5. H. H. Rowley, "Sanballat and the Samaritan Temple" in *Men of God* (London: Thomas Nelson and Sons): 246–76 (rpt. from *BJRL* 38 [1955–56]: 166–98).
6. Thus Rowley ([N 5]: 256–57) is able to state that "Josephus is universally recognised to present garbled and unreliable history."
7. Since the time of Rowley's article, new discoveries have forced the reconsideration of some of these points by certain scholars; see below (pp. 154ff.) for discussion, and the excellent survey by Ralph W. Klein ("Ezra and Nehemiah in Recent Studies" in *Magnalia Dei: The Mighty Acts of God* [The Wright Festschrift; Garden City, NY: Doubleday, 1976]: 361–76).
8. The contention of Kellermann ([N 4]: 136) that Josephus dates Nehemiah to Artaxerxes I in *Ag. Ap.* 1.40 is unwarranted.
9. Josephus is here following the LXX, which renders the Hebrew *'ăḥašwērôš* (= Xerxes) as Artaxerxes.
10. A. Büchler, "La relation de Josèphe concernant Alexandre le Grand," *REJ* 36 (1898): 1–26. Büchler's summary of his findings, with which Marcus is in agreement, is quoted by the latter in *Josephus* 6 (LCL): 532. Tcherikover has argued for two, rather than three sources, but would agree with Büchler in the definition of the first. See V. Tcherikover, *Hellenistic Civilization and the Jews* (Philadelphia: Jewish Publication Society, 1961): 43–44.
11. The designation of this source as Samaritan has been accepted by Tcherikover ([N 10]: 44, 420) and G. E. Wright ("The Samaritans at Shechem," *HTR* 55 [1962]: 362), among others. Purvis feels it very likely that a Samaritan tradition lies behind *Ant.* 11.321–325; see J. Purvis, *The Samaritan Pentateuch and the Origin of the Samaritan Sect* (Cambridge: Harvard University, 1968): 105.

12. Torrey has likewise argued that 11.297–301 belongs to the same source as 11.302ff. See C. C. Torrey, *Ezra Studies* (Chicago: University of Chicago, 1910; rpt., New York: Ktav, 1970): 331–32; *The Second Isaiah* (New York: Scribner, 1928): 457.
13. Wright (N 11): 364.
14. F. M. Cross, "The Discovery of the Samaria Papyri," *BA* 26 (1963): 110–21; "Aspects of Samaritan History in Late Persian and Hellenistic Times," *HTR* 59 (1966): 201–11.
15. Cross, "Discovery" (N 14): 120; "Aspects" (N 14): 204.
16. So, among others, Kellermann ([N 4]: 143–44, 166–67); Purvis ([N 11]: 102ff.); K. Galling (*Studien zur Geschichte Israels in persischen Zeitalter* [Tübingen: J. C. B. Mohr, 1964]: 210); A. F. Rainey ("The Satrapy 'Beyond the River,'" *AJBA* 1 [1969]: 64); B. Porten (*Archives From Elephantine* [Berkeley: University of California, 1968]: 116).
17. If one might be facetious, he could ask what scholars a couple of millennia hence might do if there were but two extant accounts of American history for the 1960's, one which stated that John F. Kennedy was assassinated by a gunman while President of the United States, and another which reported that Robert F. Kennedy was assassinated by a gunman while campaigning to be President of the United States. Indeed, the incredibility of such a combination of events in modern times should caution against any easy denial of the possibility of intermarriage between different generations of official families in antiquity.
18. So, e.g., Cross ("Aspects" [N 14]: 205); Galling ([N 16]: 210); Purvis ([N 11]: 102ff.); Porten ([N 16]: 116).
19. The noteworthy exception is Cross, who recently has argued for the accuracy of the fourth-century Bagoas in Josephus' narrative, much to the delight of this author who arrived at the same conclusion independently. See F. M. Cross, "A Reconstruction of the Judean Restoration," *JBL* 94 (1975): 5.
20. See A. T. Olmstead, *History of the Persian Empire* (Chicago: University of Chicago, 1948): 437ff., 489ff., and the sources there cited.
21. Diodorus 16.50.8 (LCL 7).
22. Olmstead (N 20): 490.
23. See D. Barag, "The Effects of the Tennes Rebellion on Palestine," *BASOR* 183 (1966): 6–12.
24. That Bagoas had little regard for sacral matters is clear from the manner in which he sold the confiscated sacred scrolls back to the Egyptian priests at outlandish prices (Diodorus 16.51.2).
25. Marcus (N 10): 456–57, 499–500.
26. Porten ([N 16]: 290 n. 24), we feel, unnecessarily confuses the matter by identifying the monarch as Artaxerxes II. As a result he must allow for three men bearing the name Bagoas: the one known from Elephantine, the one mentioned by Josephus, and the eunuch of Ochus.
27. Neh 12:1–26 literally bristles with problems, most of which cannot be discussed here. See the basic commentaries; also Kellermann (N 4): 105–10; and S. Mowinckel, *Studien zu dem Buche Ezra-Nehemia* 1 (Oslo: Universitetsforlaget, 1964): 160ff.
28. Rudolph calls attention to the Jonathan of Neh 12:35 who is called Johanan in the LXX, indicating how easily these two names could be confused in transmission; see W. Rudolph, *Esra und Nehemia* (HAT 20; Tübingen: J. C. B. Mohr, 1949): 190.
29. The first position is held by such scholars as W. F. Albright (*The Biblical Period from Abraham to Ezra* [Harper Torchbook rpt.; New York: Harper and Row, 1963]: 94); L. W. Batten (*The Books of Ezra and Nehemiah* [ICC; New York: Scribner, 1913]: 277); and R. A. Bowman ("Ezra and Nehemiah," *IB* 3:787). The second is held by such as G. Hölscher ("Die Bücher Esra und Nehemia" in *Die Heilige Schrift des Alten Testaments* 2 [4th ed.; Tübingen: J. C. B. Mohr, 1923]: 553); Kellermann ([N 4]: 107ff.); and Rudolph ([N 28]: 192–93).
30. See E. G. Kraeling, *The Brooklyn Museum Aramaic Papyri* (New Haven: Yale University, 1953): 108.
31. Rudolph (N 28): 193–94.
32. However, Albright has argued for Darius I ("The Date and Personality of the Chronicler," *JBL* 40 [1921]: 112–13), and J. M. Myers (*Ezra-Nehemiah* [AB 14; Garden City, NY: Doubleday, 1965]: lxix, 198–99) vacillates between Darius I and Darius II. Among those opting for Darius II are Cross ("Aspects" [N 14]: 202 n. 4; "Reconstruction" [N 19]: 11); Bowman ([N 29]: 789); Kellermann ([N 4]: 107–08); and Rudolph ([N 28]: 193). Darius III has been posited by such as A. Bertholet (*Die Bücher Esra und Nehemia* [KHC; Tübingen: J. C. B. Mohr, 1902]: 85); Torrey (*Ezra* [N 12]: 320); H. Schneider (*Die Bücher Esra und Nehemia* [HSAT; Bonn: Peter Hanstein, 1959]: 244); and R. H. Pfeiffer (*Introduction to the Old Testament* [New York: Harper and Row, 1941]: 819).

33. Indeed it would seem that there was a whole string of high priests between 520 and the second century that bore the name Johanan (= Onias); see Cross, "Reconstruction" (N 19): 6-7.
34. For a recent attempt at a complete chronology, see Cross, "Reconstruction" (N 19): 5–6, 9ff., 17.
35. It needs to be pointed out, however, that Cross—whose expertise in this area will not be challenged here—feels the script will not allow for a dating later than 400 ("Reconstruction" [N 19]: 7). Still, after an examination of the bowl itself, questions linger regarding certain of the forms. On the other hand, it is not impossible that the Gashmu (Geshem) of the inscription was not the contemporary of Nehemiah since the practice of papponymy is also attested for the Qedarites.

12

WISDOM AND TORAH: THE INTERPRETATION OF DEUTERONOMY UNDERLYING SIRACH 24:23

GERALD T. SHEPPARD*

Sirach (or "Ecclesiasticus") is a remarkable "book of wise instruction and apt proverb" (Sir 50:27) from the early second century B.C. Scholars find in it one of the earliest witnesses to the formation of the Hebrew Scriptures. However, beyond a witness to a canonization process, its frequent dependence on specific biblical passages makes its claim to be a wisdom book particularly interesting. Indeed, the significance of this claim is confirmed by the explicit identification of wisdom in Sir 24:23 with the "book of the covenant," i.e., "the Torah." The following study examines how Ben Sira understood his scriptures in order to arrive at this concluding formulation of Sir 24:23.

The method of our investigation is first to describe the literary relationship of this verse to the preceding song of wisdom in Sir 24:3–22. Second, the content of Sir 24:23 and its citation of Deut 33:4 will be evaluated in the context of similar statements in Deuteronomy. Finally, our conclusion about Ben Sira's interpretation of Deuteronomy will be confirmed both by his address to the readers in Sir 51:26 and by a corresponding interpretation of Deuteronomy in Bar 3:9ff.

I. Sir 24:23

ταῦτα πάντα βίβλος διαθήκης θεοῦ ὑψίστου
νόμον ὅν ἐνετείλατο ἡμῖν Μωυσῆς
κληρονομίαν συναγωγαῖς Ιακωβ

*I am pleased to dedicate this article to Professor LaSor who, besides his instruction in biblical studies, first introduced me to Akkadian and Aramaic at Fuller. His inductive method substantially improved my earlier Greek and Hebrew. I remember him best for his gifted versatility in Semitic languages, his learned commitment to his classes, and his love for Scripture.

All these things are the book of the covenant of God Most High,
the Torah which Moses commanded us
(as a) possession/heritage in the assemblies of Jacob.

With the opening words ταῦτα πάντα the previous wisdom song (Sir 24:3–22) is pivoted on a transition between text and interpretation. That is, these words mark both the end of the wisdom song and the beginning of commentary upon it. A comparable use of the demonstrative pronoun as a literary transition occurs in 24:7. Also, this final portrayal of wisdom is not merely the last in a sequence, but it is critically differentiated from the preceding. While wisdom throughout the song is related to historical features or metaphors by a comparative "as,"[1] now she is identified in a more direct manner that speaks precisely to what she "is." All of wisdom's previous associations are thus grounded in a single more fundamental insight: "all these things (are) the book of the covenant." Subsequently, the writer elaborates this claim in words taken *verbatim* from Deut 33:4 without a citation formula.

It is as though the wisdom song in Sir 24:3–22 were a kind of riddle and one could speculate on how long a reader would take to discover the proper key. Now, if not before, the song is plainly a recital of the history of wisdom who resides in Israel as the Torah. The story begins (vv 3–4) with creation when wisdom is in the heavens and professes her origins in a manner not unlike that of the wisdom books (cf. Prov 8:22ff.). Then the narrative picks up (vv 5–7) the theme of a wandering in search of rest and inheritance, which coincides with Israel's same search (cf. Deuteronomy 12) in the time when Moses received the Torah in the cloud at Sinai and delivered it to the safekeeping of the priests. Again, like Israel, she receives a divine command (v 8) to possess the land and, like the Israelite priests, she settles at last in Zion with the sacred tent (vv 10,15).

The center of attention is consistently on wisdom, who is or becomes the Torah in the possession of Israel. Therefore, the song offers a selective application to wisdom of some Torah traditions which can be associated with the divine presence of Israel. The writer's economy of purpose for the song requires naturally only his selective treatment of historical traditions in the sequence of the Torah. For example, recollection of the Sinai event is not made in the song, even though the citation of Deut 33:4 in Sir 24:23 recapitulates the essence of the entire Mosaic blessing as a eulogy of the Torah which God gave to Moses and thus to the people at Sinai (cf. Deut 33:2).[2]

The closely worded opening phrase of 24:23 makes certain that wisdom is not equated with some vague or general sense of Torah, but specifies "the book of the covenant," a synonym for "the book of Torah" elsewhere in Sirach and in the Hebrew Scriptures.[3] Moreover, like the νόμος ὑψίστου in 39:1, it is a canonical expression in Sirach.[4] The radical nature of this statement must not be overlooked. The writer finds in the Torah, the five books of Moses, a witness to wisdom which provides the content for wisdom's song. In this short paper our investigation will concern only one instance of such a reading.

Whether or not 24:23ff. constitutes a later redactional addition to the earlier song is hard to decide.[5] At least, these verses represent a literary, redaction-like shift in the prose and provide a clarifying framework for the previous song. Moreover, 24:23 is worded thoughtfully with a play on the earlier prose. The title "Most High God" recalls the "Most High" in 24:2,3. The "command" to find a place in "Jacob" is the same theme and vocabulary as that of 24:8. Most importantly, by means of κληρονομία the citation of Deut 33:4 provides a verbal link with key words on the same theme throughout the entire earlier composition (see 24:7,12,20). Such learned and meticulous artistry, apparent even on the surface, is an indication that the writer's use of Deut 33:4, and Deuteronomy in general, may be just as intricate and involving.

II. Deuteronomy and Sir 24:23

The manner in which the writer incorporates Deut 33:4 into the prose of Sir 24:23 is significant. It is not a formal quotation, but is simply edited into the ongoing composition. Hence, the Scripture reference, like the allusions in the song before, does not stand out with the independence of a special biblical authority. Instead, both textual resources and interpretation mingle together. This mixture parallels that left by inner-biblical redactors who organized and commented on earlier traditions in such a way as to identify the older traditions with their new interpretations, cast in a new and presumably better literary whole. Consequently, Deut 33:4, by its placement in Sir 24:23, has been given a new redactional setting which successfully reveals the writer's own particular interpretation of it. For the writer, Deut 33:4 is not only a statement about the Torah, but it is a commentary on the proximity of wisdom in the history of Israel.

In the light of the writer's citation of Deut 33:4 and the free employment of Deuteronomic language elsewhere in the wisdom song, Deuteronomy plays an unusually prominent role in the composition of Sirach 24. It is not incidental that Deuteronomy 4 is often noted by commentators for its unique claim of an association between wisdom and Torah which, more than any other passage in Hebrew Scripture, comes closest to the assertion in Sir 24:23. However, Deuteronomy 4 does not propose the same full identification, as found in Sirach 24, between the book of the Torah and wisdom. For example, unlike Sirach 24, Deuteronomy 4 makes no mention of the Torah as a *book,* much less "the book of the covenant" as the Torah of Moses with its canonical connotations. Despite these differences, the writer's previous dependence on Deuteronomy[6]—the direct citation of Deut 33:4, together with the similarity in Deuteronomy 4—does suggest the possibility that a more profound interpretation of Deuteronomy as a whole may underlie the equation of wisdom and Torah in Sir 24:23.

One way to approach this matter is to examine the passages in Deuteronomy that share the most conspicuous vocabulary with canonical wisdom books, especially Proverbs. For example, words from the roots *ḥkm, bîn* and *y'ṣ* occur fourteen times in Deuteronomy:

a. Four are in chaps. 2 and 16.[7]

b. Four are found in chap. 4.[8]

c. Five occur in the Song of Moses (chap. 32).[9]

d. One instance (*ḥokmāʰ*) is found in 34:9.

The "a" occasions are all in connection with the appointment of "wise" judges to assist Moses. Similarly in 34:9, Joshua is endowed with the *rûaḥ ḥokmāʰ* which seems to reinforce this requirement for leaders in the Israelite community.[10] Likewise in Sirach 39, the hope of the scribe is that through his studying of both the Scriptures and all worldly wisdom he might charismatically be filled with the πνεύματι συνέσεως (lit. "wisdom of understanding"). Therefore, outside these explicit references to wise leaders in the community, only chaps. 4 and 32 (b and c) employ the same related vocabulary.

Deuteronomy 4 and 32 not only contain the remaining passages that overtly mention wisdom, but these passages share in common the same motif and themes. Each is concerned with the judgment of Israel by the surrounding nations (α), in terms of her wisdom or lack of it (β), which is directly dependent on her obedience to the Torah (γ). The repetition of these three features can be demonstrated individually for each chapter.

On the one hand, we confront in Deut 4:6 what is acknowledged as the closest parallel in the Old Testament to Sirach's more explicit assertion in 24:23a. There we find a remarkable relationship between the "statutes and ordinances" (*ḥuqqîm ûmišpāṭîm*, v 5), and the evaluation of "your wisdom and your understanding in the sight of the people" (*ḥokmatkem ûbînatkem lᵉʿênê hāʿammîm*, v 6). The last phrase (*lᵉʿênê haʿammîm*) emphasizes the consequence of Israel's obedience to "all these statutes."[11] It is that the nations may conclude, "Surely, this great nation [Israel] is a wise and understanding people." The two rhetorical questions in vv 7 and 8 provide the ultimate ground for the relationship between the statutes and wisdom in that no other nation has its God so "near" (*qārôb*) or a "Torah" (*tôrāʰ*) so righteous as Israel's. The judgment of the nations (α) can be viewed as the central motif by which the conclusion that Israel is wise and understanding (β) necessarily results from her obedience to the Torah (γ).

On the other hand, Israel is depicted in the Song of Moses (Deuteronomy 32)[12] as corrupt, and is addressed as "a foolish people, without wisdom" (*ʿam nābāl wᵉlōʾ ḥākām*, v 6). Only in Deuteronomy 32 is the designation of "foolish" (*nābāl*) used for Israel. The same concept recurs in 32:15 where a verbal form of this same root dramatizes the perfidy of a wayward generation, one that makes mockery of "the Rock of [their] Salvation." In v 21 Yahweh responds to Israel's vanities (*bᵉhablêhem*) by threatening to deliver her over to a foolish or vile nation (*lᵉgôy nābāl*). God warns of an annihilation so complete that Israel will never again be remembered among mankind (v 26).[13]

However, God does not actualize his angry gestures of destruction in

Deuteronomy 32 because his wrath might subsequently be misconstrued by the adversary nations. They would regard it as a private victory and not as the genuine retribution of Yahweh against his own people. The reason (vv 28,29) the nations would misapprehend the truth of the situation is that they, like Israel (vv 6,15), lack "counsel" (*ʿăṣôt*) and "understanding" (*tᵉbûnāʰ*) and are neither "wise" (*ḥākᵉmû*) nor "discerning" (*yābînû*) of their "end" (*ʾaḥărît*).[14] Still, the nations must judge (v 31). Finally, in the hortatory address immediately after the song, Moses adjures the people on the basis of his song "to observe to do all the words of this Torah" (*dibrê hattôrāʰ hazzêʰ*, v 46b). Once again, we find the nations judging Israel (α), but now Israel too is foolish and without wisdom (β), which is the circumstance under which Moses demands as remedy a renewed obedience to the Torah (γ).

In the context of the present redaction of Deuteronomy, chaps. 4 and 32 bracket the legal corpus and complement one another by connecting Israel's hope of wisdom before the nations with her adherence to the Torah. Together they serve to reinforce the same ideas. Moreover, alongside these two chapters Deuteronomy 30 must also be mentioned. Like Deuteronomy 4 and 32, Deuteronomy 30 is once again engaged with the question of the place and significance of the Torah in Israel.

Deut 30:10 conditions promises of salvation and prosperity (30:3–4) by an obedience to "his commandments and statutes which are written in this book of the Torah" (*sēper hattôrāʰ hazzêʰ*). Israel is assured that "this commandment" is not hard or far off (v 11); neither is it in heaven nor beyond the sea (vv 12–13). Rather, "the word" (*haddābār*, v 14) "is very near you so that you can do it." "The word" in v 14 clearly refers back to "this commandment" which finds its definition in v 10, in the "commandments and statutes," viz. "the book of the Torah."

The parallels with Deuteronomy 4 are particularly important. Only in Deuteronomy 4 and 30 do we find the same concern in that book for the *nearness* of God by means of the Torah (both Qal passive participles of *qrb*, 4:7; 30:14). In Deuteronomy 4, as well as in Deuteronomy 32, the Torah is the ground for the recognition of Israel as a wise nation. Likewise, in chap. 4 obedience to the Torah leads the nations to acknowledge the unique nearness of Israel's God. However, unlike chap. 4, Deuteronomy 30 does not mention wisdom. Conversely, while Deuteronomy 4 has only the more general term "Torah," chap. 30 speaks explicitly of "the *book* of the Torah," similar to "the book of the covenant" in Sir 24:23. In other words, if one reads Deuteronomy 4 and 32 together alongside Deuteronomy 30 the conception emerges of a *book of Torah* (chap. 30) which comes *near* to Israel (chaps. 4 and 30) from beyond the heavens and is her *wisdom* (chaps. 4 and 32). This imagery coincides perfectly with the presuppositions of Sir 24:23 and probably reflects Ben Sira's hearing of Deuteronomy.

III. Deuteronomy in Sir 51:26 and Bar 3:29–31

The probability that the writer of Sir 24:23ff. has understood Deuteronomy as we have reconstructed is confirmed by one of the other rare first-person accounts in Sirach. In Sir 51:13–30 the writer-sage makes one of the final appeals to his potential students. An extant Hebrew copy (MS B from the Cairo Geniza) of 51:26 reads,

Bring your necks under her yoke;	וְצַוְּארֵיכֶם בְּעֻלָּהּ הָבִיאוּ
let your soul bear her burden.	וּמַשָּׂאָהּ תִּשָּׂא נַפְשְׁכֶם:
She is near to those who seek her,	קְרוֹבָה הִיא לִמְבַקְשֶׁיהָ
and whoever is determined[15] finds her.	וְנוֹתֵן נַפְשׁוֹ מוֹצֵא אֹתָהּ:

We can observe again the play on Deuteronomy. The subject is wisdom which is "near" as in Deut 4:6,7, but this wisdom is also called a "yoke," a metaphor for obedience popularly associated with the book of the Torah (30:10).[16] The endeavor to attain wisdom in Deut 30:10 is, as here, a commitment requiring total devotion of heart and soul. In harmony with the same theological ascription in Sirach 24, Ben Sira, who has studied the book of Torah as wisdom made manifest in Israel, has now offered her to his aspiring readers, "Turn in unto me, ye unlearned, and lodge in my house of instruction" (51:23). In this context we find the above citation which says that the wisdom near to Ben Sira, both in his experience and in the Torah, can now be put *near* to his students in the form of "instruction" in this, *his* wisdom book. The idea that Torah is a special source of wisdom and that the writer has learned recourse to it suggests that the wisdom book of Sirach can thus have a special claim to wisdom. In Deuteronomy, those who pursued the commands of God found them near in the Torah. Likewise, Ben Sira's book brings instruction near to those seeking wisdom.

Finally, the wisdom song in Bar 3:9ff. provides additional evidence of a similar parallel understanding. It imitates Sirach 24 in a number of features. Like the wisdom song in Sirach, the prosaic section in Baruch describes wisdom's movement from a heavenly to an earthly sphere. She is shown repeatedly to be inaccessible to those persons in canonical history outside of Israel and consequently the cause of their destruction. Wisdom is identified at the conclusion of the prose, as in Sir 24:23, with "the book of the commandments of God and the Torah which endures forever" (Bar 4:1). But, unlike Sirach's wisdom song, in the body of Baruch's prose about wisdom Deuteronomy 30 is paraphrased! A detailed examination of the passage shows how Deuteronomy 30 is interpreted.

29 Τίς ἀνέβη εἰς τὸν οὐρανὸν καὶ ἔλαβεν αὐτὴν καὶ κατεβίβασεν
30 αὐτὴν ἐκ τῶν νεφελῶν; τίς διέβη πέραν τῆς θαλάσσης καὶ εὗρεν
31 αὐτὴν καὶ οἴσει αὐτὴν χρυσίου ἐκλεκτοῦ; οὐκ ἔστιν ὁ γινώσκων
τὴν ὁδὸν αὐτῆς οὐδὲ ὁ ἐνθυμούμενος τὴν τρίβον αὐτῆς.

29 Who has gone up into heaven and taken her,
and brought her down from the clouds?
30 Who has gone over the sea, and found her
and acquired her with choice gold?
31 There is neither one who knows her way,
nor one who comprehends her path.
(Bar 3:29–31)

There is substantial verbal agreement with Deut 30:12–13:

Bar 3:29–30:	Deut 30:12–13:
29 τίς ἀνέβη εἰς τὸν οὐρανὸν καὶ ἔλαβον αὐτὴν καὶ κατεβίβασεν αὐτὴν ἐκ τῶν νεφελῶν	12 τίς ἀναβήσεται ἡμῖν εἰς τὸν οὐρανὸν καὶ λήμψεται αὐτὴν [καὶ ἀκούσαντες αὐτὸ ποιήσομεν]
30 τὶς διέβη πέραν τῆς θαλάσσης καὶ εὗρεν αὐτὴν καὶ οἴσει αὐτὴν χρυσίου ἐκλεκτοῦ	13 οὐδὲ πέραν τῆς θαλάσσης ἐστὶν λέγων τίς διαπεράσει ἡμῖν εἰς τὸ πέραν τῆς θαλάσσης καὶ λήμψεται ἡμῖν αὐτὴν [καὶ ἀκουστὴν ἡμῖν ποιήσῃ αὐτὴν καὶ ποιήσομεν]

This Deuteronomy passage is part of Moses' last address to Israel before it enters the land. In it he adjures the elect people of God to obey the commandments of God. By so doing they will gain the rewards of life and future abundant prosperity (30:8ff.). Moses emphasizes that the required laws are not hidden, harsh, or obscure, but written plainly in a public document, "the book of the Torah" (v 10). The existence of a fixed, accessible Torah means that "the word (*dābār*) is very near you" (v 14). The statements in vv 11–13 eloquently establish this point by an argument for the mundane availability and practicality of the Torah, an argument which provides the proper context for understanding the very severe statements (v 15) of the consequences of disobedience.

Within Deuteronomy the rhetorical questions of Deut 30:12 and 13 are examples of inquiry utterly ruled out by the literal accessibility of the Torah. These are for Israel the untenable questions which, after the provision of the Torah through Moses, can only be seen as illegitimate excuses not "to hear and to do it" (vv 12b,13b). The importance of this latter phrase is evident both by its repetition in these two verses and, with some elaboration of the first verb, the occurrence again in v 14 which concludes the matter: "the word is very near you; it is in your mouth and in your heart, so that you can do it." The centrality of this particular thematic phrase and its absence in Baruch are significant.

In fact, the changes made in the allusion to Deut 30:12–13 show a discernible pattern that gives valuable insight into the author's adaptation of it. In Deuteronomy the two questions are both presented as specious ones. The writer of Baruch alters this by a very simple deletion. He removes the particularity of the questions for Israel by dropping in each case the prepositional phrase, "for us" (*lānû*). Now the questions are no longer incongruous self-reflections of Israel regarding a purported hiddenness of the Torah, but they are universalized to serve as an incisive rhetoric that points up the limits of all purely human efforts to grasp "the way of wisdom" (cf. v 31). Within the presupposition of wisdom's original status in the heavenly domain of God, they satirize any pretense of grasping her by mere earthly genius and agility. By quite similar logic Prov 30:3–4 portrays "wisdom" as synonymous with "the knowledge of the Holy One" and interjects, "Who has ascended to heaven and come down?"

In addition, the central, repeated purpose clause, "to hear and to do it," has been judiciously dropped and other material has taken its place. In v 29, the verbal expression, "and take it for us" (*w^{e}yiqqāḥehā lānû*), has been slightly changed and given a new semantic context. Not only has the *lānû* been omitted in keeping with the aforementioned deletion of *lānû* in the earlier part of the question, but in the place of the Deuteronomic purpose clause the verbal idea of "taking it" has been supplemented by the sequential activity of "bringing" wisdom "down from the clouds." The resulting "clouds" in parallel with "heavens" now reflects a frequent biblical metaphor for divine transcendence. For example, this metaphorical pair is used to express God's uniqueness (Deut 33:26), the mystery of his way (Job 35:5) and his exaltation above humanity (Ps 36:5; 57:11; 108:4). Consequently, the final verb "brought down" stands in sequential contingency with "taken it (her)." By formulaic, biblical parallelism these actions have been cast as a vain human attempt to overcome divine transcendence, even as implied in Job 35:5. Moreover, this action of taking and bringing down may be reminiscent of the aforementioned Prov 30:4.

The second question in v 30 likewise omits the Deuteronomic purpose clause. The main verb in this substituted phrase, οἴσει 'to obtain' or 'to acquire,' probably translates *qānā^h* (Eccl 2:7,8; Gen 12:5; 31:1; Deut 8:17,18; Jer 17:11) rather than *sḥr* (Prov 3:14) or *'āśā^h* (cf. LXX of Hos 9:16).[17] *Qānā^h* in this case would be idiomatic to the injunction in Proverbs that one should "obtain wisdom."[18] Moreover, the Deuteronomic verb "take her" has been changed to "find her" (εὗρεν αὐτὴν, prob. *m^{e}ṣā'āh*). The resulting combination of verbs represents, as in v 29, a sequence of activity which here entails first "going up," then "finding," and finally "acquiring" with money. Like the verb *qānā^h* in relation to wisdom, *māṣā'* is also idiomatic to the canonical wisdom literature (Prov 1:28; 2:5; 4:22; 8:9; 12:17); and the combination of *lqḥ* and *mṣ'* occurs similarly in Prov 8:9,10 (cf. Sir 30:39; 51:28). At exactly this point Job 28:15–19 shares the same theme as here: "It [wisdom] cannot be obtained for gold" (v 15a).

By contrast, in the Torah and the Prophets one never speaks of "finding" or "obtaining" the Torah, but rather, as in Deuteronomy, "hearing" and "doing it" (cf. Deut 27:26; 28:58; 29:29; 31:12; 32:46). In addition, Kneucker builds a convincing case for a series of motifs in Bar 3:30b ff. reminiscent of the same series in Job 28:15–28; v 30b parallels Job 28:15–19; v 31, Job 28:20–22 (=

28:12–14); vv 32ff., Job 28:23ff.; v 36, Job 28:28.[19] Thus v 30b is the first crucial step toward a shorthand paraphrase dependent on the sequence of motifs in Job 28:15–28. The deleted Deuteronomic phrases, had they been retained, would have further distracted the reader from the controlling imagery throughout Bar 3:9ff. of "finding" (εὑρίσκειν, v 15) or "finding out" (ἐξευρίσκειν, vv 32a,36) wisdom in order that she may be known. Hence, both by omitting certain words and phrases from Deut 30:12–13 and by adding others, the writer conforms the older Deuteronomic material, which speaks exclusively of the Torah, to a new, specifically wisdom context.

The denouement of the lesson is that only God has "found out" wisdom, and he has subsequently "given her" to Israel (v 36). This conscious motif throughout Bar 3:9–4:4 of first locating wisdom and then making her accessible is the same as that now reflected in vv 29–30. The change in the verb "take" from Deut 30:13 to "find" in v 30a overtly adjusted the vocabulary to suit this larger contextual theme of a quest for wisdom consistent with that of Job 28. Here, too, Baruch stresses the *knowledge* of the way of wisdom, rather than obedience to commandments intrinsic to it. Likewise, Israel's exile is not cast sharply as a transgression of commandments, but as a "forsaking" (ἐγκαταλείπειν, prob. *'zb*) of the way, an expression used in Scripture both in reference to the Mosaic Torah and to wisdom (cf. Ps 89:30; Prov 28:4; 4:2,6). We must remember that Deuteronomy 30 does not mention wisdom but refers only to the commandments of the Torah. However, by selective citation, alteration in vocabulary and additional complementary statements, Deuteronomy 30 is intentionally conformed in Bar 3:29–30 to the special themes and vocabulary of the canonical wisdom literature. Just as Deuteronomy 4, Deut 30:12–13 now reads as a statement about wisdom.

Baruch's close interpretation of Deuteronomy 30, which was originally only about the Torah, reveals the same assumption underlying Sirach 24, namely, that the Torah which is wisdom near to Israel (Deut 4) is the same Torah which God alone brings near (Deut 30). Because there is no direct reference to wisdom in Deuteronomy 30 by itself, only our proposal regarding its resonance with Deuteronomy 4 accounts for the assumed relationship of Torah with wisdom both here and in Sirach 24. Even as Sir 51:26 stresses the yoke of "instruction" which is "near" (*qᵉrôbāʰ*) and which the diligent "find" (*môṣē'*), so the Deuteronomy 30 section in Bar 3:9ff. is interpreted in terms of a searching for and "finding" (ἐξευρίσκειν, see 3:15,32,36) of *wisdom*. Therefore, our conclusion with respect to Sirach 24 has been further complemented by the analogous, if not directly dependent, interpretive activity in Bar 3:9ff., especially 3:29–31.

IV. Conclusion

In summary, the interpretation of Deuteronomy in Sir 24:23 picks up the theme of the Torah as *wisdom* which appears the same in both Deuteronomy 4 and 32, and incorporates from Deuteronomy 30 the idea of the *book* of the Torah that is no longer in heaven but given to Israel. However, the writer of Sirach expresses the idea of *nearness* (Deuteronomy 4 and 30) more concretely in the election vocabulary found elsewhere within Deuteronomy (e.g., Deut 3:18ff.; 12:1ff.) of a divine "possession" or "inheritance" in Israel. In order to secure this connection he simply edits Deut 33:4 into his commentary. It is significant that 33:4 is the only verse in Deuteronomy that employs the same thematic catchword "possession/inheritance" (κληρονομία = *môrešet*), which was stressed throughout the wisdom song (cf. Sir 24:7,12,20).[20]

The combined interpretation of Deuteronomy 4, 30 and 32 is the conclusion that "the book of the covenant" is wisdom, and results from simply one possible selective reading of Deuteronomy. The method of employing related texts to interpret each other obviously cannot be regarded in itself as a peculiarly sapiential device. Yet, the *book* of the Torah found in Deuteronomy 30 has come to have a special meaning in Sir 24:23, like the "Torah of the Most High" in Sir 39:1. As in Sirach 39, it stands for one of the canonical divisions, the five books of Moses, and a primary source of wisdom for the sage. So, here, the giving of the book of the Torah is synonymous with the settlement and unique presence of divine wisdom in Israel. It is both a promise and a hermeneutical statement. The Torah can be read as a guide to wisdom and resides as a unique possession of Israel.

NOTES

1. The Greek is *hōs* in Sir 24:3,13(2x), 14(4x),16,17. *Hōs* is probably *k-* in Hebrew as M. H. Segal (*Sepher Ben Sira* [Jerusalem: Bialik Institute, 1953]: 145–56) has suggested.
2. While economy of purpose allows for selectivity, certain omissions like this reference to Sinai are intentionally consistent for Sirach (cf. Sir 17:11–14). If wisdom were initially linked to Israel by the Sinai event, then the midrash on wisdom at creation and particularly in Eden might be compromised (cf. Sir 17:6–7). See Edmund Jacob, "L'historie d'Israël vue par Ben Sira" in *Mélanges bibliques rédigés en l'honneur de André Robert* (Paris: Bloud and Gay, 1957): 288–94.
3. J. Marböck (*Weisheit im Wandel* [Bonn: Peter Hanstein, 1971]: 177–78) sets out the matter clearly. Cf. 2 Kgs 2:8,11 and 23:2,21. E. Kutsch ("Gesetz und Gnade," *ZAW* 79 [1967]: 30) demonstrates this for the Deuteronomistic history. Also, see Sir 17:12; 28:7. 1 Macc 1:56,57 has both phrases in parallel.
4. Segal (N 1): 149; cf. K. Hruby, "Gesetz und Gnade in der rabbinischen Überlieferung," *Judaica* 25 (1969): 33.
5. Cf. W. L. Knox, "The Divine Wisdom," *JTS* 18 (1937): 233, 236–37. Knox argues unconvincingly that 24:23ff. requires a Greek mentality distinct from the Semitic flavor of the song, for otherwise Hebrew *feminine* "wisdom" and "Torah" would be identified with a *masculine* noun, "river" (vv 24ff.). He regards 24:23ff. as a secondary interpolation originating not before 132 B.C. U. Wilckens (*Weisheit und Torheit* [Tübingen: J. C. B. Mohr, 1959]: 167–68) suggests that 24:23 represents what in a later redactor's mind "*für ihn* die zentrale Aussage des ganzen Liedes ist." M. Hengel (*Judentum und Hellenismus* [Tübingen: J. C. B. Mohr, 1969]: 289 n. 339) considers Knox's contentions of a later interpolation to be impossible. Marböck ([N 3]: 45–46, 77–78) notes the discontinuity and implies a redactional step which, in tune with the theme of the song, concludes the series of personified concretizations with a final radical "reinterpretation." For further discussion, see Otto Rickenbacker, *Weisheitsperikopen bei Ben Sira* (Göttingen: Vandenhoeck & Ruprecht, 1973): 125–27.
6. Cf. the language of "rest and inheritance" in Sir 24:7–8 with the same in Deuteronomy 12. See Marböck (N 3): 62–63.

7. 1:3(2x),15; 16:19.
8. 4:6(4x).
9. 32:6,28,29(2x).
10. The phrase *rûᵃḥ ḥokmāʰ* does not occur elsewhere in Deuteronomy.
11. For the use of *'ăšer* to introduce either purpose or result clauses in the Old Testament, see Ronald J. Williams, *Hebrew Syntax: An Outline* (Toronto: University of Toronto, 1967): pars. 465–66. Also, Carl Brockelmann, *Hebräische Syntax* (Neukirchen Kreis Moers: Verlag der Buchhandlung des Erziehungsvereins, 1956): 153 (§161bαβ). Also, its use in Deut 4:40 to introduce a purpose clause parallels somewhat the context here in 4:6.
12. For a discussion of the Song of Moses and a complete bibliography of recent studies including those concerned with its wisdom elements, see C. J. Labuschagne, *De Fructu Oris Sui* (ed. I. H. Eybers, *et al.;* Leiden: E. J. Brill, 1971): 85–98, esp. 92.
13. Cf. Sir 44:10–15.
14. For a discussion of this phrase as a possible wisdom feature, see Moshe Weinfeld, *Deuteronomy and the Deuteronomic School* (Oxford: Clarendon, 1972): 316–17.
15. Lit. "gives his soul."
16. E.g., Jer 5:5; *Pirqê 'Abôt* 3.6. Cf. Hruby (N 4): 38–39. It is not used in the Old Testament in association with wisdom.
17. J. J. Kneucker, *Das Buch Baruch* (Leipzig: F. A. Brockhaus, 1879): 304.
18. See, e.g., Prov 4:5,7; 8:22; 16:16; 17:16; cf. 1:5; 18:15; 19:8.
19. Kneucker (N 17): 303.
20. The Hebrew for κληρονομία in the previous song is probably *naḥălāʰ*, which is the conventional expression for "inheritance" in the Deuteronomic phrase "rest and inheritance." Cf. Sir 24:7,8; see Deut 3:18–20; 12:1–11; 25:19; Josh 11:13–15 and Marböck (N 3): 62. Nevertheless, the Hebrew word in Sir 24:23b is probably *môrešet* as in the MT of Deut 33:4. The two Hebrew terms are quite similar in meaning; both terms are commonly translated in the LXX with κληρονομία: usually for the former and in one-third of the occurrences (12) for the latter. Clearly, the probability of a lexical distinction is overshadowed in Sirach 24 by the conceptual agreement between the two words and the importance of that agreement in the interpretation of the wisdom song. That κληρονομία is the translation equivalent in the LXX to the term in Deut 33:4 confirms its contextual agreement in meaning with the use of *naḥălāʰ* in the preceding song.

13

HOSEA THE STATESMAN

GERALD G. SWAIM

Although one of Isaiah's most famous messages was a form of political advice to Hezekiah at the time of the Syro-Ephraimite crisis,[1] and though Amos was accused of treason[2] (clearly a political offense), Hosea is often thought of as being concerned only with the spiritual adultery of Baal worship and related sins, and with God's merciful response. It is little wonder that Hosea is seen in this way, since on the one hand the fact that he used an unhappy relationship to his wife[3] as a symbol of Yahweh's relationship to Israel is obvious to the most casual reader, while on the other hand, the exact details of his marriage[4] or marriages[5] are so confused that there is no consensus regarding these details, and most critical scholars who deal with the book expend much effort to understand them.[6] Nevertheless, a careful reading of the book in the light of the known situation in Hosea's day indicates that he was quite interested in politics. To see this clearly, it will be helpful to sketch the political scene from sources outside Hosea's book.

Judah and Israel had enjoyed a period of unparalleled prosperity for about forty years under the almost simultaneous reigns of Uzziah and Jeroboam II, respectively.[7] They were on their thrones during a period when there were no truly strong aggressive states in the Near East, and jointly they had regained control of nearly all the territory formerly held by David and Solomon. Mesopotamia, Egypt and even Damascus were all relatively weak, and so the small Hebrew states were able to flourish. It was in the middle of this period, about 760 B.C.,[8] that Amos spoke out against the rich in Samaria (4:1) and against those who were "at ease in Zion" (6:1). When Amos spoke to foreign countries, he was content to confine his message to the small states contiguous with Judah and Israel, and was relatively unconcerned with Assyria and Egypt.

But in 746–45 things changed radically on two fronts. Jeroboam II was succeeded by his son, Zechariah, who was assassinated only six months later by Shallum ben Jabesh. Shallum lasted only one month before being replaced by Menahem ben Gadi. Thus the internal scene had shifted quickly from the long, stable reign of Jeroboam to a situation of assassination and civil war. Externally, just at this time Tiglath-pileser III came to the Assyrian throne and embarked on a career of serious aggression. He soon had his armies in such condition as to threaten the entire Near East. The era of small states was almost over. As early as 743 Tiglath-pileser drove west, returning several times until, in 734, he conquered Gaza and the Philistines, thus apparently intending to confine Egyptian influence to Egypt itself.[9] In 732 he conquered Damascus, potentially the strongest of the western states. It is no surprise that Menahem offered him tribute to avoid having the Assyrians attack Israel. And perhaps Menahem hoped thereby to strengthen his own hold on the Israelite throne as well.

In any event, it was into this general milieu that Hosea came with his message from Yahweh, and much of his message has political overtones. Political statements in Hosea may be divided into three categories: (1) those that refer to international relations with Assyria and Egypt; (2) those that speak of the kings of Israel, always in a rather negative tone; and (3) those that refer to Judah in some way. Let us examine these in order.

There are about a dozen references throughout the book to Assyria and/or Egypt. From the way these nations are mentioned, it seems obvious that there were those, like Menahem, who favored appeasement, even alliance with Assyria. Others apparently favored looking to Egypt for help against Assyria, but Hosea lumped the two groups together and castigated both at once in 7:11–12:

> Ephraim is like a dove, silly and without sense,
> calling to Egypt, going to Assyria.
> As they go, I will spread over them my net;
> I will bring them down like birds of the air;
> I will chastise them for their wicked deeds.

Similarly, in 5:13–14 he spoke of God's opposition to an alliance with Assyria:

> When Ephraim saw his sickness,
> and Judah his wound,
> then Ephraim went to Assyria,
> and sent to the great king.
> But he is not able to cure you
> or heal your wound.
> For I will be like a lion to Ephraim,
> and like a young lion to the house of Judah.
> I, even I, will rend and go away,
> I will carry off, and none shall rescue.

Although those who favored an alliance with Assyria must have been bitterly opposed by those who looked toward Egypt for help, Hosea consistently treated them as if they were one party and offered them similar judgments from Yahweh:

> They shall not remain in the land of the Lord:
> but Ephraim shall return to Egypt,
> and they shall eat unclean food in Assyria. (9:3)

They shall return to the land of Egypt,
  and Assyria shall be their king,
  because they have refused to return to me. (11:5)

The poetic parallelism here clearly suggests that residence in either Assyria or Egypt should be viewed by an Israelite as a judgment from God, and apparently Hosea saw little ground for choice between Assyria and Egypt. Thus, he opposed alliances with those whom he might logically see as enemies of Yahweh.

Regarding internal affairs, he was strongly opposed to and disappointed by the kings of Israel.[10] This is first seen as early as his prophecy against the house of Jehu (i.e., Jeroboam and his son Zechariah) in chapter one. Here he named his own firstborn "Jezreel" as a constant reminder that the blood shed by Jehu in the Valley of Jezreel must be avenged. Hosea certainly lived to see this prophecy fulfilled, but he hardly seemed pleased with the assassination of Zechariah or with the anarchy ushered in by succeeding assassinations. He stated in 3:4 that "Israel shall dwell many days without king or prince," and went on in 5:1 to castigate both priests and king:

Here this, O priests!
  Give heed, O house of Israel!
Harken, O house of the king!
  For the judgment pertains to you.

He summed up his rejection of the usurpers of the Israelite throne in 9:15: "All their princes are rebels," but he also hinted elsewhere that the anarchy of assassination was not all that he objected to. The kings of Samaria lacked legitimacy because they were not chosen by Yahweh and because they perpetuated the worship related to the golden calves originally set up by Jeroboam I[11] and associated early with Bethel and Dan—later also with Samaria:

They made kings, but not through me.
  They set up princes, but without my knowledge.
With their silver and gold they made idols
  for their own destruction.
I have spurned your calf, O Samaria.
  My anger burns against them. (8:4–5a)

Thus there were at least three political positions in Israel that Hosea opposed—external reliance on either Assyria or Egypt and internal reliance on the Israelite kings, including the dynasty of Jehu and the rapid succession of usurpers who followed that dynasty. Was Hosea merely a religious crank who opposed any practical approach to the huge dilemmas of a small state threatened externally by the Assyrian menace and internally by civil strife, or did he have some kind of alternative to offer? Obviously, Hosea wanted the people to return to Yahweh and to trust in him, but what this meant practically remains obscure if we follow those critical scholars[12] who excise all references to Judah as later additions by some scribe who wanted to make Hosea's book palatable to a southern audience after the demise of the northern kingdom.

The basic argument for removing the references to Judah is the supposition that no one in Israel would make such positive references to his southern neighbor. That is to say, there is no textual evidence for omitting the mention of Judah in Hosea. Since we have no textual reason for removing even the most positive references to Judah, let us reexamine the text on the assumption that most of them actually do come from Hosea. Perhaps Hosea did offer a positive political program.[13] Perhaps Hosea's position was that the best answer to both the internal chaos of kingship by brute force and usurpation and the external threat of Assyria lay in a reunion of all those who truly worshiped Yahweh, i.e., Israel and Judah. Hosea saw no one in Israel who could claim any right to the throne. The succession of assassins who followed Zechariah ben Jeroboam apparently did not even bother to claim divine sanction through anointing by a prophet. But Judah still had a Davidic monarch; why not unite under him? Hosea's main concern was for purity of religion, and while the religious commitment and expression of Judah was far from perfect, at least the Davidic house still had prophetic support in Judah. Perhaps a reunion could lead to the purification of the whole state. This may sound like a desperate move politically, but the situation itself was desperate. Let us examine the references to Judah in Hosea in terms of this hypothesis just as the book has been transmitted to us by tradition.

There are three kinds of references to Judah: (1) those in which Judah seems preferred over Israel, (2) those in which Judah is criticized, and (3) those in which Judah and Israel are treated so much alike as to be almost synonymous. To the first category belongs 3:5, which is virtually a statement of our hypothesis. After a period without king or prince, "the children of Israel shall return and seek the Lord their God, and David their king; and they shall come in fear to the Lord and to his goodness in the latter days." This shows a strong commitment to the legitimacy of the Davidic house, but it ties in well with 2:2 (1:11E), "And the people of Judah and the people of Israel shall be gathered together, and they shall appoint for themselves one head;[14] and they shall go up from the land, for great shall be the day of Jezreel." This sounds almost as if Hosea expected the overthrow of the house of Jehu to lead directly to the reunion of North and South. Admittedly, seeking a common, Davidic king would make sense as an addition by an editor from Judah perhaps in the days of Josiah, but why would he tie his statement to Jezreel? The Jezreel statement fits better in the early days of Hosea's ministry than at any later time.

It might be thought that these two passages merely treat Israel and Judah alike under a Davidic monarch. Judah is clearly preferred to Israel in two other passages. The first is 1:7, which follows a statement that Israel will no longer be pitied with the assertion that Judah will be pitied, but will not be delivered by military means. The other is 11:12, which states:

Ephraim has encompassed me with lies,
  and the house of Israel with deceit;

but Judah is still known by God,
  and is faithful to the Holy One.

Such statements may be viewed as the theological underpinnings of Hosea's desire for reunion with Judah. He has observed the relatively greater stability of Judah as well as the *relative* purity of Yahwistic worship in the southern kingdom.[15] But these observations do not blind him to problems in the southern state. Indeed, he has several biting comments for his desired ally—5:10 and 8:14. These may be taken together as opposed to Judah's military preparations, perhaps specifically as they affect boundaries and relations between the two Yahwistic kingdoms:

The princes of Judah have become
  like those who remove the landmark;
upon them I will pour out
  my wrath like water. (5:10)

Israel has forgotten his Maker, and built palaces;
  and Judah has multiplied fortified cities;
but I will send a fire upon his cities,
  and it shall devour his strongholds. (8:14)

These passages show a willingness to criticize Judah for anything it might do to prevent the reunion of the people of Yahweh in total dependence upon Yahweh, and so are similar to those references to Judah which present it alongside Israel as an equal, sometimes as the poetic parallel of the northern kingdom. Hosea 5:5 shows this:

The pride of Israel testifies to his face;
  Ephraim shall stumble in his guilt;
  Judah also shall stumble with them.

And so does 5:12–14a:

Therefore I am like a moth to Ephraim
  and like dry rot to the house of Judah.
When Ephraim saw his sickness,
  and Judah his wound,
then Ephraim went to Assyria,
  and sent to the great king.
But he is not able to cure you
  or heal your wound.
For I will be like a lion to Ephraim,
  and like a young lion to the house of Judah.

The same attitude is seen in 6:4:

What shall I do with you, O Ephraim?
  What shall I do with you, O Judah?
Your love is like a morning cloud,
  like dew that goes early away.

And in 10:11:

> Ephraim was a trained heifer that loved to thresh,
>   and I spared her fair neck;
> but I will put Ephraim to the yoke,
>   Judah must plow,
>   Jacob must harrow for himself.

Ephraim and Judah are here seen as parallel branches of Yahweh's people. Indeed, this is the way Hosea looks at the two kingdoms throughout his book.

There are other passages in the book of Hosea that mention Judah, but none is harder to explain in terms of this hypothesis than the ones we have examined. To be sure, they are usually explained as later additions, but this leaves Hosea as a man who is critical of every position that his contemporaries espouse regarding foreign and domestic policy but without anything positive to offer in place of foreign alliances and succession by assassination. If these passages actually come from Hosea, he was a man with a very positive program. If his program had been adopted, it might possibly have been as successful as Hezekiah's refusal to capitulate to Sennacherib.

We have moved beyond[16] thinking of prophets of doom who could not offer a word of hope.[17] Is it not time to move beyond Hosea the critic of domestic and foreign policy to Hosea the statesman?

NOTES

1. Isa 7–8.
2. Amos 7:10–17.
3. H. H. Rowley, "The Marriage of Hosea" in *Men of God* (London: Thomas Nelson and Sons, 1963; rpt. from *BJRL* 39 [1956–57]: 200–33).
4. Abraham J. Heschel, *The Prophets* (New York: Harper & Row, 1962): 52ff. Adolphe Lods, *The Prophets and the Rise of Judaism* (London: Routledge & Kegan Paul, 1937): 90–98. George Adam Smith, *The Book of the Twelve Prophets* 1 (*The Expositor's Bible;* New York: George W. Doran, 1896): 232ff.
5. Ernst Sellin and Georg Fohrer, *Introduction to the Old Testament* (Nashville: Abingdon, 1968): 421. J. M. P. Smith, *The Prophets and Their Times* (2nd ed.; Chicago: University of Chicago, 1941): 70–76. Robert H. Pfeiffer, *Introduction to the Old Testament* (New York: Harper & Brothers, 1941): 567–69.
6. Thus, e.g., Artur Weiser devotes approximately two pages out of five on Hosea to the problem of Hosea 1-3 in *The Old Testament: Its Formation and Development* (New York: Association, 1961): 232–38.
7. John Bright, *A History of Israel* (2nd ed.; Philadelphia: Westminster, 1972): 267ff. Martin Noth, *The History of Israel* (2nd ed.; New York: Harper & Row, 1960): 253ff.
8. For the date of Amos' earthquake, see James L. Mays, *Amos* (Philadelphia: Westminster, 1969): 20.
9. For records from Tiglath-pileser III's western campaigns see *ANET*[2]: 282–84.
10. A. Gelston, "Kingship in the Book of Hosea" in *Oudtestamentische Studien* 19 (Leiden: E. J. Brill, 1974): 71–85. Cf. Roy L. Honeycutt, Jr., "Hosea" in *The Broadman Bible Commentary* 7 (Nashville: The Broadman Press, 1972): 57.
11. Roland de Vaux, "The Religious Schism of Jeroboam I" in *The Bible and the Ancient Near East* (Garden City, NY: Doubleday, 1971): 97–110.

12. Pfeiffer (N 5): 566–67; cf. Samuel Sandmel, *The Hebrew Scriptures: An Introduction to Their Literature and Religious Ideas* (New York: Alfred A. Knopf, 1963): 71.
13. I have not seen the work of Caquot referred to by Sellin–Fohrer (N 5): 424, which apparently has a thesis regarding Hosea's political views.
14. James L. Mays (*Hosea* [London: SCM, 1966]: 32) argues that Hosea here uses *rô'š* as an indication of his opposition to kingship. But cf. 1 Sam 15:17, where Saul is recognized as *rô'š* and (therefore?) Yahweh makes him *melek*.
15. The evidence for the common assumption that the worship of Yahweh was purer in Judah than in Israel deserves further study.
16. Cf. John Mauchline, "The Book of Hosea" in *IB* 6 (New York: Abingdon, 1956): 559–60.
17. Contra Pfeiffer (N 5): 573.

14

A QUESTION-ANSWER SCHEMA IN HAGGAI 1: THE FORM AND FUNCTION OF HAGGAI 1:9–11

J. WILLIAM WHEDBEE

Many commentators continue to have a low view of the style and substance of Haggai's prophetic message. C. Stuhlmueller is typical: "The first prophet of post-exilic Israel, Haggai, was truly a 'minor prophet,' with a meagerness of words and a crabbed style."[1] Part of this sort of negative assessment is no doubt due to the extreme shortness of the book; but part of it is also sometimes due to a pejorative view of the religious developments of postexilic Israel—a view which more often than not displays a prejudice toward the relative significance of the rebuilding of the temple and the reemergence of the priestly hierocracy.[2] Moreover, Haggai as a representative of the prophetic movement is often seen as a side eddy when set against that mighty stream of prophetic figures we call collectively the classical prophets. I would agree with an increasing number of scholars who argue that classical prophecy has been allowed to dwarf other key prophetic dimensions in ancient Israel. P. R. Ackroyd's review of R. E. Clements' recent monograph, *Prophecy and Tradition,* expresses well the persistent problem of an unbalanced, monolithic presentation of Israelite prophecy: "An excellent and stimulating survey; but there is very little concern with prophecy apart from the main figures, with little or no mention of Joel, Nahum, Habakkuk, Haggai, or Zechariah. It is essentially one prophetic pattern that is examined here; one has the uneasy feeling that if we knew more about other kinds of prophecy . . . we might see more clearly how this 'main style' has imposed itself and made us read all prophecy in one way."[3]

Although I have no interest in serving as an apologist for Haggai or in pressing unwarranted claims for this "minor prophet," I do think it important to develop a more diversified, balanced approach to Israel's prophets. As a small effort toward this end I propose to examine a relatively neglected text in Haggai. It is my hope that a careful form-critical and traditio-historical analysis of Hag

1:9–11 will reveal a greater depth and richness to Haggai's prophetic message than first meet the eye.

> You looked for much, but see, it came to little; and when you brought it home,[4] I blew it away. Why?—oracle of Yahweh of hosts—Because of my house that lies waste (*ḥārēb*), while each of you runs for his own house. Therefore the heavens above you have held back the dew, and the earth has held back its produce. I have summoned a drought (*ḥōreb*) upon the land and the hills, upon the grain, the new wine, and the oil, upon what the ground brings forth, upon men and cattle, and upon all the work of their hands. (Hag 1:9–11)

I

At first glance the delimitation of Hag 1:9–11 from its literary context seems relatively easy. A formula ("says Yahweh") separates 1:8 from 1:9ff.; moreover, 1:8 with its demand plus promise forms a climax in the preceding speech. At the other end (1:12ff.) the shift to the reportorial style marks a clean break as the narrator portrays the response of leaders and people to the prophetic demands.

Other considerations, however, give one pause before separating 1:9–11 too sharply from the preceding section. The long-noted parallelism in style and theme between vv 9–11 and 4–6 suggests a self-conscious attempt to forge a strong link between the two sections. Again, the reportorial frame (1:1 and 1:12ff.) leads one to view 1:2–11 as one speech—at least that would seem to be the intention of the final redaction.

Once 1:9–11 is set in the perspective of the larger literary setting the interpretative options increase dramatically. First of all, many critics point to repetition and unevenness in 1:2–11 and seek to remove the apparent difficulties either by rearrangement or deletion.[5] Secondly, form critics have oscillated between two approaches: (1) the quest for the smallest original units, which results in a dismemberment of the text into several originally disparate sayings now fused together by redactional links;[6] (2) the quest for larger, more comprehensive genres, which attempts to demonstrate an original continuity and cohesiveness among various parts of 1:2–11. The latter approach has much to commend it, because it at least tries to deal more adequately with the generic configuration of the present form of the text while at the same time recognizing the tensions and breaks in the material. This approach helps to overcome the atomizing tendency of some form-critical work on prophetic literature.

Three scholars in particular represent the last-named approach and offer distinctive and significant contributions toward the form-critical interpretation of Haggai 1; their researches must form the starting point for a form-critical analysis of Hag 1:9–11. First, W. A. M. Beuken describes 1:3–11,12b as a "sketch of Haggai's appearance and its historical success."[7] Here he follows a lead of H.

W. Wolff, who has identified such a genre in Hosea (cf. Hos 5:1–7).[8] Although Beuken is keenly aware of the uneven, differentiated character of the various elements in Hag 1:2ff., he nevertheless argues that they all finally fit into that genre Wolff describes as a "traditionists' sketch."[9] Thus diverse parts of the prophet's speech, which belong to the same scene and are focused on the same theme, are combined in an eyewitness report. Beuken therefore affirms both a thematic and generic continuity between 1:9–10(11?) and the preceding speech. He calls 1:9 a "disputation" comprised of a "futility curse" (9a) plus an accusing element (9b);[10] 1:10–11 is a "retrospect on the announcement of judgment" (v 11 may be a later addition).[11] Thus in the end he denies generic integrity to 1:9–11. What is especially lacking in his analysis is his failure to deal with the question-answer schema in 9b except as it falls into the broad category of disputation.

In the same year that Beuken's book appeared, K. Koch published a penetrating form-critical analysis of Haggai concerned particularly with the identification of "this people" and "this nation" in 2:14.[12] To get a proper fix on the highly debated placement of 2:15ff., Koch analyzed the structure and genre of the major units in Haggai. According to Koch, 1:2–8 forms a clearly defined genre, which he identifies as an original speech unit and which he names a "prophecy of salvation."[13] To Koch 1:9–11 is a second speech on the same theme which is given in an abbreviated form, but he suggests the possibility that even it can be identified as the concluding part of the older prophetic speech.[14] It would then function structurally as a "concluding characterization." Thus Koch is equivocal as to whether or not 1:9–11 really belongs to the preceding speech; it would seem he means to argue that its earlier form has been altered so that now it appears as a shortened version of another speech. In fairness to Koch, however, it must be said that his principal purpose is not to interpret precisely the form and function of 1:9–11, so that in light of his assessment of its present role in the literary context he can leave it out of consideration. But at least he gives us some preliminary clues as to his understanding of the generic character of 1:9–11.

The most recent form-critical analysis of Hag 1:2–11 is from the pen of O. H. Steck; it is clearly the most incisive and thorough treatment to date and it represents therefore the sharpest focal point for subsequent form-critical work on Haggai 1.[15] He has a different thesis from either Beuken or Koch and criticizes the proposals of both scholars. Like Koch, he argues for the generic integrity of 1:2–8 (contra Beuken who contends that v 2 belongs to the later redactional frame). Steck, however, differs from Koch in the identification of genre: 1:2–8 is best defined as a discussion or disputation rather than a prophecy of salvation.[16] Steck's careful delineation of the argumentative character of the speech is convincing and deals most adequately with the individual parts of 1:2–8. But what of 1:9–11? To Steck 1:9–11 is not a continuation of the preceding speech but is a *parallel* unit, which likewise is to be defined as a discussion speech, but which now is in fragmented form, lacking a demand such as we have in 1:8a.[17] It is the identification of the audience which really sets apart Steck's view. Whereas the first speech (1:2–8) was directed to those Judeans who had remained in the land, 1:9–11 was addressed to those who were recent returnees from the Babylonian exile.[18]

I have no quarrel with Steck's explanation of the speech as a disputation, but I am not convinced by his proposal as to the different audience. Even he admits that the differentiation of the two audiences has now all but been obliterated in the present form of the text.[19] Moreover, his evidence for the proposal hangs on a slender thread. His case is founded principally on the descriptions of the alleged difference in the housing situations represented in vv 4 and 9: in the former the addressees already possess houses, whereas in the latter they do not have houses as yet and must therefore build them.[20] This differentiation is based more on assertion than solid evidence. The phrase "run to or for his house" (*râṣîm l^{e}-bêtô*) may indeed be read idiomatically or metaphorically ('busy oneself in or about'), but to assert that this phrase in the context unequivocally means that the addressees do not have houses is most questionable. If that had been the intent, there are much clearer ways to say it. Moreover, reading the clause, "you brought it into the house" (*habbayit*), as a reference to the temple is unconvincing.[21] Finally, Steck's acknowledgment that the separation of the addressees into two groups is now obscured in the text is a damaging admission indeed. Thus in the end one must say that Steck's interpretation is ingenious and even possible, but given the available evidence it is improbable.

In summary we are left with three explanations as to the form and function of 1:9–11, none of which is completely convincing. All three scholars recognize that in *some sense* 1:9–11 both parallels and advances the thought of the preceding speech, but in what precise sense they differ. What is interesting is that each one attempts to go behind the text to recover a prior stage of tradition. To Beuken 1:4–10 is a part of an eyewitness sketch of Haggai's appearance (v 11 is some kind of later addition); Koch speaks vaguely of a stage in which 1:9–11 may have served as a "concluding characterization" of a prophecy of salvation, but now it is a second speech on the same theme; finally, Steck argues that it was originally a separate speech and recovers a different audience for it. In my judgment, none of the three scholars adequately interprets the text as it stands—despite some of their claims to the contrary.[22] All three still represent that type of form criticism which sees as its chief goal the recovery of an earlier setting. Moreover, what is especially surprising is that none of the three adequately analyzes the most prominent structural feature of 1:9–11: the question-answer schema. Steck and other scholars who recognize the argumentative character of the speech and label it variously as disputation or discussion are on the right track,[23] but they have not gone far enough in discriminating more precisely the particular type of disputation speech that is involved. Now I wish to interpret first of all the repetitive and parallel character of the external relationships between vv 9–11 and the preceding speech; then, secondly, I want to focus on the internal pattern of vv 9–11 to attempt to interpret more adequately the form and function of the question-answer schema.

II

A structural analysis serves best to highlight the external and internal arrangement of the different parts of the text.

I. Introduction: A Messenger Formula (1:2a)
II. The Unfolding of the Disputation Speech (1:2b–11)
   A. The Problem Defined (2b–7)
      1. The basis of dispute: The quotation of the people's word (2b)
      2. Word reception formula (3)
      3. The people's position attacked (4)
      4. A call for reflection on present conditions (5–7)
         a. A general call prefaced by a messenger formula (5)
         b. Specific object of reflection: The frustration and futility of economic conditions (6)
         c. A repeated general call prefaced by a messenger formula (7)
   B. The Solution Advanced: The Command to Rebuild the Temple (8)
      1. A series of imperatives (8a)
      2. A rationale for rebuilding (8b)
   C. The Problem Reiterated and Further Defined (9–11)
      1. A reflection on present conditions: The frustration and futility of economic existence (9a)
      2. An explanation and justification: A question-answer schema (9b–11)
         a. Question: "Why?" (9bα)
         b. Answer (9bβ–11)
            (1) "Because . . .": Statement of people's guilt (9bβ)
            (2) "Therefore . . .": Statement of divine judgment (10–11)

In contrast to most structural analyses of 1:2–11, this approach takes the text as it stands and attempts to see an organic unity in it. Rather than positing a secondary origin for 1:9–11 (or parts thereof) or arguing for another audience (now all but lost from view), I would contend that the repetitive, parallel character is integral to the structure of the speech (here Koch's suggestion that 1:9–11 is a "concluding characterization" has possibilities). So viewed the command to rebuild the temple (v 8) is now the center of the whole speech, not the climax of the so-called first speech (which allegedly ran from v 2 to v 8). As the center of the speech it is framed in a kind of envelope structure in which the problem is initially defined (vv 2–7) and then reiterated and further defined or refined (vv 9–11). Both parts support the central demand. In particular, v 9 stands in an inversely parallel relationship to vv 4 and 6: v 9a is matched by v 6, and v 9b by v 4. There is similarity in specific formulation as well as general theme. For example, vv 6 and 9a are strikingly alike, involving so-called "futility curses."[24] Standing as a kind of frame around the command to rebuild, this application of the curse tradition forces the people to reflect on the futile, frustrating economic conditions of past and present and gives the command to rebuild a special urgency.

It is important, however, to see that v 9a is more than a mere repetition of v 6. It introduces for the first time the divine "I" ("When you brought it home, I blew it away."): Yahweh identifies himself as the primary cause for the people's economic disasters; Yahweh is the one responsible for the judgment.[25] Moreover, continuing the first-person style, Yahweh uses a kind of didactic question-answer schema which goes beyond the first movement of the speech. Yahweh himself poses the inevitable question "Why?" and then gives his own answer: "because of my house that lies waste, while each of you runs for his own house" (9b). Again there is repetition of the same theme as in v 4: "Is it a time for you yourselves to dwell in your paneled houses, while this house lies waste?" But since the repetition is now set in an elementary form of question-answer, it serves to make even more patently clear the root cause of the people's economic plight. The addition of the "therefore" clause to the basic answer brings out the deeper implications of the economic disasters: the drought is directly linked with the ruined temple and Yahweh is explicitly identified as the divine cause (vv 10–11). A wordplay on the root *ḥrb* further cements together the themes of devastated temple and devastating drought ("my house lies in ruins" [*ḥārēb*]; "I summoned a drought" [*ḥōreb*]).

In sum, the repetition here exactly matches Muilenburg's classic definition of its rhetorical function: it "serves . . . to center the thought . . . , to focus the richness of varied predication upon the poet's varied concern . . . , to give continuity to the writer's thought; the repeated word or phrase is often strategically located, thus providing a clue to the movement and stress of the poem."[26] The repetition, which both forms an envelope structure around the central command to rebuild the temple (v 8) and advances the thought, illustrates the adroitness of Haggai's utilization of the age-old technique of parallelism.

III

Although Steck has given a fascinating form-critical analysis of 1:9–11, he gives scant attention to the question-answer schema except for the correct observation that elements from the prophetic judgment speech have been given the stamp of a disputation.[27] So the highly stylized question-answer schema still needs more precise delineation than has hitherto been the case. A question "why" (*ya'an mê*^{h}) is posed about the frustrating economic conditions and is then followed by an answer prefaced by "because" (*ya'an*), which in turn leads to a statement of consequences introduced by "therefore" (*'al-kēn*). The schema is the glue that holds together the different parts of the speech. The pattern is striking because of its rationalized, didactic cast. It attempts to deal with a pivotal theme in exilic and postexilic Israel: the problem of divine judgment which takes the form of economic disasters. It then correlates this theme with the problem of the destroyed temple.

It would appear that such a seemingly stereotyped schema with its accompanying complex of themes would find analogues in biblical and Near Eastern literature. In fact, it would be most surprising if the data did not cast some light on such a pattern. Steck's analysis points to some of the generic components taken from the prophetic judgment speech, but Haggai's question-answer schema also has significant affinities with other such schemata in ancient Israelite literature and the content embedded in the schema reveals some of the traditio-historical roots of Haggai's message. Haggai appropriates this sort of stylized pattern to deal with the problem of most urgency to his contemporaries—the dire economic straits of the community—but he seeks to resolve the problem by seeing it as a consequence of a far deeper issue: Yahweh's punishment of the people for their refusal to rebuild the ruined sanctuary. We must now attempt to define more precisely any traditional analogues which may have been available for Haggai's use.

Credit belongs to B. Long for providing a most insightful and discriminating examination of question-answer schemata in prophetic literature.[28] Among the various sorts of question-answer patterns, he distinguishes two principal types. The first (which he calls type A) is easily discernible in texts characterized by Deuteronomistic style. 1 Kgs 9:8–9 is typical:

> And this house will become a heap of ruins; every one passing by it will be astonished, and will hiss; and they will say, "Why has the Lord done thus to this land and to this house?" Then they will say, "Because they forsook the Lord their God who brought their fathers out of the land of Egypt, and laid hold on other gods, and worshiped them and served them; therefore the Lord has brought all this evil upon them."

(Note the parallel in 2 Chr 7:21–23; cf. also Deut 29:24–27; Jer 22:8–9.) Long identifies three major elements in this schema: "(1) a *setting* for the question, mentioning those who ask it; (2) the *question,* given as a direct quotation; (3) the *answer*, given as a direct quotation."[29] Although the contexts for the schema are varied, the examples are all found in exilic literature—a fact which Long considers important for the question of *Sitz im Leben*. In Long's view, "The question and answer expresses a peculiar sort of pedagogical historiography which sought to place the destruction in the context of a broken covenant and a realized covenantal curse (Deut 29:20–27)."[30] Long then surmises that the type A question-answer schema is "embedded in the literary style of the deuteronomistic historian or a like group" and also cites some striking Near Eastern parallels drawn from Assyrian historiographical texts.[31]

The second question-answer schema (type B) which Long isolates likewise consists typically of three parts: "(1) a *setting,* mentioning a future time when people will ask; (2) a *question* envisioned and formulated; (3) an *answer* prescribed."[32] He cites the following texts as examples of the basic pattern: Jer 5:19;

13:12–14; 15:1–4; 16:10–13; 23:33; Ezek 21:12; 37:19. In this schema Long finds that "an address of Yahweh to the prophet envisions a question and prescribes an answer."[33] Type B seems to have roots in the practice of consulting a prophet for an oracle and then asking for its significance. From this setting it was drawn into a variety of patterns, one of the most interesting of which being its use in showing the significance of symbolic actions (cf. especially Ezek 21:6–12 [1–7E] and 37:15–28 where the schema is attached to reports of symbolic actions). The type B schema is interwoven with type A in Jer 16:10–13, apparently under Deuteronomistic influence.[34] In fact, to quote Long: "The question and answer schema became a special vehicle for Deuteronomistic theology. Perhaps in light of the literary device of type A, type B was picked up and made to answer the exilic question, 'Why has Israel suffered this catastrophe?' In such cases, a speech pattern originally associated with oracles became a ready tool for scholastic commentary of another sort."[35]

When Haggai's question-answer schema is set over against the two types outlined by Long, it does not fit either category exactly—which no doubt is the reason Long does not even mention it. The differences are quite apparent, but the similarities are not to be overlooked. In type A the pattern is stylized as a third-person narration that envisages a *future* situation when a group or individual asks the question "why?" (*ʿal-māʰ*) about a destroyed site, to which the answer introduced by "because" (*ʿal*) is given. Conversely, the primary distinguishing mark of type B is that it is divine speech addressed to the prophet with the question anticipated and the answer prescribed. Like type A, Haggai's question-answer schema has a "why-because" sequence, though in contrast to type A it has *yaʿan mêʰ* and *yaʿan* for "why-because" and the whole speech is in the form of a first-person Yahweh speech. Like type B, Haggai's schema is divine speech: Yahweh asks "why?" and then answers his own question with a "because. . . ." Whether this question presupposes a prior question addressed to the prophet is hard to say, but it is a possibility despite Steck's contrary contention.[36] Thus Haggai's pattern has elements in common with both type A and B. Of course it is possible that Haggai's schema is so disparate that it cannot be brought into illuminating alignment with Long's two types; perhaps the similarities are only coincidental.

I would suggest, however, that both formal structure and thematic concerns show some significant links between Haggai's schema and these other patterns. The sequence "why-because-therefore" coupled with the situation of disaster is a favorite pattern within exilic and postexilic literature, and thus one might expect some sort of connection. Moreover, the content of Haggai's question-answer schema tightens the relationship and suggests the possibility at least that more is involved than coincidence. First of all, the schema is preceded and followed by the prophet's use of the "futility-curse" (vv 6,9a)—a key motif of Deuteronomic and prophetic preaching as well as an element in Near Eastern treaty language (cf. Deut 28:38–40; Hos 4:10; 5:6; 8:7; 9:12,16; Amos 5:11; Mic 6:14–15).[37] Likewise, Long has argued convincingly for the covenantal ambiance of the type A question-answer schema and its prominence in Deuteronomistic circles.[38] Also, the specific answer in Yahweh's speech invokes the image of the ruined temple, which was a concern of the Deuteronomistic historian and which is dealt with explicitly in one of the prime examples of the type A schema (cf. 1 Kgs 9:8–9). Here, however, the difference is as striking and significant as the similarity: to the Deuteronomistic historian the symbol of the ruined temple is a mute but horrifying witness to the disobedience of the people; the breaking of the covenant has eventuated in the divine curse (cf. 1 Kgs 9:8–9; Deut 29:20–28). But Haggai gives a crucial twist to the problem of the ruined temple: the people's reluctance or even resistance to the rebuilding of the temple is now construed as a new act of disobedience which continues to elicit the divine curses threatened by the Deuteronomic preachers.[39] Nonetheless to Haggai Israel stands before the possibility of the full measure of divine blessing; all she has to do is obey the prophetic—yea, the divine—command to rebuild the fallen temple and thereby experience the fullness of Yahweh's presence and the new era of prosperity (cf. the related oracle in 2:15–19).

It would not seem, therefore, to go beyond the evidence to suggest that Haggai stands in the same tradition that produced important strains within the Deuteronomistic school as well as classical prophets such as Amos and Hosea. He perceives that the same sorts of divine curses that struck preexilic Israel are continuing to affect the postexilic community; he simply lessens their severity and shifts the focus as to what constitutes the people's failure to obey and honor Yahweh. This new act of disobedience is the people's refusal to rebuild Yahweh's house and so to honor him (cf. Hag 1:2,4,9). Haggai employs the conventional structure of a question-answer schema as a pedagogical device to make crystal-clear what the failure of the people is and why they are experiencing the continued curses threatened for covenant breakers.

IV

In conclusion, it is indeed the case that Hag 1:9–11 picks up and reiterates themes already found in 1:4–6, but the repetition serves to intensify and reinforce Haggai's view as to the fundamental cause for the people's plight. His didactic intention is enhanced by the use of a question-answer pattern. So he stands in a long and vital tradition in his attempt to point out the folly of Israel's way and to return her to a course of true devotion to Yahweh. His is also the way of the Deuteronomistic school and the classical prophets. To be sure, he concentrates on the necessity to rebuild the fallen temple as the primary condition for Yahweh to manifest his glory.[40] If he does this to the seeming exclusion of "the great moral teaching" of the classical prophets, we must remember that to Haggai the people's attitude toward the destroyed temple demonstrated their attitude toward Yahweh's honor. For Haggai this was the burning issue in sixth-century Israel. And we must recall that the great classical prophets saw no necessary contradiction between the enactment of justice and righteousness and a temple dedicated to

Yahweh's honor (cf. Isa 2:2ff.; Ezek 40–48). One should not falsely isolate one theme from the other in Israel's prophetic heritage. The pivotal issue for Haggai as well as for Isaiah or Ezekiel was the honor of Yahweh—and this above all else is what unites Israel's prophets. Haggai may indeed be a "minor prophet," but he deserves better treatment than he often has received by critics who fail to see clearly his devotion to Yahweh's honor and his concern to bring traditional genres and themes to bear on the needs of his own generation.

NOTES

1. C. Stuhlmueller, *The Jerome Biblical Commentary* (Englewood Cliffs, NJ: Prentice-Hall, 1968): 387. Of course there are noteworthy exceptions. Cf., e.g., H. W. Wolff, *Haggai* (Neukirchen: Buchhandlung der Erziehungsverein, 1951); P. R. Ackroyd's several studies of Haggai: "Studies in the Book of Haggai," *JJS* 2 (1951): 166ff.; 3 (1952): 1ff.; the relevant portions of his book, *Exile and Restoration* (Philadelphia: Fortress, 1968); and his interpretation of Haggai in *Peake's Bible Commentary* (London: T. Nelson, 1962): 643–44. See also the exemplary studies by W. A. M. Beuken, K. Koch, and O. H. Steck which are discussed extensively below.
2. Cf. again Stuhlmueller ([N 1]: 388): "He did not demand any great interior moral reform, but merely the rebuilding of a place of worship. . . ."
3. P. R. Ackroyd, *Book List 1976* (London: The Society for Old Testament Study): 49.
4. F. Peter argues that the term *habbayit* refers here to the temple ("Zu Haggai 1:9," *TZ* 7 [1951]: 150). His arguments are not compelling, however, as pointed out by W. A. M. Beuken (*Haggai-Sacharja 1–8* [Studia semitica neerlandica 10; Assen: Van Gorcum, 1967]: 187 n. 1).
5. O. Eissfeldt's assessment is representative of this view: ". . . i, 1–11, does not seem to be in order. Vv. 5–11 give the impression of being overloaded, for vv. 5–6 provide a parallel to 7 + 9–11. Usually this is eased by deletion (of v. 7 or 7b only) and by transposition (v. 8 or v. 7a + 8 after v. 11), but the possibility must be considered that we have here the combination of parts of two small collections, namely of a memorial to Haggai . . . and of a loose collection of his sayings" (*The Old Testament: An Introduction* [New York: Harper and Row, 1965]: 428).
6. There is no need to rehearse the various proposals; see the various introductions and above all the thorough review of the possibilities in O. H. Steck, "Zu Haggai 1:2–11," *ZAW* 83 (1971): 356–79, esp. 358 n. 11.
7. Beuken (N 4): 184ff.
8. H. W. Wolff, *Hosea* (Philadelphia: Fortress, 1974): 96.
9. Beuken (N 4): 204f.
10. Beuken (N 4): 188.
11. Beuken (N 4): 200ff.
12. K. Koch, "Haggais unreines Volk," *ZAW* 79 (1967): 52–66.
13. Koch (N 12): 56. Here he explicitly rejects the form-critical approach that would atomize the text: "Hinter v. 2–8 mehrere ursprünglich selbständige Einzelsprüche zu vermuten . . . besteht kein Anlass" (58).
14. Koch (N 12): 58. His suggestion as to the function of 1:9–11 in the older speech is found on the same page, n. 16a.
15. Steck (N 6): 355ff.
16. Steck (N 6): 362ff., esp. 368 and n. 39.
17. Steck (N 6): 368ff., esp. 371.
18. Steck (N 6): 372ff.
19. Steck (N 6): 372; also see n. 51 on the same page.
20. Steck (N 6): 370.
21. Here Steck ([N 6]: 370 n. 46) follows the view of Peter (N 4); the more natural translation is "brought it home," i.e., *habbayit* is used adverbially and generally; there is no necessary reference to the temple *per se*. No indictment of cultic sacrifice at the temple site seems to be in view here.
22. Notably Steck, who argues that one must deal seriously with the redactional problems ([N 6]: 359); even he, however, puts his main efforts into the discovery of an earlier setting for 1:9–11 in

which it was directed to a different audience (370ff.). He deals only peripherally with the question of why the redactor chose to obscure the identity of the original audience by dropping the original conclusion and fusing the remaining fragment to the preceding unit: "Ob aus Unkenntnis oder mit Absicht, ist schwer zu sagen. Dass der Redaktor so verfährt, hängt jedenfalls damit zusammen, dass sich Haggai nach ihm nur an eine einzige Bevölkerungsgruppe wendet, die heimgekehrte Gola . . ." (370 n. 51).

23. Steck (N 6): 37; cf. also Beuken (N 4): 189.

24. This generic label is proposed by D. R. Hillers in his *Treaty-Curses and the Old Testament Prophets* (Rome: Pontifical Biblical Institute, 1964): 28ff. See also the discussion in Beuken ([N 4]: 190ff.) and Steck ([N 6]: 364f. and 378, *addendum* to n. 32). The latter argues that one must differentiate between vv 6 and 9–11 on the degree of affinity each text has to the curse catalogs; he succeeds in showing some of the differences in formulation, severity in tone, and particular application to Israel. However, he still holds to the view that Haggai's words are rooted in the curse tradition, whatever the changes that the prophet has made.

25. See the nicely nuanced discussion of this theme in Steck (N 6): 371 and 378 (*addendum* to n. 32).

26. J. Muilenburg, "A Study in Hebrew Rhetoric: Repetition and Style" in *Congress Volume* (VTSup 1 [1953]): 99.

27. Steck (N 6): 369 n. 43, 371f. and nn. 49 and 50 (in the latter note he cites Mal 2:10–16 as a generic parallel, but see my discussion below on question-answer patterns).

28. B. O. Long, "Two Question and Answer Schemata in the Prophets," *JBL* 90 (1971): 129–39.

29. Long (N 28): 130.

30. Long (N 28): 131.

31. Long (N 28): 131ff.

32. Long (N 28): 134.

33. Long (N 28): 134.

34. Long (N 28): 137.

35. Long (N 28): 138.

36. Steck (N 6): 371; cf. Gowan's interesting study of the word *ya'an,* which appears to be a technical term used in the process of oracle-giving (D. E. Gowan, "The use of *ya'an* in Biblical Hebrew," *VT* 21 [1971]: 168–85, esp. 184f.).

37. Cf. the discussion in Beuken ([N 4]: 190ff.) and Steck ([N 6]: 364ff.).

38. Long (N 28): 133ff.

39. Cf. also Beuken (N 4): 197. See n. 24 above for Steck's important discussion of the use of the curse tradition in Haggai, though I would question whether there is as sharp a differentiation between 1:6 and 1:9ff. in their dependence on the curse catalogs as he asserts.

40. Cf. also the related oracle in 2:15ff. In these passages Haggai shows clearly his deep roots in the mythological conceptions connected with the Jerusalem temple (cf. Psalms 46,48,65,132; Ezekiel 47; etc.).

15

THEY LIVED IN TENTS

D. J. WISEMAN

It would seem appropriate, in a volume to honor the sixty-fifth birthday of an academic colleague, to remind him that, according to some ancient Semitic thought, such an age is but midway between "maturity" and "long life."[1] It is then but a stage on life's journey. Since Dr. LaSor has long been concerned with the study of the Old Testament and its relationship with ancient Near Eastern languages and literatures, this brief contribution to the discussion of a single aspect of the "nomadism" reflected in the patriarchal narratives is offered to him as a friendly tribute *ana ša'āl šulmišu*.

Among current criticisms of a historical Abraham an argument is being adduced to indicate that the Genesis narratives cannot have originated earlier than the first millennium B.C. As put forward by J. Van Seters, "It is a curious fact that tents are not mentioned in the Mari archives at all and only rarely in other second millennium sources. This is in contrast to the tent encampments of the bedouin, which are a most distinctive feature by the mid-first millennium B.C."[2] Such a conclusion can only be reached by consideration of evidence selected on the a priori basis that the biblical narratives of any pre-Israelite settlement in the land originate no earlier than the Exile.[3] The argument is, moreover, associated with, and confused by, a concept of patriarchal nomadism similar to that known from the Mari texts which may well be only one possible interpretation of both the Genesis and extra-biblical sources and legitimately contradicted.[4] It is the intention of this brief essay to consider whether tents are, in fact, more indicative of first- than second-millennium life in the ancient Near East on the basis of extant textual evidence.

The traditional view of the patriarchs is clearly that of a pre-settlement "tent-dweller," for "when Abraham made his home in the promised land, like a stranger in a foreign country, he lived in tents as did Isaac and Jacob" (Heb 11:9 *NIV*). It is observed that in the Genesis narrative no reference is made to his having, or using, tents on the journey from Ur[5] via Harran to Canaan. Silence is of itself no argument against such use, as it is a characteristic of ancient texts to mention the mode of dwelling only in exceptional, and usually legal, circumstances. Tents might not be necessary on a staged journey along a regular trade route where villages or other habitations normally marked the way.[6] At larger towns or settlements, inns or other places of hospitality were readily available to passing strangers, whether as individuals or as a group.[7] It is noteworthy that the first mention of tents was when Abraham moved outside normally inhabited areas. This was when at the sanctuary at Moreh near Canaanite Shechem he was told by God that he would be given the land where he now was encamped. Abraham built an altar to mark this theophany and the promise of land-tenure (Gen 12:7). It is not impossible that at this time he pitched his tent there (cf. Gen 33:18), for this was his normal action when he moved further into the hill-country between Bethel and Ai and "pitched his tent . . . and there built an [other] altar to the Lord" (Gen 12:8). The act of erecting a tent and an altar in association at a sacred site may be symbolic of assuming territorial possession or at least of the adoption of the territory for the tribe, for these same acts are noted with some emphasis as "the place where his tent had been at the beginning and where he had made an altar at the first . . . and had called on the name of the Lord" (Gen 13:3–4).

Tents are only mentioned again when Abraham was forced to move out from the Bethel area because the neighboring grazing was insufficient for the large herds of cattle now owned by Abraham and Lot and, probably, because of the stated and associated local opposition (13:5–7). On parting, Lot first stayed near settlements in the Jordan valley before moving his tent near Sodom (13:12) pending taking up accommodation in a house in town there (19:2–3). Meanwhile, Abraham once again moved his tent (*'āhal*)[8] in order to stay and build an altar to the Lord at the sacred site[9] at Mamre near Hebron, again perhaps as a mark of, or associated with, territorial possession (13:18). It was at this same "tent-site" that a further theophany occurred and Abraham received the three "strangers" and the promise of a son and heir on whom any continued possession of the promised land would depend. It was appropriately to this same "tent-site" that Isaac brought his bride Rachel (24:67).[10]

A move further south to the Beersheba area (Gen 22:19) led to the foundation of a new "sacred-site" marked by a covenant affirmation, a symbolic "tamarisk" tree, and served by newly opened wells. This southernmost occupation of territory was to become the typical settlement marking the boundaries of the land "from Dan to Beersheba." Abraham's son Isaac returned to this same "tent-site" after camping in the valley of Gerar as a "foreigner" among the Philistines. Here he is said to have pitched his tent, (re)built the altar and called on the name of the Lord (26:17,25). It may well be that it had been a "tent-site" of Abraham also, significantly called "the gate of their enemies," on the trade route to Egypt. This action by Isaac to reaffirm occupation of land constitutes the only occasion when it is specifically noted that Isaac was a tent-dweller. His son Jacob is described as one "who lived a settled life and stayed among the tents," which here may begin to encompass the use of *'ōhel* as 'settlement, home,' in contradistinction to Esau who was a man of the open country (Gen 25:27).[11] The only occasion in Jacob's life when "nomadic" tents (and camels) are clearly mentioned was during his flight from Laban along the direct desert route normally taken by semi-nomads through Gilead east of Jordan (Gen 31:25,33–34). Jacob certainly built himself a house near Paddan-Aram at Succoth (33:17).[12] A separate untimed incident in his life tells how he also camped near Shechem and bought the land on which his tent had been pitched and on which he too (re)built an altar named or dedicated to "El—the God of Israel" (Gen 33:18).[13] After Rachel's death he moved his tent to the vicinity of the tower of Edar near Hebron. If this were near Arad (as Gen 35:21 LXX) it would mark the eastern border of later Judah.

This picture of the patriarchs is hardly one of even the "enclosed nomadism"[14] characteristic of the Mari documents or of the Middle Bronze Age or of the wider ranging nomadism of the first-century Arameans. The references to tents are confined to a limited period, yet to widely dispersed sacred sites which might be interpreted as denoting the marking of land-tenure. They do not preclude an association with the common but limited transhumance undertaken by town or village communities moving into tents for the summer pasturage of cattle or sheep,[15] for special religious festivals[16] or for work at harvest time.[17]

As would be expected, references to tents increase in the accounts of the Exodus wanderings before Israel entered their "promised" land, i.e., at the latest, in the thirteenth century B.C. Here it is again noteworthy that they were pitched around, or close by, the "Tent-Shrine" (Num 1:52–53) which, even if fashioned according to contemporary Egyptian precedents,[18] might reflect a known earlier tribal or patriarchal custom. The use of tents by such nomadic groups as the Midianites (Judg 6:5; Hab 3:7) or Qedar could be instances of reference to a mode of dwelling in special circumstances, for normally such designation would not be necessary. There is little support in the Old Testament for a "nomadic" or "desert" ideal as regards habitation. Certainly the later Rechabites were praised for their spiritual constancy rather than for the fact that they lived in tents rather than in houses, or for their abstinence from wine (not the beverage of nomads) or from agriculture (Jer 35:6–10).[19]

Against this background, extra-biblical evidence for tent-dwelling now needs to be examined. In a tale of tranquility depicted in a letter from Šulgi of Ur to Puruš-Numušda of Susa (Elam), c. 2050 B.C., he says that "a man can go wherever he wishes . . . he has filled the vast steppe . . . you set up my tent (*kuštaria*) . . . workers and laborers pass their time in the fields. . . ."[20] This bilingual text in syllabic Sumerian and Babylonian is to be dated at the latest to the Middle Babylonian period, though the editor argues plausibly for Hammurapi (c. 1700 B.C.) because of the association with literary texts and the date of the copies.[21] The Sumerian word for tent (ZA.LAM.GAR)[22] is used also for, or in association with, other terms for 'encampment' in general.[23] Edzard has shown that in the Old Babylonian texts from Mari *nawûm* denotes not merely the 'steppe' outside towns and villages but also the settlements of the nomads there.[24] While no specification is given to these as tented or otherwise, other texts from the same period designate a number of place names as "tented."[25] These are presumably semi-nomad settlements.

Second-millennium references to tents are predictably primarily to nomads. Contrary to Van Seters and Thompson, who argue against any "Amorite" background to patriarchal customs,[26] the Babylonian tradition names the ancestors of the Assyrians as "17 kings who lived in tents" (*āšibūtu kultari*), presumably at or near the sacred site of Assur which later became the national capital. This text dates back to the time of Šamši-Adad I, c. 1750 B.C.[27] The "Myth of Martu" (Amurrum) refers to the Amorite as a "tent-dweller [buffeted?] by wind and rain," as "one who does not know [var. build] a house." This reference occurs in one of only twenty non-administrative texts to mention the Amorites dated in the Ur III—early Isin-Larsa periods, i.e., c. 2000–1800 B.C.[28] There is also evidence for early "Aramean" nomadic groups such as the *Aḫlamu Ar(a)māya* already in the deserts near the Persian Gulf in the fourteenth century B.C.,[29] and as a contingent in the Syrian (Ḫatti) army opposing Shalmaneser I (1274–45 B.C.)[30] or interrupting messengers from Babylonia to Syria north of Hit.[31] Middle Babylonian administrative texts tell of tent-canopies (MB *zaratu;* MA *zarutu*) made of leather or cloth,[32] both available, whether the latter was woven from sheep's wool or goats' hair, in the Middle Euphrates area from at least 2300 B.C. onward.[33]

Egyptian texts (dated before c. 1800 B.C.[34]) of the "Tale of Sinuhe" tell of this Egyptian official of the Middle Kingdom in exile in Asia c. 1960–1928 who, challenged in his camp, responded by doing to a man of Retenu what the latter had planned to do to him: "I took what was in his tent and stripped his camp."[35] Similarly, Rameses III (c. 1192–1161 B.C.) records, "I devastated Se'ir (Edom) among the nomad tribes. I pillaged their tents (*'hr*), their people, their property and their cattle as well, . . . I carried off into captivity."[36]

The references to tents in the first millennium are fewer than the thirty or more cited for the second millennium. In the latter period, of some thirteen extant references to tents or tent-dwellers (*āšib kultari*) two are late references to the earlier Aḫlamu[37] or Amurru,[38] three to a king or queen of the Arabs,[39] only five to the Arameans or Sutê,[40] one to a royal tent taken as booty from Sardurri of Urarṭu[41] and one in which the ideogram É.EDIN (*bīt ṣēri*) 'house of the steppe' is glossed as 'tent.'[42] It is therefore suggested that the use of a supposed more frequent reference to "tents" in the mid-first millennium B.C. cannot be made a support for Van Seters' main thesis that "the few nomadic details that occur in the stories, such as the references to camels and tents, the patriarchs' presence and movements primarily in the Negeb, and their contact and political agreement with the established 'Philistines' in the border region, all point strongly to the social and political circumstances of the mid-first millennium B.C."[43] Nor would it be academically appropriate to dismiss the second-millennium evidence for the use of tents as "apologetics," as is done of the evidence for camels in the same period.[44]

NOTES

1. O. R. Gurney and P. Hulin, *The Sultantepe Tablets* 2 (London: The British Institute of Archaeology at Ankara, 1964): 400:46; i.e., between 60 GAL *bēlūtu* 'supreme power' and 70 U$_4$.MEŠ GÌD.DA.MEŠ 'long days'; cf. the Hebrew concept of 60 for 'attaining old age' and 70 'for the hoary head' (*Pirqê 'Abôt* 5.24).

In addition to the abbreviations employed in this volume, the following are used in this article:

CT *Cuneiform Texts from Babylonian Tablets, etc. in the British Museum* (London: Harrison & Sons, 1896ff.)

KAH *Keilschrifttexte aus Assur Historischen Inhalts* (ed. O. Schroeder; Leipzig: J. C. Hinrichs, 1911)

MSL *Materialen zum sumerischen Lexikon* (Rome: Pontifical Biblical Institute).

R *The Cuneiform Inscriptions of Western Asia* (ed. H. C. Rawlinson; London: R. E. Bowler, 1861ff.)

TLB *Tabulae Cuneiformae a F. M. Th. de Liagre Böhl Collectae* (Leiden: Nederlandsch Instituut voor het Nabije Oosten, 1957)

2. J. Van Seters, *Abraham in History and Tradition* (New Haven: Yale University, 1975): 14.
3. As also by T. L. Thompson, *The Historicity of the Patriarchal Narratives* (Berlin: Walter de Gruyter, 1974): 315–30.
4. For a recent reappraisal of nomadism in the second millennium see now M. B. Rowton, "Dimorphic Structure and the Problem of the 'Apirû-'Ibrim," *JNES* 35 (1976): 13–20; cf. "Enclosed Nomadism," *JESHO* 17 (1968): 1–30.
5. Irrespective of the location of Ur (of the Kasdim); though the revival of the suggestion that this was a northern site by C. H. Gordon ("Abraham and the Merchants of Ura," *JNES* 17 [1958]: 28–31) is adequately answered by H. W. F. Saggs ("Ur of the Chaldees, A Problem of Identification," *Iraq* 22 [1960]: 200–09) in favor of the S. Mesopotamian site.
6. E.g., W. W. Hallo, "The Road to Emar," *JCS* 18 (1964): 63,84. (The argument is not changed whether the stages were those of a caravan or army.) See now the article by B. J. Beitzel in this volume.
7. D. J. Wiseman, "Rahab of Jericho," *Tyndale House Bulletin* 14 (1964): 8–11.
8. Note the rare use of this denominative form in Gen 13:12,18; cf. Isa 13:20.
9. The common tamarisk or 'terebinth tree' (*'ēlā^h^*), like the oak (*'allôn*), was condemned as a place of worship (Hos 4:13; Isa 6:13). This may not have necessarily been because of association with Canaanite practices or have been occasioned by the similarity of name with *'ēl* or a holy place (cf. Akk. *ellu*) marked by a sworn oath (*'ālā^h^*).
10. Cf. Gen 18:1–2,6,9–10 for allusions to the women's section of the tent.
11. Heb. *'ōhel*; Ug. *ahl* is compared with Akk. *ālu* (*AHW*, 39a) which is used of a group of dwellings of any type, whether city, village, manor or estate (*CAD* A/1, 378–89; to be distinguished from *a'lu* 'confederation, amphictyony' [p. 374] = Syr. *iahlā,* Ar. *ahl* 'people').
12. The 'booths' (*sukkôt*) were temporary shelters for his cattle and not necessarily a mark of incipient sedentarization.
13. Shechem is described as *'îr* which, usually a walled settlement, town or village of any size or part thereof, is the equivalent of Akk. *ālu*. It is possible that the *šālēm* of Gen 33:18, usually taken as 'safely,' could denote a mutual agreement to take up land (cf. Akk. *šulmu* and its synonym *šulummû*).
14. Rowton, "Nomadism" (N 4).
15. Gen 4:20 considers Jabel "the ancestor of herdsmen who live in tents"; cf. Cant 1:8; Isa 38:12.
16. E.g., A. Goetze, *The Hittite Ritual of Tunnawi* (AOS 14; New Haven: American Oriental Society, 1938): 8 (I 40; fourteenth-twelfth century B.C.).
17. As Noah during viticulture (Gen 9:21) and armies during campaigns.
18. K. A. Kitchen, "Some Egyptian Background to the Old Testament," *Tyndale House Bulletin* 5–6 (1960): 7–11.
19. Contra R. de Vaux, *Ancient Israel* (London: Darton, Longman & Todd, 1961): 14f.; the prohibition against possessing vineyards is inappropriate for full nomads. M. V. Fox, "Jeremiah 2:2 and the 'Desert Ideal,'" *CBQ* 34 (1973): 441–50.
20. D. O. Edzard, "Deux lettres royales d'Ur III en Sumérien ≪syllabique≫ et pourvu d'une traduction accadienne" in *Textes littéraires de Suse* (ed. R. Labat; Paris: Geuthner, 1974): I i 22.
21. Edzard (N 20): 11. The Sumerian text reads ZA.LA.AM <GÀR MAŠ>.KÁN.BI.DA UM.MA.NI IN.GAR.GAR.

22. Given its Old Babylonian equivalent (= [*ku*]-*uš-ta-ru-um*) in R. Hallock and B. Landsberger, "Old Babylonian Grammatical Texts" (*MSL* 4; Rome: Pontifical Biblical Institute, 1956): xi.19′.
23. Edzard (N 20): 18. Sumerian MAŠ.KÁN may be a loanword from Semitic *maškān*. Edzard ([N 20]: 26) argues that it is so used in the course of the sedentarization of nomads in this text and cites the element in second-millennium place names of the type Maškan-Šapir, Maškan-abi. Cf. MAŠ.GÁN = *ašāšu* used of encampment and temporary shelters as Heb. *miškān* in relation to the Tabernacle (Exod 25:9; 26:7–8).
24. D. O. Edzard, "Altbabylonisch *nawûm*," *ZA* 53 (1959): 170; "Mari und Aramäer," *ZA* 56 (1964): 146; *Die zweite 'Zwischenzeit' Babyloniens* (Wiesbaden: O. Harrassowitz, 1957): 168; J.-R. Kupper, *Les nomades en Mésopotamie au temps des rois de Mari* (Paris: Société d'Edition "Les Belles Lettres," 1957): 12 n. 6.
25. E.g., *ina Kuštarātim* (*CT* 8 44a 10); URU.KI *Kuštaratum* (*TLB* I 63:14), *Kuštari*[KI] (R. Harris, "The Archive of the Sin Temple in Khafajah (Tutub)," *JCS* 9 [1955]: 39, 66 no. 26.8; 103 no. 101.4).
26. Thompson (N 3): 67–88; Van Seters (N 2): 23–26.
27. F. R. Kraus, *Könige, die in Zelten wohnten* (Amsterdam: Noord-Hollandsche Uitg. Mij., 1965).
28. Cited by G. Buccellati, *The Amorites of the Ur III Period* (Naples: Istituto Orientale di Napoli, 1966): 92.
29. In a Kassite letter (P. B. Cornwall, "Two Letters from Dilmun," *JCS* 6 [1952]: 137–45). *Aḫlamu* (var. *āramu*?) and *Ara/i/mū*, like the latter *Arabu*, may, like *'Apiru/Ḫabiru*, simply be a general designation for a person of no fixed abode (cf. W. F. Albright, "Syria, the Philistines and Phoenicia" in *CAH* II/2, 530).
30. J. M. Munn-Rankin, "Assyrian Military Power 1300–1200 B.C." in *CAH* II/2, 281.
31. Munn-Rankin (N 30): 283.
32. A. Goetze, Review of J. Friedrich, *Hethitisches Wörterbuch, JCS* 22 (1968): 24; cf. *CAD* Z, 66 (sub *zaratu*) for references.
33. As at Ebla (Tell Mardīḫ); see G. Pettinato, "Testi cuneiformi del 3. millennio in paleo-cananeo," *Or* 44 (1975): 370ff.
34. For the latest date see Thompson (N 3): 109.
35. "Sinuhe," 145 (cf. *ANET*², 20b).
36. As *ANET*², 262a.
37. J. A. Craig, *Assyrian and Babylonian Religious Texts* 1 (Leipzig: J. C. Hinrichs, 1895): 81:5.
38. V *R* 35,29 (Cyrus; "the kings of Amurru-territory who live in tents.").
39. Nūr-Adad of Tēma' (*KAH* 2 84:71); Haza'el (*OIP* 2, 92,24).
40. C. J. Gadd, "Inscribed Prisms of Sargon II from Nimrud," *Iraq* 16 (1954): 192 (vii, 58); R. Borger, *Die Inschriften Asarhaddons Königs von Assyrien* (Graz: R. Borger, 1956): Ep. 18 A v 15; D. J. Wiseman, "A Late Babylonian Tribute List?" *BSOAS* 30 (1967): 496, lines 12–13; Marduk-apla-iddina II (H. Winckler, *Die Keilschrifttexte Sargons* [Leipzig: 1889]: 34,129); Marduk-balassu-iqbi (I *R* 31 iv 44).
41. P. Rost, *Die Keilinschrifttexte Tiglat-Pilesers III* (Leipzig: E. Pfeiffer, 1893): 14,71.
42. Assurbanipal 82 viii:10; for Šamši-Adad V, see I *R* 31 iv 44; Sennacherib in his Annals (*OIP*) 58,23; 67:11 refers to the tents of Aramean tribes. The royal expedition tents of Sennacherib and of Assurbanipal are the only tents portrayed on Assyrian bas-reliefs.
43. Van Seters (N 2): 121.
44. Van Seters (N 2): 17 n. 15. This dismissal of the evidence for the presence of camels in the second millennium B.C. as a "case of special pleading for apologetic reasons and not a judgment of historical probability" is not worthy of a serious historian. He rightly quotes R. de Vaux (*Histoire ancienne d'Israël* [Paris: Lecoffre, 1971–73]: 216) against the entirely unconvincing view that the reference to camels could be glosses replacing earlier mention of donkeys, but fails to note the same author (*Histoire:* 215 n. 10) among those (including J. A. Thompson, K. A. Kitchen) who admit the possibility that the patriarchs had a limited number of camels which were already domesticated, but only infrequently employed, in the second millennium B.C.

16

A NEW LOOK AT THREE OLD TESTAMENT ROOTS FOR "SIN"

RONALD YOUNGBLOOD

> In all of the laments and reproaches made by our seers and prophets, one misses any mention of "sin," a word which used to be a veritable watchword of prophets. It was a word once in everyone's mind, but now rarely if ever heard. Does that mean that no sin is involved in all our troubles—sin with an "I" in the middle? Is no one any longer guilty of anything? Guilty perhaps of a sin that could be repented and repaired or atoned for? Is it only that someone may be stupid or sick or criminal—or asleep? Wrong things are being done, we know; tares are being sown in the wheat field at night. But is no one responsible, no one answerable for these acts? Anxiety and depression we all acknowledge, and even vague guilt feelings; but has no one committed any sins?
>
> Where, indeed, did sin go? What became of it?[1]

Karl Menninger's pointed questions are surely relevant to our modern situation, as his recent volume on the subject of sin details *in extenso*. Apart from scattered voices heard here and there, analysts of every stripe place the blame for our current moral and spiritual crisis on ignorance, environment, social inequities and the like—in short, on factors either beyond or stubbornly resistant to human control. Rarely do we hear anyone talking about sin as the root cause of the spiritual and moral defection that we see all about us. If the world is going to hell in a hand-basket, people do not seem to know why.

Although modern "seers and prophets" may be looking in the wrong places for reasons that will serve to explain man's inhumanity to man (and to God, if theism be granted!), no blinders restricted the peripheral vision of their divinely ordained Old Testament counterparts. The prophets and seers of ancient Israel, inspired by the God who had created and called them, told it like it was. For them, sin was sin—in all of its horrible diversity—and they developed a rich and varied vocabulary to describe its permutations.[2]

Among the numerous Hebrew roots for "sin" and its synonyms, three are generally recognized as being the most important:[3] *ḥṭ'*, with its verbal form, *ḥāṭā'*, occurring 237 times (in four stems) and its various nominal forms 354 times (*ḥattā't*, 293; *ḥēṭ'*, 33; *ḥaṭṭā'*, 18; *ḥăṭā'āh*, 8; *ḥaṭṭā'āh*, 2), a total of 591; *'wy*, with its verbal form, *'āwāh*, occurring 17 times (in four stems) and its nominal form, *'āwôn*, 230 times, a total of 247; and *pš'*, with its verbal form, *pāša'*, occurring 41 times (in two stems) and its nominal form, *peša'*, 93 times, a total of 134.

Statistics alone, of course, do not tell the whole story. Although it is universally acknowledged that each of the three roots has a slightly different nuance (otherwise three distinct roots would be unnecessary!), it has been observed that two or even all three roots are often "used together in such a way as to appear synonymous."[4] Indeed, they are found together, sometimes in a single verse or pair of verses, in all three sections of the Hebrew canon: *tôrāh* (e.g., Exod 34:7), *nebî'îm* (e.g., Isa 59:12; Ezek 21:29 [24E]; Mic 7:18–19), and *ketûbîm* (e.g., Ps 51:3–4 [1–2E]; Job 13:23).

In what, however, does their "synonymous" nature reside? Is it merely that all three have to do, in a vague sort of way, with sin in general? Or is there a more specific aspect of sin—or, perhaps better, a sin-related motif or metaphor—around which all three roots tend to gather?

A partial answer to these questions has already been provided by such writers as Erich Fromm, who reminds us that *ḥṭ'* means basically 'miss the road' and that *'wy* means basically 'err from the road.'[5] We would emphasize from the outset that the difference between "missing" and "erring from" is not that the first is passive (as some have tended to suggest[6]) and the second active. As its Greek equivalent, *hamartanō/hamartia,* is "any departure from the way of righteousness"[7] and is therefore premeditated disobedience, so also *ḥṭ'* is "more than ignorance or error, more than erroneous *thought;* it is wrong action, the will applied to a wrong aim."[8]

The basic meaning of *pš'* is usually said to be 'transgress, rebel,' and I do not wish to deny the helpfulness of that insight. I shall attempt to demonstrate, however, that *pš'* is also frequently used in contexts in which the advisability of walking on the right road and/or the folly of walking on the wrong road are prominent. In other words, I hope to show that the transgression/rebellion inherent in *pš'* is often that of willful "deviation from" the road of godly living, and that *pš'* therefore takes its place alongside *ḥṭ'* and *'wy* as a root intimately associated with the idea of walking along a road other than the one God wants us to use.

The imagery of "walking," "roads," "ways" and the like is exceedingly common in Scripture. Enoch "walked with God" (Gen 5:22), in contrast to his immediate ancestors and descendants, who merely "lived" (see, e.g., 5:19,26). Noah, too, "walked with God" (6:9), in contrast to all other men of his generation, all of whom had "corrupted their way" (6:12). Characteristic of the book of Proverbs are expressions such as "paths of justice" (2:8), "all your ways" (3:6), "the way of wisdom" (4:11), "the path of the wicked" (4:14), "walk in the way of righteousness" (8:20), "the path of the upright" (15:19), "a way which seems right" (16:25), and so forth; additional examples could easily be adduced.

The New Testament continues the same motif in numerous formulations. In the Sermon on the Mount, Jesus says that "the way is easy, that leads to destruction," but "the way is hard, that leads to life" (Matt 7:13–14). Paul in Colossians utilizes the verb "walk" in metaphorical fashion at least once in each chapter (1:10; 2:6; 3:7; 4:5). The early church used "the Way" as a technical term for faith in Christ and his teachings (Acts 9:2; 19:9, 23; 22:4; 24:14, 22; see also 16:17; 18:25–26). Again, further examples could be added without difficulty.

So the witness of Scripture from beginning to end is that there are two ways: the way of godliness, and the way of sin. On the one hand, living according to God's law leads one along the pathway of godliness; on the other, rebelling against God's law is the same as walking along the road of sin. "Everyone who commits sin commits lawlessness as well; in fact, sin *is* lawlessness" (1 John 3:4; my translation). And the Old Testament triad of words for sin—*ḥṭ'*, *'wy* and *pš'*—underscores the seriousness of forsaking God's ways for lesser options.

That one of the primary meanings of *ḥṭ'* (the most common Old Testament word for "sin") is 'miss the road' can be demonstrated by noting the many passages in which it occurs in context with *hālak* 'walk'; *derek* 'way'; *sûr* 'turn aside'; *šûb* 'turn to/from'; *'ōraḥ* 'path'; and so on. Classic passages include Prov 19:2b: "He who makes haste with his feet *misses* his *way*"; 8:32b,36a: "Happy are those who keep my *ways* . . . but he who *misses* me injures himself"; Ps 25:8b: "(The Lord) instructs *sinners* in the (right/good) *way*" (see also 1 Sam 12:23; 2 Chr 6:27); Neh 9:29: "Thou didst warn them in order to *turn* them back *to* thy law. Yet they . . . *sinned* against thy ordinances." Passages that connect *ḥṭ'* 'sinning' with "walking" are 1 Kgs 15:3,26,34; 16:2,19,26,31; 22:53 [52E]; 2 Kgs 10:31; 13:2,6,11; 17:7–8,21–22; Ps 1:1; 26:9,11; Prov 1:10,15; 13:20–21; Isa 33:14–15; 42:24; Jer 5:23,25; 44:23; Ezek 16:47,51; Mic 6:7–8,13,16; Zeph 1:17. Other passages that portray "sinning" in association with "way" are Num 22:32,34; Deut 9:16; 1 Kgs 13:33–34; 15:26,34; 16:2,19,26; 22:53[52E]; 2 Chr 7:14; Ps 1:5–6; 51:15[13E]; Prov 1:10,15; 5:21–22; Isa 42:24; 58:1–2; 64:4[5E]; Jer 2:35–36; 3:21,25; 36:3; Lam 3:39–40; Ezek 3:19,21; 16:47,51; 28:15–16; Hos 4:8–9; 9:7–9. Passages in which "sinning" is found in context with "turning aside" are Deut 9:16; 1 Sam 12:19–21,23; 1 Kgs 15:3,5; 2 Kgs 3:3; 10:29,31; 13:2,6,11; 14:24; 15:9,18,24,28; 17:21–22; Isa 31:6–7; Jer 5:23,25; Dan 9:5,11. Other passages that place "sinning" in context with "turning to/from" are Num 22:34; 32:14–15; 1 Kgs 8:47–48; 13:33–34; 2 Chr 6:24–26; 7:14; Neh 9:35,37; Ps 51:15[13E]; Isa 1:27–28; 31:6–7; Jer 36:3; Lam 1:8; 3:39–40; Dan 9:13,16; Hos 8:13. Two passages that use "sinning" in association with "path" are Ps 119:9,11 and Prov 10:16–17.

Needless to say, not all of these examples will prove equally convincing to everyone with respect to the main point at issue. But their cumulative weight is impressive, especially when an extended passage like the following is taken into consideration: "... sinned ... turn to ... sin ... sinned ... turn from ... sin ... way ... walk ..." (1 Kgs 8:33–36).

That one of the primary meanings of *'wy* (the nominal form of which is conventionally translated as 'iniquity') is 'err from the road' can be demonstrated by observing the large number of passages in which it is found in context with 'way,' 'turn to/from,' 'walk,' 'turn aside,' and so forth. As we did in the case of *ḥṭ'*, we cite here a few classic passages, including Lam 3:9: "He has blocked my *ways* ... , he has *made* my *paths crooked*" (root *'wy*); 2 Sam 22:22a,24b: "I have kept the *ways* of the Lord, ... I kept myself from *iniquity*" (see also 22:23b: "From his statutes I did not *turn aside*"; cf. Ps 18:22,24[21,23E]); Prov 16:6–7a: "... *iniquity* is atoned for, ... a man *turns aside* from evil ... a man's *ways* please the Lord ..."; Isa 57:17a,c: "Because of the *iniquity* of his covetousness I was angry, ... but he *walked* on, *backsliding* (root *šwb*) in the *way* of his own heart" (see also Jer 14:7); Jer 14:10: "They have loved to *wander* (root *nw'*) thus, they have not restrained their feet; ... he will remember their *iniquity* and punish their *sins*." Other passages that associate "erring/iniquity" with "way" are Ps 25:8–12; Prov 5:21–22; Isa 30:11,13; 53:5–6; Jer 3:21–22; 16:17–18; Ezek 16:47,49; 28:15; 36:31; Hos 4:8–9; 9:7–9; with "turn to/from": 1 Kgs 8:47–48 (see 2 Chr 6:37–38); Jer 3:12–13,21–22; 11:10; 36:3; Ezek 14:6–7; Dan 9:13,16; Hos 8:13; 14:2–3[1–2E]; Mal 2:6; with "walk": Lev 26:40–41; Ps 89:31,33[30,32E]; Ezek 16:47,49; Mal 2:6; with "turn aside": 2 Sam 22:23–24 (see Ps 18:23–24[22–23E]); Isa 30:11,13; Dan 9:5; with "path": Job 13:26–27; with "go astray" (root *t'y*): Ezek 44:10. Note further these extended contexts: "... turned aside ... walked away ... iniquities ... turned away (root *nṭy*) ... sins" (Jer 5:23,25); "... way ... iniquity ... way ... iniquity ... iniquity ... sin ... sin ... sin" (Ezek 3:18–21)—and, even more impressive, this passage: "... turns from ... sin ... walks ... iniquity (root *'wl*) ... sins ... way ... way ... turns from ... iniquity (root *'wl*) ... turns from ... way ... ways" (Ezek 33:14–20; see also Prov 29:27, where the opposite of "a man of iniquity" [root *'wl*] is "he whose way is straight").

Passages that relate *pš'* (the nominal form of which is conventionally rendered 'transgression') with 'way,' 'turn from/to,' 'walk,' 'turn aside,' and the like are less frequent than in the *ḥṭ'* and *'wy* groups, but they are common enough to show that one nuance of the root is that of 'deviating, straying.' We begin with a highly significant citation from the Ugaritic Aqhat epic: *laqryk bntb pš'* [ ] *bntb gan*, "I will meet you in the path of arrogance, [*encounter you*] in the path of presumption" (17[2AQHT].6.43–44). The phrase *ntb pš'* 'path of arrogance' would be vocalized as *n^e^tîb peša'* in Hebrew. As for the Old Testament itself, the crucial passages include Amos 2:4: "For three *transgressions* of Judah, and for four, I will not revoke (the punishment); ... their lies have *led* them *astray* (root *t'y*), after which their fathers *walked*"; Isa 59:13a, 15a: " ... *transgressing*, and denying the Lord, and *turning away* (root *swg*) from following our God, ... and he who *turns aside* from evil makes himself a prey"; Hos 7:13a: "... they have *strayed* (root *ndd*) from me! . . . they have *rebelled* against me!" Other passages that connect "transgressing/rebelling" with "walk" are Ps 89:31,33[30,32E]; Hos 7:12–14; 14:10[9E]; Mic 6:7–8; with "way": Exod 23:20–21; Josh 24:17,19; Ps 25:7–8; 51:15[13E]; Isa 53:5–6; Jer 5:4–6; Lam 3:40,42; Hos 14:10[9E]; with "turn to/from": Isa 1:27–28; Jer 3:12–13; Lam 3:40,42.

Again, not all of these examples will prove equally convincing. But the widespread use of our three roots for "sin" in connection with numerous roots relating to walking along a particular way or turning from a certain path serves to stress the fact that sin is comprehensively viewed in the Old Testament as the deliberate act of veering off the road that God wants us to travel. Perhaps the interpenetration of the various roots is no better exemplified than in Ezek 18:14–31: ". . . sins . . . iniquity (18:17, with LXX) . . . walks . . . iniquity . . . iniquity . . . iniquity . . . sins . . . iniquity . . . iniquity . . . turns from . . . sins . . . transgressions . . . turn from . . . way . . . turns from . . . iniquity (root *'wl*) . . . sin . . . sinned . . . way . . . way . . . ways . . . turns from . . . iniquity (root *'wl*) . . . iniquity (root *'wl*) . . . turns from . . . turned from . . . transgressions . . . way . . . ways . . . ways . . . ways . . . turn . . . turn from . . . transgressions . . . iniquity . . . transgressions . . . transgressed . . . turn . . . ."[9] In short, if meaning is determined by context, then "sinning" and "walking/turning" (in their various Hebrew lexical forms) are surely related.

The ways of God's choosing for us are always for our good and his glory. Our sinful propensities inevitably cause us to wander from those ways. Karl Menninger has defined sin in a rather penetrating manner as "a refusal of the love of others."[10] I would only add that, at heart, sin is a refusal of the love of our God (Ps 51:6[4E]).

NOTES

1. K. Menninger, *Whatever Became of Sin?* (New York: Hawthorn Books, 1973): 13.
2. See, e.g., O. J. Baab, *The Theology of the Old Testament* (Nashville: Abingdon, 1949): 84–91.
3. Th. C. Vriezen, *An Outline of Old Testament Theology* (2nd ed.; Newton, MA: Charles T. Branford, 1970): 416–17, is typical.
4. G. Fohrer, *History of Israelite Religion* (Nashville: Abingdon, 1972): 194.
5. E. Fromm, *You Shall Be as Gods* (New York: Holt, Rinehart and Winston, 1966): 168. See also C. C. Ryrie and R. A. Killen in C. H. Pfeiffer *et al.*, eds., *Wycliffe Bible Encyclopedia* 2 (Chicago: Moody, 1975): 1595.
6. See, e.g., J. Barr, *The Semantics of Biblical Language* (London: Oxford University, 1961): 118.
7. Ryrie and Killen (N 5): 1595.
8. Fromm (N 5): 169 (italics his).
9. I wish to express publicly my gratitude to Mr. Donald Storrs, my research assistant, for helping me in the tedious task of gathering pertinent Old Testament passages for this article.
10. Menninger (N 1): 19.

III. Ancient Near Eastern Studies

17

FROM ḪARRAN TO IMAR ALONG THE OLD BABYLONIAN ITINERARY: THE EVIDENCE FROM THE *ARCHIVES ROYALES DE MARI*

BARRY J. BEITZEL

I. Introduction

Modern demographic and toponymic research encounters considerable difficulties when attempting to localize the peoples, countries, districts and towns cited in ancient Near Eastern literature. Vast reconstruction is severely thwarted, on the one hand, because modern cartographical efforts differ markedly from one another and, on the other hand, because geographical images are largely unclear from this literature, owing to the shortcomings and comparative paucity of ancient maps.[1] One has also to consider that the circumferences of a particular town or district were not the same at all times, and that the same stretch of geography frequently carried disparate names in different periods of time.[2]

Nevertheless, with some entail of those dangers implicit in every step, this writer submits that there are three potential bases upon which an ancient place name may be identified with relative certainty. First, there are towns whose names have remained static since antiquity. Here one could mention Aleppo, Tadmor, Hamath and Beirut.[3] In such cases, where the attribution conforms to grammatical structure and known vocabulary and the meaning is *prima facie* suitable as the designation of the place, the problem of identification does not have to arise.[4]

Regrettably, most place-names are not of this variety.[5] Now, one has two possible means of identification at his disposal. The more direct and conclusive method is to identify a place-name through an inscription unearthed from a site, though instructive caution has been expressed by Astour: "Only if one and the same place name recurs in letters addressed to local rulers, in administrative records, in royal seals impressed upon legal documents—only then can one be sure that this was the name of the site."[6] Examples such as Mari = Tell Ḥariri, Kahat = Tell Barri, Sam'al = Zinçirli, Ugarit = Ras esh-Shamra and Qaṭna = Mishrifeh illustrate this method.[7]

A third method consists in the assemblage and critical appraisal of texts relating to neighboring place-names already identified and then in the comparison of these with the landmarks of the terrain. One must guarantee that the subliminal considerations of correspondence (insuring that the extent and character of a site fill the equation requirements) and synchronization (insuring that the remains on a site date from a period required by the proposed equation) are fully met.

Inherent in the employment of this latter method is the thesis that there is a primacy of geographic data contained in certain categories of original sources. To the degree that caravan itineraries and, to a lesser extent, military campaigns are plainly annalistic, this genre of text should be given the highest geographic priority.[8]

Assyriological and biblical scholars interested in the Old Babylonian period in general and in the Mari age in particular unanimously concur that the itinerary texts fundamental to the historical geography of the Upper Mesopotamian valley have been published by Albrecht Goetze[9] and W. W. Hallo.[10] The itinerary's importance and chronology are established beyond cavil,[11] and Old Babylonian scholarship is especially indebted to these men for their comprehensive and stellar treatments of the itinerary. Both tablets describe the station by station march of an army between Larsa and Imar,[12] Hallo's text recording the outbound (northwest) journey and Goetze's text recording the inbound (southeast) march.

However, texts from Mari largely published subsequent to Hallo's tablet in 1964 call into question the localization of what this essay will designate as the "northwest sector" of the itinerary texts. Diagrammatically set forth are the stations along the northwest sector according to the itinerary texts:

Hallo's text	*Goetze's text*
URU.ŠÀ.KASKAL	Ḫarranum
Apqum ša Baliḫa	Apqum ša Baliḫa
Ṣaḫlala	— —
Zalpaḫ	Zalpaḫ
Ṣerki	Aḫuna
Tultul	Tultul
Abattum	Abattum
BA.AḪ.RA	— —
Imar	[text broken]

While differing only in slight details, both Hallo and Goetze chart the route of the northwest sector from Apqum and the Baliḫ River westward to the Euphrates River and then downstream (southward) to Imar. On the contrary, this essay seeks to establish that the topographic evidence from the Mari archives singularly and unequivocally requires that the northwest sector extended from Ḫarran southward paralleling the Baliḫ River to the Baliḫ-Euphrates confluence and then upstream (westward) to Imar (see below, *Figure A*).

II. Ḫarran and Apqum

Ḫarranum (= Ḫarran) is the Akkadianized semantic equivalent of the Sumerian KASKAL (cf. morphology of Hallo's text), meaning 'a caravan, a roadway.'[13]

Ḫarran corresponds to the modern Ḫaran, a site immediately to the north of and between the Jullab-Daisan confluence,[14] and some ten miles south of Sultantepe.[15] Ḫarran was one of the major centers for the cult of the moon god Sîn in the Old Babylonian period,[16] and it was the city from which the patriarch Abraham emigrated.[17]

By common consensus,[18] the first stop along the itinerary downstream of Ḫarran—Apqum ša Baliḫa—is to be located near the headwaters of the Baliḫ at 'Ain al-'Arus (= "the well of the betrothed"), some fourteen miles south-southwest of modern Ḫaran, at the place traditionally associated with the meeting of Eliezer and Rebecca, and later with the meeting of Jacob and Rachel.[19]

III. Ṣaḫlala and Zalpaḫ

While no conclusive evidence has yet emerged to support the claim that the Baliḫ River was employed for navigation in the Old Babylonian period, Mallowan[20] points out the existence of an ancient road immediately to the east of and running parallel to the Baliḫ. Along that road lay a number of sites, two of which are important in this context: (1) Tell Sahlan (c. 12.5 miles south of 'Ain al-'Arus, just west of the Baliḫ, and along the west bank of Nahr al-Turkman, this massive mound was occupied from the second millennium),[21] and (2) Tell Aswad (c. 200 feet upstream of Tell Sahlan and on the opposite bank of the Baliḫ, this high mound was occupied from neolithic times).[22] Since the station after Apqum in Hallo's text is Ṣaḫlala, Tell Sahlan, on linguistic, chronologic and geographic grounds, becomes a likely candidate as its modern analogue, as Hallo[23] is quick to point out.

Zalpaḫ might have been localized at a point equidistant from Apqum and Tuttul since it was a two-day journey from each of them according to the Hallo text. However, since Ṣaḫlala was one day's journey from Apqum according to Hallo's text, whereas Zalpaḫ was one day's march from Apqum according to Goetze's text, Ṣaḫlala and Zalpaḫ must have lain close to one another, possibly representing alternate stops along the route. Such a conclusion is not at all obviated by the fact that both stops are listed in Hallo's text. By anyone's interpretation, this is a detour leg in the trip and may be likened to the Shuna–Harṣi–Shubat-Enlil zigzag also attested in the itinerary.[24] Accordingly, while a Tell Aswad equation would not be crucial to the overall argument and is not advanced here unequivocally, it would fit the itinerary description of Zalpaḫ and is not at all contradicted on chronological or archaeological grounds.

Furthermore, it is abundantly clear from a Mari text that Zalpaḫ was located *on the Baliḫ* and upstream from Tuttul, and not southwest of Ḫarran, as Hallo supposes.[25] *Naram ša 2 awiluti*^{MEŠ} *i-ša-ap-p*[*a*]*-ru-ši iš-t*[*u*] *me-e* ^{nar}*Ba-l*[*i*]*-iḫ ul-la-nu-um-ma sà-ak-ru ba-lum me-e Tu-ut-tu-ul*^{KI} *mi-nam i-ip-pé-eš ù be-lí i-de Za-al-pa-aḫ*^{KI} *iš-tu pa-na w*[*a*]*-ar-ki T*[*u*]*-ut-tu-ul*^{KI}*-ma i-la-ak i-na-an-na Za-al-pa-*[*a*]*ḫ*$^{\text{[K]I}}$ *am-mi-nim ú-da-ab-ba-bu-šu be-lí dan-na-tim a-na* ^{d}*Iškur-Lú-til li-iš-pu-ur-ma* ("[How can] two men control a river? Previously they cut off the waters of the Baliḫ, [leaving] Tuttul without water which [it] needs. My lord knows that in the past Zalpaḫ has gone to [i.e., depends on] Tuttul. Now why does Zalpaḫ dispute with him [i.e., Tuttul]? May my lord write sternly to Ishkur-Lutil").[26] Tell Aswad, of course, is altogether compatible with these textual demands.

IV. Aḫuna and Ṣerki

According to the Goetze itinerary, the Mattiwaza treaty (*KBo* I.1.rev.10) and the Annals of Ashurnaṣirpal (III.71), Aḫuna is to be localized between Tuttul and Zalpaḫ. Such a localization is generally corroborated by a Mari letter.[27] In this letter, citizens from Aḫuna and Zalpaḫ made accusations against a Ḫardanum and his herd. Since Ḫardanum's herd was grazing in the Tuttul district, and since the ten accusers came from the towns of Aḫuna and Zalpaḫ, it is reasonable to conclude that Aḫuna lay close to both Zalpaḫ and Tuttul.

Of far more significance, however, is the fact that whereas Aḫuna was the lone station between Zalpaḫ and Tuttul on the inbound route, Ṣerki was the only stop between Zalpaḫ and Tuttul on the outbound trip. As in the case of Ṣaḫlala and Zalpaḫ, this indicates that Aḫuna and Ṣerki represent alternate stations along the route and must be sought in the same geographic proximity. And here the Mari archives provide irrefutable evidence. ^{nar}*Ba-li-iḫ a-na Tu-u*[*t-tu-ul*^{KI}] *gu-um-mé-ra-ma er-ša-am ma-*[*da-am-ma*] *li-ri-šu i-na Ṣé-er-da*^{KI} *eq*[*lum i-iṣ*] *ù ru-uq še-um ša i-na-an-na aš-*[*ra-nu-um*] *i-ba-aš-šu-ú ma-an-nu-um i-le-eq-*[*qé-šu*] *a-na pu-uḫ Ṣé-er-da*^{KI} *ugaram-ma ša T*[*u*]*-ut-tu-ul*^{KI} *li-ri-šu an-ni-tam be-lí ú-wa-er-šu-nu-ti i-na-an-na er-šu-um ma-du-um-ma i-na Tu-ut-tu-ul*^{KI} *e-ri-iš ù Anum-Ú-ri a-na Za-al-p*[*a-a*]*ḫ*^{KI} [*i*]*l-l*[*i*]*-kam-ma me-e ša* ^{nar}*Ba-li-iḫ* [*ú-s*]*à-ki-ir ù ikkari*^{ri} *ša aš-ra-nu-um* [*ú*]*-še-ši-bu ú-ka-aš-ši-id* ("Bring the water of the Baliḫ to Tuttul and let them raise an abundant crop. The field at Ṣerda is small and remote. Who would [want to] take the grain which is now there? As a substitute for Ṣerda, let them raise [a crop] in the field at Tuttul. This is how my lord had ordered them. Now there is an abundant crop at Tuttul, but Anum-Uri has gone to Zalpaḫ and has cut off the water of the Baliḫ and has chased away the plowmen who were living there").[28]

As Dossin[29] has already affirmed, both the photograph and the facsimile copy of Hallo's text[30] reveal that the station between Zalpaḫ and Tuttul in his itinerary text should be read *Ṣe-er-di,* and not *Ṣe-er-ki.* Not only does the Mari text tend to confirm this improved reading Ṣerdi, but also it clearly locates all three sites—Zalpaḫ, Ṣerdi, Tuttul—*along* the waters of the Baliḫ, a point fatal to the contentions of Hallo and Goetze.[31]

Approximately equidistant between Tell Aswad–Tell Sahlan and Tell al-Biya' (c. 24 miles downstream of Tell Aswad–Tell Sahlan and c. 23 miles upstream from Tell al-Biya')[32] and adjacent to the east bank of the Baliḫ are the comparatively insignificant sites of Ḫnez and Tell Damir. This writer would postulate that the Aḫuna and Ṣerdi of the itinerary and the Mari archives are to be sought in this general section of the Baliḫ valley.[33]

V. Tuttul

Beside the transtigridian homonym cited by Gelb,[34] the Mari archives know of two cities which bear this namesake. One was located along the west bank of the Euphrates, some 165 miles downstream from Mari.[35]

However, germane to the itinerary discussion is the localization of the northern Tuttul. Goetze[36] and Hallo[37] have sought to equate northern Tuttul with Tell Aḥmar (Til Barsib), twelve airline miles south of Carchemish and along the Euphrates. On the other hand, the Mari texts place Tuttul near Zibnatum,[38] Shubat-Shamash,[39] downstream from Ẓalpaḫ,[40] between Samanum and Abattum,[41] and probably near to Zalmaqum.[42] The inference of one Mari text is that Tuttul was nearer to Mari than Shubat-Shamash was to Mari. Only when

Figure A

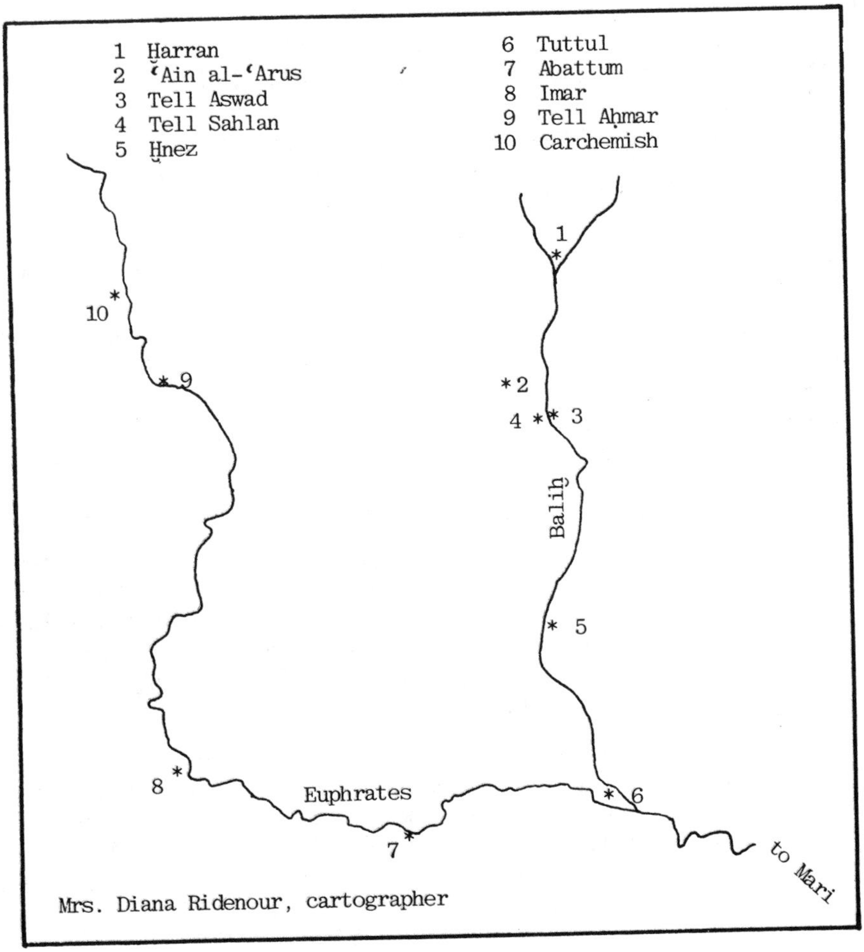

Iasmaḫ-Addu had consolidated Mari and Tuttul was he in a position to ask his father for jurisdiction of Shubat-Shamash. And based on the evidence from Mari, there is absolutely no possibility that Shubat-Shamash was located to the north or northwest of Tell Aḥmar. *As-sú-ur-ri Šu-ba-at-*^{d}*Šamaš*^{KI} *te-er-ri-iš-ma ù šarrum ki-a-am i-qa-ab-bi [u]m-ma-mi iš-de Ma-ri*^{KI} [*ù*] *Tu-ut-tu-ul*^{KI} [*ú-u*]*l ir-k*[*u-ú*]*s-*[*ma ù Šu-ba-at-*^{d}*Šam*]*aš i-ir-ri-*[*i*]*š a-*[*n*]*a la qa-b*[*i-e-em*] *i-ša-ak-ka-an-ka iš-tu iš-de* [*Ma-ri*^{KI}] *ù Tu-ut-tu-ul*^{KI} *t*[*u-ki-i*]*n-nu w*[*a-ar*]*-ka-nu-um Šu-*[*ba*]*-at-*^{d}*Ša-maš*^{K}]^{I} *it-ti šarrim e-ri-*[*i*]*š-ma i-na ḫi-du-ti-šu i-na-ad-d*[*i-n*]*a-kum* ("If you [i.e., Iasmaḫ-Addu] request Shubat-Shamash, then the king [i.e., Shamshi-Addu] will speak as follows: he has not [yet] made firm the foundations of Mari and Tuttul, yet he asks for Shubat-Shamash! He will charge you to not speak [of it again]. After you have consolidated the foundations of Mari and Tuttul, ask the king for Shubat-Shamash and he will give it to you joyfully").[43]

While Hallo,[44] on linguistic grounds, rejected the Tultul = Tuttul equation, Goetze[45] admitted that it would be impossible to deny such an equation (cf. *KAV* 183.23, [*Tu*]*-ul-tu-ul*^{KI} = ^{al}*I-i*[*t*]*/I-tu* ["Tuttul = Hit"]). On the other hand, Hallo,[46] unlike Goetze, asserted that the Tutul of the Iaḫdun-Lim inscription had to be localized near the mouth of the Baliḫ (cf. I.34; II.136 for Tutul/Tuttul). In 1974, Dossin[47] published what has become the most significant text relating to Tuttul's localization, at once destroying the Tuttul = Tell Aḥmar equation proposed by Hallo and Goetze. Lanasum, the governor of Tuttul, reports as follows: *Awilu*^{MEŠ} *Up-ra-pí-i-iú*^{KI} *a-na awile*^{MEŠ} *Tu-ut-tu-li-i*^{KI} *il-<li>-ku-nim aš-šum wa-aš-šu-ur me-e ša Ba-li-iḫ <tup?>-pí-šu-nu id-di-nu ù ki-a-am iq-bu-ú-*[*nim?*] *um-ma-a-mi šu-nu-ma iš-*[*t*]*u-ma Zi-im-ri-Li-im* [*m*]*e-e ú-ul ú-wa-a*[*š*]*-ša-ra-ku-nu-ši-im ṭe*$_{4}$*-e-em-ku-nu gu-um-me-ra-ne-ši-im-ma ù me-e ša Ba-li-iḫ i nu-ga-am-me-ra-ak-ku-nu-ši-im an-ni-tam Up-ra-pí-i-iú*^{K}[^{I} *i*]*q-bu-ú ù aš-šum an-ni-tim-ma* [*awil*]*u*^{MEŠ} *Tu-ut-*[*t*]*u-*[*l*]*i-iú*^{KI} *tup-pí-šu-nu* [*i*]*š-šu-ú ù ṭe*$_{4}$*-e-em-šu-nu iš-n*[*e-ú*] ("The Uprapean citizens have come to the people of Tuttul. Concerning the distribution of the water of the Baliḫ, they have given their agreement [lit. tablet] and they have spoken as follows: since Zimri-Lim does not wish to release water to you, give us your full agreement [lit. complete your news] and we will completely release the water of the Baliḫ for you. This is what the Uprapeans have said. On account of this, the people of Tuttul have given up their [former] agreement and have made another agreement").[48] Since Tuttul had already been shown to be on the Euphrates,[49] this new evidence meant that Tuttul had to be located at the Baliḫ–Euphrates confluence. In describing his on-the-site examination, Dossin stated as follows:

> Lors du premier jour de la reconnaissance que nous fimes aux tells des environs de Raqqa, notre attention fut attirée par un groupe de collines, situées à trois ou quatre kilomètres à peine au nord-est de la Raqqa actuelle. Du sommet de la plus centrale et de la plus élevée d'entre elles, nous fûmes frappés de la présence des vestiges d'une enceinte, qui attestait du coup l'importance de la ville ancienne que recouvraient ses ruines.[50]

Again, the intervening three days' journey between Ḫarran and Tuttul and the eighty or so airline miles separating the two cities are mutually sustaining and corroborating facts. The Mari textual evidence requires that the northern Tuttul = Tell al-Biya', a mound located at the Baliḫ–Euphrates confluence just to the northeast of modern Raqqa.

VI. Abattum and Imar

The Mari archives make it clear that Abattum was a village occupied by the Mar(u)-Iaminum subtribe known as the Rabbeans, who were seasonal migrants.[51] In his masterful study of the tribal groups attested at Mari, Luke demonstrated that the geographic distribution of the Mar(u)-Iaminum at Mari ranged along the Baliḫ valley (from Ḫarran to Tuttul), along the Ḫabur valley (from the Sagaratum and Qattunan districts), in the Jebel Bishri district, and in the Euphrates valley (from Ganibatum to Abattum).[52] Now for Goetze and Hallo, such information would require that the Mar(u)-Iaminum migrated upstream along the Euphrates midway between Imar and Tell Aḥmar, or somewhere north of Tell Ḫudan. Yet, everywhere in the Mari archives where a Rabbean subgroup is associated with a place name, that site, on other grounds, is located either in the Mari or Terqa districts.[53] No clear evidence exists from Mari to substantiate the claim that the Mar(u)-Iaminum were operative, even in a migratory sense, as far upstream as Imar, much less two days' travel north of the city.

On the other hand, predicated on the Tultul = Tuttul equation, Abattum would have lain upstream from Tuttul approximately equidistant from Imar, at or near the southern bank of the Euphrates, and in close proximity to a location on the river easily traversed.[54] Accordingly, based on this dual evidence, this writer would be inclined to look for Abattum in the neighborhood of the modern village of Tabqa.

Imar was the terminating point in the itinerary texts. Though Goetze[55] had sought Imar at Qara Membij, situated between Imar and Carchemish, Arnaud, one of the excavators of Tell Meskene, has deciphered the following phrase on a cuneiform tablet from the site: KI ^{awilut}*ši-bu-ut alim E-mar* ^{KI} ("The elders of the city of Imar").[56] Such evidence certifies the equation Imar = Tell Meskene[57] and fixes the terminal point of the itinerary.

VII. Conclusion

Arrayed against the inherently improbable conclusions of Hallo and Goetze is the incontestable textual evidence from Mari. The central conclusions which emerge include three absolutely fixed points along the northwest sector of the itinerary—Ḫarran, Tuttul, Imar; three points positively localized *on* the Baliḫ River—Zalpaḫ, Ṣerda, Tuttul; and one location incontestably situated *upstream* from Tuttul: Zalpaḫ. Any affirmation which proposes that the northwest sector of the Old Babylonian itinerary ran from Apqum and the Baliḫ westward to the Euphrates and then downstream collides with and manifestly denies all of these propositions.

Following are the probable modern locations of the northwest sector of the itinerary proffered by this writer:

Station	*Modern location*
Ḫarranum	Ḫaran
Apqum ša Baliḫa	'Ain al-'Arus
Ṣaḫlala	Tell Sahlan
Zalpaḫ	Tell Aswad (?)
Ṣerdi/Aḫuna	Ḫnez—Tell Damir region
Tuttul	Tell al-Biya'
Abattum	Tabqa region
BA.AḪ.RA	(?)
Imar	Tell Meskene

NOTES

1. The abbreviations throughout this essay will conform to those employed in this volume, with the following additions:

AIPHOS	*Annuaire de l'Institut de Philologie et d'Histoire Orientales et Slaves* (Bruxelles)
Annales	*Les Annales Archéologiques de Syrie*
AnSt	*Anatolian Studies*
Arch	*Archaeology*
BARB	*Academie Royale de Belgique. Bulletin de la classe des lettres et de sciences morales et politiques*
KAV	*Keilschrifttexte aus Assur verschiedenen Inhalts*
KBo	*Keilschrifttexte aus Boghazköi*
SH	(siglum for the tablets from Tell Shemshara)
UIOM	(siglum for the tablets in the collection of the University of Illinois at Urbana)
YBC	(siglum for the tablets in the collection of the Yale Babylonian Collection, New Haven)

For a survey of modern works treating ancient maps, the reader may consult W. W. Hallo, "The Road to Emar," *JCS* 18 (1964): 57–61.

2. See this writer's "The Place-Names in the Mari Texts: An Onomastic and Toponymic Study" (Ph.D. diss., The Dropsie University, 1976): 1–4, where it is argued at length that the so-called unknown antiquity theory cannot be employed against the use of place-names in toponymic studies.

3. The complexities of orthography are profound when dealing with place-names, and homogenized forms must be employed. On the risks involved in using classical and/or medieval sources, see Hallo (N 1): 63 n. 3; cf. J. Mellaart, "Anatolian Trade with Europe and Anatolian Geography and Culture Provinces in the Late Bronze Age," *AnSt* 18 (1968): 187. Refer also to M. Astour, "The Partition of the Confederacy of Mukiš-Nuḫašše-Nii by Šuppiluliuma: A Study in Political Geography of the Amarna Age," *Or* 38 (1969): 398–405; G. Dossin, "Le Site de la ville Kahat," *Annales* 11–12 (1961–62): 198.

4. E.g., Aleppo < Semitic *hlb* 'forest.'

5. Cf. above, n. 2.

6. M. C. Astour, "Tell Mardīḫ and Ebla," *UF* 3 (1971): 17.

7. Pilot studies on this subject include A. Reiner, "The location of Anšan," *RA* 67 (1973): 57–62; J. E. Reade, "Tell Taya (1972–73): Summary Report," *Iraq* 35 (1973): 155–87; J. Renger, "*mārat ilim:* Exogamine bei den semitischen Nomaden des 2. Jahrtausends," *AfO* 24 (1973): 103–07.

8. J. D. Muhly ("Copper and tin; the distribution of mineral resources and the nature of metals trade

in the Bronze Age," *Transactions of the Connecticut Academy of Arts and Sciences* 43 [1973]: 299) is correct in assuming that the Larsan itinerary is a detour route controverting Mari, therefore dating from a time when Mari and Larsa were hostile. While they disagree on specific details, the common underlying predication of Goetze, Hallo and Lewy is the approximate geographic accuracy of an itinerary. Itinerary texts also pertinent to Mari include J. Lewy, "Studies in the Historic Geography of the Ancient Near East," *Or* 21 (1952): 1–12, 265–92, 393–425; G. Dossin, "La route de l'étain en Mésopotamie au temps de Zimri-Lim," *RA* 64 (1970): 97–106; one should also consider *ARMT* I.7, 21, 93; V.51; VI.23. For the Cappadocian itinerary routes, consult L. L. Orlin, *Assyrian Colonies in Cappadocia* (Paris: Moulton, 1970): 36ff.; K. R. Veenhof, *Aspects of Old Assyrian Trade and its Terminology* (Leiden: Brill, 1972): 240. For Tukulti-Ninurta II's itinerary, see S. Horn, "Zur Geographie Mesopotamiens," *ZA* 34 (1922): 123–56. Sargon I's itinerary is treated in W. F. Albright, "A Babylonian Geographical Treatise on Sargon of Akkad's Empire," *JAOS* 45 (1925): 193–245. For a second copy of the Naram-Sin itinerary recovered from Mari, refer to G. Dossin, "Les archives économiques du Palais de Mari," *Syria* 20 (1939): 99; J. Laessøe (*The Shemshāra Tablets; a preliminary report* [Copenhagen: Munksgaard, 1959]) refers to a text (*SH* 809) which lists an itinerary from Zaslim to Ḫaburatum.

9. A. Goetze, "An Old Babylonian Itinerary," *JCS* 7 (1953): 51–72; "Remarks on the Old Babylonian Itinerary," *JCS* 18 (1964): 114–19.

10. Hallo (N 1): 57–88. Other significant studies on the toponymy of Mari include M. Falkner, "Studien zur Geographie des alten Mesopotamien," *AfO* 17 (1958): 1–37. This study was superseded only in a chronological sense by F. M. Tocci, *La Siria nell'età di Mari* (Rome: University of Rome, 1960).

11. So Muhly (N 8): 299.

12. I am here employing Mari orthography.

13. W. F. Albright, "Abram the Hebrew: A New Archaeological Interpretation," *BASOR* 158 (1961): 47; T. L. Thompson, *The Historicity of the Patriarchal Narratives* (Berlin: Walter de Gruyter, 1974): 20; cf. Paddan-Aram, "Aramaic road" (Gen 25:20, *et al.*). E. I. Gordon, "The Meaning of the Ideogram ^{d}KASKAL.KUR='Underground Water-Course' and its Significance for Bronze Age Historical Geography," *JCS* 21 (1967): 70–88.

14. For this equation, see W. W. Hallo, "Haran, Harran," *The Biblical World* (ed. C. Pfeiffer; Grand Rapids, MI: Baker Book House, 1966): 280–83.

15. Although A. Glock ("Warfare in Mari and Early Israel" [Ph.D. diss., The University of Michigan, 1968]: 265) equates Ḫarran with Sultantepe.

16. For the worship of Sîn at Ḫarran, as seen in the *ARM*, refer to G. Dossin, "Benjaminites dans les textes de Mari" in *Mélanges syriens offerts à Monsieur René Dussaud* (Paris: Paul Geuthner, 1939): 986; *ARMT* XV.162.

17. Gen 11:31, *et al.*

18. Goetze, "Itinerary" (N 9): 61; Hallo, "Road" (N 1): 77–78.

19. Gen 24:11; 29:10.

20. M. E. L. Mallowan, "Excavations in the Baliḫ Valley," *Iraq* 8 (1946): 112.

21. Mallowan (N 20): 126, 138–39. Tell Solola, approximately one hour north of 'Ain al-'Arus, has also been put forth as the modern Ṣaḫlala. However, all references to Tell Solola and 'Ain Solola known to this writer emerge ultimately from the description of E. Sachau, *Reise in Syrien und Mesopotamien* (Leipzig: Brockhaus, 1883): 228–29 and map. Here he records his journey from Urfa to Raqqa in 1879. As indicated by Hallo, L. Dillemann (*La Haute Mésopotamie orientale et les pays adjacents* [Paris: Paul Geuthner, 1962]: 168 n. 2) finds the geographic situation quite confused and seems to question the very existence of Tell Solola.

22. Mallowan (N 20): 126.

23. Hallo, "Road" (N 1): 78.

24. Hallo ("Road" [N 1]: 78) points this out as an unintended detour.

25. Hallo, "Road" (N 1): 78.

26. Text published by G. Dossin, "Le site Tuttul-sur-Balîḫ," *RA* 68 (1974): 28 (A.4188.24–33). A Cappadocian itinerary text cites a Zalpa (along with a Mardamam, Elaḫut, Abrum, Ḫaga and Dadania) as a station between Admum and the Euphrates; cf. Veenhof (N 8): 243, 292 n. 423; and Orlin (N 8): 38. One should consult as well J.-R. Kupper, *Les nomades en Mésopotamie au temps des rois de Mari* (Paris: Société d'Edition "Les Belles Lettres," 1957): 51.

27. I.118. For a translation of this passage see my dissertation, 288–89.

28. For the text see G. Dossin, "Tuttul" (N 26): 28 (A.4188.3–16); cf. *CAD* G, 30a; I/J, 219b, 49b;

K, 280b; *AHW,* 995b. One should point out that on p. 33 of this article, Dossin looks to Tell Zeidan as the modern analogue of Ṣerda.
29. Dossin, "Tuttul" (N 26): 27.
30. Hallo, "Road" (N 1): 58, for photograph; 60, for the facsimile copy. For Hallo's discussion of Ṣerki (= Seruj), refer to p. 78.
31. However, the orthographic feature is not central to the argument.
32. It is most reasonable to assume that one day's travel encompassed c. 17 to 23 miles when traveling overland or upstream by boat and c. 20 to 26 miles when traveling downstream by boat; cf. Hallo, "Road" (N 1): 63, 66, 84; Lewy (N 8): 280; G. Dossin, "Le royaume de Qaṭna au XVIIIe siècle avant notre ère d'après les 'Archives de Mari,'" *BARB* V/40 (1954): 420; "Iamḫad et Qatanum," *RA* 36 (1939): 52. This explains why, although Shubat-Enlil was closer in miles to Apqum than to Mari, it was a five (or three) day journey from Shubat-Enlil to Mari and six days from Shubat-Enlil to Apqum. On the one hand, the route was downstream water navigation and, on the other hand, it was a rugged mountainous route. The estimate of Goetze ("The Roads of Northern Cappadocia in Hittite Times," *RHA* 15 [1957]: 99) of fifty miles per day on good roads and on good horses is unsubstantiated for the Mari epoch, and he elsewhere ("Itinerary" [N 9]: 58, 64, 67) proposes more reasonable figures. Obviously, different circumstances in travel (administrative, military, economic) would dictate the distance traveled in a day.
33. Cf. above, n. 28.
34. I. J. Gelb, "Studies in the Topography of Western Asia," *AJSL* 55 (1938): 75.
35. Obviously referred to in I.20; IV.17.
36. Goetze, "Remarks" (N 9): 118–19.
37. Hallo, "Road" (N 1): 81. Though not actually making such an equation, S. Smith ("Yarim-Lim of Yamḫad," *RSO* 32 [1957]: 158) remarks that the northern Tuttul should be sought just south of Carchemish, arguing against a Baliḫ location because the river was not navigable.
38. I.18.19–24, 34–42; for a translation of these passages, see my dissertation, 326–27. Cf. A. Marzal, "The Provincial Governor at Mari: His Title and Appointment," *JNES* 30 (1971): 209.
39. I.118.10′–23′; cf. above, n. 27.
40. Cf. above, n. 26.
41. G. Dossin, "L'inscription de fondation de Iaḫdun-Lim, roi de Mari," *Syria* 32 (1955): 7–8,14 (col. III.3–21). For a translation of this passage see my dissertation, 263–64.
42. Dossin, "Benjaminites" (N 16): 987 (11. 8–12); for a translation of this passage see my dissertation, 307. Cf. the text published by A. Finet ("Les médecins au royaume de Mari," *AIPHOS* 14 [1954–57]: 128 [A. 675.5–11]), which describes an epidemic that struck Tuttul and Dunnum, the latter of which is downstream from Lasqum. In discussing the *kurullum,* Finet tentatively suggests that it refers to a malady whose symptoms perhaps correspond to the malady derived from a fruit tree; cf. III.78.25.
43. IV.27.18–28; cf. *CAD* Ḫ, 183ab, I/J, 238a. Other texts associating Tuttul and Shubat-Shamash include I.12, 60, 73, 118; V.5.
44. Hallo, "Road" (N 1): 79.
45. Goetze, "Remarks" (N 9): 118 n. 50.
46. Hallo, "Road" (N 1): 79.
47. Dossin, "Tuttul" (N 26): 25–34.
48. Dossin, "Tuttul" (N 26): 30 (A.2769.5–19).
49. E.g., I.102; II.137; cf. *ARMT* XV.137.
50. Dossin, "Tuttul" (N 26): 33.
51. The Mar(u)-Iaminum subgroups are the Uprapum, Amnanum, Iaḫrurum and the Rabbum. The circumstantial evidence of I.42.29–33 provides the possibility of including the Iariḫum. For the extensive argumentation supporting the Mar(u)-Iaminum orthography, vis-à-vis Benjaminite, the reader is referred to my dissertation, 227–29. See also I.6; IV.6, 21. It would be difficult to prove that the political clout of Zimri-Lim, much less of Iasmaḫ-Addu, extended as far as Tell Aḥmar. The so-called equality text, first published by Dossin ("Les archives épistolaires du Palais de Mari," *Syria* 19 [1938]: 117), precludes the extension of the Mari domain as far as Tell Aḥmar. Glock ([N 15]: 62 n. 78) demonstrates that Zimri-Lim exercised a suzerainty over some twenty vassals. From the letters published by C.-F. Jean ("Ḫammurapi d'après des lettres inédites de Mari," *RA* 35 [1938]: 109), one observes that Ḫammurapi addresses Zimri-Lim as "brother" (i.e., a salutation usually accorded an equal).
52. J. T. Luke, "Pastoralism and Politics in the Mari Period: A Re-examination of the Character and

Political Significance of the Major West Semitic Tribal Groups on the Middle Euphrates, ca. 1828–1758 B.C.'' (Ph.D. diss., The University of Michigan, 1965): 69–75. Though understood by numerous authors to represent the expression ''sons of the right hand'' (= southerner), the phrase was taken to represent various phenomena. Smith ([N 37]: 159) took it to mean ''men of the right bank of the Euphrates''; J. Muilenburg (''The Birth of Benjamin,'' *JBL* 75 [1956]: 200) understood the expression as ''south of Ephraim''; cf. K.-D. Schunck (*Benjamin: Untersuchungen zur Entstehung und Geschichte eines Israelitischen Stammes* [Berlin: Töpelmann, 1963]: 55–56), who affirmed that south of Ephraim connoted dependence on the northern tribe. Thompson ([N 13]: 185) espoused the position that the name had reference to ''south of the hill country.''

53. Cf. my dissertation, *s.v.* Rabbum, 254–55.

54. Cf. Dossin, ''Benjaminites'' (N 16): 985 (11. 12′–15′); IV.6.21.

55. A. Goetze, ''Remarks'' (N 9): 119. Hallo (''Road'' [N 1]: 81) finds Tell Meskene to be compatible with the textual demands for Imar; cf. A. Goetze, ''The Syrian Town of Emar,'' *BASOR* 147 (1957): 22–26.

56. Dossin (''Tuttul'' [N 28]: 26) provides this datum.

57. Tell Meskene is separated from Tell Aḥmar by some fifty-seven airline miles. However, the two locations are separated by some eighty-five land miles, following the course of the Euphrates. See now J. Margueron, ''Quatre Campagnes de Fouilles à Emar (1972–1974): Un Bilan Provisoire,'' *Syria* 52 (1975): 53–85.

18

THE SUFFIXES *-NE* AND *-NA* IN HURRIAN[1]

FREDERIC WM. BUSH

The Hurrian suffixes *-ne* and *-na* have been subjected to diverse understandings in the course of the interpretation of the language. F. Thureau-Dangin interpreted them as definite articles, singular and plural respectively.[2] In this he was followed by A. Goetze, who noted that these suffixes interchange in identical position with the pronominal suffixes, strongly suggesting a "determining" force.[3] On the other hand J. Friedrich noted the parallel between the Hurrian *-ne*-suffix and the suffix *-ni-* of Urartean, referring to both as "suffix-joining" particles.[4] The fullest treatment is that of E. A. Speiser in *Introduction to Hurrian* §§136–41, where he interpreted the suffix *-ne* primarily as a relational suffix in attributive construction whose function is to mark the relation of the attribute or descriptive adjective to the head noun. Yet the evidence is such that he also felt compelled to state that "*-ne* seems to have developed in certain instances the value of a derivational element" (i.e., an element that modifies the root meaning of the word rather than relating it to the sentence).[5] In the most recent treatments of the subject, these particles have been understood either as a type of definite article or determining particle, singular and plural.[6] It is so treated by Laroche in *PRU* 3, *passim,* and in the grammatical section of his study of the Hurrian materials from Ugarit in *Ugaritica* 5, and by A. Kammenhuber in her article on the morphology of the Hurrian noun.[7] In J. Friedrich's most recent treatment, he seems to have abandoned his former views of these suffixes and treats them as "eine Art bestimmten Artikels."[8]

Such a wide divergence in interpretation suggests that not all the basic facts have yet been correctly identified. It is the intent of the present study to throw sufficient light on the situation that a few more of the fundamental facts can be elucidated, even though the present state of interpretation of the language as a whole precludes a complete solution. Since my introduction to the fascinating field of Ancient Near Eastern Languages and Literature came under the teaching and inspiration of William S. LaSor, it is a pleasure to dedicate this study to him.

The first basic fact that must be taken into account in seeking to interpret these suffixes is their distribution. It has not previously been sufficiently stressed that these particles occur in two different positions in the nominal chain.[9] They occur on the one hand added directly to the root (or root plus root-complement), and on the other hand they occur in positions further down in the nominal chain between certain other suffixes under conditions that can be rather precisely defined. For ease of reference let us refer to the first as "position one" and to the second as "position two."

At this point it is suggestive to bring to mind one of the basic principles of Hurrian word formation, namely, the positional connotation of the suffixes, both verbal and nominal. This basic principle can be stated succinctly as follows: the closer a suffix stands to the root in its position in the nominal chain the more it functions to modify or add to the meaning of the root, whereas, conversely, the further its position from the root the more it functions to relate the word to the sentence.[10] This principle can be established beyond cavil by an examination of Hurrian suffixal order.[11] In the light of this basic principle, it seems logical to expect, a priori, that the suffixes -*ne*- and -*na*- in position one (attached to the root) will function to modify or add to the root meaning, while in position two (further along in the nominal chain) they will function more to relate the word to the sentence. For ease of reference let us refer to the function of these particles in position one as *derivational,*[12] and their function in position two as *relational.* As we proceed with our analysis of the usage of these forms, we shall see that they do indeed conform to this basic principle of Hurrian word formation.[13]

In our analysis, let us first look at those uses that are clear and unambiguous and then turn our attention to problematic areas. Two uses of the suffixes can be said to be unambiguous in the present stage of interpretation of the language. One is a relational use in position two, the other a derivational use in position one.

I. The Unambiguous Use of -ne- and -na- in Position Two (Relational Use)

This use occurs in certain types of nominal phrases, namely, those consisting of a nominal plus its modifier when the attribution is accomplished by the use of (1) the genitive suffix -*we* (e.g., *ewri-we šala* "the daughter of the lord"), (2) the adjectival suffix -*ḫe* (e.g., *Ḫurro-ḫe* ^{KUR}*omini* "the Hurrian land") or (3) the verb nominalized by -*šše* (e.g., *niḫari ar-oš-au̯-šše* "dowry given+past+by-me+nom.-part.," i.e., "the dowry which I gave").[14] In these types of nominal phrases the suffixes -*ne*- and -*na*- function as "suffix-connectors" in the annexation of the same relational (or "case") suffixes that the governing noun carries to the modifying members of the phrase, a phenomenon termed "suffix-duplication." In Hurrian the relational (or "case") suffixes of the governing noun of a phrase are added (pleonastically from our point of view) to the modifying members of the phrase. Thus: *šen-iwwə-u̯e ašti* (ML 3:21), "brother+my+of wife," i.e., "my brother's wife"; but *šen-iwwə-u̯e-ne-we ašti-we* (ML 4:48), "brother+my+of+*ne*+of wife+of," i.e., "of my brother's wife."

A. The Use of the Suffix -ne- *in Position Two*

The evidence is totally unambiguous in regard to *-ne*. To establish the pattern in full, compare the following pairs of nominal phrases:[15]

(1) The modifier is a nominal with the adjectival suffix *-ḫe:*

(a) The governing noun adds the genitive suffix *-we:*
Ḫurroḫe ^KUR^*omini* (ML 3:6), "the Hurrian land." *Ḫurwoḫe-ne-we omin-ne-we ew*[*re-n*]ne (ML 2:72), "Hurrian-*ne*-of land-*ne*-of king," i.e., "King of the Hurrian land."

No other minimal pairs involving a modifier with the adjectival suffix are known to me, but several isolated forms involving other relational suffixes occur:

(b) The governing noun has the dative suffix *-wa:*
KUR URU*Ḫattu-ḫe-ne-wa*[16] KUR[17]*-ne-wa*[16] KUR URU*Šapinuwa-ḫe-ne-wa* KUR*-ne-w*[*a*][16] (*KUB* XII 44 II 17f.), "for the Hittite land, for the Šapinuwa land."

(c) The governing noun has the directive suffix *-ta:*
KUR URU*Šapinuwa-ḫe-ne-ta* KUR URU*Ḫattu-ḫe-ne-ta ḫurati-ne-ta* (*KUB* XII 44 II 15), "to the Šapinuwa- (and) Hittite soldier."

(2) The modifier is a nominal with the genitive suffix *-we:*

(a) The governing noun adds the ergative suffix *-š:*
šen-iwwə-u̯e ašti (ML 3:21), "wife of my brother." *šen-iwwə-u̯e-ne-š ašti-š* (ML 3:7), "brother+my+of+*ne*+by wife+by," i.e., "by my brother's wife."

(b) The governing noun adds the genitive suffix *-we:*
šen-iwwə-u̯e ašti (ML 3:21), "wife of my brother." *šen-iwwə-u̯e-ne-we ašti-we . . . zalamši* (ML 3:76–77), "brother+my+of+*ne*+of wife+of . . . statue," i.e., "(the) statue of my brother's wife."

(c) The governing noun adds the dative suffix *-wa:*
šen-iwwə-u̯e+man kelti (ML 4:43), "my brother's well-being." *šen-iwwə-u̯e-ne-wa kelti-wa* (ML 4:44), "brother+my+of+*ne*+for well-being+for," i.e., "for my brother's well-being."

(d) The governing noun adds the directive suffix *-ta*.
No examples with *-ne* are known to me, but note the example with the plural suffix *-na* below.

(e) The governing noun adds the comitative suffix *-ra*.
No examples with *-ne* are known to me, but note the examples with the nominalized verb (sec. 3,c below) and the plural suffix *-na-* (sec. 5,b below).

(f) The governing noun adds the suffix *-nna:*[18]
tiša+man šen-iwwə-u̯e (ML 4:32), "my brother's heart." *šen-iwwə-u̯e-ne-nna tiša-nna*[19] (ML 3:13), "brother+my+of+*ne*+stative heart+stative," i.e., "the state of my brother's heart."

(g) The governing noun adds the compound suffix *-nnuḫḫa:*

tiša+man šen-iwwə-ue (ML 4:32), "my brother's heart." *šen-iwwə-ue-ne-nnuḫḫa tiša-nnuḫḫa* (ML 2:10), "the (?)[20] of my brother's heart."

(3) The modifier is a nominalized verb.[21]

(a) The governing noun adds the genitive suffix *-we:*
niḫari ar-oš-au-šše (ML 4:48), "the dowry which I gave." *tuppe niḫar-re-we ar-oš-au-šše-ne-we* (ML 3:40–41), "tablet dowry+*ne*+ of given+past+by-me+*ne*+of," i.e., "(the) tablet of the dowry which I gave."

This is the only minimal pair involving the nominalized verb that I have noted. However, singular forms regularly occur in ML in the zero-suffix form without *-ne,*[22] exactly analogous to *niḫari ar-oš-au-šše* in example (a) above, e.g.,

GUŠKIN . . . *kepan-oš-a-šše we-š+ša+an* . . . *kepan-oš-o-šše* (ML 3:67–69), "the gold which (thy father) . . . bestowed and which you . . . bestowed."

In this light the following isolated forms with the indicated relational suffixes are significant:

(b) The governing noun carries the ergative suffix *-š:*
anaḫite-ne-š tat-o-šše-ne-š[23] (*KUB* XXXII 49a, 8), "by the a., by the one which you love."

(c) The governing noun carries the comitative suffix *-ra:*
[t]at-u[k]ar-impu-šše-ne-ra+an (ML 4:96; the context is broken and the governing noun has not been preserved).

B. The Use of the Suffix -na

With the particle *-na-,* however, the evidence is somewhat ambiguous. This is due to the following difference between the forms with *-ne* and those with *-na:* In the forms with *-ne,* the *-ne* suffix is regularly lacking in the zero-suffix form (the form cited first in the examples of minimal pairs given above), but is present whenever the phrase adds one of the relational suffixes. In the forms with *-na,* however, the *-na* is regularly present in the zero-suffix form as well as in the forms with the relational suffixes. This difference is very probably to be explained by the fact that the *-na* suffix regularly expresses the plural. This will be discussed in more detail below.[24] However, for our purposes here it means that with the *-na* forms there is not the contrast present between phrases in which the nominal is in the zero-suffix form and those in which it has one of the relational suffixes, as there is with the forms in *-ne.* It is nonetheless striking that every example of suffix-duplication in which the nominal is plural finds the suffix *-na* inserted between the modifier and the phrasal relational suffixes it carries due to its relationship to the head noun. Note the following examples:

(4) The modifier is a nominal with the genitive suffix *-we:*

(a) The governing noun carries the plural ergative suffix *-šuš:*

itkalzi-ne-we-na-šuš . . . šiye-na-šuš (*KUB* XXIX 8 II 29f.), "*itkalzi* +*ne*+of+*na*+by water+*na*+by," i.e., "by the waters of *itkalzi*."

(b) The governing noun carries the plural genitive suffix *-še:* *elarti-iwwə-ue-na-še+mmaman niḫar-iaš-(w)e tupp-iaš* (ML 3:44–45), "sister-relations[25]+my+of+*na*+of+(?) dowry+their+of tablet+their," i.e., "their tablet(s), the ones of the dowries of my sister-relations."

(c) The governing noun carries the plural dative suffix *-ša:* *ᵈTeššup-pe-na-ša talḫi-na-ša* (*KUB* XXVII 42 obv. 36), "Teššup+of+*na*+for *talḫi*+*na*+for," i.e., "for the t.'s of Teššup."

(d) The governing noun carries the plural directive suffix *-šta:* *ašḫošikkonne-ne-we-na-šta* (*KUB* XII 44 II 6), "sacrificer+*ne*+of+*na*+to," i.e., "to the ones of the sacrificer."

I have noted no examples with the plural comitative suffix *-šura,* but note the example with the nominalized verb below.

(5) The modifier is a nominalized verb:

(a) The governing noun carries the plural dative suffix *ša:* *kera-šše-n[a-ša+ . .]*[26]*. . .šawal-na+ša* (ML 1:79), "to-be-long+nom.-part.+*na*+through year(s)+*na*+through," i.e., "through the long years."

(b) The governing noun carries the plural comitative suffix *-šura:* *[. . .]t-iwwə-ra tat-au-šše-na-šura* (ML 1:71), ". . . +my+with loved+by-me+nom.-part.+*na*+with," i.e., "with my . . . which I love."

C. Concluding Remarks Relative to the Use of -ne- *and* -na- *in Position Two*

In the use of *-ne-* in the pairs of examples in section *A* above, the first example exhibits a phrase in which the governing noun is in the zero-suffix form, while the second exhibits a phrase in which this noun adds the indicated relational suffix. As can be seen, it is striking that the zero-suffix forms regularly do not append the *-ne-* suffix, but it is appended without exception[27] when the relational suffixes are added. It is this fact that demonstrates that this suffix cannot have the force of marking the relation of the attribute to its head that was assigned to it by Speiser (*IH*, §§136–41), for the zero-suffix forms exhibit a phrase that is just as much an attributive construction as is its parallel *with* one of the relational suffixes.[28] It simply serves to connect the "phrasal" relational suffixes to the modifying nominals in the process of suffix-duplication.

II. The Unambiguous Use of *-ne-* and *-na-* in Position One (Derivational Use)

A. The Derivational Use of -ne-

In this use of the suffix, it is added directly to the nominal root (or root plus root-complement). The force thus imparted can admit of no doubt given the evidence of the Ug. Quad. Voc. where *ewre* = Akk. *bēlu* = Ug. *ba'alu*,[29] 'lord,' whereas *ewer-ne* = Akk. *šarru* = Ug. *malku* 'king.' Here the suffix clearly imparts an "individualizing" or "singularizing" force, i.e., "one in particular."[30]

Several details of the use of the suffix in ML and elsewhere strongly support this interpretation. The form *ewer-ne* occurs in ML 4:127–28 in a reasonably intelligible context:

m.*Tušrat*[*ta*+*n*] KUR*Ḫurwoḫe ewer-ne* [. . . *i*]*š* m.*Immuria*+*n* KUR*Mašri*[*an*]*ni ewer-ne*[31] "Tušratta, the Hurrian King, [. . .] Immuria, the Egyptian king."

Secondly, it can be noted that personal divine names, such as *Teššup, Šauška, Šimike, Kušuḫ* etc., rarely append the suffix *-ne-* when they occur as the divine element in personal names or when they occur simply as names of divinities, except in certain cases when a relational suffix is added.[32] However, in divine apellatives and divine elements in personal names, where such nominal epithets as *allay-* 'lady,' *šala* 'daughter,' *ela* 'sister,' *šena* 'brother' occur, they are invariably written with the *-ne-* suffix attached, i.e., they occur as *alla-ne, šal-ne* (regularly written *šal-le*), *el-ne* (regularly written *el-le*) and *šen-ne*.[33]

Thirdly, as Goetze noted for the forms in the material from Boghaz-köi,[34] forms with the pronominal suffixes almost never occur with the suffixes *-ne-* or *-na-*. This fits well with an "individualizing" or "singularizing" force. This usage is not absolute, however. There are significant exceptions.[35]

Finally, this may explain the use of *-ne-* in a form in the Akkado-Hurrian bilingual inscription from Ugarit. Here the phrase *Kušuḫ-uta+an elam-ul-upp-a-šše-ne* renders the Akk. *tâmê ana nâri,* "he who swears by the river." Here the verb *elam-* 'to swear,' nuanced by the root-complements *-ul-upp-,* of unknown meaning, is nominalized by the suffix *-šše,* giving "who/which swears." This form, which regularly functions in an attributive capacity in ML,[36] is then "individualized" by the suffix *-ne,* yielding "the one who swears." The interpretation is rendered suspect only by the fact that clear parallels seem lacking among the many uses of the forms in *-šše* in the long letter from Mitanni (ML). The only analogous form is the word *tiḫan-ol-um-a-šše-ne* (ML 3:8) which, unfortunately, is in an obscure context.

B. The Derivational Use of -na-

It is very clear that *-na-,* when attached directly to the root (or root + root-complement), is used to express plurality, not "definiteness" or "determination." Such frequent forms in ML as *tiwe-na*MEŠ (ML 1:99,105,108; 2:80; 3:53,56; 4:30), *taše-na*MEŠ (ML 1:88), and DINGIR.MEŠ *en-na-šuš* (ML 1:78; 2:52; 4:117), etc., make this abundantly clear. Another clear evidence of this is the following passage:

tumne išiḫḫe-na šin šiniperuḫḫe-[*n*]*a* [. . .] (ML 2:59), "four i.'s,[37] two ivory [. . .]'s."

Here the words modified by the numerals "four" and "two" append the *-na* suffix, clearly fortifying its interpretation as an indicator of plurality. Finally, the following passage strongly suggests a plural force but not "definiteness" or "determination":

> *ištan-iwwaš-a+tilla+an šen-n(a)-uḫḫa* (ML 4:120–21), "mutuality+our+in+we+and brother+*na*+qual.-adj.+stative," i.e., "in our mutuality we are like brothers" (specifically "in a state of the character of brothers").

III. Ambiguities and Difficulties With the Interpretation

Thus far the evidence and its interpretation seems reasonably clear and unambiguous. But other evidence raises questions and presents problems that are difficult to answer and solve, given the present stage in the interpretation of the language, and especially given our seriously deficient knowledge of Hurrian lexicography. No attempt will be made here to present solutions, but only to elucidate more of the evidence.

A. Ambiguities in the Use of -ne *in Position One (Derivational Use)*

Given the clear evidence of the Ug. Quad. Voc. (cited in II *A* above), one would expect to be able to correlate some such force as that suggested there with the use of *-ne* in this position. Surprisingly, no such correlation seems possible in ML, except for the use of *ewer-ne* itself (as cited above)! The general use of *-ne* in this position in ML is as follows: singular nominals in the zero-suffix form (or "stem-case," i.e., without any of the relational suffixes) that do not have a pronominal suffix regularly do *not* append any *-ne* suffix. In the rare instances that they do, no such force as that expected from II *A* above seems to fit the usage.[38] However, singular nominals *do* frequently add the suffix in position one when they appear as the modifier in nominal phrases;[39] e.g., note *omin-ne-we* in example 1,a above (where the modifier is the adjectival form *Ḫurroḫe*), *niḫar-re-we* in example 3,a above (where the modifier is a nominalized verb), and for the genitival modifier note ^{KUR}*Mizir-re-we-ne-š ewre-š* (ML 1:84–85). Yet one also finds *šen-iwwə-u̯e-ne-we* ^{KUR}*omini-we eroškinna* (ML 1:97), "the e.'s of the land of my brother," where *omini* occurs in exactly the same position without *-ne*. No circumstances seem apparent that could condition the presence or lack of *-ne*. If *-ne* attached directly to the root imparts an "individualizing" force, why should most nominals appear without *-ne* in the zero-suffix form, yet frequently append it in nominal phrases?

Further, if this is the force of *-ne* when attached directly to the root, several specific usages seem just the opposite of what one would expect. The word *ašti-* 'woman' is used regularly in ML in the specific sense 'wife.' It occurs four times in the zero-suffix form without pronominal suffixes[40] and six times in a nominal phrase,[41] yet never with the *-ne* suffix. One would certainly surmise that the force of *-ne* derived from II *A* would here be appropriate.

Exactly the opposite phenomenon is found with *Šimike-* 'Sun(-god).' It occurs once in the zero-suffix form in ML without *-ne*,[42] but seven times with relational suffixes with *-ne*.[43] Again the force of *-ne* here does not fit that suggested by II *A* above.[44]

The only solution that suggests itself is that *-ne* carries the special sense suggested by II *A* above only when attached to the word in the zero-suffix case. It is interesting to note that *ewre* occurs elsewhere in ML in the singular in nominal phrases three times, referring to both the Pharaoh and Tušratta, but without the *-ne* suffix.[45]

B. Ambiguities in the Use of -na- *in Position One (Derivational Use)*

Although it is clear that *-na* indicates plurality when it occurs, it is not clear at present under what conditions it is required. In one construction it is regularly present: when a plural nominal is modified by a nominalized verb, both the nominal and the nominalized verb regularly append *-na,*[46] e.g.,

> *unto+man ya+lle+nin tiwe-na*^{MEŠ} *šuallaman šen-iwwə-uš kat-oš-a-šše-na u̯ur-iya-šše-na* (ML 4:30–31), "now+and what+them+indeed things+*na* all+them brother+my+by communicated+past+by-him+nom.-part.+*na* desired+by him+nom.-part.+*na*," i.e., "now then, all the things which my brother has communicated and desires."

It is not, however, absolutely necessary on plural nominals as rare occurrences such as *tiwe*^{MEŠ} (ML 1:80), and especially *Ḫurwoḫe+man* ^{KUR}*omini*^{MEŠ} KIR.KIR.NI^{MEŠ} *nuli*^{MEŠ} (ML 3:113) and ^{KUR}*Mašrianni* ^{KUR}*omini*^{MEŠ} KIR.KIR.NI^{MEŠ} *nuli*^{MEŠ} (ML 3:117–18) show. In the latter case there is no morpheme anywhere in the sentence to express the plurality clearly indicated by the MEŠ-sign.

It is also quite striking that forms which carry the pronominal suffixes regularly do not append the *-na* suffix when plural,[47] even when there is no other morpheme in the sentence to mark the plurality, e.g.,

> *unto+n* $^{\text{m.}}$*Mane+n+an šen-iwwə-u̯e paššitḫi unto+n* $^{\text{m.}}$*Kelia+n+an* $^{\text{m.}}$*Arteššupa+n+an* $^{\text{m.}}$*Asali+nna+an paššitḫ-iwwə* (ML 4:35–36), "now then, Mane is my brother's envoy; now then, Kelia, Arteššup, and Asali are my envoys."

Hurrian apparently felt no absolute need to mark the plural when the fact of plurality was obvious from the context or from the nature of the word.

C. Concluding Remarks

In spite of the apparent clarity of the interpretation of *-ne* given by the Ug. Quad. Voc. (Sec. II *A* above) and the evidence supporting such an interpretation from ML and elsewhere, the pattern of use of the suffix in ML is extremely difficult to correlate with this meaning. No conditions have been noted in the present stage of interpretation that can explain its presence or lack in this position. At this point one can only make a sharp distinction between the way the suffix is used with certain nominals to modify the meaning in a distinct way and the general pattern of usage, at least in ML. As suggested above, perhaps *-ne* has this force only in the zero-suffix form. Or are we, perhaps, dealing here with dialectal differences? On the other hand, the use of both *-ne* and *-na* to connect the "phrasal" relational suffixes to the modifiers of a nominal phrase is extremely regular.

One thing seems clear, however, in the light of the present study. It is hardly descriptive of the use of these suffixes to call them "definite articles." Such a term can in no way relate to the way in which they are used in position two in the process of suffix-duplication; nor can it accommodate the fact that the suffix *-ne* is regularly lacking in the zero-suffix form in the singular, whereas the suffix *-na* is regularly present to express the plural. Here the criticism of E. A. Speiser is still very much to the point: if they are definite articles, we "have the anomalous pattern of plural forms being always determined while the singulars employ the article selectively" (*IH*, §137).

NOTES

1. The following symbols and abbreviations have been used in this study:
(a) symbols:

-      separates suffixal morphemes in morphemic transcription and individual cuneiform signs in normal transliteration.

\+   separates associative morphemes in morphemic transcription and all morphemes in literal translation.

[. . .]   indicates broken or uncertain readings in transliteration and morphemic transcription.

< >   indicates scribal omissions in transliteration and morphemic transcription.

In the morphemic transcription of Hurrian I have used the most common values of the signs of the various syllabaries (and the Ugaritic alphabet), without thereby intending any conclusions of a phonetic nature. Double writing in the syllabary has been represented by double writing in morphemic transcription. To avoid the confusion inherent in the representation of stop phonemes within and among the various syllabaries in use, I have arbitrarily used the voiceless variant of the labial, dental and velar stops in all positions. In order to represent the clear phonemic difference between *U* and *Ú* in ML, I have represented the former by *-o-* and the latter by *-u-* in morphemic transcription without intending any phonetic conclusions thereby. On occasion I have used *-o-* in the morphemic transcription of forms from Nuzi and Boghaz-köi (where the syllabaries in use make no such distinction) whenever to do otherwise would obscure the comparison between apparently identical morphemes.
(b) abbreviations—in addition to the standard abbreviations adopted for this volume, the following have been used:

GHL   F. W. Bush, "A Grammar of the Hurrian Language" (Ph.D. diss., Brandeis University; Ann Arbor, MI: University Microfilms, 1964).

IH   E. A. Speiser, *Introduction to Hurrian* (AASOR 20; New Haven: American Schools of Oriental Research, 1940–41).

KUB   *Keilschrifturkunden aus Boghazköi.*

ML   The so-called "Mitanni Letter," text 200 in *Die Tontafeln von El-Amarna* (Vorderasiatische Schriftdenkmäler 12; Leipzig: J. C. Hinrichs, 1915), used in conjunction with the transliteration by J. Friedrich in *Kleinasiatische Sprachdenkmäler* (Berlin: de Gruyter, 1932).

Ug. Quad. Voc. = The quadrilingual vocabulary from Ugarit, studied by E. Laroche in *Ugaritica* 5 (1968): 448–62.

2. "Vocabulaires de Ras-Shamra," *Syria* 12 (1931): 254–56.
3. A. Goetze, "The Genitive of the Hurrian Noun," *RHA* 39 (1940): 200ff.
4. J. Friedrich, "Zum Subaräischen und Urartäischen," *AnOr* 12 (1935): 122, 127 n. 6. He uses the term "Suffixanreihenden Elements -ni."
5. *IH*, §137, sec. 5.
6. The evidence has been set forth in detail, including quotations, in my article "The Relationship between the Hurrian Suffixes *-ne-/-na-* and *-nni/e- /-nna*," *Orient and Occident* (AOAT 22 [Gordon Festschrift]; Kevelaer: Butzon & Bercker, 1973): 39–52; see pp. 40f.
7. A. Kammenhuber, "Morphologie hurrischer Nomina," *Münchener Studien zur Sprachwissenschaft* 23 (1968): 49–79.
8. *Altkleinasiatische Sprache. Handbuch der Orientalistik* 1/2 (Leiden: Brill, 1957) *s.v.* "Churritisch," 1–30.

9. It ought to be noted at the beginning that the use of these particles is strictly limited to nominals and nominalized verbs. They never appear in verbal suffix chains.
10. This principle was first elucidated by Speiser in *IH,* §§133, 178.
11. See also, and especially, *GHL,* §5.4.
12. This term is that used by Speiser, *IH,* §133a and *passim,* to distinguish the function of suffixes attached directly to the root (although he nowhere specifically so defines the term).
13. Another hint that our interpretation is well grounded can be found by observing that the same pattern can be noted in the diverse interpretations that have been given these particles in the past. Thus, Thureau-Dangin and Goetze on the one hand interpret them as articles, giving primacy in their interpretations to those occurrences in which they stand next to the root. On the other hand Speiser and Friedrich interpret them basically as relational suffixes, giving primacy in their interpretations to those occurrences in which they stand removed from the root.
14. Not included are those phrases consisting of a nominal modified by apposition, as in *tiwe anti* (ML 1:83 etc.) or *taše apli* (ML 1:85).
15. As much as the extant literature would permit, I have attempted to locate minimal pairs, i.e., pairs in which the only difference is the indicated suffix.
16. The Boghaz-köi orthography uses the *pa*-sign here to represent the dative suffix. I have normalized it *-wa* to avoid confusion.
17. I.e., *omin-ne-wa,* using the Sumerogram KUR 'land' to represent Hurrian *omin(i)* 'land.'
18. The interpretation is complicated at this point by the identification of the third person singular pronominal associative as *-nna,* not recognized by Speiser in *IH,* and suggested very tentatively in *GHL,* §9.324, pp. 255–58. For the identification see W. Farber, "Zu einige Enklitika im Hurrischen," *Or* 40 (1971): 29–66. However, the position and function of the *-nna* in forms such as are referred to here strongly suggest a ***homograph*** whose use in contexts that are clear in ML suggests a meaning in the range of "stative" as interpreted by Speiser, *IH* §156, pp. 113–14. See also *GHL,* p. 147. Note that the *-nn-* element is present in the compound form *-nnuḫḫa* (see sec. 2,g), showing that it is independent of the final *-a*.
19. The observance of this pattern, plus the fact that the form in ML 3:13 is governed by the verbal form *šira+n,* means that we must emend ML 4:34 to read *šen-iwwə-u̯e-ne-n<na> tiša-nna šira-šše,* for the phrase there is also governed by the verb *šir-* (in the nominalized form).
20. This form occurs in an obscure passage. Yet the mention of "the dowry of my brother's wife" in the previous line clearly suggests interpreting the *-ḫḫa* as the qualitative or adjectival suffix *-ḫe/-ḫḫe* followed by the stative *-a,* as does Speiser, *IH,* p. 144. The difference in meaning between the forms in *-nna* and those in *-nnuḫḫa* is not clear.
21. On this form see *GHL,* pp. 172–76.
22. I have noted twelve such verbs, vs. one opposed: *tiḫan-ol-um-a-šše-ne šue-ne* (ML 3:8), which case may be conditioned by the following *šue-ne*. However, it must be noted that all other phrases involving *šue-ne* as a second element do not involve such agreement, e.g., *mana šue-ne* (ML 1:69,73; 2:55; 3:5,6).
23. In the syllabary in use for writing Hurrian at Boghaz-köi, *U* (o) and *Ú* (u) are not distinguished as in ML, but seem to be free variants (see *IH,* §28, pp. 22f.). I have used *-o-* in the morphemic transcription, however, to avoid confusion.
24. See sec. II *B*.
25. The term is a kinship collective referring to sisters and aunts.
26. Although the form is broken and part must be restored, the restoration admits of little doubt; see Speiser, *IH,* p. 120 n. 155.
27. The only exception I have noted is the phrase $^{\mathrm{K[UR]}}$*Mizir-ne-we* ^{KUR}*omin-ne-we allay* (ML 1:62). Unfortunately it is in totally broken context, so there is no syntactical relationship to a sentence to help in interpretation. The form contrasts markedly with such a phrase as ^{KUR}*Mizir-ne-we-ne-we ewre-we ašti+nna* (ML 3:104), "wife of the lord of Egypt." Given the pattern established in our analysis, one must either translate "lady of the land, (lady) of Egypt," or else assume haplography on the part of the scribe and emend to ^{KUR}*Mizir-ne-we<-ne-we>* ^{KUR}*omin-ne-we allay* "lady of the land of Egypt."
28. Further, note that forms with the adjectival suffix *-ḫe*, which Speiser sought to contrast with the forms using *-ne* [*IH,* §137, 1(c)], pattern equally with the genitival modifiers in the employment of *-ne* when the nominal they modify bears a relational suffix; see the examples in I *A* (1) above.
29. Written *ba-a-lu-ma* (130 III 14; 137 II 30,33).
30. Laroche compares the usage of Greek βασιλεύς vs. ὁ βασιλεύς (*Ugaritica* 5, 451 n. 1). Too

much cannot be made of the fact that both Akkadian and Ugaritic are forced to use different words to render the contrast since neither language possessed the equivalent of a definite article.

31. What difference, if any, exists between this form and the form *ewre-nne,* as in ML 2:71–72, is unclear; see Bush (N 6): 39–52.

32. On this phenomenon, see below.

33. Note the discussion of these forms in Gelb, Purves and MacRae, *Nuzi Personal Names* (Chicago: University of Chicago, 1943).

34. See A. Goetze (N 3): 200ff.

35. The forms in ML with both the suffix *-ne-* or *-na-* and the pronominal suffixes are discussed in Bush (N 6): 50.

36. See the examples cited in *A* 3 and *B* 5 above.

37. The passage, unfortunately broken, could be read: *tupe-na*+[. . .] *tumne išiḫḫe-na šin šini-peruḫḫe* [. . .], "four i. *tupe*'s, 2 ivory [. . .]'s," understanding *išiḫḫe* as an adjectival form modifying *tupe-*. In favor of this is the ending *-ḫḫe*, which could be adjectival. In favor of the reading in the text is the order of the second phrase. Whatever interpretation is adopted the point made above is not affected: nominals modified by the numerals "four" and "two" carry the *-na* suffix.

38. Thus, note the usage of *tiwe-ne*+*n* in ML 4:32 (translated in *GHL,* pp. 154–155). Contrary to the general principle, *eše-* 'heaven' occurs twice without relational or possessive suffixes, both times with *-ne: eše-ne* (ML 3:30, 4:125), unfortunately in totally obscure contexts.

39. It is this anomalous fact that led Speiser to assign to it the force of marking the relationship of the modifier to the head noun in attributive constructions (*IH* §137). In fact its frequency of occurrence is enough to suggest that it does function under special circumstances to join the relational suffixes to the noun in such phrases. However, it is missing so frequently and in such a random manner, and this contrasts so radically with its invariable presence when used as a suffix-connector further down in the nominal chain, that the explanation for its usage here must certainly lie in some other function.

40. ML 3:1,11,21; 4:33. It also occurs with the compound stative suffix *-nna* in 3:105, also without *-ne: ašti-nna*.

41. ML 2:6,9; 3:7,76–77; 4:46–47,48.

42. ML 4:122; for translation see *GHL,* p. 234.

43. ML 1:77,86,87,94,105,106; 4:125. In ML 1:101 the form is broken.

44. It is interesting and significant to note that the same usage is true in the alphabetic texts from Ras Shamra published in *Ugaritica* 5, pp. 497–544, where the divine name occurs without relational suffixes as *ṯmg* three times, but when the directive suffix *-d (ta)* is added it occurs as *ṯmgnd* six times. This usage is to be sharply contrasted with the very similar divine name *Kušuḫ-* 'moon,' which occurs twice as *kḏǵ,* and seven times as *kḏǵd,* never with the suffix *-ne*. Why 'sun' and 'moon' should be treated differently as regards a particle with the force that has been assigned to *-ne* on the basis of II *A* seems inexplicable.

45. *Ewri-š* (ML 1:85) and *ewri-we* (ML 3:105), referring to Amenophis III; and *ewri-we* (ML 3:104), referring to Tušratta.

46. The one exception is *tiwe*^MEŠ^ (ML 1:80).

47. Yet in rare occurrences the *-na-* suffix is used; see Bush (N 6): 50f.

19

TWO ARAMAIC INCANTATIONS

CYRUS H. GORDON

It was a widespread custom in Babylonia, especially during the Sassanian period (third to seventh centuries A.D.), to protect families from the mischief of demons by incantations inscribed on ceramic bowls. Most of the spells are in any one of three Aramaic dialects, written in three corresponding forms of the alphabet. The Jews preferred to have their spells written in the Aramaic of the Babylonian Talmud, in characters approximating the familiar Hebrew letter-forms. The Christians preferred the Syriac dialect and script. The Mandeans preferred their own Mandaic dialect and script. We say "preferred" because adherence to a religion did not prevent a client from patronizing, on occasion, a magician of another sect who used the dialect and script of that sect. Magic tends to be more interconfessional than official religion.

The earliest known form of bowl magic is found in Egypt during the third and second millennia B.C. Egyptologists call the documents under consideration "Letters to the Dead" because of their epistolary form. The Egyptians believed that their deceased relatives, friends or foes, were still in a position to help or harm them. They therefore sent messages to the dead, either asking their aid, or threatening to take legal action against them. Some of the Letters to the Dead are inscribed on ceramics. The Letters to the Dead were "posted" in tombs, in the belief that inhabitants of the spirit world frequented burials and thus the messages would somehow be delivered to the addressees, even if the burial was not the grave of the addressee himself.[1]

The Minoans also inscribed magic bowls, two of which were excavated at Knossos and date from about the middle of the second millennium B.C. The strong influence of Egypt on Minoan Crete suggests that the writing of the magic bowls in Minoan Linear A may have been inspired by Egyptian usage, though the Minoan language and script are not Egyptian.[2]

Neither Egypt nor Crete has yielded the large number of magic bowls that have been found in Babylonia. There are in any case resemblances in detail that suggest a historic relationship linking the Egyptian, Cretan and Babylonian bowls. Inscribed Babylonian bowls have been found inverted, as is also the case with Minoan magic bowls whether inscribed or not. In the Babylonian bowls, the clients are named matronymically (a person is always called the child of the mother, not of the father), a usage anticipated in a Letter to the Dead. A Babylonian bowl refers to a demonic spell as "a letter,"[3] and a number of the incantations are exorcisms in the form of bills of divorcement that Jewish law required to be served as a letter.[4]

Any channel of transmission from Egypt to Mesopotamia is at this time hypothetical. It is unlikely that the Jews of the Babylonian Exile remembered such an institution from the days of their bondage in Egypt; at least there is no evidence for it. Tentatively, I suggest that the custom may have been transmitted to Babylonia by the Mandeans, who preserve a number of Egyptian elements, including the angelic names Ptahil ("Ptah is God") and Preil ("The Sun/Re is God"). Also the Mandeans apply the word *ba,* as the Egyptians do, to the soul in the form of a bird with the human head of the deceased.[5]

The two charms herewith published are interrelated paleographically and in content. The letter-forms (note particularly the *l*) are close enough to suggest that they emanate from the same school, though not from the same hand. The magic acts reflected in both texts have similarities; e.g., the evil spirits are offered three traditional tokens of hospitality (food, drink and rubbing oil) so that they should with good will depart from the clients who are thus left protected from demonic harm.

The longer and better preserved of the two bowls is Number 48 in the collection of antiquities belonging to the ZRL (Zion Research Library, Boston, MA). The other is Number 9731 of the IM (Iraq Museum, Baghdad, Iraq). I thank the directors and curators of both institutions for permission to copy and publish these texts.

James A. Montgomery's *Aramaic Incantation Texts from Nippur* (Philadelphia: University Museum, 1913) includes the classical introduction to the subject despite its growing need for updating. Between 1934 and 1952, I published a series of bowls in various American, British, French, Scandinavian, Turkish and Iraqian museums. Since 1946 I have given courses on the magic bowls, every third year or so, to my graduate students. William S. LaSor was one of the first to study this subject with me. His fellow student, William H. Rossell, composed a grammar of the Aramaic bowls as his doctoral dissertation, and later revised it as the introduction to his *Handbook of Aramaic Magical Texts* (Ringwood, NJ: Shelton College, 1953). Subsequently Baruch A. Levine wrote a study of "The Language of the Magical Bowls" as an appendix to Jacob Neusner's *History of the Jews in Babylonia* 5 (Leiden: Brill, 1970): 343–75.

For the convenience of scholars working on the bowls, the chief desideratum was the gathering of the known texts into comprehensive *corpora*. The incantations that various authors had published in scattered journals were difficult to track down. Accordingly, in the 1960's and 70's I directed a triad of Ph.D. theses designed to cover the field. The first was Edwin M. Yamauchi's *Mandaic Incantation Texts* (republished as AOS 49; New Haven: American Oriental Society, 1967). The second was Victor P. Hamilton's *Syriac Incanta-*

tion Bowls (a Brandeis University thesis reproduced and distributed by University Microfilms in Ann Arbor, MI, 1971). The project was completed with Charles D. Isbell's *Corpus of the Aramaic Incantation Bowls* (republished as SBLDS 17; Missoula, MT: Scholars Press, 1975).

There are still many obscurities that frustrate the scholar who prepares new texts for publication. It is often impossible to transcribe the incantations into normal Hebrew characters accurately, even when the writing is clear, unless the interpretation is certain. This is so because two, and often more, letters may look alike. The letters *h* and *ḥ* are not distinguished (probably because they fell together phonetically in the Babylonian Aramaic dialect, even as they do in Mandaic). Sometimes, *w* and *y* look alike; the same goes for *d* and *r; b* and *k;* or *s* and final *m*. A whole series may be similar in appearance such as *w, z, y, n* and final *n,* as happens now and then in ZRL 48. The reader must constantly refer to the facsimiles to know what is in the text.

The following transliteration renders what is certain in large Hebrew letters. Letters in small Hebrew type indicate doubt not only in the case of defectively preserved letters, but whenever the translation is in doubt. This editorial device should be more convenient for the reader than a host of half-brackets, question marks, and subscript dots.[6]

I. ZRL 48

[1]שמע ישב ישראל בסתר מגיה רפא מגיה פא מגיה קפא מגיה שפא אנחנא מנמלכא בת
[2]אימאי וזרמזד ומהינדד בני {מנלמכא} מן מלכא ואימאי בת מחלפתא ומחלפתא בת
אימאי ואנוש בת אימא [3]וכל ירתיהון וכולה איסכופתה וכרמכרכה וכל קיניניהון
בביתא דפרזלא יתבין באיריה נידכוכורגו וישמע מלתא [4]קימא על ראשיהון וכד
תקאד נחשת מיתרין קיטריהון ודשא דפרזלא תפיא על ב---ז ושמאל סטנא קאים על
בביהון [5]זיניה בכפיה תלילא פלגיה לימיניה ופלגיה לשמאל<י>ה אריא רבי על
בבין מכרכא גופתיה על סוכרא בתיהון -- מן מלכא בת אימאי [6]כניש מן חרשי
ותרבציה קמן גולייא גולווא אפרואתי חרשי בישי וראזי אפוכי סליקית לאיגרא מן
מלכא בת אימא<י> ואמרית להון על [7]מא אתיתון חרשין בישין וראזין אפוכין אם
כפיניתון עול איכל איכול אם צחתון עול עול אישתו אם חרביתון עול אידהן אם
לא כפינין אתון ואם [8]לא צחואתון ואם לא חרביתון אתון איזדעזעו ופוקו מינהון מן
מנמלכא בת אימאי ומן זרמזד מן מהינדד בני מנמלכא מן אימאי בת מחלפתא מן
מחלפתא [9]בת אימאי מן אנוש בת אימאי מן כל ירתיהון ומן זרעיהון מן קיניניהון
ומן כולה איסכופתיהון דהון בה מוגייא ומן בריא אית בכול ימינהון הדרו באורחא
דאתיתון [10]בה ועולו לביתא דנפ{כ}קתון מיניה וכולו לח<מא> בסלא דלחמא
{מ מבניכון} דיאכל<ו>ולא ישבעו מנא ומנא דמיא דישתו ויפקו במנא דמשחא
דישוף ויכעבו וכעיב בשום [11]ארגורגור בשמיה עבדנכון ובשום טרליטא טרליטא
אמיץ אציק ו{ל}יהפוך חרשי על עבדיהון בעגל בעגלה ויאמר יהוה אל הסטן יגער
יהוה בך הסטן יגער [12]יהוה בך הבוחיר בירושלים הלו זה אוד מוצל מאש
. . .

The opening words are magical formulae, not plain text. We decipher *šm‘ yšb yśr’l bstr* as the first two words in each of two prophylactic Old Testament passages intertwined. The first and third words *šm‘ yśr’l* "Hear, O Israel (Yahweh, our God, Yahweh is 'One')," are taken from Deut 6:4. The second and fourth words start Psalm 91: *yšb bstr* "He who dwells in the secret (place of the Most High)." There follows a rhyming formula (possibly an encipherment):

mgyh rp'
mgyh p'
mgyh qp'
mgyh šp'

Then the plain text opens with the matronymic names of the clients to be protected.

A. Translation

We, (to wit) *Min-malka* daughter of (2) Immay, and *Zarmazd* and *Mahindad* sons of *Min-malka,* and Immay daughter of Maḥlafta, and Maḥlafta daughter of Immay, and *Anuš* daughter of Immay; (3) and all their heirs, and all her threshold (= *Min-malka's* house) and her *walled vineyard,* and all their possessions (are protected) within the house of iron, sitting in ---------- and he hears the *word,* (4) standing over their heads, and when ---- *of copper,* loosened are their knots. *And* the *doorway* of iron ---- over ----- and *Śama'el,* the Satan, standing by their gates (5) with his weapons in his hands, half held up on his right, and half on his left. ------- by *our* gates, his *tube* wrapped around the bolt of *their house*. *Min-malka* daughter of Immay (6) *is protected* from spells and ----------------------------- (and) evil spells and upsetting mysteries. I, *Min-malka* daughter of Immay, went up to the roof and said to them: "Wh(7)y have ye come, O evil spells and upsetting mysteries? If ye are hungry, enter, eat, eat! If ye are thirsty, enter, enter, drink! If ye are dry, enter, be anointed! If ye are not hungry, and if ye are (8) not thirsty, and if ye are not dry, move and get out from them: from *Min-malka* daughter of Immay, and from *Zarmazd* (and) from *Mahindad* sons of *Min-malka,* from Immay daughter of Maḥlafta, from Maḥlafta (9) daughter of Immay, from *Anuš* daughter of Immay, from all their heirs, and from their seed, from their possessions, and from all their threshold, *(and) what may be therein* ------ and from ---- *is in all* their right hand. Return on the road whereby ye came, (10) and enter the house whence ye went out, and eat bread from the basket of bread *of* your children that they may eat and not be satisfied *(with) the stint,* and the *stint* of water that they may drink and *go out* with the *stint* of oil that one rubs and they shall (still) be pained, for it hurts! In the name (11) of *Argurgur,* in the name of the one who wrought you, and in the name of *Ṭarliṭa Ṭarliṭa Amiṣ Aṣiq* so that the spells shall be overturned against those who wrought them, speedily, speedily!" "And Yahweh said to Satan: 'May Yahweh rebuke thee, O Satan! May (12) Yahweh who has chosen Jerusalem, rebuke thee! Is this not a brand plucked from the fire?' "

B. Notes

On the exterior surface there is no trace of ink for writing or drawing. In the center of the interior is depicted a demon with a tail and scaly(?) mid-section; its feet are hobbled with a chain to render it harmless. The writing is spiral from near the center, toward the rim.

Lines 1, 11–12: For the use of Deut 6:4 (l. 1), Zech 3:2 (ll. 11–12) and Psalm 91 (l. 1) in previously published bowls, see the list of Old Testament passages quoted in these texts compiled by Isbell, *Corpus of the Aramaic Incantation Bowls,* 195.

Line 1: the *n* of *mn-mlk'* is in the sequel sometimes written as a final *n,* suggesting that *mn* is the preposition *min* 'from' forming the first element of the personal name. "Min-Malka" ('from the king') could indicate that the one who bore the name came into being through the blessing or agency of the (human or divine) king.

Lines 1–2: The family is named matronymically and seems to be limited (at least for magical purposes) to women and young children. The only males are two sons (both bearing Persian names) of *Min-malka,* who appears as head of the menage. She is the daughter of an Immay, who is in turn the daughter of Maḥlafta, who is in turn the daughter of an Immay. This means that members of five successive generations lived in this extended family protected by this incantation. The two sons, belonging to the most recent of the five generations, were presumably quite young.

Line 3: *krm* 'vineyard' + *krk'* 'walled settlement' suggests the tentative translation "walled vineyard."

Line 4: A noise-making act precipitates the loosening of knots, i.e., the cancellation of spells wherewith the clients had been bewitched. Metals (iron, and probably copper, and possibly bronze[7]) are mentioned in the text for the noisy praxis designed to scare away the forces of evil.

Line 4: *Śama'el,* here called "the Satan," is an arch-demon and sometimes the Angel of Death in rabbinic lore.[8] The spelling with *ś* instead of *s* is unique and noteworthy. (Note *śm'l* 'left,' below, which is etymologically correct.) For it suggests that the destroying angel's name is associated here with the unlucky ("sinister") left hand.

Line 5: The Angel of Death also carries two lethal weapons, one in each hand, in a magic bowl from Nippur graphically indicated by a drawing. See the discussion of that bowl, including the drawing, together with a Ugaritic anticipation of the motif in David Toshio Tsumura's Brandeis University dissertation, "The Ugaritic Drama of the Good Gods" (Ann Arbor: University Microfilms, 1973): 32–33, 188.[9]

Line 5: *gwpt';* cf. *gwbt'* 'tube' according to M. Jastrow, *Dictionary of the Targumim . . .* (New York: Choreb, 1926): 218a.[10]

Line 6: Roof rituals have a long history. They occur, *i.a.,* in the Gilgamesh Epic and the Ugaritic Epic of *KRT;* C. H. Gordon, *The Common Background of Greek and Hebrew Civilizations* (New York: Norton, 1965): 67. Here the demons are offered hospitality so that they should leave satisfied and without any grudge.

Lines 9–10: The demons are ordered back to their point of origin so that they no longer molest the clients. Demons were always thought to have come from somewhere else and it is the bowl sorcerer's task to turn them back where they came from. This oft-mentioned process of overturning the forces of evil may explain why magic bowls, starting with the Minoans, and continuing into later Babylonia, are often found inverted.

Line 10: The names of potent (demonic or angelic) forces, along with the name of the wizard who sent the demons to plague the clients, are invoked to return the demons without delay to those who had sent them against the clients.

Lines 11–12: Zech 3:2 is often quoted in the bowls because it establishes, on biblical authority, the precedent whereby God foils Satan. The deviations from the *textus receptus* are limited to *matres lectionis*. *Hbwḥyr* is simply written *plene* for Masoretic *hbḥr*. The second *y* in *byrwšlym* follows the *q^e^rê perpetuum* for the standard *k^e^tîb, yrwšlm*. *Hlw* is a simplified phonetic spelling for the Masoretic *hlw'*.

Line 12: After the final word of the text the scribe adds two successive dots; contrast the Masoretic device of ending every verse with two dots, one set over the other.

II. IM 9731

This text is shorter and less well preserved than the preceding one. The overlapping praxis and phraseology in the two bowls help establish some of the readings and interpretation. And yet IM 9731, as the following transliteration reflects, is full of unsolved difficulties. One wonders whether all the magicians sufficiently understood the formulae they were copying (or repeating from memory). The opening lines are not preserved.

... [3]מרת בת מאיתא ---------- אנא ------- בת [4]אימא בביתא דפרזלא
-------------- דגללא ושמי [5]דפרזלא פריסא על ---- ואיסכופתא דנא
---------------- דשא דפרזלא לבאבי [6]קימא ומיתחדא בסוכרא זוטא קשא
------------- על בבין ומכרכא גנבתיה על [7]סוכרא בתאן בנימין מן חרשי
ותרבצ ----- [ושמא]ל סטנא דקאים על בבין וזיניה בכפיה [8]תלילה פלגיה מן
ימיניה ופלגיה מן שמאליה אפיכין ואת<ו>ן חרשי בישי וגאלי אפיכין סליקית
לאיגרא בליליא [9]ואמרית להון <אם כפניתון איתו> איכלו ואם צחתון איתו
אישתו ואם חרביתון איתו אידהנו ואם לא כפניתון ולא צחתון ולא חרביתון
[10]הדרו ואזילו באורחא דאתתון בה ועולו לביתא דנפקתון מיניה ועולו בפומא
----------דנפקתון מינה ועבשום [11]אפרפר טורדאטא ובשמיה דאי–דאגורגור בשמיה
עבדיתכון ובש [מיה] דסנסנא וקנקפתא – נעקב קץ בת ------ תיפכמך וברגבר

A. Translation

------- (3) X daughter of Y --------- I, PN, daughter (4) of Imma in the house of iron -------------- of stone *and heavens* (5) of iron split over ---- *and this threshold* ---------------- the doorway of iron for my gate, (6) standing and fastened with a hard, little bolt ------------- by our gates, with its *tube* wrapped around (7) the bolt ---------- from spells and ----------

and [*Śama'e*]*l*, the Satan who stands by *our* gates with his weapons in his hands, (8) half held up on his right, and half on his left. Upset are ye evil and *filthy* spells, upset. I went up to the roof at night (9) and said to them: "<If ye are hungry, come,> eat! And if ye are thirsty, come, drink! And if are dry, come, be anointed! But if ye are not hungry, nor thirsty, nor dry, (10) return and go on the way by which ye came and enter the house whence ye went out, and enter into the *mouth* ---------- from which ye went out!" And in the name of (11) ------------ *and in the name of* ------------. *In his name* I have wrought you *and in the name of* --

B. Notes

Line 6: *gnbtyh* vs. *gwptyh* in ZRL 48. The difference between the labials *b* and *p* poses no problem. It is possible that the *n* should be read as a *w*, which would bring the two variants together.

Line 8: Both times *mn* corresponds to *l* in ZRL 48 in the same formula. Since the impact of Ugaritic on Northwest Semitic studies, *l* 'from' (as well as *b* 'from') is no longer surprising in Hebrew, Aramaic and Phoenician. We need not go into the problems in translating the Semitic prepositions into English. All that concerns us here is the interchangeability of *l* and *mn* in one and the same formula occurring in these two magic bowls.

Line 8: *wg'ly*—Hebrew has a root *g'l* 'defiled, loathsome.' See also Mandaic *gal* 'dirty place'; E. S. Drower and R. Macuch, *Mandaic Dictionary* (Oxford: Clarendon, 1963): 76a.

Line 10: *w'bšwm* is to be pronounced *wivšum*. The ' is used as the *mater lectionis* for the *i*/*e* vowel as in Mandaic. In the Babylonian Masorah *w-* > *wi-* when prefixed to words beginning with a cluster of two consonants, even if the cluster starts with a labial.

Plate I

ZRL 48

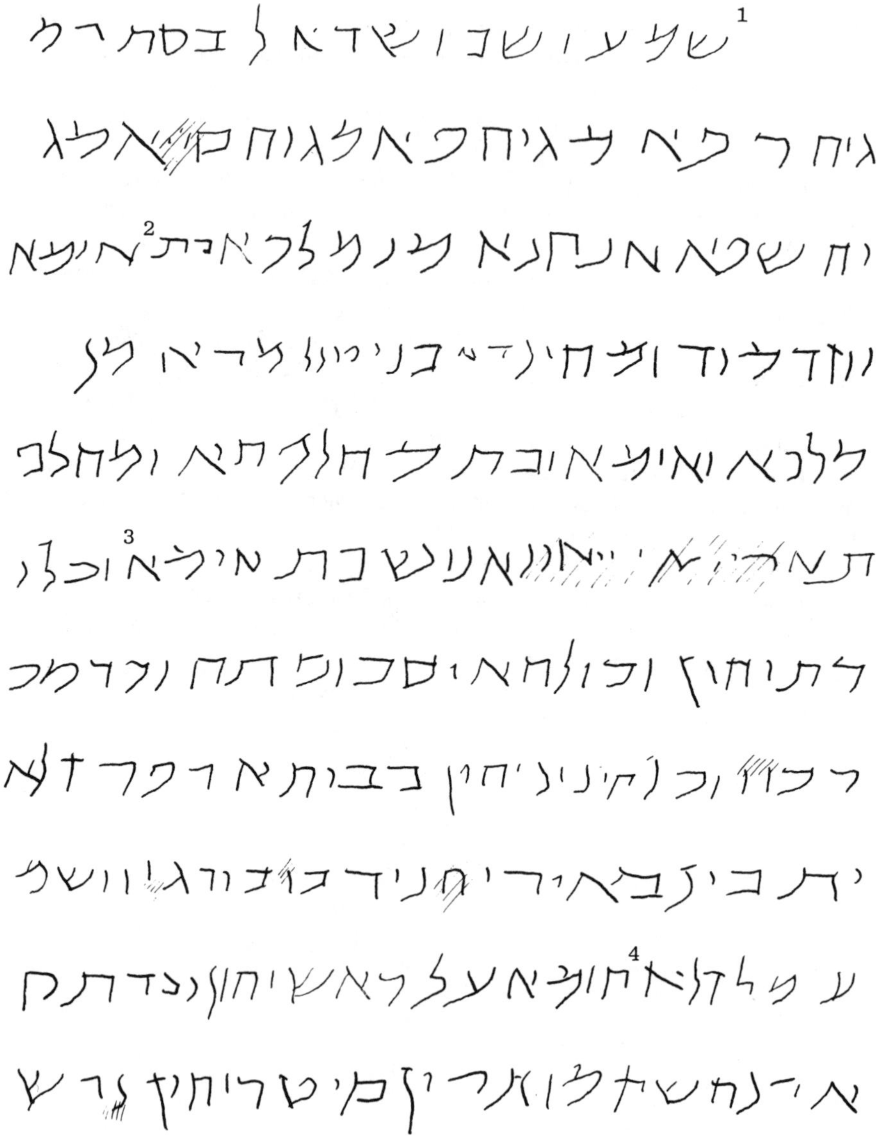

Plate II

ארכרזלאתתניאעלבה///ויעל

אלסטנמיאיסעלכבומחין⁵זיויתכל

כיהתלי/לאלכלעהליעינוחובנאחלשא

אלהארואדניועלכבין שכרעאגיקת

וחעלסודרא בתויחין///כלן עלכאהרת

איעיאⁿוכנישלןחרשיותרבצי יחקמן

גולייאגולונאאכדרואחורחלשובי

שיורלאדיאאפירה ליקיתלאוגרא

מנעלעאדתאולבאואעלדירתלחון

עלעאⁿאתיתיןחרשיןבושין

ורא//איכניריןאסטלפיניתחיעולאי

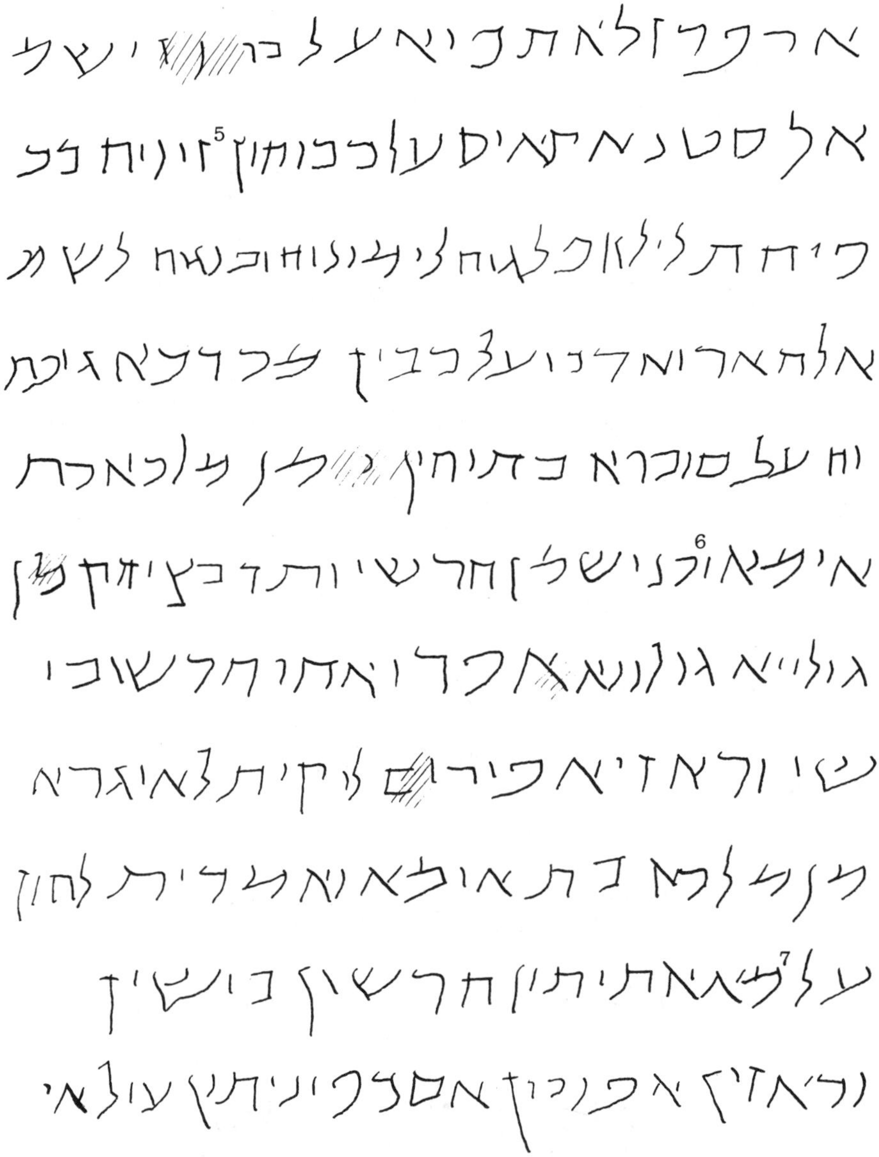

Plate III

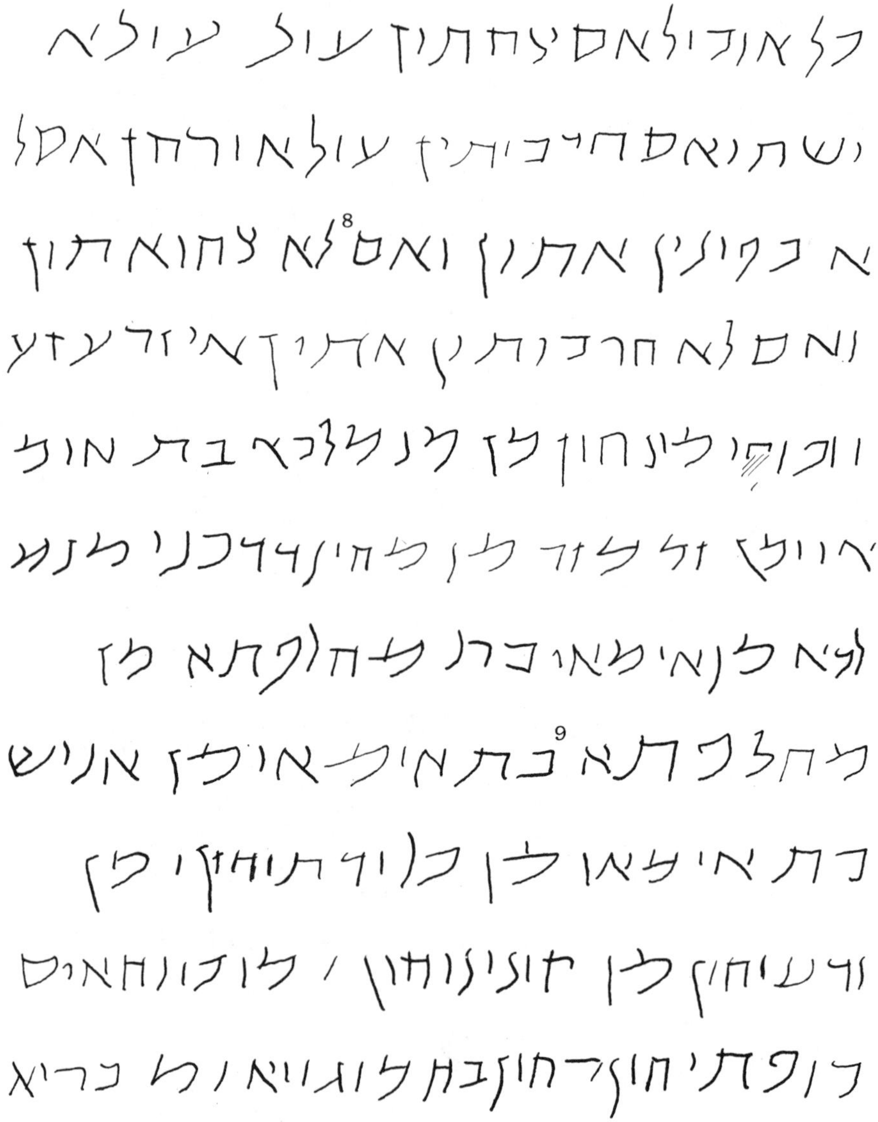

Plate IV

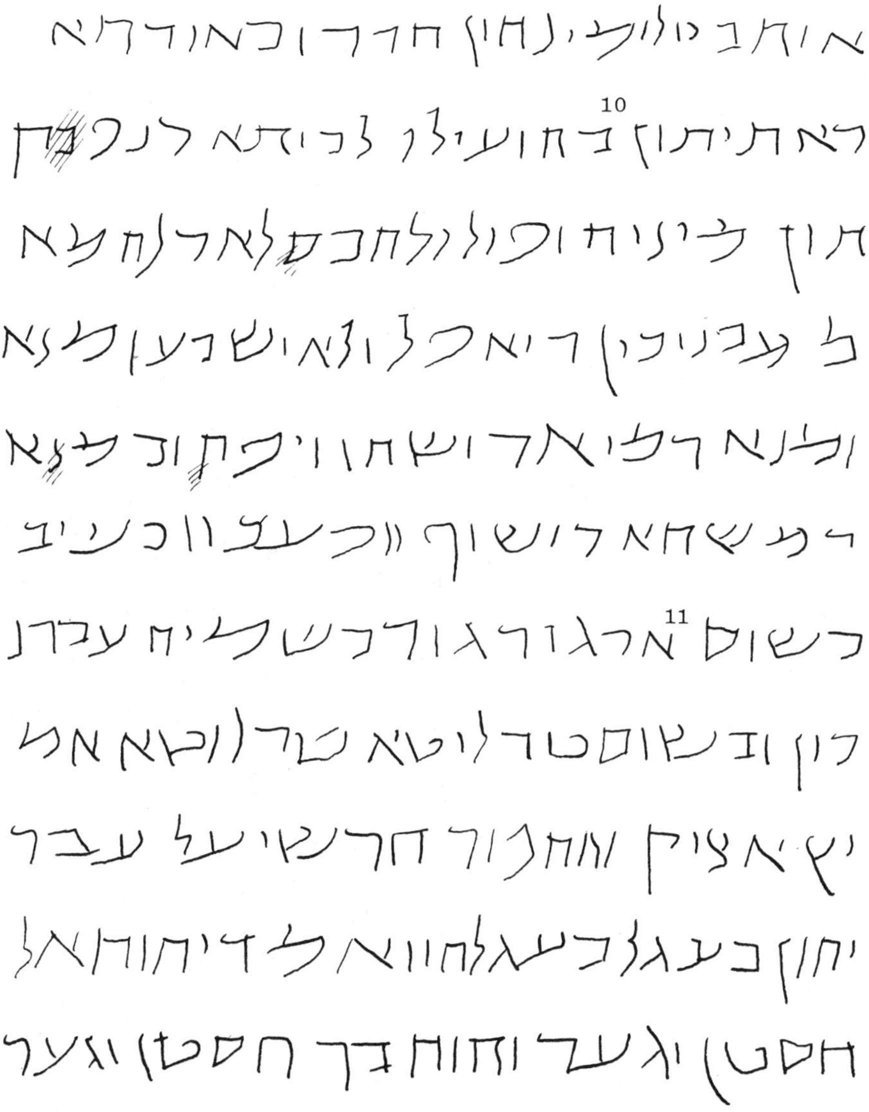

Plate V

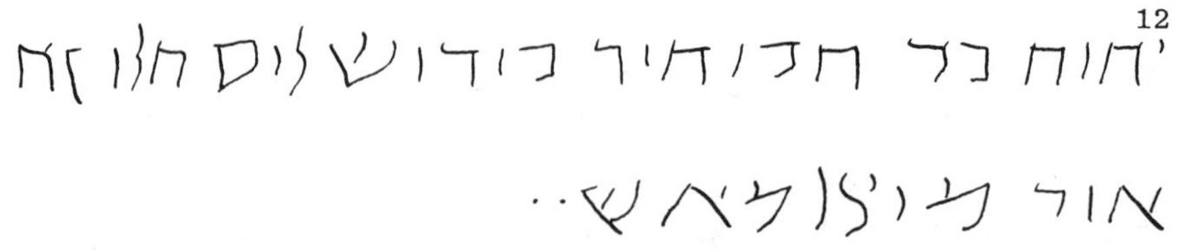

IM 9731

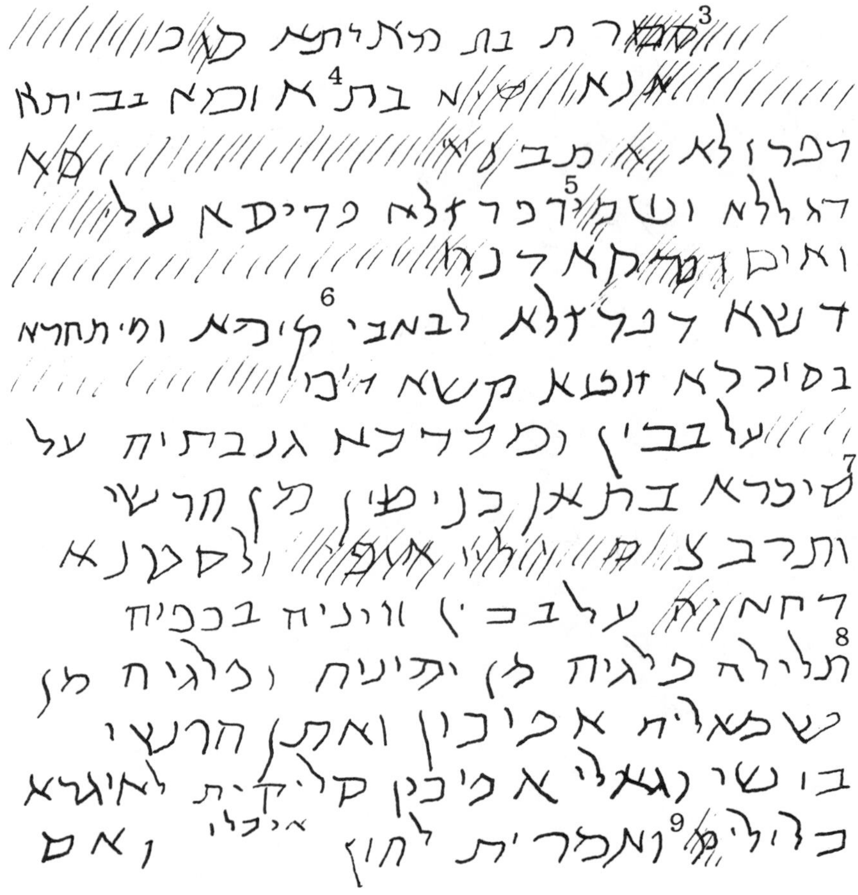

Plate VI

תחתון אי תו אישתו ואם תל ביתון
אותן אודחני ואם לא כוויתון ולא
עחתון ולא חרבימתן¹⁰ חדרו ואזילו
באורחא דאתתון ב   ועולו
לביתא דנפקתון מיניה ועולן
בביתא דמית מגיכון דנקקתו
מינה ועבשום¹¹ אמרבר טוירא
קא וכשפי דאים דאיתא ורבט מלה
עבד יתכין נבנגרסמנא
וקנקמיתאמב נעקב קמיד בתחיצה
תי נבסך ובר גבר

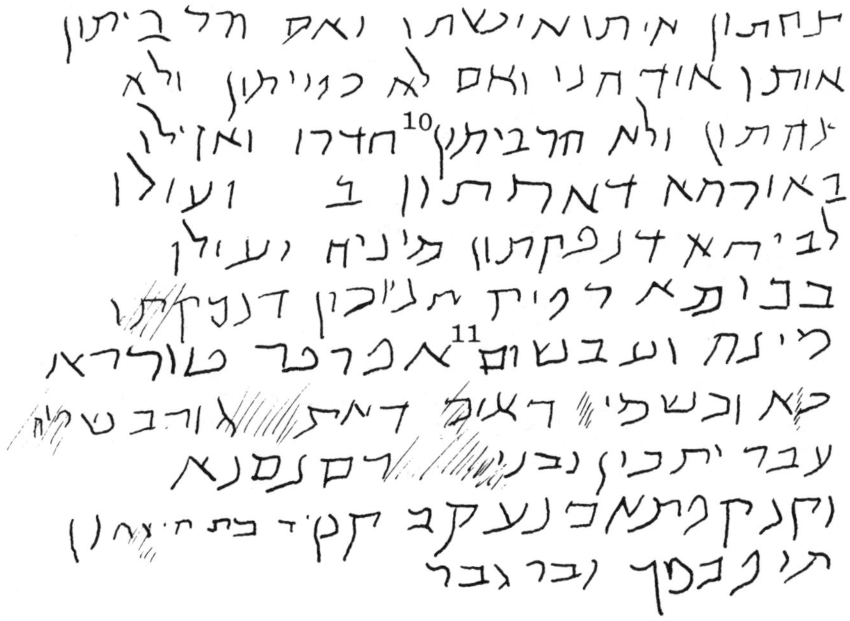

NOTES

1. I have discussed the subject in "Egypto-Semitic Magic Bowls" (in Hebrew), *Hagut Ivrit be'Amerika* 1 (Tel Aviv: Yavneh, 1972): 165–73; and in less technical form under the title "Ancient Letters to the Dead and Others," *Natural History* 78 (Feb. 1969): 94–99.
2. See my *Evidence for the Minoan Language* (Ventnor, NJ: Ventnor Publishers, 1966): 27 and pl. IX.
3. Note *'grt'* 'letter' in text L:4,6,7,9,10 in C. H. Gordon, "Aramaic and Mandaic Magical Bowls," *ArOr* 9 (1937): 98.
4. The potent letters of dismissal (= bills of divorcement) served on demons and demonesses are attributed in the bowls to Rabbi Joshua ben Peraḥya. He is among the celebrated pairs of rabbis quoted in the Mishnah, *Pirqê 'Abôt* 1.6.
5. For various facets of Mandaic culture, see the many publications of E. S. Drower including *The Mandaeans of Iraq and Iran* (Leiden: Brill, 1962). I have called attention to Egypto-Mandaic relations in "Egypto-Semitica," *RSO* 32 (1957): 269–77.
6. However, I have found it necessary to use, on occasion, parentheses for words added in translation, square brackets ([ ]) for restorations, angle brackets (< >) for scribal omissions, and braces ({ }) for erroneous scribal additions. Italicized translations are uncertain.
7. If in 1. 3, which seems to have *nḥšt, 'yr'h* is derived from Akk. *erû,* the two words should mean 'copper' and 'bronze.' One of the puzzling features of Bronze Age texts is that they often do not distinguish bronze from copper verbally. Thus ancient Hebrew has no distinct word for bronze. Hebrew *nḥšt* 'copper' apparently covers bronze as well.
8. See Louis Ginzberg, *Legends of the Jews* 5 (Philadelphia: Jewish Publication Society, 1925): 121, for a very doubtful etymology; and 7 (1938): 414–15 for a detailed descriptive index.
9. See now D. T. Tsumura, "A Ugaritic God, MT-W-ŠR and His Two Weapons (UT 52:8–11)," *UF* 6 (1974): 407–13.
10. Actually *b* occurs in the IM 9731 variant; see our note on 1. 6 of IM 9731.

20

TEXT AND COMMENT

A. R. MILLARD

> "Do you understand what you are reading?" Philip asked.
> "How can I," he said, "unless someone explains it to me?"
> (Acts 8:30,31 *NIV*)

I

The Nubian chancellor journeying from Jerusalem believed the book of Isaiah had something to teach him, yet it did not make sense to him, and he recognized his need of help to understand it. Philip interpreted the text to him in terms of Jesus of Nazareth; he gave its meaning in the light of recent history and his own faith. While the details of his exposition cannot be recovered, clearly it followed the pattern of similar exercises in the gospels and Acts, a pattern which made Jesus the fulfillment of the whole of the Old Testament. This pattern and its products have been studied intensively for generations.[1] Kinship with the approach of rabbinic Judaism, seen in Targum and Midrash, has long been apparent, a kinship arising from the common parentage of the Scriptures and the aim to show their relevance in a current situation. With the recovery of the documents from Qumran containing quantities of biblical interpretation written shortly before A.D. 70, discussion has been reinvigorated. The first Christian writers shared with the men of Qumran a belief that the key to the sacred text lay in their hands alone, that the divine records' meaning could be truly seen only in the light of the particular revelation brought by their respective leaders. With their key they could actualize the biblical words. In an early study W. H. Brownlee claimed thirteen "Hermeneutical Principles" common to the Qumran Habakkuk Commentary and to classical Jewish midrash.[2] The majority of the principles appear improper to the modern exegete, e.g., use of variant or special readings, secondary meanings of synonyms, rearrangement or redivision of letters or words. Rabbinic examples are plentiful (Brownlee gave illustrations), and it should be recalled how their influence reached through to the Authorized Version in the famous "shadow of death," in "white of an egg," and in several other renderings.[3] Occasional instances of the less involved comment using simple wordplay appear in the Old Testament etymologies of personal names (as in Gen 29:32–35; 30), and there may be rare cases of reinterpretation.[4]

Until the Dead Sea Scrolls supplied evidence for the habitual use of midrashic techniques in the Herodian period, knowledge about the history of biblical interpretation in the period before the fall of Jerusalem was vague. Now it is plain that the practices well known later were actually in force as early as tradition claimed (codified as the Seven Rules of Hillel and the Thirty-two of Eliezer ben Jose ha-Gelili). Lately two independent lines of study have converged to reveal the antiquity of some of the midrashim themselves. By refined historical research Geza Vermes has established that several pieces of biblical exegesis preserved to us in the Talmuds, Targums or Midrash exist as far back as the second century B.C., indeed, that much of the material in the Targums has descended from pre-Christian times.[5] In a detailed scrutiny of peculiarities in the Septuagint text, on the other hand, D. W. Gooding has been able to show the presence of typically midrashic processes underlying some parts of the Greek. Furthermore, some instances of material in the Septuagint different from the Masoretic Text turn out to be Greek forms of interpretations known in the early medieval rabbinic collections, and there is a strong possibility that some passages of this sort were integral to the first Greek version.[6]

Alexandria, the home of the Septuagint, also nurtured the scholarship that edited and preserved the Greek classics, and produced commentaries upon them. It is possibly from those Greek scholars that methods of commenting upon a traditional text were derived by Hellenistic Jewry—certainly there was much in common, as S. Lieberman has demonstrated.[7] Yet Lieberman minimizes any dependence, arguing for a purely native development in this field. We wish to look in another direction.

II

Before ever the Alexandrians had begun their work, traditional literature in another culture had attracted commentators. This was the Babylonian. There cuneiform writing had been employed to record literary works from early in the third millennium B.C., at first, so far as is known, in Sumerian, then in Semitic Akkadian. The coexistence of the two languages, continuing in academic circles long after Sumerian ceased to be spoken, resulted in translations of Sumerian compositions into Akkadian, both line by line and as occasional glosses. When wholesale translating began we do not know; numerous examples survive from the eighteenth and seventeenth centuries B.C. The complexity of a script having syllabic and logographic signs, many of them with several values as one and the other, or as both, stimulated scribal ingenuity in wordplay. Riddles were collected in the middle of the third millennium B.C. and others copied in schools centuries later.[8] Late in the second millennium B.C. available documents suggest that major works of literature, science and divination were revised to make what became almost canonical texts. Whereas manuscripts of the same work from earlier times may vary widely, after this time there is much greater standardization. Successive generations copied them thereafter with care until the demise of the cuneiform script. However, the language of these old texts could not always be readily understood, especially as Assyrian and Babylonian gave way to Aramaic under the late Assyrian and Babylonian emperors. In the eighth century B.C., perhaps earlier, scribes were composing commentaries to explain some of the traditional works. Whether their purpose was private edification, instruction of students, or something else, we cannot tell. At least they were considered suitable for inclusion in the library of Ashurbanipal at Nineveh, and some are extant in several copies.

In style the commentaries are simple, either excerpting words for comment (*ṣâtu* 'extract' type), or citing a line of text to comment upon one or more words in it (*mukallimtu* 'explanatory' type), with a few following other patterns (other terms used are *maš'altu* 'inquiry,' *šūt pî* 'opinion'). The comments themselves are mainly lexical, showing variant spellings, identifying a verbal form by its infinitive, supplying synonyms, and especially giving Akkadian meanings for Sumerian logograms, sometimes providing several possible equivalents, sometimes breaking them into separate elements, each with its own value and Akkadian rendering.[9]

Three examples display the methods. A commentary on the Babylonian Theodicy, l. 97, reads: [ŠUB]: *na-du-u* : ŠUB: *e-ze-bi* : *ṣú-ṣur-tú* : *par-ṣi* [ ]. The logogram ŠUB has here the Akkadian meaning *nadû* in the sense of *ezēbu* 'to leave'; *uṣurtu* 'design, plan' is synonymous with *parṣu* 'decree,' a conjugated form of *nadû* and the noun *uṣurtu* occurring in the text proper.[10] Secondly, in an astronomical omen, "If the moon is early and darkens at even, an eclipse will occur at an unusual time, the twelfth or thirteenth day," *ba-ra-ri* 'evening watch' is explained as Sumerian BARA = Akkadian *la-a* 'not,' logogram RI = Akkadian *a-dan-nu* 'period,' yielding "at an unusual time" to link with the phrase occurring in the apodosis (*ina lā adannišu*). Thus the sense of the two halves of the prognostication is brought closer.[11] The "analysis" of the word in this instance is typical of the more learned commentaries which may indulge in extended etymological fantasies.[12] In the third example identification advances beyond elementary lexical equations. The phrase "the night, the veiled daughter-in-law" in an incantation is expounded "the veiled daughter-in-law is (the goddess) Gula because no one may look at her even from a distance."[13] Explanations like this occur together with the second kind.

These examples are scribal products, presumably intended for scribal use. Others are known in a less academic scene. Divination of every sort was integral to the daily life of the king above all, for the state relied upon his well-being. From the Nineveh archives numerous letters addressed to the later kings of Assyria have been recovered, among them a large group sent by scholars to inform the king on a variety of matters. Frequently the king asked for elucidation of a recent phenomenon, the scholars being expected to supply the answer from their books. One letter cites an omen, "If the star Shanûmma approaches the god Enmesharra, the country will be happy," and comments, "Shanûmma is Mars; good fortune for the king my lord." It continues with another omen, "If Mars appears in Ayar, there will be hostilities; affliction of the Ummān-manda," with the comment, "Ummān-manda is the Cimmerians."[14] In the same way, a letter about an eclipse that had worried the king states, "This lunar eclipse which took place affected all countries, it heaped all its evil upon the Westland"; then the writer observes, "Westland is the Hittite country, or Chaldea."[15] The identifications involve synonymy in the case of Mars, interpretation equating archaic names with current usage in the cases of the Ummān-manda and the Westland (Amurru).

Related to these letters is a collection of reports to the king about events of ominous nature, usually astronomical, with advice on their significance and action to be taken to avoid unhappy consequences. One specimen announces, "Tonight Saturn approached the Moon," with the comment, "Saturn is the star of the Sun. Its interpretation is as follows: it is good fortune for the king; Saturn is the star of the king."[16]

The writers of these letters and reports were encyclopedists whose duty was to answer every problem presented. They could discover from their store of knowledge a text that was exactly or nearly appropriate, then show how it suited the incident by means of their comments. In the last text cited, the omen's significance is introduced by the word *pišeršu*. This is translated 'its interpretation,' although the noun *pišru* and the verb *pašāru* have a wider range, covering the ideas of solving problems, effecting release from spells and oaths, in short, of supplying a satisfactory answer.[17]

Similarities between these interpretative techniques and those observed in Jewish literature are plain: synonymy, double meaning, analysis of words, reinterpretation of old names. Do the similarities give a basis for proposing the passage of these practices from Babylonian to Jewish scholarship? Beside them there are other hints of a connection. First is the obvious opportunity of the Babylonian Exile and the continuing life of Jewish communities under Persian rule in Mesopotamia where cuneiform commentaries still flourished, communities that later produced the great Hillel whose rules of interpretation have been noted, and ultimately the Babylonian Talmud. Second is the use of *pšr* 'interpret,' in the Aramaic of Daniel and the Hebrew of the Dead Sea Scrolls (and Eccl 8:1). If this were a loanword from Akkadian, it would be a weighty factor. However, that cannot be demonstrated; at best its employment in these technical, exegetical contexts might be owed to Babylon, but even that is as natural a use of the word within Aramaic as any other.[18] The third hint is the trace of other Babylonian influences in Daniel. There are the titles of the wise men in 2:8 (*kśdym, 'špym*), and the word *'dn* 'time' employed in the sense of Akkadian *adannu* 'the time within, or after which some event is to take place'[19] in chaps. 4 and 7, and the various accurately represented historical items.[20]

Even granted these connections, which are themselves tenuous, Lieberman's conclusion of an indigenous origin for Jewish exegetical processes after setting them beside the Alexandrian may obtain here. Wordplay and popular etymologizing are commonplace in Semitic and other languages. Nevertheless, their development into regular tools for exegesis applied wholesale to traditional texts will have created a climate in Babylonia where, as the normal procedures, they could encourage other circles of scholarship to follow them.

III

While display of cleverness may have been the motive for some rabbinic and Babylonian comments, the majority seriously aimed to explain received texts and to apply them to current affairs. Now production of a commentary presupposes the existence of a text the commentator thought worthy of his attention, presumably a text accepted by others, too, else his commentary would hardly be worthwhile except for his own eyes. Accordingly, only when a text recognized as authoritative was circulating were commentaries likely to be composed. That appears to be true in ancient Mesopotamia, where all known commentaries belong to the eighth century B.C. and later, and are concerned with works from the repertoire normal throughout the scribal houses, works that show little variation from place to place from that time onward. How much earlier commentaries may have been made is not clear because very few literary tablets written between c. 1150 and 750 B.C. have been unearthed. As mentioned, it seems that the end of the second millennium B.C. saw the "canonization" of much of the literature copied faithfully during the next centuries. Accidents of discovery and survival have left us with some commentaries upon works no longer available, and there are other books that do not appear to have received comment, notably the legends of Gilgamesh and others. It may be that these were reckoned old stories without current application. What is important is the distinction maintained between text and commentary; there is no sign of any confusion of the two. Of course, physical circumstances hindered scribes who would add comments to a clay tablet long after it had been inscribed. Scribes and copyists who included glosses or translations at the time of writing took care to mark them by smaller script or a separating stroke.[21] Once a text is "canonized" it may engender commentaries which, in turn, aid preservation of the text.

The same attitude can be seen in the Dead Sea Scrolls, both the biblical manuscripts and the commentaries. No notes or comments were written in the margins, only corrections of copyists' errors. Not until later medieval times, when the Hebrew text of the Old Testament had been established beyond dispute for generations, did scholars add textual notes and eventually commentaries in the margins, resulting in the splendid rabbinic bibles of the sixteenth century. That Hebrew text, we are now aware, was the approved edition of one out of several current in the Herodian period, at least among the Bible students of Qumran. There the copies of that traditional text are more numerous than copies akin to the Septuagint or other traditions. Moreover, the commentaries from

Qumran rest on the traditional text almost entirely, so far as their fragmentary nature allows us to judge, making use of variants in the comments.[22] From these observations we may surmise that that was already accepted as the preferable text, the others being on the decline, a process reaching completion after the fall of Jerusalem.

Here comparison with the picture of Hellenistic Greek scholarly activity derived from the papyri by E. G. Turner is helpful. In the case of Homer either wide circulation of a resultant text, or acceptance of one manuscript as authoritative brought a change: "from about the middle of the second century before Christ such papyri conform more closely than those of the third century to the standard text. They no longer present whole series of additional lines or exuberant random variants; but neither do they contain more than a small proportion of the emendations and readings of the great Alexandrian Homeric scholars. These latter, most of them not in the manuscripts either, are preserved in the Homeric scholia."[23] In discussing the Greek commentaries extant from the first century B.C. and later, Turner emphasizes how they were kept apart from the text proper—various critical signs in the margins directed readers to the commentaries which were copied separately and with less respect. Two frequent critical signs "seem to mark a meaning that needed a commentary to make it precise." (The marks in the margins of the first Isaiah Scroll, lQIs^{a}; of a commentary, 4QpIsa^{c}; and others of the Dead Sea texts may have served thus.) Notes that do appear beside the text in the papyri are "primarily jottings about" it, but "already by the second century after Christ some annotations reach a greater length . . . by the sixth century it is possible to point to well-developed systems of marginal annotation." The advent of the codex form of book in the first and second centuries A.D. encouraged the placing of comments in margins where their reference could be more easily seen than between the columns of a scroll.

Babylonian, Hebrew and Greek scholarship shared the tendency to adopt a single text out of a confusion of varieties, a text either resulting from editorial labor, or existing beforehand, and to record divergences, observations and explanations in separate books thereafter. The impetus to such standardization is not discernible in any of the cultures. No commentaries are known from the previous stage in Babylonian or Hebrew; some may have been composed in Greek just before the transition. At that time manuscripts might diverge strikingly, sometimes falling into definable families. Whether or not comments were incorporated into texts in that situation is a subject for future study; the steps taken to indicate glosses by scribes using cuneiform may imply they would not do it easily. Another consideration against its occurrence is Babylonian scribal concern for accurate copying, evident in line counting and independent collation. Editorial work to produce the "canonical" texts, on the other hand, may have included the deliberate introduction of glosses and explanatory notes. The same attitude, we suggest, prevailed among the Hebrew scribes. Explanatory glosses and longer comments are often presumed to be present in the text of the Old Testament; our argument means that of any there are, most entered the text before the second century B.C., at a time in which it is all too easy to imagine far-reaching changes since we have no manuscript evidence at all! To trace such insertions is a perilous operation, very rarely approaching certainty, unable to obtain assurance without that manuscript evidence.[24] The greater part of ancient interpretation will have been handed down verbally, as were the older parts of the Mishnah.

The Old Testament grew in a world where writing was valued by those who knew of it, and written documents were respected, a world where editing and exact reproduction coexisted, and where important texts were given explanations and preserved for the future. Even those who believed they had been given the final solution to the meaning of the Scriptures did not cease from copying them in their plain, unelaborated state. And to that we owe a debt, else we might have been left with the Habakkuk Commentary, but no Habakkuk, the New Testament, but no Old Testament.

Preservation of the Scriptures is no longer a problem; their true interpretation remains the task of every generation that prizes them. W. S. LaSor has earned his place as a faithful interpreter and reliable teacher in the footsteps of Philip.

NOTES

1. The recent book by R. N. Longenecker, *Biblical Exegesis in the Apostolic Period* (Grand Rapids: Eerdmans, 1975), gives references to the previous studies.
2. W. H. Brownlee, "Biblical Interpretation among the Sectaries of the Dead Sea Scrolls," *BA* 14 (1951): 54–76; reproduced in *BA* 39 (1976): 118–19.
3. D. Winton Thomas, "צלמות in the Old Testament," *JSS* 7 (1962): 191–200; A. R. Millard, "What Has No Taste? (Job 6:6)," *UF* 1 (1969): 210.
4. Cf. J. F. A. Sawyer, "The Place of Folk-Linguistics in Biblical Interpretation" in *The Fifth World Congress of Jewish Studies* 4 (Jerusalem: World Union of Jewish Studies, 1973): 109–13; J. Weingreen, *From Bible to Mishnah* (Manchester: Manchester University, 1976).
5. G. Vermes, "Bible and Midrash: Early Old Testament Exegesis" in *The Cambridge History of the Bible* 1 (ed. P. R. Ackroyd and C. F. Evans; Cambridge: Cambridge University, 1970): 199–231; reprinted with related essays in *Post-Biblical Jewish Studies* (Leiden: E. J. Brill, 1975).
6. D. W. Gooding, *Relics of Ancient Exegesis* (Cambridge: Cambridge University, 1976); "On the Use of the LXX for Dating Midrashic Elements in the Targums," *JTS* 25 (1974): 1–11; "Problems of Text and Midrash in the Third Book of Reigns," *Textus* 7 (1969): 1–29.
7. *Hellenism in Jewish Palestine* (New York: Jewish Theological Seminary, 1962): 47ff., esp. 53.
8. R. D. Biggs, "Pre-Sargonic Riddles from Lagash," *JNES* 32 (1973): 26–33.
9. The only study devoted to the topic is R. Labat, *Commentaires Assyro-Babyloniens sur les Présages* (Bordeaux: Imprimerie-Librairie de l'Université, 1933).
10. W. G. Lambert, *Babylonian Wisdom Literature* (Oxford: Clarendon, 1960): 76.
11. Cited in *CAD* A/1, 101b.
12. Others may be read in L. W. King, *The Seven Tablets of Creation* 1 (London: Luzac and Co., 1902): 157ff.; W. G. Lambert, "An Address of Marduk to the Demons," *AfO* 17 (1956): 310–21 (with attention to rabbinic parallels on p. 311); 19 (1959): 118–19; R. D. Biggs, "An Esoteric Babylonian Commentary," *RA* 62 (1968): 51–58, notably ll. 14–18; M. Civil, "Medical Commentaries from Nippur," *JNES* 33 (1974): 329–38.
13. G. Meier, "Kommentare aus dem Archiv der Tempelschule in Assur," *AfO* 12 (1937–39): 240 n. 26; cf. *CAD* K, 82a.
14. Re-edited by S. Parpola, *Letters from Assyrian Scholars to the Kings Esarhaddon and Assurban-*

ipal (AOAT 5.1; Neukirchen-Vluyn: Neukirchener Verlag des Erziehungsvereins, 1970): no. 110.
15. Parpola (N 14): no. 278.
16. Parpola (N 14): no. 326.
17. See A. L. Oppenheim, *The Interpretation of Dreams in the Ancient Near East* (Transactions of the American Philosophical Society 46; Philadelphia: The American Philosophical Society, 1956): 220.
18. See S. A. Kaufman, *The Akkadian Influences on Aramaic* (Assyriological Studies 19; Chicago: University of Chicago, 1974): 81.
19. C. J. Gadd, "Some Babylonian Divinatory Methods and their Inter-relations" in *La Divination en Mésopotamie ancienne* (ed. J. Nougayrol, XIVᵉ Rencontre Assyriologique Internationale, Strasbourg, 1965; Paris: Presses Universitaires de France, 1966): 31; cf. *CAD* A/1, 97–101.
20. Cf. A. R. Millard, "Daniel 1–6 and History," *EvQ* 49 (1977): 67–73.
21. See J. Krecher, "Glossen" in *RLA* 3, 431–40.
22. P. W. Skehan ("The Biblical Scrolls from Qumran and the Text of the Old Testament," *BA* 28 [1965]: 87–100) surveys the manuscripts. For the text see H. M. Orlinsky, "Notes on the Present State of the Textual Criticism of the Judean Biblical Cave Scrolls" in *A Stubborn Faith* (W. A. Irwin Volume, ed. E. C. Hobbs; Dallas: Southern Methodist University, 1956): 117–31, supported by later finds.
23. E. G. Turner, *Greek Papyri* (Oxford: Clarendon, 1968): 109. Following quotations are taken from pp. 117 and 122.
24. Two cases have been argued recently upon apparently cogent grounds by M. H. Goshen-Gottstein ("Hebrew Syntax and the History of the Biblical Text," *Textus* 8 [1973]: 100–06) on Isa 9:13,14, and A. Hurwitz ("On the Form נעל . . . שלף—Ruth 4:7" (in Hebrew), *Shnaton* 1 [1975]: xii,xiv) on Ruth 4:7. The former has been disputed, however, by T. Muraoka, "On the Nominal Clause in the Old Syriac Gospels," *JSS* 20 (1975): 30 n. 4.

21

CASE VOWELS ON MASCULINE SINGULAR NOUNS IN CONSTRUCT IN UGARITIC

GARY A. TUTTLE

I

The purpose of the present study is to attempt to ascertain whether case vowels are preserved on masculine singular nouns in the construct state in Ugaritic. The inquiry is motivated on the one hand by the inconclusive evidence provided by comparative Semitic data,[1] and on the other hand by the assumption of L'Heureux that case vowels may be dropped from divine names in Ugaritic *metri causa*.[2] The vocalizations by Cross in his *Canaanite Myth and Hebrew Epic*[3] clearly indicate his advocacy of this same principle.[4] In fact, Cross seems to go even further, dropping case vowels from more than simply divine names.[5]

The three *aleph* signs, with their inherent vowels, contain the potential for revealing the presence or absence of a case vowel in the position in question. Our inquiry will thus be limited primarily to nominal forms ending in *aleph*. We shall also look to nouns ending in *yod*. In this case, depending upon the nominal pattern, the loss of a case vowel in construct could result in the elision or contraction of the *yod*, and its disappearance from the orthography. So, e.g., if nouns of the form *CCayu*,[6] *CCiyu* or *CCyu* lost their case vowel in the construct state, the following developments would presumably obtain: *CCayu* > *CCay* > *CCê*; *CCiyu*> *CCiy* > *CCî*; and *CCyu* > *CCy* > *CCî*. All three forms would therefore appear in the orthography as *CC*. If, however, the singular construct form appears as *CCy*, this could be an argument for the presence of a case vowel.

The matter of *CC'* nouns is somewhat more complicated. The complexity resides in the disputed question of the syllabic nature of the signs. There is general agreement that when a vowel follows the *aleph*, the *aleph* sign employed is the one with that inherent vowel.[7] The problem arises with vowelless *aleph*. The most recent discussion of this problem, and in our opinion the most convincing, is that of D. Marcus, "The Three Alephs in Ugaritic."[8] Marcus gives a brief, but complete, survey of the scholarly discussion of the Ugaritic *aleph*'s,[9] so there is no point in presenting a detailed summary here. The three most probable views are recorded by Gordon: (1) the inherent vowel reflects the vowel preceding the *aleph;* (2) only *aleph-i* is used for vowelless *aleph;* (3) any *aleph* sign may be used.[10] Although Gordon admits that "where comparative Semitic grammar calls for vowelless aleph, the scribes nearly always write *i,*" he concludes his discussion by saying, "it is likely that vowelless aleph tends to be represented by the aleph-sign containing the vowel that precedes it."[11] This conclusion requires that Gordon assent to the principle formulated by Harris that *Ca'* > *Ce'*,[12] in order to explain those forms which exhibit *aleph-i* where *aleph-a* would be expected.

Perhaps Gordon would have done better to conclude that the use of *aleph-i* for syllable-closing *aleph* was by design. Marcus' study shows clearly that the vast majority of forms with *aleph* in Ugaritic can be convincingly explained according to the principles first articulated by Ginsberg,[13] viz., *a* = *'a, 'â; u* = *'u, 'û, 'ô; i* = *'i, 'î, 'ê* or *v'*. This view of the *aleph*'s is prompted mainly by the generally accepted contention by Ginsberg that Barth's law (regarding the vocalization of the imperfect in Hebrew[14]) is applicable to Ugaritic.[15] Moreover, Rainey has maintained that the attenuation of **yaqtōl* > **yiqtōl,* characteristic of biblical Hebrew, is not present in the "true glosses" of El-Amarna. Rainey suggests that this vocalic shift is "very late according to all indications,"[16] and is thus probably not present in **yaqtul(u)* forms in Ugaritic. This lends support to Ginsberg's and Marcus' understanding of *aleph-i* being used for syllable-closing *aleph* (thus, e.g., *yiḫd* was probably vocalized **ya'ḫudu,* rather than **ye'ḫudu*). It is this pervasive usage of *aleph-i* for syllable-closing *aleph* which allows a resolution to the problem of the case vowel in masculine singular construct nouns.

II

If the case vowel had been lost from masculine singular nouns in construct in Ugaritic, such nouns from *CC'* roots should end in *aleph-i*. Thus, e.g., "the king's throne" should appear as *ksi mlk* no matter what the phrase's syntax. The best possible example to prove that the case vowel is still present would be a masculine singular construct *CC'* noun in the accusative which appears with final *aleph-a*. The genitive case is not helpful because it would appear with final *aleph-i* whether the case vowel were present or not. With most masculine nouns the nominative case contains the possibility for confusion with the plural. The long *ū* of the masculine plural nominative would, of course, be preserved even in the construct state.[17] Only context would determine if the construct noun were singular or plural. Context is a valid criterion for such a determination, but we eliminate all possible confusion by seeking a masculine singular construct noun in the accusative.

Such a noun as we have been describing exists in Ugaritic in a clear context. It is a form of the ubiquitous *ks'*. The passage reads as follows:

špš [23]*tṣḥ lmt*	Šapš cries to Môt:
šm' m' [24]*lbn ilm mt*	"Hear now, O divine Môt.

ik tmt[ḫ][25]*ṣ ʿm aliyn bʿl*	Why do you con[te]nd with Mighty Baʿl?
[26]*ik al yšmʿ[k] ṯr* [27]*il abk*	How will Bull-El, your father, but hear [you]!
lysʿ alt [28]*ṯbtk*	Surely he will pull out the stays[18] of your dwelling,
lyhpk ksa mlkk	Verily he will overthrow the throne of your kingship,
[29]*lyṯbr ḫṭ mṯpk̩*	Indeed he will break your judgment-staff.'' (6[49].6.22–29)[19]

Here clearly *ksa mlkk* (l. 28) is the direct object of *lyhpk,* and there can be no doubt that *ksa* is a masculine singular noun in construct with *mlkk*. Thus we would vocalize something like **kussi'a mulkika*. The *a* on *ksa* must designate the case ending. Had the case vowel been lost, one would have expected the final syllable closed with *aleph* to be represented by *i*. A parallel passage is found in 2.3[129].18, but the word *ksa* must there be restored. The phrase *ksa mlk(y/h)* has been restored by some in 22.1[123].17, one of the *rpum* texts,[20] on the basis of the parallelism of *ks' ṯbth* and *kḫṯ drkth* elsewhere.[21] However, the only certain example of *ksa* as a masculine singular construct noun in the published Ugaritic texts is that cited above.[22]

Another, somewhat problematical, example of a *CC'* noun in the accusative case and in construct occurs in 4[51].6.40–43:

[40]*ṭbḫ alpm [ap]* [41]*ṣin*	He slaughtered oxen [and] sheep;
šql ṯrm [w]m[42]*ria il*	he felled bulls [and] choicest fatling
ʿglm d[t] [43]*šnt*	yearli[ng] calves,
imr qmṣ l[l]im	kids from the abundance[23] of l[am]bs.

Here the noun *mria* is in construct with *il*[24] and this phrase is a second object of the verb *šql*. Thus *mria* is masculine singular construct and accusative, and so meets the criteria defined earlier for illustrating that the case vowel is not lost in construct. The double *aleph* on *mria* is a bit problematical (the word also occurs as *mra*). Marcus intimates that the form contains *i* as a vowel, with no consonantal value, and *a* as *'a: *marī'a*.[25]

A third example of a masculine singular construct noun in the accusative from a *CC'* root which still exhibits the case ending is found in 15[128].5.16–18:

[16]*ʿrb špš lymǵ* [17]*krt*	At sunset verily will Krt arrive,
ṣbia špš bʿlny	at the setting[26] of the sun, our lord.

The form *ṣbia* in this passage is analogous to *mria* in the preceding passage. *Ṣbia* is in construct with *špš,* and the two words serve as a temporal phrase used adverbially, hence the accusative case ending on *ṣbia*.[27] The counterpart of *ṣbia* without the *i, ṣba,* is used similarly in 16.1[125].36:

[32]*aḫtk* [33]*ydʿt krḥmt*	Your sister I know is truly compassionate;
[34]*al tšt bšdm mmh*	she will surely place in the fields her water,
[35]*bsmkt ṣat npšh*	in the heavens[28] the expiration of her breath.
[36]*[ ]mt[ ] ṣba rbt* [37]*špš*	Await(?) the setting of Dame Šapš
wtgh nyr rbt	and the repairing of Lady Illuminator.

This passage entails many difficulties. The lines previous to these depict Krt's son, Ilḥu, lamenting the impending death of his father whom he had thought to be immortal. Finally, Krt bids his son not to weep, but to call his sister, Ṯtmnt, about whom he says *tbkn wtdm ly* "she shall weep and wail for me" (1. 30). Ilḥu is then instructed to speak to his sister (*ǵzr al trgm laḫtk,* 1. 31), the *al* apparently being asseverative, since in 11. 39–45 the message he is to give is stated, and in 11. 46ff. Ilḥu sets off. Thus our passage, which follows the instructions to "tell your sister" and a partially broken line, probably also uses *al* as asseverative rather than negative. This interpretation is reinforced by the usage of the asseverative *kap* in *krḥmt* in the preceding line. The second and third lines apparently depict with poetic hyperbole the probable grieving which Ṯtmnt will demonstrate, punctuated with weeping and sighing. Unfortunately, the beginning of 1. 36 above is broken, which causes ambiguity in interpreting *wtgh* in the following line. It is clear that if [ ]*mt*[ ] is a verb, the activity mentioned takes place "at the setting of Dame Šapš." If [ ]*mt*[ ] is a verb which is omitted in the parallel line, then *wtgh* may be a *t*-formation noun from **wgh* 'to repair, go, turn, head' (cf. Ar. *wajuha*), and would mean 'repairing, going,' or the like. The phrase *nyr ṭbt* 'goodly Luminary' parallel to *špš* in lines 18–19 of the newly published RS 34.126 makes it clear that *nyr rbt* here is a parallel to *špš*. In view of the fact that Ilḥu meets Ṯtmnt when she is coming forth to draw water (11. 50–51), an activity commonly done at eventide,[29] Ginsberg[30] (followed by Caquot[31]) may not be far wrong in restoring a verb from Mishnaic Hebrew: *mtn* (H- 'to wait'). If such an interpretation is correct, *ṣba* is accusative because it is direct object,[32] and, being in construct with *rbt,* illustrates once more that case vowels are not lost from masculine singular construct nominal forms.

We turn now to a consideration of passages containing those words we earlier eliminated as primary evidence, namely, masculine singular construct nouns from *CC'* roots which stand in the nominative. If we may convincingly argue that in particular contexts these nouns are singular, they will provide corroborating evidence that case vowels are not lost from masculine singular nouns in construct in Ugaritic. The word *ks'* is particularly productive, for its plural has feminine morphology: *ksat*. Thus no possibility of confusion with the masculine plural nominative in *ū* exists. *Ksu* can only represent the masculine singular nominative. A first example demonstrates the usage of *ksu ṯbt* // *arṣ nḥlt:*

[10]*idk al ttn* [11]*pnm*	Thereupon do thou set face
tk qrth [12]*hmry*	midst his city Hmry;
mk ksu [13]*ṯbth*	Low is the throne of his sitting,
ḫḫ arṣ [14]*nḥlth*	Base, the land of his inheritance.
	(4[51].8.10–14)

In discussing this passage,[33] M. Pope inserts the line *'m bn ilm mt* before *tk qrth hmry,* an emendation[34] apparently based on the similar passage, 5[67].2.13–16:

[13]*idk* [14]*lytn pn*<*m*>	Thereupon they set face
'm bn ilm mt	toward the divine Môt
[15]*tk qrth hmry*	midst his city Hmry;[35]

mk ksu [16]*ṯbt*<*h*>	Low is the throne of <his> sitting,
ḫḫ arṣ nḥlth	Base, the land of his inheritance.

However, Pope misinterprets the syntax of the last two lines, as Held has recently shown.[36] Pope translates, "Ruin the throne where he sits // Infernal filth his heritage," taking *ḫḫ arṣ* as a construct phrase, comparing *ḫḫ* to Akk. *ḫaḫḫu* 'spittle, slime, mucus,' and construing *arṣ* as a reference to the netherworld.[37] However, a parallel passage (noted by Held) makes clear that *ksu ṯbth* must parallel *arṣ nḥlth*. The passage reads:

[12]*idk al ttn* [13]*pnm*	Thereupon do thou set face
tk ḥqkpt [14]*il klh*	midst Ḥqkpt[38] (and) the god of all of it;[39]
kptr [15]*ksu ṯbth*	Caphtor is the throne of his sitting,
ḥkpt [16]*arṣ nḥlth*	Ḥkpt,[40] the land of his inheritance.
	(3['NT vi].6.12–16)

In this passage clearly *kptr // ḥkpt*, thus *ksu ṯbth // arṣ nḥlth*. Moreover, *ksu* must be in construct with *ṯbth*, the phrase forming the subject of a nominal sentence. It is obvious from morphology that *ksu* is singular. Here, then, is a masculine singular construct noun from a *CC'* root which occurs in the nominative, and whose case vowel is preserved. The syntax of *mk ksu ṯbth // ḫḫ arṣ nḥlth* in the two previous passages (4[51], 3['NT vi]) is analogous. Each colon is a nominal sentence with *ksu ṯbth // arṣ nḥlth* serving as a grammatical subject, while *mk // ḫḫ* are the respective predicates.[41] Again, *ksu* is a masculine singular construct noun with its case vowel present.[42]

We considered earlier the phrase *ṣb(i)a špš*. This phrase also occurs twice in the nominative, *ṣbu špš*, in text 35[3].47,53, but the text, which apparently deals with sacrifices for various gods, and possibly ritual acts, is too broken to provide a clear context.[43] The word *ṣbu* also occurs in the sense of 'soldier, army.' The phrase *ṣbu anyt*[44] sheds no light on the problem we are discussing because *ṣbu* is undoubtedly plural, "soldiers of ships" / "sailors." However, in the *Krt* text the word seems to occur in the singular, although the passage is fraught with difficulties.

[85]*'dn ngb wyṣi*	A crowd supply,[45] and let it go forth,
[86]*ṣbu ṣbi ngb*	a supplied super-army;
[87]*wyṣi 'dn m'*	and let go forth the crowd together,
[88]*ṣbuk ul mad*	your army, a great host,
[89]*ṯlṯ mat rbt*	three hundred ten-thousands.
	(14[KRT].85–89)

In spite of the difficulties, it seems likely that *ṣbuk* is singular, since its appositive (or predicate), *ul mad*,[46] is almost surely singular. We consider *mad* a singular attributive adjective modifying *ul*, a singular noun. *Ṣbu*, the cognate of Hebrew *ṣābā'*, in the form *ṣbuk* is in construct with its suffix: **ṣaba'uka*. The construct phrase *ṣbu ṣbi* offers a clear example of the same word with the nominative case vowel still present: **ṣaba'u ṣaba'i*. The construction appears to be a superlative, "an army's army," i.e., "a mighty/powerful/excellent/super army." The syntax at first blush seems peculiar, but we view *ṣbu ṣbi ngb* as the grammatical subject of *wyṣi,* even though *ad sensum* the phrase is in apposition to *'dn,* and thus, if it were grammatically so interpreted, would require the accusative. The key words are abraded in the parallel passage (14[KRT].176–81), so we do not have an unambiguous control on the syntax. However, it is clear there that the case ending is present on *ṣbu* before the third person masculine singular suffix:

176*'dn ngb w[yṣi]*	A crowd he supplied and [let it go forth],
[ṣbu] 177*ṣbi ng[b]*	a suppli[ed sup]er-army.
[wyṣi 'dn] 178*m'*	[He let go forth the crowd] together,
[ṣ]buh u[l mad]	his [a]rmy, a [mighty ho]st,
179*ṯlṯ mat rbt*	three hundred ten-thousands.
180*hlk lalpm ḫḏḏ*	They went by the thousands like rain,[47]
181*wl rbt kmyr*	and by the ten-thousands like showers.

A third *CC'* form in the nominative which is in construct demands our attention and holds out the possibility of further confirmation of the existence of case vowels in the construct state in Ugaritic. In the description of the ideal son in the *Aqht* poem, one reads the following:

31*[a]ḫd ydh bškrn*	who [s]eizes his hand in (his) drunkenness,
m'msh 32*[k]šb' yn*	who carries him [when] he is sated with wine,
spu ksmh bt b'l	who eats his meal[48] in the temple of Ba'l
33*[wm]nth bt il*	[and] his [po]rtion in the temple of El.
	(17[2 AQHT].1.31–33)[49]

Clearly the forms *aḫd, m'ms* and *spu* are participles which are in construct with their respective complements, thus forming asyndetic relative clauses. There is little doubt but that *spu* is singular, since just prior to the beginning of the description of the son's activities (1. 27) one reads *wykn bnh bbt // šrš bqrb hklh* "that there may be his son in the house // a root in the midst of his palace," where "root" can only be singular. *Bnh* and *šrš* are the antecedents to which the following series of participles refer. Thus it must be conceded that *spu* is a masculine singular construct substantive whose case vowel is preserved.

We have not treated masculine singular construct forms which are in the genitive. These were eliminated, it will be remembered, because if *i* may represent both *'i* and syllable-closing *aleph,* no certain information about the retention of case vowels would be provided, since the orthography would be the same in both cases (i.e., "to the throne of his sitting" = *lksi ṯbth* whether the case vowel is present on *ksi* [**kussi'i*] or absent from it [**kussi'*]). On the basis of the accusative and nominative singular forms we have investigated, which consistently do indicate the presence of case endings on masculine singular construct nouns, we would maintain that in the genitive the case ending is also preserved.

Of course, we have also not dealt with *CC'* nouns which are in the absolute. It is almost universally agreed that case endings are preserved on such nouns. However, we would like to draw attention to one prominent *CC'* proper name which has suffered some abuse at the hands of vocalizers because of the presupposition that a case vowel may be dropped from a divine name *metri causa*. This is the name *rp'*, which is attested frequently in UG 5.2.[50] Cross' rendering of part of the reverse of this text has appeared in at least two places.[51] We give it here *sans* his vocalization:

[6][*yṯpṭ?*] *rpi mlk 'lm b'z*[*h*]	Let Rapi' the eternal king [judge?] in might,
[7][*yṯpṭ? m*]*lk 'lm bḏmrh*	Let [the eter]nal king [judge?] in strength,
bl [8][*ymlk*] *bḥtkh bnmrth*	Verily let him [rule] his offspring in his grace:
lr[9][*mm b*]*arṣ 'zk*	To ex[alt(?)] thy might in the earth
ḏmrk l[*pn*][10]*n(?) ḥtkk*	Thy strength be[fore] us(?) thy offspring,
nmrtk btk [11]*ugrt*	Thy grace in the midst of Ugarit
lymt špš wyrḫ	As long as the years of Sun and Moon
[12]*wn'mt šnt il*	And the pleasance of the years of 'Ēl.

A key to the understanding of this text resides in the significant repetition of the five elements:

'z, ḏmr, l[ ], *ḥtk, nmrt*
'z, ḏmr, l[ ]*n, ḥtk, nmrt.*

Cross' restoration of *l*[*pn*]*n* in the second series (11. 9–10) is highly suspect. The autograph clearly shows the *l,* followed by a break large enough for one letter. Line 10 begins with a sign which can be little else than *n,* which is followed by a clear *k*. The reading is therefore *l*[ ]*nk*. In two recent articles, Fisher has noted the results of his recollation of this text.[52] He affirms without equivocation that the reading of the word in question is *lank*. Therefore, it is very probable that *anh* is to be restored in the first series, broken over 11. 7–8. Thus Cross' restoration of *ymlk* at the beginning of 1. 8 is without foundation.

As for Cross' restorations at the beginning of the text quoted above, the preceding discussion of case endings on *CC'* nouns, as well as Marcus' study,[53] suggests that *rpi* in 1. 6 cannot be nominative as Cross construes it, but must be genitive.[54] As such, it is doubtful that a finite verb should be restored preceding it. More likely, a substantive in construct or a preposition has been abraded. Furthermore, in each of the three occurrences of *rp'* in UG 5.2, the epithet *mlk 'lm* follows immediately.[55] Very probably, then, a form of *rp'* is to be restored at the beginning of 1. 7 preceding [*m*]*lk 'lm*. Since there is no indication of an abrasion at the end of 1. 6, the *h* restored by Cross is inappropriate.[56] Therefore, it seems likely that *'z* at the end of 1. 6 is in construct with [*rp' m*]*lk 'lm* of 1. 7, so the appropriate form of *rp'* to be restored in 1. 7 is the genitive: [*rpi m*]*lk 'lm*. Thus the *yṯpṭ* restored by Cross at the beginning of 1. 7 is eliminated. With these notes in mind, and allowing the repeated five-member series to be a guide,[57] the following stichometry emerges:

[6][ ]*rpi mlk 'lm*	[ ] of Rp', king eternal
b'z [7][*rpi m*]*lk 'lm*	by[58] the power of Rp', king eternal
bḏmrh bl[8][*anh*]	by his protection, by [his] predomi[nance],

bḥtkh bnmrth	by his superintendence, by his strength.
lr^{9}[b b]arṣ ʻzk	May your might in[crease in] the land,
ḏmrk la^{10}nk	your protection, your predominance,
ḥtkk nmrtk	your superintendence, your strength
btk ^{11}ugrt	in the midst of Ugarit
lymt špš wyrḫ	for the days of Šapš and Yariḫ
^{12}wnʻmt šnt il	and the most pleasant years of El.

III

We may now turn to a consideration of the evidence provided by *CCy* forms. We admit that the evidence gained from *CCy* forms is inferential. However, it is known that **ay*-diphthongs monophthongize in Ugaritic,[59] and that **-iy* contracts as well, becoming long *-î*.[60] Thus if a *CCy* noun vocalized *CCayu* or *CCiyu* had lost its case vowel in the construct, one of the following developments would have occurred: *CCay* > *CCê* or *CCiy* > *CCî*. The result would be that the *y* would disappear from the orthography. Therefore, if in a given context it can be convincingly argued that a *CCy* nominal form is singular and in construct, and the *y* is still present, then we may conclude that the case vowel is still present. Several examples are offered by the Ugaritic literature.

It may be helpful simply to delineate the examples in alphabetical order. We note first *any* 'boat' (Heb. *'ŏnî,* Amarna *a-na-ya*[61]) which appears in the nominative and in construct in text 2056.1:

^{1}any al[šy?]	the ship of Al[šy]
^{2}db atlg(?) [ ]	which is in Atlg [ ].

It is certain that the noun in question is singular, because the plural is amply attested as *anyt*.[62] Hence an appropriate vocalization might be **'anayu,* with the case vowel still present. Text 2059.24–25 provides an example of *any* with a suffix (Virolleaud's translation):

^{24}wanyk št	Et maintenant ton navire est stationné[63]
^{25}by ʻky ʻryt	dans[64] Acre (après avoir été) déchargé.[65]

Here again *any* is singular construct, in the accusative case.[66] The presence of the *y* argues for the maintenance of the case vowel: **wa'anayaka.*

Numerous examples of the word *ary // aḫ* are found in which *ary* is in construct with a suffix. No example is yet available of *ary* in construct with another noun. Moreover, it cannot be convincingly shown that *ary* is singular in any case, and, in fact, in most cases it may be decisively shown that *ary* must be plural. Typical is:

^{44}ṣḥ aḫh bbhth	He (i.e., Baʻl) calls his brothers into his house,
a[r]yh ^{45}bqrb hklh	his s[i]bs into the midst of his palace:
ṣḥ ^{46}šbʻm bn aṯrt	he calls the seventy children of Aṯirat.

(4[51].6.44–46)

The "seventy children of Aṯirat" is a synonym for "the gods,"[67] and clearly argues for construing *aḫ* and *ary* as plurals also. In the same vein we may note 4[51].4.48–51:

[48]*yṣḥ* [49]*aṯrt wbnh*	Aṯirat and her children cry out,
ilt wṣbrt [50]*aryh*	the goddess and the group of her sibs:
wn in bt b'l [51]*km ilm*	"Lo, there exists no house of Ba'l as (for) the gods
wḥẓr kbn aṯrt	nor court as (for) the children of Aṯirat."[68]

Here the obvious plural *ilm* is parallel to *bn aṯrt* and, since the *bn aṯrt* are identical with *bnh* in the first line, *aryh* must be plural as well. The only passages where it may be suggested that *ary* is singular occur in the *Aqht* poem, of which the following is typical:

[16]*mk bšb' ymm*	Lo, on the seventh day
[17][*w*]*yqrb b'l bḥnth*	Ba'l approaches during his supplication
abynt [18][*d*]*nil mt rpi*	the misery of [D]nil, man of Rpu,
anḫ ǵzr [19][*m*]*t ḥrnmy*	the sighing of the hero, [m]an of the Harnamite,[69]
din bn lh [20]*km aḫh*	who has no son as his brother(s)
wšrš km aryh	nor root as his sibling(s).
	(17[2 AQHT].1.16–20)[70]

There is nothing in the *Aqht* poem which requires that Dnil have more than one brother. So it might be argued that *aḫ* and *ary* are here singular. On the other hand, it cannot be established that Dnil had only one brother. When Dnil's daughter, Pǵt, makes reference to her slain brother,[71] which reference must necessarily be singular, the problematic *'l umt* is found parallel to *aḫ* where one might have expected *ary*. This may, of course, simply be poetic variation. However, it might indicate that *ary* is used in Ugaritic only in the plural, or else that it is collective. If the former, the word is not germane to our inquiry. If the latter, however, the word would be singular in form, and so those examples cited above in which *ary* is nominative or accusative are apropos, and support the argument that case vowels are preserved in construct.

Another, somewhat more convincing, example may be provided by a nominal form from *bky:*

[26]*y'rb hḥdrh ybky*	He (i.e., Krt) enters his room, he weeps,
[27]*bṯn* [*r*]*gmm wydm'*	while repeating[72] [wo]rds he sheds tears.
[28]*tntkn udm'th*	His tears pour out
[29]*km ṯqlm arṣh*	like shekels to the ground,
[30]*kmḫmšt mṭth*	like five-shekel pieces to the bed.
[31]*bm bkyh wyšn*	While he is weeping he falls asleep;
[32]*bdm'h nhmmt*	while shedding tears (there is) slumber.
[33]*šnt tluan* [34]*wyškb*	Sleep prevails and he reclines;
nhmmt [35]*wyqmṣ*	slumber, and he reposes.[73]
	(14[KRT].26–35)

In 1. 31 one finds *bm bkyh,* the latter element of which is probably an infinitive

construct with suffix, indicating a temporal clause. The form is in the genitive following the preposition *bm,* and is simultaneously in construct with its suffix. The preservation of the *y* suggests the presence of the case vowel.[74]

Evidence for the retention of the case vowel in the construct may also be provided by the epithet of El, *bny bnwt,* frequently translated, "Creator of creatures,"[75] but literally, "Builder of built ones."[76] The epithet occurs in the accusative in text 4[51].2.8–11:[77]

[8]*štt ḫptr lišt*	She (i.e., Aṯrt) put a pot on the fire,
[9]*ḫbrṯ lẓr pḥmm*	an ewer[78] on top of the coals.
[10]*t'pp ṯr il dpid*	She importunes Bull-El, the merciful;
[11]*tǵẓy bny bnwt*	she entreats the Creator of creatures.

Here *ṯr il dpid* and its parallel *bny bnwt* are the objects of the verbs in their respective clauses. The presence of the *y* on *bny* makes likely the retention of the case vowel. The epithet *bny bnwt* is never used in the nominative, but it occurs in the genitive on several occasions, both as object of the preposition *l*[79] and as *nomen rectum* in a construct phrase.[80] If *bny* is to be vocalized as an active participle *(*bāniyu),* its genitive would be **bāniyi.* The fact that the final **-iyi* did not contract to *-î* and the *y* disappear from the orthography may mean one of three things: (1) such a contraction is not regular with the participle; (2) the phrase *bny bnwt,* being an epithet, is a frozen form not readily susceptible to phonological alteration; (3) *bny* should be vocalized as a *nomen professionis* rather than participle: **bannāyi.* In our opinion explanations 1 and 2 seem the more probable,[81] but the very ambiguity lessens the value of *bny bnwt* for our inquiry.

The form *diy,* representing two different nouns, one meaning 'wing' (// *knp*),[82] the other meaning 'bird,' or the like (// *nšr*),[83] provides no evidence relevant to our study. The former word, occurring with reference to *nšrm,* is undoubtedly dual, while the latter is not attested in the construct.

The epithet of Aṯirat's messenger, *qdš amrr,* is *dgy,* which Gordon translates "fisherman."[84] It occurs in construct in both of its attestations, and is in each case vocative, hence it would probably end in *-u* since it is in apposition to the subject ('you,' inherent in the imperative verb in each case). Thus we read:

[31]*dgy rbt aṯr[t ym]*	O fisherman of Dame Aṯira[t of the Sea],
[32]*qḥ rṯt bdk* [ ]	Take a net in your hand(s) [ ],
[33]*rbt 'l ydm* [ ]	a dragnet on your hands [ ].[85]
	(4[51].2.31–33)

The syntax seems fairly clear. *Qḥ* is imperative and *dgy* . . . specifies the addressee. In the second passage, the vocative-*lamed* is present:[86]

[9]*šmšr* [10]*ldgy aṯrt*	Proceed, O fisherman of Aṯirat.
[11]*mǵ lqdš amrr*	Go, O Qdš-amrr.
	(3['NT].6.9–11)

Here there is little doubt that *dgy aṯrt* // *qdš amrr* are vocatives, each in apposition to the inherent subject of the imperatives.[87] If *dgy* is gentilic or participial, and if Gordon is correct in assuming the vocalization **-iyy-* for the gentilic,[88] the presence of the *y* on *dgy* suggests the preservation of the case ending on this construct noun. Had the case vowel disappeared, one might have expected the following developments: **dagiyyu* > **dagiyy* > **dagiy* > *dagî, or *dāgiyu* > **dāgiy* > **dāgî*. Either way the orthographic representation would be *dg*.

A uniquely attested noun may be of some help in our investigation. The word is *mnḥyk,* which appears in the following passage:

36*[wy'n] ṯr abh il*	[Then answered] Bull, his father, El:
'bdk b'l y ymm	"Your servant is Ba'l, O Yamm,
'bdk b'l 37*[l'l]m*	Your servant is Ba'l [forev]er.
bn dgn asrkm	Dagan's son is your prisoner.
hw ybl argmnk kilm	He will bring your tribute[89] as the gods
38[ ] *ybl k!bn qdš mnḥyk*	[ ]will bring as the holy ones your offering."
	(2.1[137].36–38)

The word *mnḥyk* is surely cognate with the Heb. *minḥāʰ* (cf. Ar. *manaḥa* 'to grant, give, bestow'). This form may provide further evidence of a nominal feminine ending in *-y* in Ugaritic.[90] Moreover, it argues for the preservation of a case vowel in the construct (albeit in the feminine). If the ending is *-ay,* the loss of the case vowel would have produced **manḥayaka* > **manḥayka* > **manḥêka,* which would have appeared as *mnḥk* in the orthography.

IV

It may be well now to summarize what we have demonstrated. From a consideration of singular *CC'* nouns in construct, several cases were identified where the construct noun is in the accusative, and ends in *a,* thus showing that the case vowel was still present. Secondly, we considered *CC'* nouns in the nominative whose morphology or context make clear that they are singular. In these cases considerable evidence corroborating our view that case vowels are retained in construct was set forth. A consideration of the proper name *rp'* suggested that Cross' treatment of *rpi* in UG 5.2.2.6 as a nominative is untenable. Finally, we investigated nouns ending in *-y,* most of which are from *CCy* roots. The evidence here is of lesser value because of possible frozen formulae, occasional contextual ambiguity and unique attestations. However, fairly reliable inferential evidence was mustered to suggest once more that case vowels are preserved on singular nouns in construct in Ugaritic. Thus we conclude that Cross' frequent omission of case endings from divine names, epithets and an occasional common noun in the construct in his vocalization of Ugaritic is unwarranted. It may also be doubted that case vowels may be dropped from divine names in the absolute *metri causa*. Certainly the assumption may not be granted *a priori*. Thus a certain skepticism about Cross' methodology in dealing with Ugaritic poetry may be voiced. It is founded in part on questionable presuppositions.[91]

NOTES

1. In a paper of this scope we cannot survey the behavior of case vowels on masculine singular construct nouns throughout Semitic. Very generally speaking, Akkadian and Arabic form the dipoles, the former exhibiting the loss of case vowels in the masculine singular construct, while the latter attests their preservation. Closer scrutiny, of course, presents a more complicated picture, but the lack of uniformity supports no *a fortiori* conclusion regarding Ugaritic. The Eblaic material holds no immediate promise of clarifying the matter (see G. Pettinato, "Testi cuneiformi del 3. millennio in paleo-cananeo rinvenuti nella campagne 1974 a Tell Mardīkh = Ebla," *Or* 44 [1975]: 361–74).
2. Conrad E. L'Heureux, "El and the Rephaim: New Light from *Ugaritica* V" (diss. Harvard University, 1971): iv. In his preface, L'Heureux gives a brief apologetic for presenting the Ugaritic texts he discusses with vocalization. One reason to vocalize, he says (iv, and n. 1), is to test the hypothesis that "the fundamental parameter in the meter of Ugaritic poetry is the number of syllables in each colon." Yet he assumes *a priori* "that the case endings may be omitted from divine names *metri causa*"!
3. F. M. Cross, *Canaanite Myth and Hebrew Epic* (Cambridge: Harvard University, 1973).
4. One finds, e.g., *'il* (nom.): *CMHE* (N 3): 15(2x) and 37; *'il* (gen.): 36(3x) and 38–39(2x); but *'ilu:* 16(2x), 21(2x), 184(2x); and *'ili:* 21, 37(2x), 117. The name *b'l* is used with the case ending fairly consistently (nom.: 37, 64, 114[4x], 115, 116, 117[2x], 118, 183 n. 162[2x], 184[2x]; but nom. without case ending: 117, 118; gen.: 114, 184). *Aṯrt* sometimes has the case ending (21, 28, 31[2x], 33, 184[2x]) and sometimes not (20, 67[2x]). The name *rpu* is vocalized with the case vowel on p. 20, but without it on 21 and 67.
5. E. g., Cross eliminates the case ending on divine epithets—*malk* (nom., epithet of El; *CMHE* [N 3]: 15, but cf. *malki* on 36 and 39), *rabbat* (nom., epithet of *Aṯrt*, 33; but *rabbatu* on 184), especially those which constitute a construct phrase—*rpu's* epithet, *malk 'ôlami* (20, 21[2x]); the last two elements of Ba'l's epithet, *ẓbl b'l arṣ*, vocalized *ba'l 'arṣi* (64, 117, 118); Ba'l's epithet *bin dagani* (114, but *binu Dagni* on 183 n. 162); Ba'l's epithet *rkb 'rpt*, vocalized *rākib 'arapāti* (67, but *la rākibi 'urapāti* on 114); Môt's designation *bin 'ili-mi* (117). In at least two instances Cross omits the case ending from predicate adjectives—*'ôlam* (nom., 15) and *dārdā<r>* (nom., 15). Twice he has eliminated the case ending from common nouns in construct—*la-yāmāt šapši* (gen., 21) and *ḥayyat* (nom., 184; but cf. *ḥayyatu* on 16, though in this case the next word, *ḥiẓẓata* [gen.!] has the wrong case ending). Cross also uses case endings irregularly on prepositions. E.g., the word *'m* is found vocalized three different ways in *CMHE: 'im* (36, 37, 38); *'ima* (16, 184); and *'immaka* (with suffix; 116 n. 17[2x]). Whether the *m* is doubled is moot, but surely a case vowel would preserve the doubling whether a suffix followed or not. Precisely what determines the presence or absence of case endings on prepositions in Cross' vocalizations is not clear. One suspects meter might be the governing factor, but some examples lead to confusion. One reads, e.g.:

'im 'il mabbikê naharêmi
qirba 'apiqê tihāmatêmi (CMHE, 36).

The syllable count as Cross vocalizes is 9:10. However, a case vowel on *'im* would provide the syllable needed for perfect balance. On p. 37 one finds:

tôk ğūri <'i>li
'im puḫri mô'idi.

Here the count is 5:6. Addition of a case vowel on *tôk* would have balanced the two lines. Like *qrb* (vocalized *qirba* on 36, and *baqirbi* on 178 n. 135), *tk* maintains its character as a substantive, occurring both independently (vocalized *tôk* by Cross; 37, 38[2x]), and governed by a preposition: *btk* (vocalized *ba-tôk*; 21). If, as Cross suggests, by vocalizing, "the morphology and syntax of the interpretation are made plain" (*CMHE,* 21 n. 50), one would suspect that *tôka* would be the syntactically least ambiguous form.

Cross' vocalizations are replete with errors and inconsistencies. The most blatant is the following (4[51].4.41ff.):

taḥmuka 'il ḥakamu	*tuḥumuka 'ilu ḥakama*
ḥakamu (sic!) 'ima 'ôlami	*ḥukmuka 'ima 'ôlami*
ḥayyatu ḥiẓẓati taḥmuka	*ḥayyat ḥiẓẓati tuḥumuka*
(CMHE, 16)	*(CMHE,* 184).

Other errors include *Pidrayya bitta rabbi* (for *bitta 'āri,* 116 n. 17); *Yamma la-mitu* (for *yammu,* 116); *wa-yadlup tamūnihū* (for *tamūnuhū,* 115); *'āy-yammarī* vs. *'āy-yamarrī* (115); *'itê* (64, for *'iṯê*); *ḏimrika, namirtuka* (21) should both be accusative; *na'īmatu* (21) should be genitive, governed by the preposition in the preceding line; *yaširu* (21, for *yašīru*); *rā'iyu* (21, for *rā'iyi);* the third radical *n* of *ttḥnn* is misconstrued as the dual morpheme (*tiṯḥānannū,* 117).

Excluding those already mentioned, the inconsistencies include: vocalizing the preposition *l* as *li* (36) but *la* elsewhere; *b* is apparently vocalized *ba* throughout, in spite of the spelling *by* (2059.13,25 *i.a.*) and *bi-i*[ ] (UG 5, 130, III.6′); *la-tattin panīma* (36), but *la-yatinu panīma* (38); *kī ḥayya 'al'iyānu ba'lu* (64), but *wa-himma ḥayyu 'al'iyānu ba'lu* (118; the parallel lines *kī 'iṯê* and *wa-himma 'iṯê* indicate that the two lines just noted have the same syntax); *zubulu* (64, 117, 118), but *zubūlu* (114); *titrapū šamāmi* (118), but *titrapū šamūma* (150); *šamāmi . . . tamaṭṭirūna* (118), but *šamūma . . . tamaṭṭirūna* (151); *la-šamêmi* (117), but *šamêma* (119); the third person masculine singular suffix is vocalized *hu* (15[2x], 21[4x], 36, 37[2x], 117[2x]) and *hū* (115[6x], 178 n. 135[2x], 184), *nu* (117) and *nū* (117[4x]); the first person plural suffix occurs as *nu* (115[2x]) and *nū* (184[2x]).

Though these errors and inconsistencies tend toward obfuscation, rather than making the syntax plain, the evidence mustered above at least suggests the serious possibility that for Cross case vowels may be eliminated. Whether the determination to do so is based solely (or primarily) on metrical considerations is not absolutely clear.

6. "C" designates "consonant." This generalized system of root characterization is employed in Wm. S. LaSor, *Hebrew Handbook* (Pasadena, CA: privately published, 1951; 3d ed., 1961): §§14, 27.22, and 29.

7. Gordon, *UT* §4.8.

8. D. Marcus, "The Three Alephs in Ugaritic," *JANES* 1 (1968): 50–60.

9. Marcus (N 8): 52–53.

10. Gordon, *UT* §4.8.

11. Gordon, *UT* §4.8.

12. Gordon, *UT* §5.16. Cf. Z. S. Harris, "A Conditioned Sound Change in Ras Shamra," *JAOS* 57 (1937): 151–57, esp. 154.

13. H. L. Ginsberg, "נוספות לעלילת אלאין בעל," *Tarbiz* 4 (1933): 382; "The Rebellion and Death of Ba'lu," *Or* 5 (1936): 175.

14. J. Barth, "Zur vergleichenden semitischen Grammatik," *ZDMG* 48 (1894): 4–6.

15. H. L. Ginsberg, "Two Religious Borrowings in Ugaritic," *Or* 8 (1939): 318–22.

16. A. F. Rainey, "Observations on Ugaritic Grammar," *UF* 3 (1971): 164 (§9.9).

17. The plural of *ks'* is a significant exception, for its plural is *ksat;* thus, wherever *ksu* occurs, it is masculine singular nominative (see pp. 256–57).

18. For a discussion of *alt* see J. C. de Moor, *The Seasonal Pattern in the Ugaritic Myth of Ba'lu* (AOAT 16; Kevelaer: Butzon & Bercker, 1971): 236–37.

19. Textual references are given according to R. E. Whitaker, *A Concordance of the Ugaritic Literature* (Cambridge: Harvard University, 1972). The first numeral is that assigned by A. Herdner in *Corpus des tablettes alphabétiques découverts à Ras Shamra—Ugarit de 1929 à 1939* (MRS 10; Paris: Imprimerie Nationale, 1963). The number in brackets is that assigned by Gordon in *UT*.

20. Most recently by L'Heureux, 151; but as early as Virolleaud, "Les Rephaim. Fragments de poèmes de Ras Shamra," *Syria* 22 (1941): 10–14.

21. 3['NT].4.46–47; 16[127].23–24; 10[76].3.12–15.

22. Whitaker ([N 19]: 359) lists the clause *y'bd ksa nḫš* as occurring in UG 5.7.23–24, but a comparison with Virolleaud's transcription shows this to be an error. Whitaker has inadvertently changed the order of the lines. He has transposed Virolleaud's line 23 to follow Virolleaud's l. 20.

23. The meaning of *qmṣ* is not certain. It has been connected by Aistleitner with Ar. *qamaṣa* 'to bind'; by Albright, Ginsberg, Driver and Jirku with Heb. *qāmaṣ* 'to take in the hands,' hence 'to strangle'; and by Rin, de Moor and Caquot with the Heb. noun *qᵉmāṣîm* (Gen 41:47) in the sense of 'abundance.' The word may be in construct with *llim*. One might take the phrase *qmṣ llim* in apposition to *imr,* but since *imr* is normally not collective, and is here parallel with three plural nouns (*alpm, ṯrm, 'glm*), we prefer to consider it masculine plural construct, "kids of (= partitive) the abundance of lambs." (Another understanding would see *llim* in apposition to the construct phrase *imr qmṣ*.) Even if this understanding is erroneous, the point being made about *mria* is unaffected.

24. This superlative construction is exemplified several times earlier in text 4[51], when the superior furniture fashioned by Kṯr-wḪss is described in col. 1. This fact was originally overlooked by Albright and Gaster, who had an extended dialogue in *BASOR* 91, 93 (1943, 1944) regarding "The Furniture of El in Canaanite Mythology." See now A. van Selms ("A Guest-room for Ilu and Its Furniture," *UF* 7 [1975]: 469–76), who doubts that "such a way of expressing the superlative occurs in Ugaritic" (470).

25. Marcus (N 8): 50 n. 1, 54; Gordon, *UT* §4.5. However, it would be more consistent with Ginsberg's and Marcus' view of the *aleph* signs to consider the *a* as having vocalic quality only, and the preceding *i* as being, in effect, syllable-closing.
26. Cf. Ar. *ḍaba'a* 'to cower, to hide.' The parallel of *ṣbia špš* with *'rb špš* makes the meaning of the former clear. The same parallel occurs in APP II[173].51–52; 35[3].47.
27. The usage of *ṣbia* here, which form clearly must be singular, would seem to make Gordon's assertion in *UT* §19.1544 that *mria* is plural unlikely, besides which the *a* on a masculine plural noun would be anomalous.
28. Cf. Ar. *samk* 'roof, ceiling.' So here perhaps 'vault, heavens.'
29. See, e.g., Gen 24:11.
30. H. L. Ginsberg, *The Legend of King Keret, A Canaanite Epic of the Bronze Age* (*BASOR* Sup. Stud. 2–3; New Haven: American Schools of Oriental Research, 1946): 45.
31. A. Caquot, M. Sznycer and A. Herdner, *Textes Ougaritiques* 1, *Mythes et Légendes* (Paris: Les Editions du Cerf, 1974): 553 n. q.
32. The other possibility is that *ṣba* is adverbial, modifying the elliptical verb.
33. M. H. Pope, "The Word שחת in Job 9:31," *JBL* 83 (1964): 277.
34. The emendation may well be correct since the third person masculine singular suffixes on *qrth*, *tbth*, and *nḥlth* are without antecedents in the text as it stands. Môt is not mentioned until 11. 16–17. However, it should be noted that the last lines of col. 7 are missing and could have made reference to Môt.
35. Pope (N 33) translates "Slushy," relating the word to Ar. *hamara* "which is connected with liquids and wetness," and to the *hapax mhmrwt* in Ps 140:11 "which designates '(watery) pit(s)' from which one cannot rise." The word *mhmrt* is used parallel to *npš* in 5[67].1.7–8 in reference to Môt's gullet. M. Held ("Pits and Pitfalls in Akkadian and Biblical Hebrew," *JANES* 5 [1973; The Gaster Festschrift]: 188) suggests, following H. L. Ginsberg (כתבי אוגרית [Jerusalem: The Bialik Foundation, 1936]: 41), that *npš* in this passage means 'tomb,' and therefore that *mhmrt* does too. Moreover, he notes that *mhmrwt* in postbiblical usage means 'pit' or 'grave' and has nothing to do with rain or water. In a personal communication, Pope notes that Ginsberg was discussing another text (4[51].7.47–49) in the place cited by Held, and that Ginsberg has since abandoned the interpretation of *npš* = 'tomb' in that text (see Ginsberg's translation in *ANET*³, 135a, where *npš* is rendered 'soul'). Moreover, Pope notes that Ginsberg's treatment of 5[67].1.7–8 (where *npš* // *mhmrt*—still translated 'tomb' // 'pit' by Ginsberg in *ANET*³, 138b) is based on one of Ginsberg's rare misunderstandings of the stichometry. Furthermore, Pope argues that later inscriptional evidence makes a clear distinction between the tomb and its *npš*, i.e., the funerary monument. A. Caquot ([N 31]: 221 n. e) says *hmry* can only be related to Ar. *hamara*.
36. M. Held (N 35): 188–89.
37. Pope (N 33): 277.
38. Gordon (*UT* §19.860) regards *qk* as a double writing for a "foreign palatal intermediate between k and g"; Caquot ([N 31]: 178) writes Ḥ{q}kpt.
39. We understand this line in terms of 17 [2 AQHT].5.20–21 *b'l ḥkpt il klh* "Lord of Ḥkpt, god of all of it," which has reference to Kṯr-wḪss. Perhaps here we have an asyndeton indicating the lord and his realm (provided *ḥqkpt* = *ḥkpt*). Or, the preposition *tk* could serve a double purpose, "towards Ḥqkpt, (towards) the god of all of it." The phrase *il klh* occurs in 6.1.65 [49.1.37] with reference to 'Aṯtar's descent from Ba'l's throne to rule *barṣ il klh* "over the earth as god of all of it." For a different interpretation see J. C. de Moor (N 18): 204, as well as M. Dijkstra and J. C. de Moor, "Problematical Passages in the Legend of Aqhâtu," *UF* 7 (1975): 182.
40. *Kptr* and *ḥkpt* designate the abode of the artisan god Kṯr-wḪss. Cf. H. L. Ginsberg, "Two Religious Borrowings in Ugaritic Literature," *Or* 9 (1940): 424; C. H. Gordon, *Ugarit and Minoan Crete* (New York: W. W. Norton, 1966): 58 n. 24; W. F. Albright, *Archaeology and the Religion of Israel* (Garden City, NY: Anchor Books; Doubleday, 1969): 80. The identity of *ḥkpt* with Eg. *ḥ.t-k3-ptḥ* = Bab. *ḫi-ku-up-ta-aḫ* 'Memphis, Egypt' is contested by Driver (*Canaanite Myths and Legends* [Edinburgh: T. & T. Clark, 1956; rpt., 1971]: 169) and Caquot ([N 31]: 99).
41. We follow Held ([N 35]: 189) contra Pope ([N 33]: 277) in translating *ḫḫ* as "base," since it must surely be a synonym of *mk* (< *mkk;* cf. Heb. and Aram. מכך, a synonym of *špl,* both having the antonym *rwm*). No etymology is offered. It should be noted, however, that Akk. *ḫaḫḫu* is not a generic term for filth, but is "primarily a medical term denoting 'spittle (as a result of a coughing fit)' " (Held, 189; cf. *CAD* Ḫ, 28b).
42. *wkšu b'lt* occurs in a broken "religious text" (see Gordon, *UT* §17.1, no. 33), 47[33].7, which

may be another example: "and the throne of the Mistress."

43. Restored in APP II[173].51 on the basis of 35[3].47.

44. 79[83].1,7,10.

45. Cf. Akk. *nagāb/pu* 'to supply with provisions' (von Soden, *AHW,* 710a).

46. The etymology of *ul* is difficult. One might compare Ar. *'āl* (< *'wl*) 'family, kinsfolk, clan, partisans, people.' *Mad* is probably to be equated with Akk. *mādu,* 'mighty' (cf. Marcus [N 8]: 58 n. 128). Another possibility (suggested privately by F. Rosenthal) is (Ar.) **'ulāy* > *'ulê,* i.e., "your army, those of might" (*ṣbuk* could still be sing.).

47. The description of the marching army has been variously interpreted, but it seems clear enough that the large number is of primary importance. Thus raindrops would provide a fitting comparison, so we take *ḫḏḏ* and *yr* as the equivalents of Heb. חזיז and יורה respectively. The vocable *ḫdd* we consider as accusative, having the same force as the following *km yr*. In the latter case the development seems to be **kimā yāriyi* > **kimā yārî,* with contraction of *y* with the surrounding homogeneous vowels. Cf. my note "*DI DIT* in UG 5.2.1.8" (*UF* 8 [1976]: 465–66) for a similar phenomenon, and Cross, *CMHE* (N 3): 150 n. 14. For חזיז see M. Pope, *Job* (3d ed., AB 15; Garden City, NY: Doubleday, 1973): 205–06.

48. Following Gordon, *UT* §19.1283.

49. Cf. 17 [2 AQHT].2.4–5, 19–22.

50. Ch. Virolleaud, "Les nouveaux textes mythologiques et liturgiques de Ras Shamra (XXIV[e] campagne, 1961)," *Ugaritica* 5 (1968): 551–55, 557.

51. *CMHE* (N 3): 21–22 (vocalized); *TDOT* 1, 246. The beginning of the text, besides appearing in these two places, also finds expression in F. M. Cross, "The 'Olden Gods' in Ancient Near Eastern Creation Myths" in *Magnalia Dei: The Mighty Acts of God* (the Wright Festschrift; Garden City, NY: Doubleday, 1976): 331.

52. L. Fisher, "A New Ritual Calendar from Ugarit," *HTR* 63 (1970): 489–90 n. 20; "New Readings for the Ugaritic Texts in *Ugaritica* V," *UF* 3 (1971): 356.

53. Marcus (N 8).

54. The nominative *rpu* appears twice in the text (obv. line 1, rev. 1. 4).

55. UG 5.2.1.1; 2.4–5,6.

56. Even Cross does not translate the suffix.

57. Whereas in the first occurrence of the series Cross has *'z* // *ḏmr,* and *ḥtk* in collocation with *nmrt,* in the second occurrence he has *'z* // *ḏmr* // *nmrt,* while *ḏmr* and *ḥtk* stand in the same line.

58. Due to the broken state of the text preceding 1. 6 the exact nuance of *b* cannot be determined.

59. Gordon, *UT* §5.18.

60. Cf., e.g., *dit* < **dā'îtu* < **dā'iytu* in UG 5.2.1.8 and my article in *UF* 8 (1976), where *g't, mṭt* and *ḥmt* are noted. To this list may be added *kst* (<*ksy*), *mštt* (<*šṯy*) and probably *ǵlt* (<*ǵly*). Note the gloss of *ḥmt* as *ḫa-mi-tu,* and see Rainey (N 16): 171.

61. EA 245:28; on the text see Ch. Virolleaud, *PRU* 5 (1965): 74.

62. 84[319].1.1; 1040.1; 2160.11,16; 2008.2.11,13; 2061.13; 2106.12; 2110.3 and probably 79[83].1.7,10.

63. Translation of Virolleaud, *PRU* 5 (1965): 82. We assume *št* is understood as third person masculine plural < *šyt,* an indefinite third plural used as a passive.

64. Here the *y* is probably a vowel letter. See Simon Parker, "Studies in the Grammar of the Ugaritic Prose Texts" (diss. Johns Hopkins University, 1967): 11, 13, and Gordon, *UT* §§4.5, 19.435.

65. The vocable *'ryt* is perhaps to be related to the root *'ry* 'to be naked, bare, stripped, denuded, divested'; perhaps vocalized **'ariyatu*.

66. This if *št* is as described in n. 63, or if it is taken as perfect first singular, which seems less likely. If *št* is passive, *anyk* is subject; the case ending is present, nevertheless.

67. M. H. Pope, *El in the Ugaritic Texts* (Leiden: Brill, 1955): 49.

68. Cf. 4[51].1.7–12; 6.1.40–43[49.1.12–15]. Cf. 4[51].2.24–26. The passage in 12[75].2.45–48, which displays the parallelism *a[ḫh]—aryh* with reference to Ba'l, mentions 77—88 kin in the succeeding lines. Cf. 5[67].1.22–23.

69. S. B. Parker, "The Ugaritic Deity Rāpi'u," *UF* 4 (1972): 99–100.

70. Cf. the parallel of the last two lines in 17[2 AQHT].1.21–22; 2.14–15.

71. 19[1 AQHT].196–97, 201–02.

72. The word *ṯn* may belong to a class of nominal forms from III-weak roots which regularly appear in Ugaritic without their third radical: *šd, bk, mṭ, qn, pr* and *m'n*. Cf. J. C. de Moor, "Studies in the New Alphabetic Texts from Ras Shamra," *UF* 1 (1969): 175.

73. The parallelism of the frequently misunderstood lines 33–35 was established by M. H. Pope, *El in the Ugaritic Texts* (N 67): 40 n. 76. S. B. Parker ("Parallelism and Prosody in Ugaritic Narrative Verse," *UF* 6 [1974]: 291) has arranged the cola correctly.
74. Whether unaccented short vowels syncopated in Ugaritic is a question which merits further investigation (Gordon [*UT* §5.15] suggests vowels are not lost in any position). O. Aram. *bn'ly* suggests an original vocalization **banayu* > **banay* > **banê* (but see P.-E. Dion, *La Langue de Ya'udi* [Waterloo, Ontario: The Corporation for the Publication of Academic Studies in Religion in Canada, 1974]: 194). So here, perhaps, **bakayihū >? *bakyihū* (though Ar. *bukā'* may indicate **bukyihū*).
75. E.g., Gordon, *UT* §19.483.
76. Pope, *El in the Ugaritic Texts* (N 67): 50.
77. Parallel: 4[51].3.29–32.
78. For an explanation of *ḫptr* and *ḫbrṯ* as Hurrian loanwords, see, *i.a.*, M. H. Pope, "The Scene on the Drinking Mug from Ugarit" in *Near Eastern Studies in Honor of William Foxwell Albright* (Baltimore: Johns Hopkins University, 1971): 349.
79. 17[2 AQHT].1.24–25.
80. 6[49].3.4–5, 10–11.
81. Cf., e.g., *lapy mr[i*] (1133.5) **la'āpiyi* (vocalizing according to biblical Heb. אפה); perhaps *diy* in *km diy* (// *km nšr* in 18[3 AQHT].4.18,28) is further evidence, if, as is commonly assumed, *diy* is a participle. The problem needs further investigation.
82. 19[1 AQHT].3.107–08 (restored), 114–15, 122–23, 128–29, 136–38, 142–43, 148–50.
83. 18[3 AQHT].4.18,20,28,31; 19[1 AQHT].1.33; UG 5.2.1.8.
84. Gordon, *UT* §19.642. Cf. de Moor, *Seasonal Pattern* (N 18): 143, 227.
85. De Moor, *Seasonal Pattern* (N 18): 143, restores *qdš* and *amrr* in the two lacunae.
86. A. D. Singer, "The Vocative in Ugaritic," *JCS* 2 (1948): 1–10.
87. On the imperative of *CCy* verbs, see Gordon, *UT* §9.52 (p. 89).
88. *UT* §8.51.
89. Objective genitive: "tribute to you."
90. The evidence so far includes the numerous feminine names ending in *-y: pdry, ṭly, arṣy* (Ba'l's daughters), *dmgy* (Aṯirat's handmaid), *dnty* (Dnil's wife), *ḥry* (Krt's wife), *rḥmy* (Anat?). Cf. Gordon, *UT* §8.51, .54. Gordon mentions *n'my* as a possibility (see 5[67].6.6–7, 28–30; 6[49].2.19–20). *N'my* occurs in construct with *'rš* in 17[2 AQHT].2.41, which phrase is paralleled by *ysmsmt 'rš*. The word may be a feminine abstract 'loveliness,' or the like. In parallel passages *brkt* 'pool' and *brky* occur (UG 5.4.1.6 and 5[67].1.16). It has been suggested that *tply* in UG 5.3.1.5 is a feminine noun (= biblical Heb. Aram. תפלה; see M. H. Pope and J. H. Tigay, "A Description of Baal," *UF* 3 [1971]: 125). On the matter of a nominal feminine ending in *-y* see the bibliography in de Moor, "Studies" (N 72): 172 n. 33 and 186 n. 138, who cites *ṣrry* as a feminine adjective.
91. D. K. Stuart's *Studies in Early Hebrew Meter* (HSM 13; Missoula, MT: Scholars Press, 1976) came to hand too late to be treated in detail in this paper. One comment may be permitted. "The most significant problem in vocalization [of Ugaritic] is perhaps that presented by the case ending in a construct chain," according to Stuart (p. 51). He continues, "The case ending, containing a minimum amount of semantic information precisely when part of a construct chain, would have been liable to omission *metri causa*." The extant Ugaritic data does not support such an assumption, as our study has shown.

22

TWO EXAMPLES OF EDITORIAL MODIFICATION IN 11QtgJOB*

BRUCE ZUCKERMAN

It is generally recognized that the text of the recently published targum of Job from Qumran Cave 11[1] follows a tradition very close to that preserved in the Masoretic text; still, 11QtgJob also attests a number of interesting departures from the Masoretic tradition. Perhaps the most intriguing of such departures are those which appear to be the product of specific biases of the translator or of an editor of the Hebrew manuscript on which the translation was based. Some of these editorial modifications are of a kind we would almost expect. For example, the Hebrew בני אלהים, "the sons of God," in Job 38:7b is rendered in 11QtgJob 30:5, מלאכי אלהא, "the angels of God," thereby avoiding the theologically inappropriate use of בני. Similar circumlocutions can also be found in some of the versions; the Standard Targum[2] of Job renders כיתי מלאכיא, "bands of angels"; the LXX, ἄγγελοι μου, "my angels"; and the Peshitta, *bn̈y ml'k'*, "the sons of Angels."[3] But other editorial modifications are quite exceptional and highly revealing. Many of these changes have been collected by E. W. Tuinstra in his dissertation on hermeneutical aspects of 11QtgJob.[4] But Tuinstra's collection is not comprehensive and his analysis and conclusions can in many respects be questioned.[5]

In a short study such as this, we cannot hope to deal with the broad question of the nature and import of editorial bias in 11QtgJob. This will have to await another occasion.[6] Rather, we propose to focus attention upon two examples of editorial modification which are particularly interesting because they allow us some insight into the mechanics of hermeneutical interpretation in 11QtgJob.

The first of these is 11QtgJob 27:8 = MT 36:14b. The passage is from Elihu's fourth speech. In describing men of impious mind, Elihu declares, תמת בנער נפשם וחיתם בקדשים, "their soul dies in youth, and their life among the

*This study has been adapted from material for my dissertation, currently in progress, in the department of Near Eastern Languages and Literatures at Yale University. The intent of my dissertation is to give a comprehensive picture of the process of translation in 11QtgJob.

sodomites.'' Only the equivalent of the last part of this verse is preserved in the Qumran Targum: [ומ]דינתהון בממתין, ''[and] their [c]ity by killers/pestilences.'' Aramaic ממתין has been given a double translation because two interpretations are possible. Below, we will consider which of these is to be preferred.

The equivalence of מדינתא 'city, district,' to חיה 'life' may at first appear difficult to explain; but actually the correspondence is easy to elucidate. As M. Sokoloff has recognized, חיה 'life, living thing,' has a homonym which means 'a place where one lives.'[7] Note, for example, חית פלשתים in 2 Sam 23:13, which is translated, משרית פלשתאי, ''the encampment of the Philistines,'' in Targum Jonathan.[8] This term can also be found in Aramaic; cf. חיתא in Tg. Jonathan 2 Sam 23:11.[9] Therefore, the translator either misunderstood חיה in Job 36:14b or chose to interpret it as מדינתא for his own purposes. Since there is a lacuna of some length preceding [מ]דינתהון in 11QtgJob 27:8, we do not have enough evidence to determine which is the case. However, a simple misunderstanding could easily have happened, for the common meaning of חיה in biblical Hebrew is 'living thing, animal,' which obviously cannot fit the context of Job 36:14b. The targumist may not have been aware that חיה on rare occasions is used in the Bible in the more general sense, 'life.'[10] This could have led him to conclude incorrectly that חיה could only be understood as 'settlement' in the context of this verse.

The correspondence of מדינתא to חיה is not, however, as significant as the other we must consider: Hebrew קדשים to the Qumran Targum's ממתין. The Hebrew term refers to the male cult prostitutes of the Canaanite fertility cult,[11] and the Standard Targum's translation, מרי זנו, ''masters of prostitution,'' shows understanding for this sense of the word. The LXX, on the other hand, has confused *q*[e]*dēšîm* with *q*[e]*dôšîm* 'holy ones,' as its translation, τιτρωσκομενη ὑπο ἀγγελων, ''wounded by angels,'' indicates. The key to understanding the Qumran Targum's rendering is found by referring back to Job 33:22 (not found in the preserved portions of 11QtgJob). There, in another of Elihu's speeches, where he refers to the man chastened by God, we find the following passage: ותקרב לשחת נפשו וחיתו לממתים, ''And his soul approaches the pit, and his life to the killers'' (vocalized: *lam(m)*[e]*mîtîm*). Note the defective orthography for the form ממתים (instead of ממיתים). This has caused some confusion in the versions as to how the Hebrew form should be understood. The Standard Targum and Peshitta, in respectively rendering למיתותא, ''to death,'' and *lmwt'*, ''to death,'' have apparently connected ממתים with *m*[e]*môtîm* 'deaths.'[12] The LXX appears to reflect a double tradition, translating ἐν ᾅδῃ, ''in Hades,'' in v 22, but in the next verse rendering מלאך 'angel,' as ἀγγελοι θανατηφοροι, ''angels of death,'' showing the influence of the reading *m*[e]*mîtîm*. The Vulgate's *mortiferis,* ''to dealers of death,'' appears to follow the Masoretic vocalization.

However ממתים was understood, we can see that the translator of the Qumran Targum has appropriated the form from Job 33:22 and substituted it for קדשים in his translation of 36:14b. Thus, we know how ממתין entered 11QtgJob in 27:8; but the question remains, why?

The explanation involves our recognition that the targumist or a predecessor misunderstood קדשים in Job 36:14b to mean 'holy ones,' just as the LXX translator did. But if "holy ones" are referred to in this verse, this poses an interpretive dilemma. For how can one say of the impious that "their life/city is with holy ones"? This would not only seem to be a glaring contradiction in Elihu's remarks; but, more importantly, there is an apparent moral contradiction involved. This verse would seem to imply that a godless person can be on the side of the angels.

Because of these difficulties, the Qumran targumist or a previous editor felt that further clarification was necessary. If we presume that he read ממתים as *m^e^mîtîm* in Job 33:22, we can then suggest how he may have employed that passage to guide his interpretation and translation of 36:14b. He concluded that a special type of holy ones was meant in this verse, namely, the ממתים or 'divine killers, angels of death.'[13] This approach resolves all difficulties, for to say that the impious find themselves in the company of divine killers is more than satisfactory contextually and morally.[14] We might further note that the LXX translator is sensitive to the same interpretive dilemma as the Qumran targumist. But he has resolved the difficulty in a different manner, by qualifying ἀγγελων (= קדשים) by the insertion of τιτρωσκομενη ὑπο, "wounded by."

This interpretation, if correct, allows us important insights. Not only are we made aware of the targumist's or a previous editor's sensitivity to an apparent moral contradiction, but we have also been able to catch a glimpse of his hermeneutical approach. For in substituting ממתים/ן for קדשים he has made two assumptions: (1) that contextually ממתים = קדשים, and (2) that the justification for this is that the two words are used in nearly identical phrases. Perhaps it is not insignificant that the translator or a previous editor could justify his modification/clarification of קדשים in Job 36:14b on the grounds of such an assumption. For he seems to have exemplified a principle of hermeneutics which is also known in the rabbinical tradition, and which Hillel listed as the sixth of his seven *middôt* or "norms of interpretation": כיוצא בו ממקום אחר, "exposition by means of another similar passage."[15]

Indeed, because we may see in 11QtgJob 27:8 the possibility that the translator is thinking hermeneutically, the approach outlined above seems preferable to one suggested by Sokoloff. Sokoloff has maintained that ממתין in 11QtgJob actually reflects a reading of *m^e^môtîm* 'deaths' in Job 33:22 by the targumist, and that the translator therefore employed the closest Aramaic cognate of this Hebrew form in his rendering of Job 36:14b. Thus, ממתין in 11QtgJob 27:8 should be vocalized *m^e^mātîn* and be understood as "types of death."[16] (I prefer a somewhat looser rendering like "pestilences" if this approach is followed.) Two arguments can be mustered to back Sokoloff's interpretation: (1) probably both the Standard Targum and Peshitta, as previously noted, have interpreted ממתים in Job 33:22 as *m^e^môtîm;* and (2) if "killers" were meant, the form in the Qumran Targum should have been written *plene,* ממיתין, since elsewhere in the scroll internal long [î] is always written *plene.* A form *m^e^mātîn,* in contrast, would conform with the orthography we find in 11QtgJob 27:8, ממתין.[17]

Sokoloff's explanation may well be correct, but from a hermeneutical standpoint it is less attractive. For in seeing קדשים 'holy ones' being replaced by ממתין 'killers,' we can trace a coherent logic in the translator's or a previous editor's approach to Job 36:14b. He has equated קדשים with ממתים and thereby resolved an interpretive dilemma. But while the equation "holy ones = (divine) killers" is relatively easy to make, the equation "holy ones = types of death, pestilences" is not so obvious. In fact, a substitution with *m^emātîn* cannot be viewed as a means of clarifying קדשים, but rather must be seen as an attempt to excise an offensive term by replacing it with a more harmless term. The change is less logical and more *ad hoc*. The phrase in Job 33:22 would serve merely as the point of departure for such a change.

The main point in favor of Sokoloff's interpretation is really the defective writing ממתין instead of the *plene* ממיתין. However, we can note that in one instance an internal long vowel [ê] is not fully written with *yod;* cf. בינהן 'between them' in 11QtgJob 36:2 instead of the expected ביניהן. The vowel [û] is also occasionally written defectively.[18] However, perhaps we should view the defective spelling here from a completely different standpoint. The Hebrew form in Job 33:22 is also defectively written, at least as we have it in the MT.[19] Possibly, ממתין in 11QtgJob 27:8 is spelled in imitation of the defectively written Hebrew form; that is, it is a partial Hebraism. The employment of such a Hebraized form would then serve to point out that the rendering of Job 36:14 has been borrowed, we might even say quoted, from Job 33:22.

If this is actually the case, we can suggest a further conclusion. Up to now we have been careful to say that editorial modification in 11QtgJob reflects either the translator's own work or that of a previous editor. However, if we can document Hebraisms in the editorial modifications of the Qumran Targum, this implies an editorial activity in the Aramaic text and not in an underlying Hebrew manuscript. Consequently, editorial modification would almost have to be viewed as coming from the hand of the translator himself.

The evidence in favor of viewing ממתין as a partial Hebraism would seem most dubious if it were the only such example we could adduce. But the Qumran Targum attests yet another example where, in making an editorial modification, the translator has quoted a Hebrew phrase in only a slightly Aramaized form. We turn now to a consideration of this passage which, besides supplying justification for our approach in 11QtgJob 27:8, is highly intriguing in its own right.

The example is 11QtgJob 25:7 = MT 34:31. Again the passage comes from one of Elihu's speeches. Elihu remonstrates to Job, כי אל אל האמר נשאתי לא אחבל, "For unto God has (one) said, 'I have suffered (although) I have not acted badly'?" The Qumran Targum preserves only the last part of this phrase where it reads: [ ]נ̇י לה איחל, "[ ] me to him I will hope." The first two letters in the targum's passage, which I have transcribed *nun-yod,* have been variously interpreted, the editors of the *editio princeps* reading ת̊י̊[ ], Sokoloff, י̊[ ].[20] Part of the problem is that the second letter has a long downstroke, more like that of a *waw*. But a check of all instances of final ני- in 11QtgJob reveals that in all cases the stroke of *yod* is extended and ligatured (or nearly ligatured] to the base horizontal stroke of the *nun*.[21] In all other respects comparison also tends to confirm that]נ̇י[is the proper reading.

It is obvious that the Qumran Targum's translation varies considerably from the Masoretic tradition. Moreover, no other version shows any similarity with 11QtgJob at this point. Various proposals made by commentators to explain this disparity have been less than satisfactory. The original editors of the scroll are content to note that Aramaic לה appears to correspond with Hebrew לא. They further propose that Hebrew חבל, understood in the sense 'to bind, associate oneself,' was loosely translated by the targumist as "I (will) hope."[22] Tuinstra proposes that the translator changed the wording so that Elihu's statement would appear to affirm Job's piety instead of question it.[23] Sokoloff connects the Qumran Targum's יחל with a Syriac verbal root and translates, "will I forsake him?"[24]

Surprisingly, no scholar except M. Pope has even suggested that the Qumran Targum's rendering recalls Job 13:15a.[25] But it is precisely this insight which gives us the key to understanding the Qumran Targum's rendering. Job 13:15a reads, according to the MT, הן יקטלני לא איחל, "if He slay me, I have no hope." In this way Job affirms the wretchedness of his position before a vengeful God. However, this is one of the few biblical passages where the Masorah indicates a scribal emendation—do not read the negative particle לא, but read לו, preposition plus third masculine singular pronominal suffix. From this, of course, comes Job's famous utterance of faith, "though He slay me, yet will I trust in Him," which is often invoked by apologists of Job to show his piety. It appears that in 11QtgJob 25:7 the translator has substituted for לא אחבל, and almost certainly for נשאתי as well, this text from Job 13:15. We can therefore restore, [הן יקטל]נ̇י לה איחל, "[if he slay] me I will hope for Him."

We can be fairly certain that the translator himself made the substitution in 11QtgJob 25:7 because of the verb that was utilized, יחל 'to hope.' This is a Hebrew root and is not attested anywhere in Western Aramaic. As noted above, *yḥl occurs in Syriac (in the aphel) in the sense 'to despair, forsake,' but it is unlikely that the targumist knew this Eastern Aramaic usage. Hence, it is best to assume that the translator is quite literally quoting the Hebrew of Job 13:15 in a slightly Aramaized form. We should emphasize that it is improbable that an earlier editor made the substitution instead of the translator himself. For if the substitution were already in the targumist's *Vorlage*, then when he came to the verb form איחל 'I will hope,' he would have used a common Aramaic verbal root with the meaning "to hope" to translate יחל. Indeed, this is precisely what he has done in 11QtgJob 21:1 = MT 32:11 where Hebrew הוחלתי is translated סברת, employing the common Aramaic root סבר, 'to hope.'

We still must consider what prompted the translator to insert the text of Job 13:15 into Job 34:31 in place of נשאתי לא אחבל. This question might be more clearly answered if we knew how the targumist rendered the first part of v 31, but his translation is lost due to a lacuna. Perhaps the translator felt that Elihu's attack on Job was simply too strident here, and that furthermore Elihu was putting words into Job's mouth that he had never really said. The translator may therefore have desired to convert Elihu's attack into praise. And what better way to achieve this end than to have him quote Job's most pious statement? This would be consistent with a tendency in the Qumran Targum, noted by Tuinstra, to upgrade the image of Job so that he will appear ever the righteous sufferer.[26]

In conclusion, the two examples of editorial modification analyzed above have given us limited but insightful access into the process of interpretation in 11QtgJob. We have seen that the targumist appears to have some awareness of a hermeneutical principle which is also utilized by the rabbis in their interpretation of biblical texts. Further, we have seen that the translator will even quote passages from Job in what closely resembles their Hebrew form. Finally, this brief study has also afforded us an unexpected bonus, viz. we have been able to establish that the famous *q^e^rê* in Job 13:15 existed in an early tradition independent of the Masoretic and rabbinical sources.

NOTES

1. The *editio princeps* of 11QtgJob was published by J. P. M. Van der Ploeg and A. S. Van der Woude (in collaboration with B. Jongeling), *Le Targum de Job de la Grotte XI de Qumran* (Leiden: E. J. Brill, 1971). The best general introductory article on the Qumran Targum is J. A. Fitzmyer's "Some Observations on the Targum of Job from Qumran Cave 11," *CBQ* 36 (1974): 503–24. On pp. 503–04 nn. 3 and 4, Fitzmyer has published the most comprehensive bibliography on the scroll to date. The following studies should be added to those he has listed. Reviews of the *editio princeps:* K. R. Veenhof, "De Job-Targum uit Qumran Gepubliceerd," *Phoenix* 18 (1972): 179–81; S. Medala and Z. J. Kapera, *Folia Orientalia* 14 (1972–73): 320–22; C. T. Fritsch, *TToday* 30 (1974): 442–43. Major Studies: B. Jongeling, *Een Aramees Boek Job* (Amsterdam: Bolland, 1974); M. Sokoloff's *The Targum to Job from Qumran Cave XI* (Ramat-Gan: Bar-Ilan University, 1974; cited by Fitzmyer) has been reviewed by B. Jongeling, *JSJ* 6 (1975): 117–20; L. H. Schiffman, *JBL* 95 (1976): 158–60; B. Jongeling, C. J. Labuschagne, A. S. Van der Woude, *Aramaic Texts from Qumran* (Semitic Study Series 4; Leiden: Brill, 1976): 3–73. Articles: A. Caquot, "Un Ecrit Sectaire de Qoumran: Le ≪Targoum de Job≫," *RHR* 185 (1974): 9–27; J. A. Fitzmyer, "The Contributions of Qumran Aramaic to the Study of the New Testament," *NTS* 20 (1973–74): 382–91, esp. pp. 386–91; A. Diez-Macho, "Le Targum Palestinien" in *Exégèse Biblique et Judaisme* (ed. J. E. Menard; Strasbourg: Université des sciences humaines, 1973): 26–31 (also found in *MS Neophyti 1* 4, *Numeros* [Madrid: Consejo superior de Investigaciones Cientificas, 1974]: 80*–84* and *RSR* 47 [1973]: 180–85); J. Gray, "The Massoretic Text of the Book of Job, the Targum and the Septuagint Version in the Light of the Qumran Targum (11QtargJob)," *ZAW* 86 (1974): 331–50; B. Jongeling, "The Job Targum from Qumran Cave 11 (11QtgJob)," *Folia Orientalia* 15 (1974): 181–96; B. Jongeling, "La Colonne XVI de 11QtgJob," *RevQ* 8 no. 31 (1974): 415–16; T. Muraoka, "The Aramaic of the Old Targum of Job from Qumran Cave XI," *JJS* 25 (1974): 425–43; R. Weiss, "זרע רומ̊א, in 11QtgJob xx,7," *IEJ* 25 (1975): 140–41. A running translation of most of the targum along with various notes can also be found in M. Pope, *Job* (3rd ed., AB 15; Garden City, NY: Doubleday, 1973).

2. We shall avoid the potentially confusing and somewhat misleading nomenclature employed by some scholars by which 11QtgJob is designated "Targum 1," and the targum of Job preserved in the rabbinical Bibles as "Targum 2." For one thing, this convention ignores the fact that there is another fragment of a Job targum (not to mention a Leviticus targum) which was found in Qumran Cave 4. One wonders what numerical designation we should assign to this targum (perhaps "1a"?). Secondly, by calling 11QtgJob "Targum 1," we imply (whether intentionally or not) that it merits a special primacy in the targumic tradition for which no evidence can actually be mustered. Consequently, numerical labels are best avoided. In this study we shall therefore refer to 11QtgJob by its *siglum* or simply call it "the Qumran Targum." We can suggest provisionally that the Cave 4 Job targum be

designated the Qumran Job-Targum Fragment, since so little of it is preserved. The rabbinical targum will be designated "Standard" since it is the standard version utilized in the Jewish tradition.

3. Cf. Van der Ploeg, Van der Woude and Jongeling (N 1): 70. Citations from the Standard Targum of Job are taken from P. de Lagarde's *Hagiographa Chaldaicae* (Leipzig: B. G. Teubner, 1873; reissued Osnabruk: O. Zeller, 1967); the LXX from *Septuaginta* (ed. A. Rahlfs; Stuttgart: Wurttembergische Bibelanstalt, 1935); and the Peshitta according to Codex Ambrosianus published in facsimile edition by A. Ceriani, *Translatio Syra Pescitto Veteris Testamenti* (Mediolani: Norgate and Loescher, 1876–77). In Job 38:7b the Vg (*filii Dei*), Theodotion and Aquila (υἱοι θεου) follow the MT. Citations from the Vg are according to *Biblia Sacra Iuxta Vulgatam Versionem* (ed. R. Weber; Stuttgart: Wurttembergische Bibelanstalt, 1969); Theodotion and Aquila are given according to the listings in F. Field, *Origensis Hexaplorum quae Supersunt*... 2 (Oxonii: E Typographeo Clarendoniano, 1875).

4. E. W. Tuinstra, *Hermeneutische Aspecten van de Targum van Job uit Grot XI van Qumran* (Gronigen: Rijksuniversiteit, 1971). This Dutch study has been conveniently summarized and expanded somewhat by Caquot, "Ecrit Sectaire" (N 1).

5. See provisionally Fitzmyer, "Observations" (N 1): 512.

6. A full treatment of this topic will be found in my dissertation.

7. Sokoloff (N 1): 138.

8. Citations from Tg. Jonathan are taken from *The Bible in Aramaic* 2, *The Former Prophets* (ed. A. Sperber; Leiden: E. J. Brill, 1959).

9. There are probably other examples in the targums of חיתא in the sense of 'settlement,' e.g., Tg Pss 68:11; 143:3 (according to Lagarde). But because the context in these instances allows for an understanding of חיתא as 'life, living thing,' as is also the case for the underlying Hebrew חיה, no certain conclusions can be reached.

10. Cf. Ezek 7:3; Ps 143:3; Job 33:18,20,22,28. These last four passages are unfortunately not translated in the preserved portions of 11QtgJob.

11. Cf. M. Pope (N 1): 269–70.

12. This interpretation may have been influenced by Ezek 28:8: לשחת יורדוך ומתה ממותי חלל בלב ימים, "To the pit they will bring you down, and you will die the deaths of the slain in the heart of the seas." Many scholars have suggested that the Standard Targum and the Peshitta translations reflect an underlying Hebrew למו מתים; see, e.g., the critical apparatus in *BH*³. But this is a more difficult approach.

13. On ממתים as "destroying angels," cf. Pope (N 1): 251. Note Ibn Ezra explained the phrase לממתים in Job 33:22 as למלאכים הממיתים.

14. Compare the somewhat similar approach of Jongeling, "Job Targum" (N 1): 194–95.

15. Cf., e.g., *'Abôt R. Nat.*, chap. 37, in the edition of S. Schecter (Vienna, 1887; corrected ed., New York: P. Feldheim, 1967): 110. For a translation see J. Goldin, *The Fathers According to Rabbi Nathan* (Yale Judaica Series 10; New Haven: Yale University, 1955): 154. See further H. L. Strack, *Introduction to the Talmud and Midrash* (Philadelphia: Jewish Publication Society, 1931): 93–98, 284–85; S. Lieberman, *Hellenism in Jewish Palestine* (2d ed.; New York: Jewish Theological Seminary, 1962): 53–54. We have employed Lieberman's terminology in describing Hillel's principles.

16. Sokoloff (N 1): 139. Note in particular his evidence for Aramaic *mᵉmāt*.

17. On the use of internal vowel letters in 11QtgJob see Sokoloff (N 1): 13–14.

18. Sokoloff (N 1): 13 n. 3. There are two instances cited by Sokoloff of internal [û] written defectively.

19. The form is also defectively written in Jer 26:15. The only other example of the hip'il masculine plural participle, 2 Kgs 17:26, shows the full spelling.

20. Van der Ploeg, Van der Woude and Jongeling (N 1): 60; Sokoloff (N 1): 76.

21. Cf. 11QtgJob 9:2; 14:2,5; 16:2,6,9(2x); 22:2; 30:1,2; 31:6 (cf. fragment "E"); 34:4; 37:7(2x).

22. Van der Ploeg, Van der Woude and Jongeling (N 1): 61.

23. Tuinstra (N 4): 24.

24. Sokoloff (N 1): 77, 135.

25. Pope (N 1): 260. Pope, however, does not follow up on his observation, but instead also appeals to the Syriac *yḥl* along lines similar to Sokoloff's explanation.

26. Tuinstra (N 4): 108, e.g.

A SELECT BIBLIOGRAPHY OF THE WRITINGS OF WILLIAM SANFORD LaSOR

COMPILED BY DAWN E. WARING

BOOKS

1935 *Six Sermons on the Person and Work of Jesus Christ* (Ocean City, NJ: privately published): 40pp.

1950 *A Basic Semitic Bibliography (Annotated)* (Wheaton, IL: Van Kampen): 56pp.

1951 *Hebrew Handbook. An Inductive Study of the Elements of Hebrew Based on the Hebrew Text of Esther* (Pasadena, CA: privately published; rev. 1953, 1955): 164pp.

1956 *Amazing Dead Sea Scrolls* (Chicago: Moody; rev. 1962): 251pp.

1958 *Bibliography of the Dead Sea Scrolls, 1948–1957* (Pasadena, CA: The Library, Fuller Theological Seminary): 92pp.

1959 *Great Personalities of the Old Testament. Their Lives and Times* (Westwood, NJ: Revell): 192pp.

1961 *Great Personalities of the New Testament. Their Lives and Times* (Westwood, NJ: Revell): 192pp.

1965 *Great Personalities of the Bible* (rpt. of 1959, 1961 volumes; Westwood, NJ: Revell): 384pp.

1964 *Handbook of New Testament Greek. An Inductive Approach Based on the Greek Text of Acts* (Pasadena, CA: privately printed; rev. 1968): 362pp.

1966 *Daily Life in Bible Times* (Cincinnati: Standard Publishing): 128pp.

1970 *Men Who Knew God* (Condensation of 1959 volume; Glendale, CA: Regal Books): 196pp.

1971 *Men Who Knew Christ* (Condensation of 1961 volume; Glendale, CA: Regal Books): 167pp.

1972 *The Dead Sea Scrolls and the Christian Faith* (pb rpt. of 1956 volume; Chicago: Moody): 251pp. Translated into Chinese.

The Dead Sea Scrolls and the New Testament (Grand Rapids, MI: Eerdmans): 281pp.

Church Alive! An Exposition of Acts (Glendale, CA: Regal Books): 429pp. Translated into Spanish.

1973 *Handbook of New Testament Greek: An Inductive Approach Based on the Greek Text of Acts* (revised and enlarged ed. of 1964 volume; Grand Rapids, MI: Eerdmans): two volumes, 570pp.

1976 *Israel, A Biblical View* (Grand Rapids, MI: Eerdmans): 108pp.
1978 *Handbook to Biblical Hebrew: An Inductive Approach Based on the Hebrew Text of Esther* (revised and enlarged ed. of 1951 volume; Grand Rapids, MI: Eerdmans): two volumes, 500pp.

TRANSLATIONS

1954 René Pache, *The Return of Jesus Christ* (Chicago: Moody).
1955 G. E. Meuleman, "Infant Baptism," *Etude Evangelique* 5: 51–72.

ARTICLES

1937 "An Adventure in Giving," *The Presbyterian* 197 (2 September): 23.
"Has Life a Meaning?" *The Presbyterian* 107 (7 October): 4–6.
1938 "God's Declaration of Independence," *Presbyterian Memorial Echo* (3 July): 2–4.
1941 "Walking on the Sea," *Revelation* 11 (February): 53, 80.
"Is There a Spiritual Law?" *Moody Monthly* 41 (June): 585, 615–16.
"The Last Word," *The Presbyterian* 111 (7 August): 6–7.
"The Peril of Taking Communion," *The Presbyterian* 111 (2 October): 2, 15. Translated into Spanish.
1942 "What Is a Christian?" *The Presbyterian* 112 (11 June): 3–5.
"The Pearl of Great Price," *Revelation* 12 (July): 305, 334.
1943 "The Duty of Men of Faith," *The Presbyterian* 113 (25 February): 3, 6.
"The Parable of the Dragnet," *Revelation* 13 (April): 149, 176–77.
"The Birth of Jesus Christ," *Revelation* 13 (December): 507, 539.
1944 "A Chaplain's Chat," *The Presbyterian* 114 (17 August): 11.
"He Is Coming," *Moody Monthly* 45 (October): 72, 113.
1945 "Victory Is of the Lord," *The Presbyterian* 115 (2 August): 6–7.
1946 "The Newness of Christ," *The Presbyterian* 116 (30 May): 3, 6.
1947 "True Christianity Is Power," *Revelation* 17 (January): 13, 42.
1950 "Symposium on the Value of a Knowledge of the Dutch Language for Biblical and Theological Studies" (with C. Van Til and A. D. Ehlert), *Fuller Library Bulletin* 5 (January–March): 7–8.
1952 "Isaiah 7:14—'Young Woman' or 'Virgin'?" (Pasadena, CA: privately published; rpt. 1976): 11pp.
"A Further Note on the Words *bethulah* and *'almah*" (Pasadena, CA: privately published; 29 December): 8pp.
1954 "The Advantages of Studying Foreign Languages" (in Hebrew), *Siyum Hasman* 7.
1955 "Beyond Biblical Criticism," *His* 15 (April): 5–6, 17, 22–23.
"Note on *'ahav, chavah, 'avah* and *'agav* and Etymological Conclusions," *Gordon Review* 1: 141–42.
1956 "Notes on Genesis 1:1—2:3," *Gordon Review* 2: 26–32.
"The Messiahs of Aaron and Israel," *VT* 6: 425–29.
"Secondary Opening of Syllables Originally Closed with Gutturals (in Hebrew)," *JNES* 15: 246–50.
"Pray Like This," *Episcopal Recorder* NS 37: 8–11, 18.
1957 "The Sibilants in Old South Arabic," *JQR* 48: 161–73.
1958 "The Dead Sea Scrolls after Ten Years," *Fuller Library Bulletin* 8 (January): 6–7.
"The Tabernacle, Types and Symbols," *The New Century Leader* (May): 13, 48.
"Significance of a Land," *The New Century Leader* (June): 12, 54.
"Justice Is Righteousness," *The New Century Leader* (August): 12, 57.

"What the Scrolls Reveal," a review article, *Eternity* 9 (October): 40–41.
1960 "Bibliography [of Qumran]," *RevQ* 2: 459–72, 587–601.
"New Finds Spur Bible Land Archaeologists," *Christianity Today* 4 (18 July): 25–28.
"Mishnah" in *Baker's Dictionary of Theology* (ed. E. F. Harrison; Grand Rapids, MI: Baker): 358.
"Monotheism" in *Baker's Dictionary of Theology* (Grand Rapids: Baker): 362–63.
"Talmud" in *Baker's Dictionary of Theology* (Grand Rapids: Baker): 511–12.
"Zoroastrianism" in *Baker's Dictionary of Theology* (Grand Rapids: Baker): 565–66.
"Was the Flood Universal?" *Eternity* 11 (December): 11–13.
"Foreword" in *Josephus, Complete Works* (Grand Rapids, MI: Kregel): vii–xii.
1961 "Bibliography [of Qumran]," *RevQ* 3: 149–60, 313–20, 467–80.
"The Last Word: You and Your Dysteleological Surd," *Eternity* 12 (October): 48.
1962 "Bibliography [of Qumran]," *RevQ* 3: 593–602.
"The Messianic Idea in Qumran" in *Studies and Essays in Honor of Abraham A. Neuman* (ed. M. Ben-Horim, B. D. Weinryb and S. Zeitlin; Leiden: Brill): 343–64.
"Can a Christian Doubt?" *Sunday School Times* 104 (24 March): 7, 13.
"The Dead Sea Scrolls and the Beginnings of Christianity," *Christian News from Israel* 13 (July): 8–13. Also in French and Spanish.
"Historical Framework: the Present Status of the Dead Sea Scrolls Study," *Int* 16: 259–79.
"The Sanctity of the Mount of Olives," *Christian News from Israel* 13 (December): 16–23. Also in French and Spanish.
1963 "Bibliography [of Qumran]," *RevQ* 4: 139–59, 311–20, 467–80.
"The Holy Spirit" in *Things Most Sincerely Believed* (ed. C. S. Roddy: Westwood, NJ: Revell): 76–85.
"Architecture" in *Zondervan's Pictorial Bible Dictionary* (ed. M. C. Tenney; Grand Rapids, MI: Zondervan): 66–69.
"Art" in *Zondervan's Pictorial Bible Dictionary* (Grand Rapids: Zondervan): 73–74.
"Dead Sea Scrolls" in *Zondervan's Pictorial Bible Dictionary* (Grand Rapids: Zondervan): 205–09.
1964 "Bibliography [of Qumran]," *RevQ* 5: 149–60.
1965 "Bibliography [of Qumran]," *RevQ* 5: 293–320.
1966 "The Use and Abuse of Archaeology," *Eternity* 17 (May): 19–21.
"Open Letter to Professor Allegro, *Hidden Secrets of the Dead Sea Scrolls,*" *Eternity* 17 (November): 21–22, 36.
1967 "The Dead Sea Scrolls after Twenty Years," *Sunday School Times* 109 (1 August): 8–9.
"Have the 'Times of the Gentiles' Been Fulfilled?" *Eternity* 18 (August): 32–34.
"Interpretation of Prophecy" in *Baker's Dictionary of Practical Theology* (ed. R. G. Turnbull; Grand Rapids, MI: Baker): 128–35.
1968 "Heart Transplants and the Bible," *Eternity* 19 (March): 17–18, 29.
"Criticism of the Anchor Bible," *Commentary* 45 (May): 5, 8.
"U.S. Involvement in Vietnam," *Theology, News and Notes* 14 (July): 6.
1969 "The Biblical Basis for Social Action," *Theology, News and Notes* 15 (January): 8–10.
1970 "1 and 2 Kings" in *The New Bible Commentary Revised* (ed. D. Guthrie, J. A. Motyer, A. M. Stibbs and D. J. Wiseman; London: Inter-Varsity): 320–68.

1971 "What Is a Theological Liberal?" *The Opinion* 10 (January): 5–6.
1974 "Ethiopia, A Land Rich in History," *World Vision* 18 (June): 10–11.
"The Inductive Method of Learning Hebrew: Its Advantages and Pitfalls," *Hebrew Abstracts* 15: 108–19.
1976 "Further Information about Tell Mardikh." *JETS* 19: 265–70.
"Major Archaeological Discoveries at Tell-Mardikh," *Christianity Today* 20 (24 September): 49.
"Archaeologists Unearth Genesis-Era Tablets," *Eternity* 27 (September): 8.
"Wilbur Smith—An Appreciation," *Theology, News and Notes* 23 (October): 16–18.
"Life Under Tension—Fuller Theological Seminary and the Battle for the Bible," *Theology, News and Notes* (special issue; October): 5–28.
"The Conversion of the Jews," *The Reformed Journal* 26 (November): 12–14.
"Tell Mardikh—The Latest Archaeological 'Greatest,'" *Theology, News and Notes* 23 (December): 19–23.
1977 "An Approach to Hebrew Poetry through the Masoretic Accents," *JQR* anniversary issue, forthcoming.
1978 "Sensus Plenior" in *Scripture, Tradition and Interpretation, Festschrift for E. F. Harrison* (Grand Rapids, MI: Eerdmans): 260–77.

BOOK REVIEWS

1940 R. C. H. Lenski, *The Interpretation of the Acts of the Apostles, The Presbyterian* 110 (4 July): 22.
1946 V. Ferm, ed., *The Encyclopedia of Religion, The Presbyterian* 116 (17 October): 22.
Nelson Glueck, *The River Jordan, The Presbyterian* 116 (26 December): 16.
1947 Lewis Browne, *The World's Great Scriptures, The Presbyterian* 117 (8 February): 22–23.
J. McKee Adams, *Ancient Records and the Bible, The Presbyterian* 117 (1 March): 15.
George Simpson, *A Book About the Bible, The Presbyterian* 117 (2 August): 15.
1948 J. Phillip Hyatt, *Prophetic Religion, Monday Morning* (9 February): 8.
G. M. Lamsa, *New Testament Origins, Monday Morning* (31 May): 8.
C. H. Gordon, *Lands of the Cross and Crescent, Monday Morning* (31 May): 8.
1950 E. F. Harrison, *The Son of God Among the Sons of Men, Bibliotheca Sacra* 107/405 (January-March): 124–25.
A. Dupont-Sommer, *Les Araméens, Or* 19: 356–58.
C. H. Gordon, *Ugaritic Literature, Bibliotheca Sacra* 107/426 (April–June): 250–53.
W. F. Albright, *The Archaeology of Palestine, Bibliotheca Sacra* 107/426 (July–September): 377–80.
1951 O. T. Ellis, *The Unity of Isaiah, Eternity* 2 (May): 29.
1952 C. R. Erdman, *The Book of Numbers, Eternity* 3 (November): 34–35.
1954 Eugène Lemoine, *Théorie de l'emphase hébraïque, JBL* 73: 118–19.
E. Leslie Carlson, *Elementary Hebrew, JBR* 25: 174.
1957 B. M. Metzger, *An Introduction to the Apocrypha, Christianity Today* 2 (14 October): 34.
1958 S. Mowinckel, *He That Cometh, United Evangelical Action* 17 (15 June): 14.
Elizabeth Hamilton, *Put Off Thy Shoes, JBR* 29: 276.
Y. Yadin, *The Message of the Scrolls, Eternity* 9 (August): 43.
Millar Burrows, *More Light on the Dead Sea Scrolls, Eternity* 9 (October): 40–41.

F. M. Cross, *The Ancient Library of Qumran and Modern Biblical Studies, Eternity* 9 (October): 40–41.

1959 Nelson Glueck, *Rivers in the Desert, Christianity Today* 3 (16 March): 37–38.

C. G. Howie, *The Dead Sea Scrolls and the Living Church, Eternity* 10 (July): 43–44.

J. M. Allegro, *The People of the Dead Sea Scrolls, Eternity* 10 (August): 45.

J. van der Ploeg, *The Excavations at Qumran, Eternity* 10 (August): 45.

1960 Jean Daniélou, *The Dead Sea Scrolls and Primitive Christianity, Eternity* 11 (August): 44–45.

F. F. Bruce, *Biblical Exegesis in the Qumran Texts, Eternity* 10 (November): 47–48.

1961 W. Corswant, ed., *A Dictionary of Life in Bible Times, Eternity* 12 (February): 42–43.

Bible Guidelines 1, 7, 11, 13, *Christianity Today* 5 (17 July): 906–07.

H. M. Morris and J. C. Whitcomb, Jr., *The Genesis Flood, Eternity* 12 (August): 43.

J. A. Sanders, *The Old Testament in the Cross, Religion in Life* 30: 640.

Ch. Pfeiffer, ed., *Baker's Bible Atlas, Eternity* 12 (November): 54–57.

1963 Emmanuel Anati, *Palestine Before the Hebrews, Christianity Today* 7 (29 March): 35.

1966 James A. Michener, *The Source, Eternity* 17 (January): 40–41.

John C. Trever, *The Untold Story of Qumran, Eternity* 17 (March): 40–41.

Gerhard von Rad, *Old Testament Theology* 2, *The Theology of Israel's Prophetic Traditions, Christianity Today* 10 (1 April): 36.

1967 *The Jerusalem Bible, Eternity* 18 (June): 41–43.

1968 *The Wycliffe Historical Geography of Bible Lands, Eternity* 19 (June): 44.

Y. Aharoni, *The Land of the Bible, A Historical Geography, Eternity* 19 (June): 44.

J. Pelikan and W. A. Hansen, ed., *Luther's Works* 30, *The Catholic Epistles, CBQ* 30: 121–23.

1969 J. Pelikan and W. A. Hansen, ed., *Luther's Works* 5, *Lectures on Genesis, Chapters 26–30, CBQ* 31: 117–19.

1972 Johannes Lehman, *Rabbi J, Eternity* 23 (October): 62–64.

Edwin Yamauchi, *The Stones and the Scriptures, Christianity Today* 17 (10 November): 21.

1973 Larry Collins and Dominique Lapierre, *O Jerusalem!, Eternity* 24 (February): 50.

G. A. Turner, *Historical Geography of the Holy Land, Christianity Today* 18 (10 May): 40–42.

Morton Smith, *The Secret Gospel, Eternity* 24 (September): 54.

1975 C. G. Montefiore and H. Loewe, *The Sources of Judaism. A Rabbinic Anthology, Christianity Today* 19 (June): 24–25.

Harry T. Frank, *Discovering the Biblical World, Eternity* 26 (September): 42–43.

1976 J. A. Fitzmyer, *The Dead Sea Scrolls: Major Publications and Tools for Study, JBL* 95: 681–82.

John Van Seters, *Abraham and Tradition, Christian Scholars Review* 6: 214–15.

Elias Auerbach, *Moses, Christian Scholars Review* 6: 214–15.

1977 *Good News Bible; The Bible in Today's English Version, Eternity* 28, forthcoming.

Henryk Muszyński, *Fundament, Bild und Metapher in den Handschriften aus Qumran, JBL* 96: 445–47.

FILMS, FILMSTRIPS, RECORDINGS, PLAYS

1938 "The Lord Is Risen! A Resurrection-Day Pageant" (Ocean City, NJ: privately published). Translated into Spanish.

1940 "The First Traveling Seminar" (Color slides of traveling seminar in Arizona and New Mexico for Board of National Missions, UPUSA).

1957 "The Prophecy of Jeremiah" (Burbank, CA: Sacred Records, recorded 13 May).

"The Lamentations of Jeremiah" (Burbank, CA: Sacred Records, recorded 14 May).

1962 "Great Personalities of the Bible" (twelve filmstrips; photography, script, narration; Burbank, CA: Film Services).

"Archaeology and the Living Bible" (30-minute film; script and narration; Burbank, CA: Film Services).

"Archaeology and the Living Old Testament" (30-minute film; script and narration; Burbank, CA: Film Services).

"Archaeology and the Living New Testament" (30-minute film; script and narration; Burbank, CA: Film Services).

1963 "Dead Sea Scrolls" (University Slide Sets, University Lecture Series; photography and script; Los Angeles: Wolfe Worldwide Films).

"The Birth and Boyhood of Jesus" (University Slide Sets, University Lecture Series; Los Angeles: Wolfe Worldwide Films).

1964 "Miracle in Black" (34-minute documentary of indigenous Christian work in Ghana; photography, story and script; Pasadena, CA: World-Wide Missions).

1974 "In the Footsteps of Paul, Part I" (30-minute videotape; photography, script, narration; Burbank, CA: Vision Communications).

SYLLABI, PAPERS, RESEARCH PROJECTS

1942 "A Study of the Exegetical Basis of Premillennialism" (Th.M. thesis, Princeton Theological Seminary): 91pp.

1947 "The Life and Teaching of Jesus Christ" (Syllabus, Lafayette College, Easton, PA): v + 71pp.

"The Beginnings of Christianity" (Syllabus, Lafayette College): 30pp.

1949 "Semitic Phonemes, with Special Reference to Ugaritic and in Light of the Egyptian Evidence" (Ph.D. diss., Dropsie College of Semitic and Cognate Learning): 240pp.

1950 "Old Testament Introduction" (Syllabus, Fuller Theological Seminary): 86pp.

1951 "Revelation in the Pentateuch" (Paper delivered to Faculty Forum, Fuller Theological Seminary, 29 March).

1952 "Report of a Photographic Survey of the Lands of the Bible" (Research proj., Univ. of S. CA): 185pp.

"Old Testament History" (Syllabus, Fuller Theological Seminary): 66pp.

1953 "A Dialect Study of the Book of Hosea" (Research proj., Univ. of S. CA): 90pp.

1955 "A Study of the Developments in New Testament Textual Criticism Since Westcott and Hort" (Research proj., Univ. of S. CA): 110pp.

1956 "A Preliminary Reconstruction of Judaism in the Time of the Second Temple in the Light of Published Qumran Materials" (Th.D. diss., University of Southern California): 488pp.

1957 "Some Observations on the Qumran Messiah" (Paper presented to Pacific Coast Section, SBL, 12 April).

1962 "Historical Method and the Dead Sea Scrolls" (Paper for Pacific Coast Branch, National Association for Biblical Instructors, 18 October).

1965 "Old Testament Interpretation—Reactions to Dr. Laurin's Paper" (Paper given at Ministers' Theological Seminar, California Baptist Theological Seminary, Covina, CA, 16 November).

1966 "Archaeology and Scripture—A Reaction" (Response to paper by D. J. Wiseman, Seminar on Scriptural Authority, Boston, 21 June).

1968 "Notes on Biblical Aramaic" (Syllabus, Fuller Theological Seminary): 56pp.

1970 "Old Babylonian Handbook" (Syllabus, Fuller Theological Seminary): 201pp.

1972 "Old Testament Prophets" (Syllabus, Fuller Theological Seminary): 123pp.

1973 "The Inductive Method of Learning Hebrew: Its Advantages and Pitfalls" (Paper presented to National Association of Professors of Hebrew, Chicago, 8 November).

1975 "Epochal Events of the Bible. An Approach to Biblical Theology" (Syllabus, Fuller Theological Seminary): v + 343pp.

"Semitic Phonemes and Some Applications for Biblical Studies" (Paper, Old Testament Graduate Seminar, Fuller Theological Seminary, 1 April).

"The Tendency to Avoid Phonetically Homogeneous Phonemes in the First-and-Second and First-and-Third Radicals of Semitic Roots" (Paper, Comparative Semitics Seminar, Fuller Theological Seminary, 4 April).

"The Religion of Israel" (Paper, Old Testament Graduate Seminar, Fuller Theological Seminary, 28 September).

"The Messiah: An Evangelical Christian View" (Paper delivered at Conference of Jews and Evangelical Christians, New York, 8 December).

EDITORIAL RESPONSIBILITIES

Contributing Editor, *Seek*, a devotional booklet (Chicago: Good News Publishing Co.): one page per month since 1941.

Co-editor, Fuller Theological Seminary Bibliographical Series (Pasadena, CA: The Library, Fuller Theological Seminary): 1950–1957.

Contributing Editor of "Bibliography," *RevQ* (Paris: Gabalda): 1959–1965.

Revising Editor, Biblical Geography and Archaeology, *International Standard Bible Encyclopedia* (Grand Rapids, MI: Eerdmans): 1961–.

Consulting Editor, Archaeology, *Eternity*, 1967–.

Editor, *Theology, News and Notes* (Pasadena, CA: Fuller Theological Seminary): volumes 1–11, 1954–1964.

Co-editor, *World-Wide Missions Magazine* (Pasadena, CA: World-Wide Missions): 1967–1972.

INDEX OF SUBJECTS

INDEX OF AUTHORS

Pre-critical

Modern

INDEX OF SCRIPTURAL REFERENCES

A. Old Testament

C. Apocrypha

B. New Testament

C. *Apocrypha*

INDEX OF OTHER ANCIENT SOURCES

A. *Cuneiform Literature*

B. *Ugaritic Literature*

C. Qumran Literature

INDEX OF NEAR EASTERN WORDS

A. *Hebrew and Aramaic*

B. *Ugaritic Words*

C. *Akkadian/ Sumerian*

D. *North Semitic Inscriptions*

E. *Greek, Roman, Early Jewish*